Praise for
## WIN WITHOUT GREED
### By Irving Burling

"Irv Burling has, by personal example, demonstrated that a disciplined proactive mindset can be a powerful catalyst for organizational renewal-a mark of enlightened leadership".

--Ed Oakley, coauthor of
Enlightened Leadership

"This is an excellent book for every business management team and Board of Directors interested in building a sustainable future in the 21st Century. The book, informal in style and well written, provides sound theoretical underpinnings as well as many practical examples of what to do and what to avoid. The reader quickly comes to know the author and can personally identify with the pressures associated with making critical decisions. It is refreshing to see that some leaders truly are looking out for stakeholders first."

--Bill Rabel, Ph.D., FLMI, CLU
Sr VP Life Office Management Association

"Using Micah 6:8 and Ephesians 4:2 as bookends to a very fine work, Irv Burling models the qualities described in these two Biblical texts and writes with a servant heart. This important work describes and demonstrates a process promising success for the corporate manager, the employee and the institutions they serve. With passion and through clear illustrations Irv provides a significant counter weight to the proliferation of greed and pride which so plague today's marketplace."

--Leroy R. Rehrer
Senior Pastor
Holy Trinity Lutheran Church

# WIN

# WITHOUT

# GREED

*An amazing story of what any leader can accomplish with intense focus on sound fundamental principles*

A Corporate Success Story

IRVING BURLING, FSA

Published in Chandler, Arizona, by Irving Burling, FSA

ISBN 0-9755204-0-7

# DEDICATION

This book is dedicated to the Cuna Mutal Life Insurance Company in Waverly, Iowa who, for 125 years, has been committed to meeting the needs of thier policyholders without greed.

*He has told you what he wants, and this is all it is: to be fair and just and merciful, and to walk humbly with your God.*

*Micah 6:8*

# TABLE OF CONTENTS

THE PROBLEM

CHAPTER 1: 100 YEARS OF COMFORT
            TURNED TO WAR                 Pg. 21

THE SOLUTION

CHAPTER 2: DOWN SIZING                    Pg. 37

CHAPTER 3: MODIFYING THE "MERGER"
            MODEL                         Pg. 43

HOW IT WAS ACCOMPLISHED

CHAPTER 4: LEADERSHIP SKILLS NEEDED
            TO MAKE THE TRANSITION        Pg. 55

CHAPTER 5: DEVELOPING A SHARED
            VISION IN THE COMPANY         Pg. 67

CHAPTER 6: I NEEDED A COACH               Pg. 79

CHAPTER 7: CAPITALIZING ON OUR
            MOST IMPORTANT ASSET-
            HUMAN RESOURCES               Pg. 91

CHAPTER 8: ELEMENTS OF SUCCESS IN
            TIMES OF CHANGE               Pg. 105

# ACKNOWLEDGMENT

I am deeply indebted to all of the editing and critiquing Fred Waldstein did on this book. When I started this book I was indefinite as to the help I was seeking. Nor was I sure how long it would take or if I would follow through to completion. Fred was always encouraging and motivating to the end. I appreciate the articulate way he can express himself in simple direct terms using a minimum of words.

Every business develops it's own vocabulary. It was very helpful that Fred was not a part of our business. His penetrating questions for clarification were invaluable resulting in a better end product.

Fred is Director of the Institute for Leadership Education, Professor of Political Science, and holds the endowed Irving R. Burling Chair in Leadership at Wartburg College in Waverly, Iowa.

In addition writing this book gives me an opportunity to thank several groups of people that were such an important part of my life during the transformation of the company in Waverly, Iowa.

First of course were the Associates in the company. I'm grateful for your trust and appreciate your creative capacity, good spirit during tough times and diligent work ethic. For 17 years I had the benefit of looking forward to work every day. You made the difference.

Secondly, it was heartwarming for a stranger to feel so welcome by the staff in Madison, WI. Your spirit of "can do" and your commitment to the client was outstanding. I regret not having had the opportunity to get to know more of you better. You can be proud of what you've accomplished.

I would be remiss if I didn't note a special word of thanks to both Boards of Directors. Your continual effort to stick to good business practices, to devote untold hours to a just and innovative solution to a problem, and of course your tireless effort to hold management accountable for results was commendable. Thank you for your trust.

Finally I must thank the citizens of Waverly, IA. These were trying days and your open and honest concerns were absolutely essential as we worked through the issues. One of my blessings in life was to have the good fortune of spending nearly a quarter of a Century in your community. It was a wonderful place to grow and raise a family. I have many memories that I will always cherish.

# INTRODUCTION

In today's climate of corruption in corporations, many people are anxious about their future. How long will my job be secure? Will I be "dumped" as I grow older? How will I find another job at my age? Will the benefits be there when I am ready to retire? Will health care be provided for me and my family?

The symbols and actions of corporate greed and mismanagement surround us and have become an all too familiar part of the daily "business beat" reported by the media. Our business and management leaders need to refocus their thinking from "what's in it for me," to "what are my responsibilities to my customer and my employees as well as to my board of directors." This orientation is linked to the term, "servant-leadership," first used in 1970 by a retired businessman, Robert K. Greenleaf, in his publication, "The Servant as Leader."[1] Greenleaf's vision of servant-leadership

[1] Greenleaf, R. K. 1970. <u>The Servant as Leader,</u> Indianapolis, IN: The Robert Greenleaf Center.

*The principles and values of servant- leadership in corporations are desperately needed.*

is "a model that puts serving others-including employees, customers, and community-as the number one priority. Servant-leadership emphasizes increased service to others, a holistic approach to work, promoting a sense of community, and the sharing of power in decision-making."[2]

The principles and values of servant-leadership in corporations are desperately needed. It is more critical than ever before in our history for business leaders to find creative ways to address these problems and provide job security for people who depend on them. I believe that transformation can happen in people's lives and in the lives of institutions.

This book focuses on the lessons learned as a result of a dedicated group of individuals doing the common thing uncommonly well. The lessons learned in this story should be of interest to every leader. This is my story of attempting to provide servant-leadership and what happened as a result in a small business and in a small Midwestern community where it was located. While the situations described are real, the names of individuals

[2] Spears, L.C. 1998. Insights on Leadership; Service, Stewardship, Spirit, and Servant-Leadership. New York; John Wiley and Sons. P. 3.

*The lessons learned in this story*
*should be of interest to every leader.*

used in telling this story are fictitious.

I spent over 50 years in the insurance business. During the last 17 years of my active career I was the CEO of a life insurance company where I had the opportunity to be the catalyst in transforming the company from certain demise to a sustainable future.

My 17 years as CEO began in a period of relative calm in the insurance business, and ended during a period of intense competition as we approached the 21st Century. It was apparent to me that the leadership skills that built the business during its first 100 years of existence were different than what would be needed to survive and build a sustainable future.

Large companies began a consolidation process through mergers. Small companies would not be exempt from this transition. The final means to the end of a successful transformation had to be some type of merger. However, 70% of the mergers negotiated in this country fail to meet expectations. We had to find a way to beat those odds.

"MERGERS SELDOM PAY OFF" an article, published on April 30, 2001 in the Arizona Republic, was based on a study done by the Chicago Tribune in conjunction with the consulting firm of A. T. Kearney. Some of the findings were as follows:

- Nearly seven in ten surviving companies lagged their industry peers in performance two years after the deals were completed, some dramatically.

- Even as the latest wave of deals transformed the corporate landscape and disrupted many lives, it failed to generate the promised returns.

- Many deals look good on paper but wither as vastly different organizational cultures, distribution channels and personal agendas surface.

- Most observers believe plenty of industries are still ripe for continued consolidation.

- WHY DO SO MANY DEALS GO AWRY?

In the 1990s there were roughly 46,000 mergers--which means 32,000 failed to meet expectations!!!! Can the probability of success be enhanced? The answer may very well be "yes". This story explains how.

# CHAPTER ONE

## 100 YEARS OF COMFORT TURNED TO WAR

In January of 1976, I was named the CEO of Century Life of America, a small life insurance company in the heartland of America, after being with the company for seven years. The company was the stable "anchor business" in Waverly, Iowa, a community of 8,000. The company's 100 year history in rural America with its inherent work ethic had produced a very competitive, financially strong, well respected insurance organization. Turnover was unusually low and never in the history of the company had there been an early retirement. It used to be said that the parents of high school graduates, in wishing the best for their children, wanted them to work for the company. Recruiting was never a problem.

We called our employees "Associates". When I first became CEO I would spend part of every day walking around and chatting with them.

I thought I was with a company that would practically run itself for the next 100 years. What would I do with my time? Was I wrong!

The history of the insurance business is punctuated with various "price wars" in specific products such as term insurance to establish inroads in market share, but these typically never lasted more than six months. Then the pricing of products would go back to what had been normal for many years. The pattern of pricing products for a stable economic environment had been built into the strategic planning models of insurance companies for many years.

The fundamental foundation of most life insurance companies in this country was built on life insurance that had long-term guarantees which meant conservative interest assumptions and life expectancies involving several generations. Furthermore to build distributions systems companies built commission schedules into the pricing of products, which increased expenses faster than revenue was earned. A typical insurance product would not pay back, what in effect had been borrowed from surplus to build the business, for ten to fifteen years.

The relationship of the three parties in an insurance contract evolved like a three-legged stool-the company, the agent and the client. During the first 100 years of the life insurance business in this country there was a type of "alliance" between the company and the agent. Because of the long term guarantees and assumptions the client didn't always understand the details of the product except to know the product was necessary and the companies kept their promises. The three-legged stool remained solid and in place. The first 100 years of the company was the "comfort zone" in the business.

But the spike in interest rates in the early 80s changed all that. Suddenly all HELL broke loose. The consumer's primary focus was now on asset accumulation products with insurance playing a secondary role of completing the consumer's long-term goal in the event of a premature catastrophe.

Now the client was saying "I didn't understand all of the guarantees and other aspects in the life insurance contract, but I understand interest and I want the best deal NOW". Life insurance products lost some of their glamour and the client demanded a whole set of interest sensitive products which were innovative, had a short shelf life and were expensive to administer. We found ourselves in a financial services "war". The "comfort zone" had passed and we were now in the "war zone". The insurance business would never be the same again.

The unwritten "alliance" in the three-legged stool suddenly changed from the company and agent to the agent and client. To satisfy the client's demands the agent, to stay in the new "alliance" and retain his/her commission income, frequently transferred the business to another company. Some of the business was transferred before it had been on the books of the originating company ten years. This meant that surplus borrowed to write the business in the first instance was never going to be repaid.

In addition, interest sensitive products, such as annuities and universal life, meant competition from financial intermediaries outside of the insurance business, such as banks and investment brokers. Also, the nature of these changes demanded improved technology, which was expensive. And regulators, in an attempt to stay on top of all the dramatic changes, imposed more regulations, which added to costs.

I remember going to insurance trade association meetings during the early years of the "war" and seeing my peers concerned about losing control of their company's destiny. Not only were agents transferring business to other companies but banks, while interest rates were so high, were telling their clients "if you have a life insurance product you're better off to borrow against it since the guaranteed rate is so low". The result was an eroding of the financial underpinnings of the company.

For 100 years insurance companies had been known as strong financial intermediaries in this country. With a stable, predictable source of income insurance companies were making long-term investment commitments on behalf of the policyholders. These investments were a source of revenue to provide long term financing to, for example, build businesses, homes, apartments, hotels, and infrastructure in this country. At the peak of the "war" demands for cash from the policyholders was exceeding cash reserves and some companies had to go to the banks for temporary help.

Truly this was a whole new ball game. The rules had changed. The higher volume of business in interest sensitive products, which were more subject to the whims of the policyholders, meant that companies had to be more careful in making long-term investment commitments.

My thoughts while "managing by walking around" building relationships of trust with Associates were totally different than in the past. Now I was thinking, "Why is this happening to me?" "How does this parochial company survive in this environment?" "What kind of critical mass

*"It takes different skills to manage as we'd done for 100 years than it does to create a sustainable future in an unknown, changing environment."*

or size is needed to survive?" "Is it possible that we could lose a significant piece of the distribution system since loyalty meant little in this "war"?" "What happens to the Associates that can't keep up? It takes different skills to manage as we'd done for 100 years than it does to create a sustainable future in an unknown, changing environment." I'd look at the Associates and say to myself, "These people and their families are counting on the business to stay in this community and not only survive but to thrive". It weighed heavily on my conscience.

As I looked to the future I felt we had three options: 1) maintain the status quo, 2) position the company-spread the resources in such a manner that the company would be in position to provide any financial product through any distribution system that policyholders would demand in the future, or 3) take a position-focus on a few strengths with the objective of being one of the best in a chos market.

Maintain the status quo
I could have "masked" what war

*Never pay back evil for evil. Do things in such a way
that everyone can see you are honest clear through.*

*Romans 12:17.*

and held on until my retirement. For example, one possibility considered by companies during this period was to sell their home office building and lease it back, and then add the value of the building to surplus. In addition, as a company we were always conservative in establishing liabilities. We could have revalued those liabilities and added the extra amount to surplus. Furthermore, while the erosion in surplus was real it would not have been noticeable for several years.

But masking the financial results would have violated the values and principles of openness and honesty that were at the core of our organization. For example, we had implemented an audit system using what was then one of the big 8 firms with no other involvement with the company (similar to legislation implemented after the Enron travesty). We did this years before mutual insurance companies were even required to have an outside auditor. Several years before state regulators required it we had made it a regular practice to furnish the Board of Directors with very detailed information about the company. We wanted to make sure everything "was on the table for everyone to see". In other words, we wanted to be a totally transparent organization to the 300,000 plus policyholders that entrusted their resources with us. These people had to be our first priority.

We could have waited and considered a traditional merger with a larger company. Typically that would eventually mean all of the business would be administered at the larger company office and most of the staff would have to look for new jobs. And there would be a high probability that the office would have limited use to the surviving company. That would have had a very significant negative impact on our staff and the community. I felt we needed to be more creative and, most important, we could do better for our policyholders than a merger would have allowed.

Position the company

This meant that we would utilize our resources to be ready for any eventuality-any type of distribution system, all product offerings and, in effect, not be a specialist in any. This would require considering, for example, the possibility of distributing our products through department stores or banks to their customers. It would also mean trying to predict which products (e.g., term insurance, disability insurance, long term care insurance, whole life, annuities, or something entirely new) would be the hot product of the future. It was obvious that to be able to offer everything to everyone we would have to spread ourselves too thin in light of our financial underpinnings.

<u>Take a position</u>

That meant to me, picking an option where we would have the opportunity to be a major force in a niche market. We would have to sell off some of our smaller lines of business and focus our resources on a few product lines where we could be a significant player in the market place. Furthermore, it is worth noting that the margins in an insurance company's annuity products were not sufficient, on their own, to support the distribution systems that insurance companies had in place.

In Thomas Friedman's book, <u>The Lexus and the Olive Tree</u>,[3] he refers to the new environment where there will be a tendency for the "Winners to take all" in the market. The giants in the business and the companies who already hold a strong market identity would take over the market. If we could position ourselves in a target market where we could both reduce our distribution cost per sale and our administrative cost with greater volume we would have an opportunity to build a sustainable future. The challenge would be to identify that lynch pin to our future.

During this time rural America was struggling. You could see it in the number of businesses closed on Main Street in the small communities. The business leaders of our community formed an economic development group to be proactive and to stop the bleeding. I was named Chairman, which created additional pressure for the company to lead in a community transformation effort.

The "comfort zone" of the first 100 years was over not only for the company but the community

[3] Friedman, T. L. 2000. <u>The Lexus and the Olive Tree</u>. New York: Random House. P.306

as well. While I had been working on methods to improve productivity in the company in my early years as CEO there was now a high degree of urgency in implementing our future strategies. My calendar became a 24/7 effort to transform the company. Change is difficult and scary for everyone involved. Small businesses were closing, unemployment was rising, and the "anchor company" in the community for the first time in its history laid off staff. People in the community understandably were nervous. On one occasion eggs were thrown at my car. There were even threats to my security. One community leader sent a letter to our Board of Directors complaining that I was out to destroy a beautiful company and the whole community. And during the height of the stress and heavy schedule I had a mild heart attack.

*I had to cut expenses and build a group of Associates that was much more proactive in building a sustainable future.*

# CHAPTER TWO

## DOWN SIZING

We did not have the economies of scale needed to offset the rising cost of doing business. For years we had tried to increase the number of new policies written in one year to exceed 30,000 but were unsuccessful. Our experience followed the national trend - about a 2% drop in life insurance policies written each year and about a 6% increase in annuities written. Furthermore, to aggravate the problem the margins on annuities could not support our distribution system and there were ominous signs of no improvement in the foreseeable future.

For the long term good of the organization we needed to form a partnership with another company. To find the right partner for a long term fit and to prepare our Associates with the major changes that would entail would take time. Furthermore, to avoid a gradual erosion of the strength of the company, we needed to stop the hemorrhaging NOW. That is, I had to cut expenses and build a group of Associates that was much more proactive in building a sustainable future.

The company had never experienced a general lay-off or early retirement in over one hundred years. The changes we needed to make would be traumatic. Some of the terminations would involve my best friends. The trust we had worked so hard to build would suffer.

We did a number of things to help in the transition:

- At our monthly meetings with the entire staff we spelled out the problem. On a huge chart we showed the trend over the last several years of the ratio of expenses to premium income. It was approaching 14% and for the type of business we were writing it should have been less than 10%. We indicated that we were working on ways to increase premiums. We asked everyone to look for ways to cut expenses.

• We held a session for senior officers to address issues such as, "how do we rollout and communicate the change-who should communicate to whom-what should we expect-how do we react". The discussions and dialogue we had were invaluable because we could anticipate reactions and were able to deal with them promptly and constructively.

• The first step we took was to offer early retirement for those individuals over a certain age. The incentive package we offered made it attractive for about ten Associates. We did not replace them.

• Our ratio of expenses to premiums kept creeping toward 14%. We sold off minor lines of business, eliminated some functions that we felt we could do without in a crunch and expanded the responsibilities of some managers so we ended up with fewer managers, each managing more Associates. This eliminated almost 1/4 of

*There is a limit on how much you can
down size an organization without hurting
the core of its operation.*

the staff. To help the Associates terminated we offered a generous severance package-the longer the service the greater the severance-and provided professional placement services to help them in the transition.

- There is a limit on how much you can down size an organization without hurting the core of its operation.Any further cuts would have to be temporary until we found a way to increase premiums. After 3 years and cutting 1/4 of the Associates we still had not reached the 10% ratio we were striving to achieve. I'll never forget the year end budget meeting we were holding trying to determine where we could cut eight more positions. I suggested to the senior officers that we sleep on it and resolve the problem the first thing in the morning.

When I returned to my desk there was a letter from the state of Washington for a $50,000 assessment!! The states operate state Guarantee Associations so if a company licensed in the state goes bankrupt the state assesses each company licensed in the state a sufficient amount so in total the policyholders are made whole and one of the domestic companies takes over the management. In effect we were covering for some company that had for years refused to make the hard decisions. The next morning I had to announce to our senior officers that we had to cut ten positions not eight-disgusting..

We cut 10 positions picking those who had the smallest impact on achieving our objective of a 10% ratio. The Associates who remained with the company understood the issue and knew that we were willing to face the tough problem. I also felt that they knew we were trying hard to find a way to increase premiums.

# CHAPTER THREE

## MODIFYING THE "MERGER" MODEL

The easiest solution to the dilemma I faced during the "war" was to merge the company and leave town. Because of the quality and history of the company I had several unsolicited opportunities to do just that. This option may have met the needs of the policyholders, but the best interests of the hard working Associates and the community in which most of them lived demanded the exploration of alternative options. We needed to see if there was a creative solution to the future so that everyone could be a winner in the long term. Because we were one of the early companies to react to what was happening in our business I thought we might have more options.

After extensive searching for a partner I finally found what seemed to be the perfect match I was seeking. The CUNA Mutual Insurance Group sold a variety of products to Credit Unions and through Credit Unions to their members. They did not market products directly to the members of the Credit Union. Century Life had the marketing and administrative expertise to sell products directly to the members of the Credit Union. It was a niche market for Century Life. It was a good fit.

In one of the first serious merger meetings I had with the CEO of CUNA Mutual and their consultant, the consultant was describing the merits of a merger and how this would meet the needs of both companies. It apparently was obvious to him that I was dragging my feet when he said to me "Are we going too fast?" I told him "I'm not interested if we're going to use a method where the professionals who work on mergers state that the probability of meeting expectations is less than 50%. We need to be more creative".

Why was I so against a merger? There were several reasons.

- When you're trying to do the right thing for those you're trying to serve, in our case the policyholders, a 30% probability of meeting expectations is not a satisfactory odds for responsible management. As good stewards of our clients' resources we ought to be able to do better than that.

- I simply didn't want our company to be swallowed up by another. In a traditional merger one of the companies disappears and the staff of the survivor takes most of the key positions and the other company's employees are let go. The increased size of the surviving entity is intended to generate greater efficiencies and thus higher productivity. Most likely in our case we would lose most of our Associates and the operations would probably have been moved out of town. Two things worth preserving would be lost first, a dedicated staff that as a unit had a capacity to deliver one of the better product values available; and second, a significant economic base for the community.

- A merger tends to be "event" driven meaning that on a certain day the operations would

*You can improve the chance of success of the venture by involving Associates throughout the organization in the end result.*

cease in the smaller company. Obviously it is very traumatic to your greatest asset, the loyal men and women who have given so much to the company.

• In addition, the merger process tends to be driven from the "top down". I believe you can improve the chance of success of the venture by involving Associates throughout the organization in the end result.

I was determined to not even use the word merger. We needed to think outside the box. I was adamant in using language and any other tools that would help us think in new ways. We named the process a PERMANENT AFFILIATION.

The concept of merger is so inborn in our culture that I probably corrected individuals no fewer than a hundred times-"It is not a merger". In fact five years after completing the very successful collaborative effort, I received a cryptic note on a Christmas card from a local businessman, which simply said, "I still say it was a merger"!

The objective was to create a sustainable, more productive joint effort by building synergistically on the strengths of each organization. The essential difference compared to a merger was that the legal entity of the smaller company remained intact. While the  name has been changed for business reasons, the financials of each entity remain separate and are reported to the state regulators as such.

What impact did the Permanent Affiliation have on our Associates?  The larger company had a staff of over 3,000 functioning as  a group operation with sales and billing, for example, done through the credit unions to the member. Our staff was fewer than 300 with marketing and administrative expertise in individual direct sales to the member. I was asked more than once, "Are you sure you know what you're doing? They will chew you up and spit you out". It never happened. For many years CUNA Mutual had tried to provide for their market place the type of products and services we provided on an individual basis to supplement their operations but had not been successful.

Therefore they were as interested as we in doing what was right for the policyholders.

As mentioned earlier, we had down sized by 1/4 before I found a solution that would generate more revenue. During this process we lost only one Associate who voluntarily chose an opportunity with another company. We broadened our distribution system and number of representatives.

Currently over eighty field and home office Associates have moved into positions in the larger company and those that remained have assumed broader assignments in the smaller company. The employment base in the smaller company increased to nearly 800 from the original 300 people and is still growing.

Additional building space and new roads are needed to accommodate the growth, which of course will necessitate additional support services in the community for the increased staff. In effect the community "anchor" company has become even stronger with a sustainable future and in turn

*The change in the company is dramatic and impressive.*

the community has benefited. On a recent trip I drove through the community again after being gone for almost ten years. It was heartening to see the growth-a new highway system, a 25% growth in the student population of the local college from its low point, over 30 million dollars of new construction at the college, a number of new home development areas, an additional golf course, added motels and businesses, a new up to date library and plans for an expansion in the insurance office to consolidate the functions which have grown into four separate buildings.

The net change in the company is dramatic and impressive.

- Because we are now in a target market the cost of distribution per unit sale decreased significantly.

- The administration of the individual business previously written by the larger company plus a dramatic increase in business written under additional distribution systems meant improved productivity gains - a greater volume of business was being processed within the same facility with proportionately less staff.

• A three-fold increase in assets is now managed by one staff instead of two.

• Integration of functions has saved millions of dollars.

• Applications for policies increased from under 30,000 per year to nearly a million per year.

I remember the time some of our professional underwriters returned from a National Underwriters meeting. The "hallway" gossip at the meeting was how most of the companies were looking for ways to reassign their professional underwriters because business was down. We were now looking for ways to employ more because of the increase in business!

*These types of managers are not well suited for an environment which requires nonincremental change as they often become paralyzed by their need for extensive analysis and their desire for support within an organizational structure that is no longer viable.*

# CHAPTER FOUR

## LEADERSHIP SKILLS NEEDED TO MAKE THE TRANSITION

The leadership skills required to function efficiently during the "comfort zone" were different than those required to function effectively in the "war zone".

In the "comfort zone" the primary emphasis was on maintaining a "status quo" management style with the main emphasis on improving organizational efficiency. Managers in this role tend to think of change in incremental terms. These types of managers are not well suited for an environment which requires nonincremental change as they often become paralyzed by their need for extensive analysis and their desire for support within an organizational structure that is no longer viable. Functioning in the "war zone" can be extremely frustrating and debilitating for these managers.

In the "war zone" the manager must always be looking for new ways to do things - past practices are not that important. The need for innovative, quick decisions means the manager must be willing to be held more accountable for results.

I frequently have used basketball to think of the difference in management styles needed in the Comfort Zone versus the War Zone. Basketball players today are much taller on average than they were when I played. To make it more challenging the Comfort Zone manager would consider raising the height of the basket. The War Zone manager would consider eliminating the basket and changing the game and the rules of how you score. Clearly different mind sets.

The balance of this Chapter will focus on the different management issues we addressed during the "comfort" and "war" periods.

## LEADERSHIP DURING THE COMFORT ZONE

During my early years with the company I worked hard to build a level of trust with Associates. For example, in the early 70s before I was named CEO there was an attempt by the Associates to organize a union to represent them in negotiations with management. The Board of Directors asked me to represent management and through that process I worked closely with the head of Human Resources and managers to understand their grievances.

When I became CEO I was always available to deal with human relations problems. Regularly we conducted attitude surveys, which measured the level of trust between Associates and management and took corrective action where necessary. After several years of working at this process the outside source we used to conduct the surveys indicated that the trust level was one of the highest they had encountered.

To get an outside perspective of the company I asked a consultant friend of mine who had been in the business for many years and worked with many different insurance companies to describe in his words the profile and culture of our company as he saw it currently. He used terms like resistant to change, methodical, reactive, paralyzed with analysis, paternalistic, a typical mutual company but also parochial.

I had an independent survey done of regional businesses and received the same statements in describing the company. In addition, I had a number of management audits done internally so I would have a good handle on not only the outside perspective, but the inside one as well.

## LEADERSHIP IN THE WAR ZONE

We had made progressive changes during the Comfort Zone but the fact remained that we were still simply another mutual insurance company among many-- strong but small among the giants and no market niche. I remember the time one of my favorite field managers from Texas said to me, "Pres why can't we operate like we did in the past? Let's go back to the good old days". But it would never happen anymore than there would be a resurrection of the small family farms in America.

*We needed to cut our cost of operations--we need-ed a niche--we needed to be more proactive--we needed to have a crisp clear vision of where we were headed-we needed to have our Associates committed to a vision with a  passion.*

We needed to cut our cost of operations--we needed a niche--we needed to be more proactive-we needed to have a crisp clear vision of where we were headed-we needed to have our Associates committed to a vision with a passion.

We wanted to build a sustainable future where our humanitarian interest and absolute integrity were very evident, that is, transparent to everyone with whom we did business. I asked myself, "What characteristics of leadership are needed to lead an organization through an extensive transformation"? "What skills do I have to hone to the point of being redundant in order to do our very best"?

We could not fail in this effort if the company was to survive.

After a considerable amount of reading and listening to a number of experts on the subject I came up with the following leadership skills and attributes I would need:
    • A capacity to establish a clear vision for the future.

- The ability to be able to effectively communicate that vision.
- A very apparent willingness to listen to others when shaping a vision.
- The tenacity of a bulldog to hold on to the vision.
- A selfless attitude with minimal ego needs.

I shared this information with our Board of Directors and told them that these attributes must apply to all of our managers and in particular to me. At the end of every Board meeting when they would hold their executive session I suggested the first agenda item should be:Do we continue to retain Irv as CEO? Can he continue to be the catalyst for change to transform the company into a viable business for the next century? The stakes were high. We could not fail.

Until you're faced with adversity you don't know if you're up to the task. But at the same time the way you deal with adversity can be a life giving experience. I decided to focus on the following:

- Find as compassionate a way as possible to down size the company to stop the eroding of the company's financial underpinnings.

- Find a partner where it would be in the best interest of both companies to work together to build a sustainable future into the 21st century.

- Develop a very deliberate process so that the vision for the future became the passion for every Associate.

- Hire a coach to make sure I stuck to the agenda as I've outlined. Create an innovative Human Resource strategy to make the most of the talent in the organization.

- Focus on our performance appraisal discipline with renewed effort at the corporate, department and individual level in order to improve the climate for performance in the company.

I traveled to Philadelphia, the location of a consulting company that was developing an instrument to measure organizational productivity, to pore over the results of the surveys where we were one of the participants. Most importantly, I reviewed my plans to change the climate including personnel changes where necessary with the consultants. We discussed my plans to implement change in great detail, going back and forth, until I felt comfortable with the plan. It was extremely helpful in this process to have the independent opinion of the consultants to continually challenge my options and conclusions. It gave me a sense of being well prepared for any course of action I took.

To keep up with all of the changes that we and other insurance companies were making to adapt to the changing economic environment we held a number of meetings for virtually all level of employees including the following:

- All of our senior officers attended a seminar in Boston on the psychology of change, understanding the psychological contract between the employees and the company, and managing an organization through such a change.

- We held a 2 day seminar conducted by a guest psychologist for senior officers and their spouses on "climate for change" issues.

- Some of our junior officers attended a University course on organizational change.

- We held dinners for all of our managers and their spouses to talk about the changes and the reasons they were being made.

- We held monthly meetings for all Associates to talk about the changes and answer questions.

- At each Board meeting or committee meeting we discussed "Organizational Renewal" and what I was anticipating in the future.

We had the advantage of an early start in creating our long term strategy for not only surviving but sustaining the operation. It worked!!

*Tell me and I'll forget; show me and I may remember; involve me and I'll understand.*

*ChineseProverb*

# CHAPTER FIVE

## DEVELOPING A SHARED VISION IN THE COMPANY

The only way the PERMANENT AFFILIA-TION was going to be a success was if the Associates could understand and adopt the vision with a passion. They had to take ownership in the vision in order to achieve a successful transformation. I'm reminded of the story of Ozzie, one of our Associates.

Ozzie's responsibilities were principally jan-itorial but he also picked up visitors at the local air-port, which was 15 miles from our office. One cold winter day he picked up a visiting consultant from Philadelphia. On the way back to the office the consultant asked Ozzie, "What's new?" He expect-ed to get a report on the weather but instead Ozzie said, "Year to date our premium income is up and the expense ratio is down". The consultant was shocked and I was thrilled. The process was work-ing. People at every level of the organization were invested in helping to shape the vision and beginning to own it.

## Fundamental beliefs that would not change

Before we established our vision for the future I felt it was important to put into writing our fundamental beliefs as an organization. We spent months reviewing input from climate for performance studies and attitude surveys discussed at length in Chapter Seven. In addition, we reviewed input from personal interviews of residents in the area and industry representatives.

Our senior officers then spent several retreats and a number of meetings simplifying into a few crisp statements the fundamental beliefs that we wanted to hold into the next century. To suggest permanence to these beliefs we printed them on granite and gave one to each Associate. That piece of granite stated:

WE BELIEVE:
   • Trust is earned by treating others with dignity and respect.

• Success depends on developing the abilities of our Associates.

• Our Associates have the creative capacity to solve problems.

• Communications should be open, honest and timely.

• Performance must be measured by long term results.

<u>A three-fold strategic vision</u>

The first strategy for our long term vision for the company was to find a partner who was in a target market that would provide unlimited growth opportunities for our distribution system. With the added volume we would be able to reduce our total cost for the underwriting of new business. Second, we wanted to administer additional blocks of business currently on the books with the same plant and staff to achieve a reduction in unit costs for both companies. And third, we wanted to consolidate similar functions to reduce duplication of effort in the two companies.

There is a lot written in the literature about keeping strategy ahead of structure. Clearly the long term strategy for the two organizations was to be successful in number one, albeit the most difficult to implement. There was a natural instinct to start focusing on numbers two and three, which tend to be more structural. Not only is it easier to grasp the possible changes but the results are more immediate.

The key to success for both organizations was the joint marketing and administrative capacity of the smaller company in the larger company's market. In the long term, if this were done effectively, it would generate more improvement in productivity than the consolidation of functions.

Every time someone suggested an integration of functions I asked, "Show me how that will impact our number one strategy and our timetable for achieving it ". It was my way of keeping strategy ahead of structure so that we would maximize the long term return to the policyholders and thus sustain the Permanent Affiliation.

## We design-built the Permanent Affiliation

The process used to create the Permanent Affiliation was patterned after the process we used when we built a new home office building. In building the office we had the architect draw detailed plans for the exterior but not the interior. While the architect was drawing the interior we began the construction. The end product was done much quicker and at a lower cost.

We used a similar model to develop the affiliation. We laid out the vision of where we wanted to be in 5 years and then, within given parameters, our Associates began to implement the plan.

I remember one of our marketing managers saying to me, "I understand where you want the organization to be in 5 years but what if it doesn't work, what is your back up plan". I said, "There

*"There isn't any back up plan.  This must work!"*
*This attitude had a tremendous advantage*
*in  bringing out the creative capacity*
*of our Associates.*

isn't any back up plan. This must work!". This attitude had a tremendous advantage in bringing out the creative capacity of our Associates.

In the insurance business there has always been a willingness to share nonproprietary information. In this instance no one had done an affiliation before and so our staff could not benefit from the experience of other companies. Furthermore I had said this must work. No one ever came into my office to tell me this or that wouldn't work. They figured it out. They had to come up with a solution.

In effect the outer design was done. The internal processes were designed by those who knew the most about them. The detail of the Permanent Affiliation was being driven from the "bottom up". People throughout the organization were being listened to and empowered to come up with solutions.

Effective communications in sharing the vision

The monthly "house organ", periodic bulletin board announcements and regularly scheduled meetings were not going to be sufficient to keep

*If we were going to reach our vision it was only
going to happen through the combined effort of
all of our Associates and they needed to have
accurate and timely information.*

Associates informed when changes were happening so fast. I remember the instance when the company was making some necessary changes to the exterior. Understandably it became a matter of curiosity for the community. When people would ask our Associates what was happening they didn't have the answer. It was an illustration of how difficult it was to keep everyone informed when changes were coming so fast. I wanted our Associates to always be "in the know" and we were constantly finding new ways to do that.

If we were going to reach our vision it was only going to happen through the combined effort of all of our Associates and they needed to have accurate and timely information. They had to own the vision. Following are some of the changes we made:

- We assigned an individual the responsibility of an information guru. Information was disseminated as soon as needed in whatever format worked the best at the moment. I was always available when he needed my attention.

- We held regularly scheduled meetings to report results and actions to be taken. We broke the meetings into sufficient size to encourage questions and participation.

- In addition to my efforts to "manage by walking around" I regularly "table hopped" during coffee breaks and lunches to be available to answer questions and encourage dialogue and openness.

- Periodically we held meetings with community business leaders to keep them informed.

- Luncheon meetings were held with spouses of managers and retiree's to keep them informed.

One of the key reasons we were successful was that Associates were well informed. Because they were well informed they were in a position to contribute to the  process. They made it happen.

# CHAPTER SIX

## I NEEDED A COACH

We had made significant and progressive changes to break away from being the parochial company we had been in the past. New products were introduced, changes were made in the organizational structure, new data processing systems were introduced and changes were made in staffing. We even changed our name from Lutheran Mutual, a name adopted in 1938, to Century Life of America to better represent our marketing efforts.

But now we were in the War Zone and the rate of change was moving exponentially. This staid old company was going to have to increase the rate of change and I would have to lead the way. There would be a great deal of misunderstanding and suspicion about motives. The bridge of trust that I had worked so hard to build over the past 7 years would be stretched to the limit. It would be a lonely job and I had no one to talk to. I needed to do everything possible to avoid making cumulative mistakes. The company had to go through a total transformation and I wanted to avoid my own blind spots and prejudices.

I decided I needed a "sounding board"-- someone I could talk to-someone who would listen to my frustrations-someone who would challenge my plans and keep asking searching questions. He or she didn't have to know our business but they needed to have an extremely high threshold of curiosity and an ability to listen and provide candid feedback. I didn't expect the "sounding board" to tell me what to do. It had to be my plan. I had to take ownership and responsibility for the future. I couldn't pass the buck but I had to minimize miscues.

In my search for the right person I checked with the head of Human Resources for one of our industry organizations for some names to consider. He gave me two names that were at the top of his list-one was an Industrial Psychologist teaching at a University just 20 miles from our office!! He was well organized, disciplined in his thinking, very curious and could ask a ton of searching questions. Our relationship developed to the point where we wasted zero time on "chit chat", got right to the heart of an issue and were openly honest and frank with each other. The synergy was amazing.

I didn't realize it at the time, but there was a new concept gaining popularity in this country called "Life Coaching". It is defined as a powerful alliance designed to forward and enhance the life-long process of human learning, effectiveness, and fulfillment. In effect I had hired my own personal coach. It was the best decision I made in picking up the pace of the transformation I had started.

Our Board of Directors, while supportive, looked with a jaundiced eye at me when I said I was retaining a personal coach. True, in a sense any member of the Board could have filled the role of coach. But what I needed was someone who would be on call 24/7.

Following are some ways where I found my coach particularly helpful.

*In creating a climate for change----*

I reviewed with my coach all the changes I had made during the Comfort Zone period. We discussed ways in which decisions could be made much quicker and with even greater sensitivity to the culture. The number of meetings with managers, all Associates, the community and local newspaper were increased.

We named a communications guru to make sure we weren't missing something.

My coach would periodically sit in on some of my meetings and we would follow them up with not only a performance appraisal of how I did but discuss what we heard and how it shaped the future.

*In dealing with individual problems-*

I called my coach late one night and set up an appointment to meet him for breakfast at Happy Chef at 6 AM to discuss a plan I had for dealing with a distribution problem. Agents were telling their companies that they would keep the clients' business with the company if the company would pay to the agent some of the high early commissions. It simply wasn't fair to the client to once again incur those extra expenses. I had to find a way to protect the interest of the policyholders.

A few companies had made changes to cope with what was happening in the economy, which had a negative impact on the agents who distributed the company's products.

The situation had become critical as agents began to take the business they had written and move it to another company. In fact in a few cases it became so serious that regulators stepped in to avoid critical impairment of the company's surplus.

I was trying to work with all of the interested parties to come up with a solution that would be a win-win for the company and the distribution system. We went back and forth on the issue and at 8 AM I held a breakfast meeting (my 2nd for the day) with the Associates affected. The meeting went

People are often unreasonable, illogical, and
self-centered; forgive them anyway.

*

*

What you spend your years building, someone
could destroy overnight; build anyway.

*

*

You see, in the final analysis it is between you and
God.  It was never between you and them anyway.

From a poem by
Mother Theresa

well because I had thought through the various options and was in a position to anticipate reactions. I was well prepared.

The "egg" throwing harassment in the community, mentioned earlier, helped me to realize there were community groups outside the company interested in what we were doing. It was necessary for me to play an active public relations role, especially in a small town where suspicion and distrust could have a negative impact on the Associates and their families in ways that could affect morale within the company. This required me to delegate a number of internal responsibilities to others if I was to be the spokesperson to the community. Otherwise I ran the risk of spreading myself too thin. As a result, I shifted some of the work assignments and reduced the number of senior officers reporting to me from six to four.

The option I considered and adopted at one of our periodic brainstorming sessions was to assign one of our bright young men to the role of sweeping up after me on detail, documentation and follow up. This young man attended all of the meetings I attended. He kept a record of decisions made and who was to do what to follow up on decisions.

A special problem arose. We had a long-term associate who was considering organizing opposition to the course of action the company was taking. In the meeting with my coach I considered two options: 1) letting him go; or 2) keeping him employed by listening to his concerns and getting him involved in the solution. I took the second option. With the blessings of his manager I used him as a resource for ideas when dealing with his phase of the business. While it meant more travel for me since his office was not within the small community he became a trusted partner and his input was constructive. It worked.

One evening I called my coach to discuss with him over the phone a situation where one of the Associates was considering bolting from my attempts to affiliate with the other company. He was one of the point individuals in my plans. I needed him involved. A misunderstanding had developed over the organization of one of the functions that was to be consolidated between the two companies.

We discussed the source of the problem and the options I had to resolve it. The next morning I called for the corporate plane, which was on another mission, picked up the Associate, took him directly to the source of the problem and within a matter of hours hammered out an amicable solution. With an effective "sounding board" I had the benefit of an objective approach to the resolution of an issue and could deal with it in a deliberate, constructive manner.

My coach was also valuable in helping me address concerns of the board and the strategies used to keep them engaged and constructive. It was in discussions with my coach that I decided there was the need for a special board committee to deal with affiliation issues. As a result the Board appointed a three member ad hoc committee of the Board. Members appointed to the committee had experienced dramatic change in their own companies. The committee met between Board meetings on an "as needed" basis and in turn reported to the total Board at the Board's quarterly meeting. From the Board's perspective they were more involved in the rapid changes that were taking place and it gave me another creative resource to work with in the change process. The result was that it strengthened the Board/CEO partnership.

*In monitoring communications----*

I asked my coach to sit in on some of our senior staff meetings so that together we could improve the process. As a result I started identifying agenda items as either a "1" or '2". A "1" meant that I would identify the issue and then solicit comments. Once I felt that everyone had provided their input, I would make the decision. We simply didn't have time to function by consensus. A "2" meant that I had made a decision but they had a "need to know" for effective communications throughout the organization.

With input from my coach I developed a plan for communicating on a regular basis to Associates. To avoid misunderstanding where people were reluctant to bring up questions in large groups we had pre-communications meetings with the managers. The purpose of these meetings was to advise them as to what I would be saying. I also asked them "Tell me what I said". By listening I could massage my communications to be more effective. Also the managers had an obligation to advise Associates if there was a misunderstanding, to say, "no, this is what was said". The procedure helped the effectiveness of communications and minimized rumors.

*God has given each of you some special abilities;
be sure to use them to help each other, passing
on to others God's many kinds of blessings.*

*1 Peter 4:10.*

# CHAPTER SEVEN

## CAPITALIZING ON OUR MOST IMPORTANT ASSET: HUMAN RESOURCES

For several years prior to the Affiliation we spent significant time and energy in developing our greatest asset, our Associates. If we integrated human resources in concert with consolidating functions between the two companies we could be assured that the Affiliation would become permanent. It was like scrambling eggs. There was no way it could be unscrambled. Permanency would be accomplished. We integrated functions in the location where there was a natural employment base.

We used the following process to de-emphasize the politics of assigning Associates to a particular job and location in affiliating the two companies:

- Three members from each Board of Directors were assigned to oversee the process.

- The integrated jobs were profiled ten years into the future.

- Candidates for the integrated jobs were all given up-to-date psychological assessments.

- The CEO from the two companies, the senior human resources person from each company, the industrial psychologist who did the assessments and a senior consultant who reported to the joint Board committee reviewed each job and prioritized candidates.

- Positions were then assigned according to ability and capacity to grow into the future role. The process worked in effect like a professional sports draft.

- Once the senior positions were assigned the process was repeated throughout the organization except the newly appointed supervisor would participate in the process for his or her unit.

The Associates from the smaller company had an opportunity in the new company. We had spent years in identifying the potential capacity of each individual Associate followed by a development plan to meet that objective. The years of work put into developing the organization paid off. Associates were prepared to accept broader responsibilities.

The remainder of this chapter is devoted to the extent to which we went to improve the traditional performance appraisal process.

To survive and sustain growth on behalf of the policyholders the company had to change its profile from a parochial, paternalistic organization to a much more productive, creative company. Before the "war" it was common practice in the business to either add a new product or change the pricing in your portfolio about every two years.

*The analysis further shows that the common climate for performance elements in what I refer to as a "tightly" managed company are high drive, open management style, excellent people and effective management structure.*

During those years it was common to become paralyzed with analysis because there was no sense of urgency coming from the marketplace.

During the "war" that all changed. In this new era you had to be prepared to make portfolio changes monthly and even weekly or daily. Our "climate for performance" analysis discussed in this chapter gave us some clues to follow. Companies which stress management adaptability, performance over job security, emphasize individual accountability and good and quick service, seem to have the best climate for performance. The analysis further shows that the common climate for performance elements in what I refer to as a "tightly" managed company are high drive, open management style, excellent people and effective management structure.

During my forty seven years in business I can count on one hand the number of times that I received an effective performance appraisal. It was usually "You're doing fine. We're increasing your compensation by X dollars!" I believe that's the experience of many but we had to do much better than that to build a "tight" organization.

A thorough performance appraisal should last from two to four hours. In addition, I chose to focus on a multifaceted "tighter" approach to our performance appraisal process-at the corporate level, the department level, and the individual level. I started by monitoring my own performance as a means for demonstrating my commitment to its use as a valuable professional development tool.

*For the total company----*

A national consulting firm from Philadelphia was trying to develop an instrument which would measure the "climate for performance" of the total company. It measured such items as understanding of corporate objectives throughout the company, weak links within the company, image of the company in the market, and crispness in the decision making process. We were one of eleven companies that was asked to participate in the study. From what I understand we were the only company that followed up the study by spending a day in

Philadelphia analyzing the results.

We developed an action plan to improve the "climate for performance". Every two years we would redo the study to measure how much progress we had made compared to our previous study and what we should do next to further improve the climate for performance.

In the year in which we were not doing a climate for performance survey we did the traditional employee attitude survey.

*For the individual departments----*

A greater volume of business and different products, for instance more asset accumulation products than life insurance, meant different expertise and staffing in the future. As we considered what the company would look like ten years into the future it became clear that some departments would have to make drastic changes. By using an outside resource we did a "physical" of the department to compare the current profile of the unit to what it would have to look like in ten years. We then developed an action plan to build the unit in order to be more proactive than reactive.

*For interoffice meeting discipline----*

My coach helped us structure meetings within the office to make sure there was an advance agenda, leaders were helped in how to effectively work the agenda, and assignments were made including a follow through process.

The market place during the first one hundred years in the insurance business did not demand quick changes in products. A linear process for making product changes had evolved over those years-each department would make its contribution to the new product and pass it on to the next department. Changes might take from one to two years. All that changed with the shelf life of products during the "war" measured in months and changes in pricing measured in days. We organized a special unit to monitor projects that were critical to the organization's future and which involved interdisciplinary attention. We needed to be more responsive to the market.

*For individuals----*

I had psychological assessments completed on all individuals that were managing Associates. We also offered the service for others who wanted it. The purpose of these assessments was to help the company manage our most important asset, human resources. We tried to be more effective in determining where in the future the Associate might have the best opportunity to utilize his or her strengths in the company. If strengths were innate but not developed we followed through with a development plan to reach the Associate's objective. Assessments were updated every three years.

Some people are threatened by psychological assessments and I have been criticized for placing too much emphasis on them. The best I could do was to lead by example and point out that the instrument is just a guide and the final cut is made between the supervisor and the Associate. Before I joined the company I asked that an assessment be done on me to see if we might have a fit.

*Periodic performance appraisals are essential but probably the most effective are the ones that immediately follow an incident.*

The assessment is just one of the instruments used in helping to shape the career of an individual. What we were after as a company was to provide a climate that would encourage the Associate to stretch, to reach his or her career objective.

*Contextual performance appraisals:*

Periodic performance appraisals are essential but probably the most effective are the ones that immediately follow an incident. These, of course, should include both affirmation and corrective change. Following is an example. At one of our senior officer meetings I described an agenda item where I needed input. I asked for opinions from everyone. After the discussion, which was divided about even, I indicated the decision. "George," who had offered a different opinion, threw his papers down with an attitude which reflected obvious disgust. After the meeting I went to see him in his office and told him what I had observed and asked him what he recalled from the incident. He didn't acknowledge what happened but it never occurred again.

Performance appraisals typically tend to be generic and not specific. Contextual performance appraisals are specific because the event is timely and fresh in ones mind and much more effective and motivating.

*Monitoring my own performance*

It was important that all employees knew that the new discipline in performance appraisal applied to everyone in the organization, including me. Periodically I had my coach sit in on meetings with my senior officers to make sure they were participative, timely and productive. He didn't participate in the meeting, but after the meeting the two of us would meet and critique the session. The purpose was to give me a performance appraisal on the meeting. Associates knew I was having the follow up meeting and why.

I wrote out performance appraisals for those reporting to me and reviewed them with my coach in advance. In addition I randomly had the coach sit in the appraisal session. He didn't speak at the session but after the meeting would offer me a critique of my performance. Again the staff member knew that this process was a part of my evaluation and I was setting an example of the importance I was placing on performance appraisal throughout the organization.

# CHAPTER EIGHT

## ELEMENTS OF SUCCESS IN TIMES OF CHANGE

What I have tried to do in the text is to focus on those elements of the management process that made the difference between success and failure in the Affiliation.

While the principles discussed in the text would be of interest to any business, if the reader is considering a merger there may be advantages in the Affiliation process. The book ACHIEVING SUCCESSFUL ORGANIZATIONAL TRANS-FORMATION (ISBN:1-56720-026-5) by David A. Whitsett and Irving R. Burling gives a history of the Affiliation. The last chapter spells out the Lessons Learned from doing the Affiliation.

Those lessons were as follows:

## STRATEGIC ISSUES:

- Keep strategy ahead of structure.
- Develop a well-thought-out strategy.
- Develop a plan so that the entire organization will keep a focus on your primary strategy.

## CULTURAL ISSUES:

- Understand the difference in corporate cultures and define what type of culture you want to create.
- Develop a method to work through differences in culture.

## COMMUNICATION ISSUES:

- Plan and orchestrate communications carefully.
- Do not delay passing on information.
- Do not oversell the change.
- Do not withhold information longer than necessary.
- Do not make promises you cannot keep.
- Be acutely aware of your comments.

## TRANSFORMATION ISSUES:

- Appoint a transformation director.
- Senior management should keep hands -on during the change process.
- Clarify the role of any consultant.
- Do not use the most extreme example of your culture as your cultural change agent.
- Have a technique for counterparts in the organizations to become better acquainted.
- Involve human resource staff on the high level transition team.

## ADDITIONAL ISSUES:

- The CEO must focus on Board integration early in the process.
- Do not depend exclusively on economies of scale to ensure your future.
- Integrate the CEO positions carefully.
- Work hard at keeping your ego in perspective
- Strive to create a transparent organization.

Successfully addressing these issues was both a personal and a collective journey of leadership development for me and my Associates. While every circumstance and environment is different, there are lessons learned from our journey that can be of practical benefit to others.

Even when the ominous signs of the future are understood there is a decided reluctance to do what eventually must be done for a variety of reasons -it's hard, the uncertainty of the end result, resistance from their Board, loss of control, too much change ….the challenges are almost limitless.

To use the analogy of Noah -its now raining and the tide is rising and many haven't yet started

*"You will find yourself by losing yourself in service to others."*

building their ark!!! Instead they continue to rearrange their chairs on the deck of the Titanic!

There is a statement that can be found in the scriptures and I believe it was also Gandhi who said something like this: "You will find yourself by losing yourself in service to others". The simple answer to the success story I've shared and the ultimate result of beating the merger odds is servant leadership. If you embark on the journey using the process I've described remarkable results can be obtained. I urge you to try it. It can be very rewarding.

*Sharing the vision with Associates*

The number one key to accomplishing our goal was the attention given to our communications plan to share the vision with all Associates. We had total commitment throughout the organization that our vision would be a reality because: 1) our Associates understood the problems the company faced; 2) we went to great lengths to communicate our vision for the future; and 3) we continu-

*"People don't resist change as much as they resist being changed."*

ally communicated our progress toward that vision.

Communications were critical in bringing all Associates into the process and allowing them to develop ownership in the vision. Ownership of the process was a critical factor. This could not have been done without a very good communications plan. Furthermore as the process of change evolved it became increasingly apparent as noted by Oakley and Krug in the <u>Enlightened Leadership</u>"...that people don't resist change as much as they resist being changed"[4].

There was never any doubt in my mind that the Affiliation would be accomplished. Perhaps an analogy helps explain my sense of resolve.

I've always been fond of Boston Bull Terriers, a special kind of bulldog. I use to play tug-of-war with them with an old sock. I believe I could have walked around all day with them hanging on to that old sock until they had lost all their teeth. That's the tenacity with which we held on to the vision of our strategy. When everyone under-

[4]Oakley, E. and Krug, D.1994. <u>Enlightened Leadership</u>. New York: Simon & Schuster P.125

".......choose trust over invulnerability."

stands what you're trying to do and they're all participating in the solution your chances of success improve significantly.

## HIRING A PERSONAL COACH

Hiring a personal coach was obviously helpful in establishing a vision-- listening to all sides of an issue and communicating effectively where we were headed as an organization. Not many stones were left unturned.

One of the frequent reasons given for the failure of mergers is the personal agenda or the ego needs of the CEO. If you make an honest personal assessment of your ego needs and conclude that they are very important, a coach is a must. An open and honest psychological contract with a personal coach can mitigate against letting ego get in the way of meeting the needs of the total organization. The relationship with the coach should be very confidential, direct and honest with no holds barred. As Patrick Lencioni stated in his book <u>The Five Temptations of a CEO</u> "choose trust over invulnerability".[5]

[5] Lencioni, P. M. 1998. <u>The Five Temptations of a CEO</u>. San Francisco, CA. Jossey-Bass P.119

A number of years ago I was Chair of the Board of Regents of a college. It was during the time when demographic trends were hurting college enrollment. There was high turnover in the CEOs of colleges. It was very obvious that those CEOs who instinctively made it a practice to solicit input from any source they could tap were surviving the traumatic changes that were occurring. We all have personal blind spots we need to avoid when changes are dramatic. A coach can alert one to those spots.

A coach can also help in pushing the CEO to the point where the vision is clear and the communications of the vision much more crisp. Being alert to how communications will be heard is extremely important.

Two references on coaching to consider are <u>Executive Coaching</u> by Mary Beth O'Neill and <u>Enlightened Leadership</u> by Ed Oakley and Doug Krug.

## FOCUSING ON PERFORMANCE APPRAISAL

Through crisp accountability standards for the corporation, the departments, and individuals we were going to be a "tighter" organization-much more creative, proactive and accountable for results. Developing a "tighter" organization inherently means the company mission evolves with a greater sense of urgency. I've often said that as the organization matured there was no way I could look at the future of the company through "rose colored glasses", that is, gloss over the trouble spots in the future and convey a very rosy picture. They wouldn't have let me get away with it. The culture of the company changed.

I wish every business leader would consider the merits of broadening and intensifying their company performance appraisal system. The climate for performance surveys, the attitude surveys, the department "physicals", reviewing individual performance appraisals with the industrial psychologist, individual development plans and my visibility in the process paid off in the end. The invento-

*Be humble and gentle. Be patient with each other,
making allowance for each other's faults
because of your love.*

*Ephesians 4:2*

ry of human resources indicated that individual development plans resulted in untapped potential. If we hadn't used it through the affiliation process the company would very likely have lost a very valuable resource.

## CAPITALIZING ON YOUR HUMAN RESOURCES

If one is sincere about sustaining the organization the first priority should be to develop and build human resources. It is the most important asset of any organization. Two examples of how I tried to nurture this asset follow.

When we started to change the culture of the company there would inevitably arise misunderstanding among Associates. I tried to explain that there are very few people in this world who wake up in the morning with the attitude of "I'll get so and so today". When there is a difference of opinion, assume good intentions -start to resolve the issue by assuming there is a misunderstanding. Anytime we saw someone consciously do this we would give them an "AGI" (assume good intentions) saying well done. This practice was particularly helpful when we were consolidating two companies with their different cultures.

I always tried to know not only all Associates by their first name but also their spouses. I'll always remember the 100th anniversary convention we held where approximately six hundred home office and field Associates and their spouses were in attendance. It was quite a challenge. Some Associates would try to confuse me by coming up to me with some one else's spouse!

The impartial manner in which future leadership was selected preserved the asset we had worked so hard to nurture. When I retired I was asked if I would consider the traditional role of "consulting". I said, "No, the Associates in place are very capable of carrying on the mission. I've done everything I can do, don't feel you need to call me, I'll call you".

## PERMANENT AFFILIATION VERSUS MERGER

The concept of permanent affiliation versus

merger could have advantages in any consolidation. For us the bottom line was that we could keep our most important asset, our Human Resources, intact and we could utilize the plant we had in a location where there was an excellent employment base. By removing the shackles of what everyone else had done for years we were able to create our own future.

## RADICAL CHANGE AS ADAPTIVE WORK

No matter how you cut it the decision to down size is a painful process. It is widely recognized that one of the challenges of leadership is to avoid taking the path of least resistance by choosing what will be popular in the short-term over long-term accountability. In our case we down-sized for the long-term benefit of the owners, the clients.

This takes authentic leadership which, in the words of Ronald Heifetz, requires "adaptive work." "Adaptive work consists of the learning required to address conflicts in the values people hold, or to diminish the gap between the values people stand for and the reality they face. Adaptive work requires a change in values, beliefs, or behavior." (Leadership Without Easy Answers, p.22) It was only through the willingness of all Associates to engage in adaptive work that we were able to survive as an organization.

## FINALE

There is extensive material written regarding the impact that different cultures have on a merger. It does not have to be a negative experience. I believe that through the joint effort of the two companies we were able to build a blended culture. Years of building a tight team in the smaller company meant that it could be a contributor to the blended culture and in effect the sum of the two ended up better than either one alone.

The Affiliation journey was long and arduous. But nothing really worthwhile is ever easy. The blood, sweat and tears are now past history but there are two stories that I will never forget.

By design the Board of Directors was a tough minded but fair group of individuals. They were not a "rubber stamp" group. They represented the policyholders and took their responsibilities seriously. I was being innovative and they of course were concerned. As my thinking evolved on the unique approach to consolidate two companies I became more articulate as to the course of action we should take. When I laid my plans out one of the more vocal Board members asked to meet me and in some very colorful language said "......I never dreamed this was what you had in mind"! Several years later he said "There are two moments in history than I"ll never forget- When Neil Armstrong stepped on the moon and when we consolidated these two companies- I never thought it would happen".

The second story is about the Associates. They had concerns of course, but they "hung in there" and made it happen. On December 8th 1989 I received a touching letter signed by all 300 Associates, which I put in a glass stand so I can read all the signatures on both sides of the letter.

Following is that letter in its entirety:

Dear Irv,

1989 has been an exciting and historic year for the company. It has been a year when a new direction has been set for our Company, and this new direction holds the promise of continued success for many, many years in the future.

These accomplishments have not come without struggle, pain, and intense effort. No one in our organization has felt this more directly than you personally. The long hours, the continuous travel, and your split home between two locations have not made life easy for you.

You came into the insurance industry when it was a relatively calm, stable, predictable business. Now, in the later years of your career, it has become difficult and chaotic. Many of your peers in other companies have apparently decided to wait out the storm until their retirement, leaving the problem solving to those left behind. You have not. Even though you have earned the right to relax and enjoy your accomplishments, you knew that the company needs more than that if it is to survive.

We thank you for your tireless visionary leadership. Today all of our associates will receive their Productivity Sharing bonuses. It would be nice if we could present you a bonus check equal to the value of your efforts, but no company could afford that. Instead, we give you our thanks, and our pledge of support to make your dreams a reality.

Thanks for a good year.
All of the Company Associates

Through misty eyes I've reread that letter many times. That letter alone made all of the hard work, difficult decisions, personal growth, perspiration.....worth it. Making a difference in the lives of those people and generations to come was what it was all about.

## ABOUT THE AUTHOR

Irving Burling is a Fellow of the Society of Actuaries. Since retiring as President and Chief Executive Officer of Century Companies of America he has coached senior executives facing a transformation of their own companies. In addition he has coached individuals regarding career changes. His previous book was <u>Achieving Organizational Transformation</u> (Quorum Books 1996).

"Win Without Greed" is available at special quantity discounts for bulk purchases for sales promotions, premiums, employee giveaways, fund-raising, or educational use.

To learn more or to order more copies of this book please visit:

**www.IrvingBurling.com**

or write:

**Burling Publishing**
P.O. Box 1228
Chandler, AZ 85244-1228

# STEPS I CAN TAKE TO APPLY THIS BOOK
## TO MY WORK OR LIFE

_____

_____

_____

_____

_____

_____

_____

_____

_____

_____

_____

_____

_____

_____

_____

_____

_____

_____

_____

_____

_____

_____

_____

_____

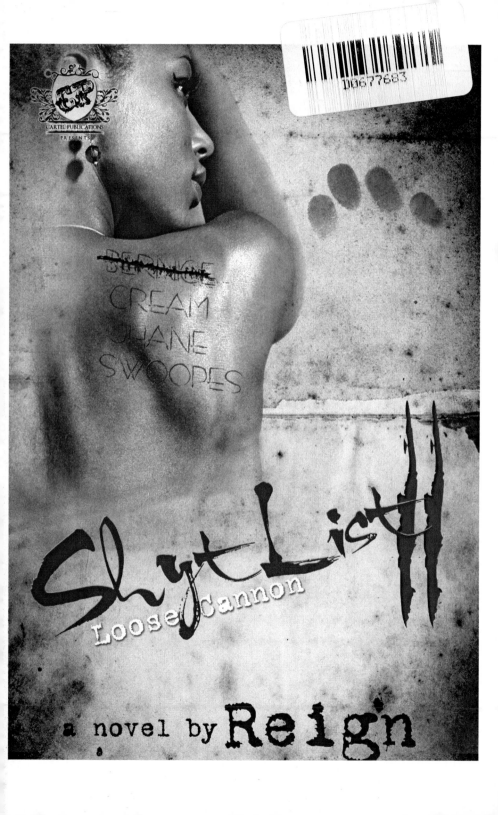

CARTEL PUBLICATIONS

PRESENTS

BERNICE
CREAM
JHANE
SWOOPES

# Shyt List II
## Loose Cannon

a novel by **Reign**

Library of Congress Control Number 2009926656
ISBN: 0-9794931-8-8
ISBN 13: 978-0-9794931-8-8
Cover Design: Davida Baldwin www.oddballdsgn.com
Editor: Advance Editing Services
Graphics: Davida Baldwin
Typesetting: Davida Baldwin

First Edition
**Printed in the United States of America**

# Dedication

This book is dedicated to my fans of the Shyt List movement who are just as nasty and crazy as me.

Thanks for opening your minds to something new in urban hip hop literature.

I hope you enjoy this one too!

theauthorreigns@yahoo.com

What up Fam!

Thanks for stopping thru and lettin' me bend ya ear. First, I gotta kick it off by sayin' thank you to all our loyal Cartel fans. Ya'll been side by side wit' us since the birth of "The Cartel Publications" and we see you still wit' us. That's love!! We really appreciate how you ride for us. Thank you for the words of encouragement and all the support you send. We continue and will always continue to put out dem bangers for you.

Now, on to the book at hand, "Shyt List 2", Yvonna's psycho ass! Well, if you didn't get enough of her wild stunts in the first one, she's back and bolder than ever. Shawty got another list and won't rest until she deals wit' everybody on it. If you thought Yvonna was out of control before, wait 'til you see what she up to now!! As always, in every Cartel Publications novel, we have to give love and recognition to our peers in the book game who are doin' it big and this is no exception. Please show love to:

*"Ashley & Jaquavis"*

Author's of, "Dirty Money"; "Diary of a Street Diva"; "The Trophy Wife"; and the already street certified, "The Cartel" These two literary geniuses are on the rise and we had to take time out to let 'em know we see their shine! Much love!!

Aight now, get some grub, get a drink, lock your doors and get comfortable, cuz one of the most anticipated sequels of the century is in the palm of your hands. Enjoy!!!

Charisse Washington
VP, The Cartel Publications
www.thecartelpublications.com
www.twitter.com/cartelbooks
www.myspace.com/thecartelpublications

P.S. Don't forget to slide down to The Cartel Café' & Books, the sexiest bookstore in the DMV (DC, MD & VA). The address is: 5011 B Indian Head Hwy, Oxon Hill, MD 20745.

# Prologue

Yvonna looked at her nude body in the full-length mirror on the bathroom door. She examined herself as she did many times before.

"Who am I?"

That question wasn't about the curves in her hips or how her breasts were still as perky as they were months after cosmetic surgery. The question was about her mental stability and why it always seemed that everything, and everyone she loved for one reason or another could never love her back.

She turned around and stared at Dave's body on the bed through the open doorway. A single tear fell down her face as she realized a love lost. The glossy blood from his throat dripped out of his body and fell against the wooden floor.

She loved him with the kind of love she had when she played with a brand new doll on Christmas day as a child. This was before her father raped her stealing any innocence or understanding she had of life. All she wanted was love. Yet a part of her, the part she called Gabriella, loved nothing more than to cause destruction to those who crossed her path. Gabriella was how she protected her feelings.

As the steam from the running shower filled the bathroom, and covered the mirror she smoothed it off with her left hand. Another tear fell down her cheek as she readied herself for what she was about to do. Kill again. Feeling extreme contempt caused Gabriella to appear behind her wearing a one-piece red tight dress.

She placed a hand on her shoulder and whispered in her ear.

1

"Think of it this way, once they're gone, you'll be happy. Isn't that what you want?"

"Yes." She nodded.

"Good." Gabriella kissed her cheek. She looks just like Taraji P. Henson from the movie *"Baby Boy"*. "Now do it. Get mad. And get even. Let's finish what you started."

Yvonna wiped the onerous tear off of her face and grabbed the knife off of the edge of the white porcelain sink.

With revenge and malice overflowing, she carved the names of the people she hated most in the flesh of her right shoulder. Although the blade tore through her soft skin, she didn't flinch. The pain was pleasurable as she watched the names of the people she despised appear with oozing blood. When she was done she wiped the red fluid off her skin with her free hand and smiled.

*Bernice*
*Cream*
*Jhane*
*Swoopes*

Yvonna was beyond crazy.

Yvonna was beyond mad.

Hate consumed her so much that at times, it was difficult to breathe. And with Gabriella being unleashed, it was impossible for her to be controlled.

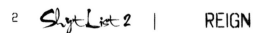

# CATCH A CO-CONSPIRATOR BY HER TOE

Yvonna and Gabriella stood quietly backstage as they watched the middle school children act out a scene from a play they wrote called, *A Midwinter Night Scream*. Colorful costumes dressed the floor, empty chairs and equipment as they ran from the stage to the back to prepare for each scene.

Like a snake waiting to attack *they* remain still. Their eyes are fixated on two children and nothing or nobody will stand in their way. They had to get them.

"Hi, I'm Mrs. Princely. Can I help you?" asks a beautiful black woman with soft curly shoulder length hair. Her face stern when she approaches Yvonna from behind.

"No, I'm just watching my niece. Isn't she beautiful?" Yvonna looks at the stage at no child in particular.

The woman's face softens immediately. After all, she looks nothing like your average abductor. In fact, she looks stylish in her dark blue custom made jeans and red leather jacket. Her hair is styled in her trademark short spiky cut. Just the way she likes it.

"Oh…which one is yours?" she smiles looking upon the stage with Yvonna as the children sing a wretched ballad.

Yvonna doesn't have an answer for the nosey bitch and she wishes she just leave her the fuck alone. She doesn't.

"Tell the bitch her name is Lil Reecy or some shit!" Gabriella yells from the sidelines wearing an all red leather jumper by Baby Phat. "Make somethin' up! Think on your feet! Haven't I taught you anything?"

"Be quiet! You makin' a scene and shit!" Yvonna tells her.

"Are you okay?" the woman asks.

"Oh…uh…yeah."

She scrutinizes her. "Well…who are you talking to?"

"No one. Just had an outburst. That's it."

Yvonna had worked so hard to control Gabriella but nothing worked. She was still convinced that Gabriella was real, just that people couldn't see her.

"If you say so. Well, which one is your niece?"

Yvonna scans the crowd of brats and picks the homeliest looking one she can find. Truth be told, not a one of them looked like they'd seen any parts of a tub, soap or water, ever.

"That one right there?" She points at the girl with pink barrettes in her hair and a bright yellow sunshine costume. "She's my niece."

"Who? Tabitha?" Yvonna can tell by the woman's expression that she could not imagine a child so afflicted being related to her in any form or fashion.

"You just had to pick *Snot-Nosed-Nancy*, didn't you?" Gabriella laughs. "Don't be surprised if she don't believe you now."

Yvonna ignores her and says, "Yes. She's my niece. I just got back in town and wanted to surprise her. So when I found out at the last minute about the play, I ran over here. I wanted to be the first person she hugs when she steps off stage."

"Wow! Oh…uh…I can't wait to see the look on her face," the woman beams. "No one ever supports her in school. Not to say anything bad about your family."

"No worries," Yvonna reassures touching her lightly on the arm. "My sister's a hot ass mess, I know it." The woman gasps.

Yvonna ignores her reaction.

"But you should get on out of my face," Yvonna stops clears her throat and says, "I mean, you should go back out there. The kids need you."

"They're fine. I want to be here to see Tabitha's face when she sees you."

This woman was causing Yvonna's blood to boil. And if she knew what was good for her, she'd get lost before she showed up missing...permanently. Because nothing or nobody was stopping Yvonna from snatching Treyana's kids and she didn't mind covering her tracks *and* witnesses if they got in her way. She never thought deceiving Treyana's sons into leaving out the back door with her would be so difficult.

"Hurry up and get rid of her! They almost done!" Gabriella yells.

Gabriella was growing agitated so Yvonna had to think quickly. Her mind wanders and she grapples with choking the fuck out of the old ass crow or smacking her down. She decided upon smacking her until she sees a little girl holding her hands between her legs, running toward the restroom. The purple glittery shoes she wore caused a devilish idea to enter her mind.

"Excuse me," Yvonna says to the woman. "I have to go to the restroom before my niece comes out."

"No problem! I'll be waiting right here when you get back. I can't wait to see the look on her face!"

*Man this whore is about to make me unleash! Why she gotta be all in my fuckin' business?!"*

Yvonna makes her way past the children who were roaming around backstage. She sees a small bucket on the floor filled with costume jewelry for the performance. She took one look behind her to see if the woman was watching...she wasn't. A little girl who needed help changing a costume had briefly taken her attention.

So she dips inside the restroom and looks under the stalls until she saw the purple shoes the little girl was wearing. When she spots them, she goes into the stall next to her and dumps the jewelry on the floor. Afterwards, she used the bucket to scoop out some water from the commode. There was shit and piss inside but Yvonna doesn't care. She stands up on the commode and dumps the foul feces all over the little girl who screams in terror.

Yvonna's laughter prohibits her from running as fast as she wants to while she exits the restroom. She manages to calm herself down moments before approaching the woman.

"I think something's wrong with one of the children in the rest-room. I saw another little girl playing an awful joke on her. Hurry!" Yvonna appears frantic. "Go help her! Please!"

The woman drops the clipboard she's holding and runs toward the bathroom. When she leaves, Yvonna regains her focus as she watches Treyana's kids come back stage after their role. She's amazed at how cute they are with their fluffy curly hair and wide-eyed smiles. This despite the costumes they are wearing that make them look like two fruity bitches. In her opinion they didn't look like Treyana or her husband.

"You boys were wonderful!" Yvonna cheers. "I'm so proud of you."

"Who are you?" one of the twins asks. "You look familiar."

Yvonna had been around them before but not often and she was surprised they remembered. One of them was slightly taller than the other but they were still identical.

"I'm your aunt Paris! You don't remember me?" Yvonna touches her heart and appears hurt.

"No," the other one responds. "I never heard of you."

"That's awful! You really haven't heard of your aunt Paris from Texas?"

The twins look at each other again and shake their heads no.

"Don't worry about that right now. We'll have plenty of time for catch up," she smiles. "But right now I need you to come with me. Your mom wants me to take you home. We'll talk about everything on the way there."

"But momma said to never leave with a stranger," one of them says.

"A stranger?" Yvonna folds her arms and stands on her back foot. "I doubt very seriously that a stranger would be dressed as good as I am. Now are you coming or not? It don't make me no never mind." Yvonna lies.

Whether the boys knew it or not, they were leaving out of that school with her, even if she had to snatch them by their undeveloped balls.

They look at each other and then Yvonna. She knows they're examining her stylish shoes, and pretty face and she smiles. To them she doesn't look harmful and she does everything she can to conceal her pleasure. Men always become her victims.

*Little do you know, the devil has many faces.* She says to herself.

The taller one shrugs his shoulders, looks at the shorter one and replies, "Ok. Let's go."

"Great! And I brought some candy for you too. I figured you'd like it."

Like all kids do when they come into contact with sweet poison...it was lust at first sight.

# WHAT GOES AROUND HAS COME AROUND FASTER

Treyana paces the living room floor in their large four-bedroom home in Largo Maryland. Her husband Avante stands by her side consoling her. Her black hair is combed back and it falls gently in the middle of her back and her long legs glisten under the cute black cotton dress she purchased from Nordstroms earlier in the week.

"What do you mean?!!! Why wouldn't you know where the fuck my boys are?!" she yells on the phone at the play director from the middle school. "It's been over two hours! How do you lose two boys…twins at that?!" She and Avante had just gotten back and their kids were not home.

Her entire body is wet from sweat and worrying and Avante opens the window, allowing the cool midevening air to seep inside. Dust from the windowsill finds its way onto his brown slacks and black cashmere sweater and he wipes it off with his hands. Although normally the blue chiffon curtains dancing in the breeze would've cooled anyone down, it does nothing for a woman who is missing her children.

"Sit down, honey." He whispers and places his hand on the small of her back.

"I'm okay!" she shoots him an evil glare and steps away from him. He backs up but looks sternly at her and she softens her stare.

"You betta, slow your roll." He warns. "I'm not the enemy."

In her mind it was his fault. Had he not pressed her out to go to a non-refundable real estate seminar, she would've been at the play with her children.

"Mam, we really have looked everywhere."

"Stop saying that shit like it's acceptable! You don't just lose kids!"

"I'm not intending it to be acceptable. Alls I'm saying is that Mrs. Princely, the Arts teacher, will find out what happened. We're trying to reach her. She was the last person who saw them. But we know they're here so don't worry."

"Bitch, if you don't find my kids, I'ma come up to that school and smoke your white ass out!" she points her finger into the air. "Now you betta find my boys, or kill yourself before I do!" she slams the phone to the receiver.

"They're probably over Jones's house or somethin'. You know how they are with that video game. They probably just lost track of time."

She ignores him and focuses on her children's faces on the picture on the wall. They were her life and she can't imagine life without them. Five minutes later, her home phone rings and she rushes toward it and answers.

"Hello! Did you find 'em?!"

"Treyana," Yvonna says coldly. "How's the life I made for you? Is it better than the piece of shit you had before?"

Treyana drops the phone and covers her mouth. Fear surges from the top of her head to the bottom of her feet.

"What is it baby?" he asks after picking up the phone. Treyana doesn't respond. "Who is this?!" he yells into the handset. "Who is this?"

Silence.

Treyana already knowing the drill musters up enough courage to take the handset from Avante.

"Baby, what's going on?" he asks again after releasing the phone to her possession.

"I...I...got it," she stutters. "H...hello?"

"Bitch, don't do that again. Do I make myself clear?"

"Yes."

"Great!" she says as if she'd just heard great news. "Now that we have an understanding let me begin. I have your boys."

Treyana sobs heavily and doubles over.

"What's wrong, baby?! Who the fuck is that? Talk to me!" He demands seeing his wife's condition.

"Don't say a word to that faggy, just listen to me."

"O…okay." She stands up straight and leans against a wall.

"As you can see you're touchable and that means I can get to you in and everywhere you are. I'll go through hell to fuck you. Always remember that."

Heavy breaths cause her chest to rise and fall hard. "What do you want?"

"What have I always wanted? Revenge."

"But I didn't do anything to you."

"You didn't do anything *for* me either, bitch! We had an agreement and you left me high and dry."

"You need help," she whimpers.

"Treyana…I'm beyond help."

Silence.

"Now…I'm going to return your kids to you on one condition."
"What's?!!!!!!!"

"I want you to help me finish what *we* started."

"How?"

"We're going to get back at all those who fucked with me. That's all you need to know for now. Anyway I don't have all the details. I'm better when I work things out as I go along," she giggles.

"Why aren't you happy? You're married now."

"Bitch, fuck that shit! I'm not playin' with you! You talking about marriage when that life you have is courtesy of me. Cleaning that fishy pussy ain't all I showed you how to do. Your entire swagger belongs to me. And as easily as I gave you back your life, I can take it away."

Although she already knew the answer she says, "And if I don't?"

"What do you think Treyana? Look at how you feel right now. Imagine if the feeling of losing your children was permanent."

"I'll kill you if you hurt them!"

Yvonna laughs and says, "Bitch, you sound like a fool! I got nine lives so the question you should be asking yourself is how many sons you got. I got away with murder…remember? They think I'm certified. If I get the right doctor I can kill your entire family and be out in two years. So do you really want it with me? You think you up for it? If you are, let's get it in."

"What do I have to do?" Treyana whines.

"That's my baby," Yvonna cheers. "Get some rest now, suga. Besides, you've been through a lot tonight. I'll call you later with the details."

"And what about my boys?!"

"Listen at you sounding like a concerned mother. Don't worry…the two little drunk bastards are lying on your front porch. I dropped them off right before I called you. And check out what I put on their backs. You'll love it!"

"What did you do?!! Why did you give my children alcohol?"

"Girl, please! The way they tossed that vodka back, it was not their first time. I just left a little something to remind you about our arrangement. I trust you won't forget this time."

Treyana rushes to the door and sees her two boys passed out. Avante walks around her. "What the fuck is going on? What happened to my sons?" He picks up one of the twins and she picks up the other. They were groggy and reek of liquor. "Let's get them inside," he leaves her alone.

Treyana remains outside for moment. She scans the street from her porch looking for Yvonna and she sees her sitting in a blue Chrysler 300. A black man with a baldhead was in the driver's seat. Yvonna winks at her and they pull off.

She lifts her son's shirt and examines his back, afterward she bawls uncontrollably. There on his skin was a tattoo that read, *'Don't Get On My Shyt List Again'*.

Yvonna paid a drug-addicted tattooist to tattoo children. And believe it or not, he was easy to find. Secretly Treyana always knew she'd resurface, but she always hoped her fury would pass her by. It didn't.

11

# HOLLYHOOD

The wind moves the leaves on the large oak trees in front of Yvonna's house. Dave's silver Suburban is parked in the driveway and the banner 'Just Married' is still hanging from the bumper.

Yvonna looks out of the window of the black Honda Accord rental car she purchased using Dave's credit card. Her eyes droop and a wave of nausea overcomes her. *What if he was the one? What if I killed the one for me?*

Had it not been for the desire to wear her high fashion clothes, and the cash he had stashed in the house, she wouldn't be anywhere near her house.

Before she get's out, she checks her surroundings. Although she killed him in Jamaica, and no one knew they were there, she was still worried that the murder would catch up with her soon. She wiped her fingerprints clean from the villa and left the torn piece of paper with the telephone number of the weed connect, in Dave's handwriting, next to his body along with the weed. She wanted it to look like a set-up and because Americans were killed all the time there anyway, she hoped it would be believable.

Wanting to get everything over with, Yvonna rushes up the driveway, snatches the banner down and jogs up the stairs and into the house. Once inside, she ransacks the house looking for money, grabbing her favorite clothes along the way. She was on her way back out when she hears his phone rang and the voicemail answers.

"Dave, it's Penny. I...I know yous not there. I...I hope things are okay with you. Please, call me. I'm worried. And tell Yvonna I asked 'bout her. Bye, honey."

Yvonna is shocked that she cared enough to ask about her. But just like Penny was calling, she knew it wouldn't be long before people reported him as missing. Dave didn't have a lot of family but he was active at the non-profit organization he started called, *Each One Teach One.*

She grabs the fifty thousand dollars in cash Dave has under the bed. Although he made honest money, he still didn't trust putting all of it in a bank. Once a hustler always a hustler. She was on her way out the door when someone knocks. Her heart pounds in her chest and her pressure rises.

"Fuck! I knew it!" she says pacing the floor. "They found out I killed him and they gonna try and take me away. I'm not going away."

"Calm down," Gabriella appears in red shorts and a white tank top. "It might not be that serious."

Yvonna tries to lower her heart rate but it doesn't work.

"Just get the door." Gabriella persists.

"What if it's the cops?"

"The door, Yvonna." She points.

Yvonna takes a deep breath, walks to the door and opens it. When she does, she sees a white man and a white woman outside. And there was a stretch black limousine waiting on them at the curb.

"Well if they cops they sure don't look like it," Gabriella says.

"What do you want?" Yvonna asks ignoring her.

"May we come in?" His short spiky red hair, looked messy but neat, a style she knew he worked purposefully.

Yvonna also takes notice to his cinema navy *Modern Amusement* button down shirt and his blue *Acne* jeans. "What the fuck do you want?"

They look at one another and flip through their pads. "You're Yvonna Harris right?"

She slams the door in their faces and gathers up all her things and throws them on the couch. She figures they're probably reporters trying to get her story again. Almost everyday she was at Green Meadows, a reporter from one paper or another attempted to get in contact with her. She wasn't interested then and she wasn't interested now. She didn't have time for bullshit.

Grabbing her things in her arms, she opens the door and they're still there.

"Why the fuck are ya'll still here? I'm busy!" they glance at the pile of clothes she has in her arms.

"Yvonna, this won't be long. I'm Tim Spicer and this is Mora Flasher." Mora looks like Cameron Diaz except her hair is brown and shoulder length. "We're with 20th Century Fox and we'd like to talk with you about your story."

"My story?" Yvonna was now curious. "What could a movie company want with my story?"

"Well, Ms. Harris. We've been following your case for some time now and we are willing to offer you a substantial amount of money for the rights to your story."

Technically all they had to do was check the court records. But they'd been doing movies long enough to know that a story was made better if the person who's story is being told participates. "We'll work overtime to be sure you're depicted exactly the way you want to be. People like you are rare. And people want to know what makes you tick," Mora says.

A sinister smirk came across Yvonna's face. "So, you want me to tell people how crazy I am?"

"No. We don't think you're crazy," Mora interjected. "We think you're unique and we want to hear it from you. We want everybody to see what you go through. This is your chance to give your side of the story. Isn't that what you want?"

"What? What did you say?" Yvonna's eyes overlook them as she talks. "Kill them? But why? They only want my story." Mora and Tim are filled with fear as they turn around and see no one behind them. "But if I kill them how will we dispose of the bodies?" She pauses. "Oh, we're going to eat them. Well we've never done that before."

"Ms. Harris, we see you are busy. We'll leave you alone. Have a good day."

They run to the car without looking back and Yvonna grips her stomach from laughing so hard. She didn't want the attention they brought anywhere near her. The more chaos the harder it would be to carry her plans out and she could not have that. And if they did become a problem, she had all intentions of making them go away.

# ALL IN YOUR MIND

The doctor's office was as drab as any of the other's Yvonna had seen since she'd been diagnosed as insane. As a part of her release program, Yvonna had to attend regular sessions at the Psychiatric Institute of Washington in DC. And Jona Maxwell, her psychiatrist in the Intensive Outpatient Program, believed from the day her case file came across her desk that Yvonna was far from healed and she cursed the officials who pronounced her sane.

Yvonna sat opposite of the psychiatrists' desk in a red plastic chair. She looked sexy in the one-piece blue, pink and green silk Chemise Tie-Back dress with her pink Versace pumps. And because she wasn't wearing any panties, one slow cross of the legs would reveal her Brazilian waxed pussy.

"So how's life?" Jona asks as Yvonna thumbs through the keys on her cell phone. She was totally uninterested in the session and Jona for that matter.

"I wouldn't even answer that bitch if I was you," Gabriella says as she stands next to her wearing a tight red cat suit large black shades and a pair of high heel laced black leather boots. Yvonna looks to her left in Gabriella's direction with frustration. She was sick of her talking in public and had warned her against outbursts in doctor's offices. "You betta watch that attitude and that expression," she laughs pointing at Jona. "You're going to make that bitch think you're *really* crazy."

Yvonna remembers where she is and softens her scowl before looking at the doctor. One check on her chart and Yvonna could be readmitted for good. There was only one problem, Jona tried to get her recommitted before but each time her supervisors examined Yvonna, she was overruled. They decided every time that she was sane.

"Are you okay?"

"Why wouldn't I be?" Yvonna asks her calmly, a light smile following. "Do I look okay to you?"

"Looks are deceiving."

"Are they?" Yvonna giggles in a condescending tone.

"Why do you say that?"

"If looks are deceiving, I wonder what they say about you."

"I'm not under psychiatric care, Yvonna. You are."

"What do you want from me? I'm here ain't I? I've never missed an appointment. So what's the problem?"

"I want to know if you're seeing people...again."

"Bitch, is you seein' people?" Gabriella yells. She's so loud that in Yvonna's mind, Jona *had* to hear her.

"Yvonna, did you hear me? Are you seeing people or not?"

"Jona, I haven't had a problem since I was released. Your facility said I was sane, so I must be sane. Now if you're done with me, I'd like to go."

Yvonna grabs her large blue Gucci bag off the floor and is preparing to leave until Jona says, "Sit your ass down before I put something on this chart that will make any hopes of a normal life outside of this facility impossible."

Yvonna stops, struts back toward her seat opposite of Jona and opens her legs so wide you would've thought she was preparing to get a pap smear.

Jona's facial expression turns from anger to disgust. "Yvonna, close your legs! That's terrible."

"Jona, its just pussy. I mean...I am sitting down. That is what you wanted isn't it?"

"You shouldn't walk around like that, Yvonna."

She laughs, "Like what? Without panties?" Yvonna keeps her legs open. "Jona...Jona...Jona. You must be interested in me or something."

"You wish."

"I sure do, because if I *did* eat that little dried up bush tree between your legs, you'd be further up my ass than my favorite La Perla thongs, when I choose to wear thongs that is. Maybe then you'd relax."

The idea of Yvonna coming anywhere near her causes her to lose composure but she must remain cool. "Well enough," she says trying to avoid looking at Yvonna's pussy lips. "I see you wanna play games so let's play them. I know you're far from cured. I've been in this business for twenty years and have seen people like you go and come right back."

"I doubt very seriously that you've seen *anybody* like me."

"Oh but I have. Just like you." She points a pencil at her. "Out there trying to deceive the world. You're a danger to society, Yvonna. A loose cannon waiting to blow. And I'm going to stop you."

"How? By lying on me?" she giggles. "Don't forget you've tried to recommit me before. I don't know, doctor," she shakes her head "maybe you're the one who's crazy."

Jona takes a deep breath and says, "I'll do what I have to, but I trust you will hang *yourself* first." She looks down at Yvonna's chart and makes notes. "I'm increasing your sessions by one more a week. That means you're to see me three times a week and I want you to be *early*. And Gabriella can come too." she says looking to Yvonna's left, where she saw her look earlier.

Unconsciously, Yvonna whips her head toward Gabriella. The moment she does, she realizes she made a serious mistake. Yvonna turns around to face Jona who is now smiling.

"Just like I thought, you're far from healed, honey. Be back tomorrow."

There was nothing Yvonna could say. She fucked up but she wasn't going to let her know it. She stands up and walks as smoothly as Grace Kelly toward the door. But once outside of Jona's office, she exhales and rubs her head profusely trying to rid herself of the throbbing migraine that was coming on.

Gabriella says, "I hope you know we can't let her live. She's too smart. She'll try to keep us in for good. We're too fly too be in a place like this."

Yvonna remains silent. How she wishes she could make Gabriella go away. She didn't need her anymore and now she was interfering with her freedom. If Gabriella hadn't spoken in the office, Jona would not have noticed Yvonna's expression. Her life was on the line, not Gabriella's. She could come and go as she pleased. As always the game was going to have to be changed. What she didn't know was how.

# THE PLAN

"So what do you want me to do, Yvonna?" Treyana asks as they sit in the car outside of Bernice's house. Yvonna's eyes stay glued on Bernice as she washes dishes in the sink of her kitchen. The yellow chiffon curtains blow around and hide Bernice's vision and the hateful glare Yvonna has on her from the car. "I haven't seen Bernice in two years. It's gonna seem weird if I knock on her door all of a sudden."

"Ask her how she's doing, and ease into what I want to know. The full name of the nigga she used to fuck. The one that was cool with Bilal's father."

"That's stupid. She's gonna see right through me."

Yvonna levels a basilisk glare at her and says, "When are you going to realize this is not a fuckin' game? Who do I have to kill to prove to you that I'm serious?" she pauses. "You? Your husband? Who, Treyana?"

Treyana looks out the window for fear that Yvonna's stare alone will kill her.

"I know you're serious. I want to be smart."

"I'm the only smart one in this car. You just do what the fuck I tell you to. Let's check your mic."

"Why do I have to where this?"

"'Cause I don't trust your dusty ass that's why."

Treyana adjusts the tiny microphone under the lime green shirt she's wearing, bends her head down and says, "Can you hear me?"

"It works," she smiles. "Now go and leave the rest to me."

Treyana was about to exit the car until Yvonna grabs her wrist, "Remember who I am. If you remember nothing else, remember my name and what I'm capable of."

Treyana exits the car, adjusts the Seven for all Mankind denim skirt she's wearing and struts with her black Christian Louboutin pumps. *That bitch is sooo trying to be like me.* Yvonna thinks.

Taking one last look at Yvonna before she reaches the steps, she walks slowly to the door and knocks softly. Yvonna can see Bernice dry her hands with the blue hand towel before disappearing from the window. Second's later, Bernice opens the door.

"Treyana? What are you doing here?" She looks Treyana over with deep suspicion.

"I was just in the neighborhood and wanted to stop by to say hello. We haven't seen each other since the case. And I wanted to make sure all's well."

"All's well?" she repeats. "You sound very proper." She jokes.

"I've changed."

"I see. But what do you want? You made it clear on what position you plan to take with the...," is all Yvonna hears before the ear set makes a loud crunchy sound due to the mic being ripped off Treyana's shirt.

Yvonna sits up slightly but not too much as to reveal herself. She's irritated and wonders what Treyana has planned. *What are you up to bitch?* Her leg shakes uncontrollably as she fights hard to resist the urge to get out of the car, and swell on Treyana's black ass. The only thing that stops her are the restraining orders. Her mind was running wild when she suddenly hears hysterical laughter in the backseat.

"You's about a dumb bitch," Gabriella teases.

Yvonna adjusts the rearview mirror and says, "I'm not up for your shit right now, Gabriella."

"Yes you are. Haven't you heard...my shit *is* your shit? We're one in the same."

"Whatever, Gabriella."

"Wake up, Yvonna! Stop bein' naïve and you're making us look bad."

"You don't know what you're talking about."

"I know what *we're* talking about. You're talking to yourself remember. That girl is in there telling her you're out here plotting and your stupid ass gonna let her get away with it. Go in there and kill 'em both!"

Yvonna's face grows warm as blood rushes to the surface. She shakes her head and closes her eyes hoping when she reopens them, she'll be gone. She desperately wants to believe the doctors and is now angry with herself for refusing to take the medicine to help her deal with the Multiple Personality Disorder.

"I'm still here, bitch." She says when Yvonna opens her eyes. "You can't get rid of me."

She sighs. "I'll handle Treyana if she tries me."

"Like you handled everybody else? Don't waste your time, if you don't do what needs to be done, I'll take care of her for you. I always do."

Little did Gabriella know that if Treyana crossed her this time, Yvonna would be more than willing to do the dirty work herself.

# THE FOLLOW UP

When Treyana comes outside fifteen minutes later Yvonna calms herself down long enough to get the details.

"So what's Tree's real name?" she asks the moment she slides inside the car and closes the door.

"My mic fell off," she offers right away.

"What is Tree's real name?"

"Tamal Green." Treyana looks guilty. "She says he's in a minimum security prison in New Jersey."

"Minimum security? Bilal said he had king pin charges." Yvonna thinks out loud.

"He did, but she thinks he snitched and will be coming home soon. She seemed scared."

Yvonna knew why she was scared but didn't tell Treyana. Bernice and Tree set Bilal's father up and took his money years ago. But when Tree got locked up, she promised she'd hold him down and she didn't. Bilal told her how his mother told him she killed his father for him. She claimed that his father was going to leave her for another woman with no money or means to care for themselves.

"How did you get the information?"

"I told her Avante is working on a case involving him. You know he works for the FBI." Treyanna's eyebrows rise as to warn her that she had access to authorities.

"Oh yeah. So did she tell you which prison?" Yvonna is unmoved by her silent threat.

"No, but you can go online to find out where now that you have his name. She says she thinks he's in FCI Fairton."

"FCI Fairton?"

A smile spreads across her face because this was the same prison Swoopes was in. In her original plan she wanted to get a hold of Tree to conspire with him to get back at Bernice but now another idea entered her mind.

Yvonna leans a little toward the passenger seat and says, "Anything else?"

Treyana backs up. Her head rests against the window and her hands raise a little to cover her face. Her chest moves up and down rapidly. She is so scared it seems as if she's about to faint.

"N...no...no. That's it."

"So...why did you take the mic off again?"

"I...thought she saw it. And I didn't...," was the last thing she said before Yvonna reaches between her legs, grabs a fist full of pubic hair and snatches it.

"Awwwwwwww...Owwwwwwwwwww!" Treyana yells covering her private area.

Yvonna wipes her hands off along with a bunch of loose hairs and says, "So you still not shaving your pussy. Even after I taught you how to clean your ass."

"Why did you do that?" she cries.

"That was nicer than what I was about to do. I advise you not to fuck wit' me again. You're my little dog and if my dog gets out of line, I check her ass. Understood?"

Treyana remains silent. Besides, there was nothing left to say. Yvonna was the boss and if she wanted to live, she'd have to remember it.

# LIKE MOTHAFUCKIN' MINDS

Yvonna walks into a crowded nail salon in Maryland looking for Ming Chi, the baddest nail designer in Maryland. Although she could use a manicure, she was interested in using her services. She was much more curious about a mutual acquaintance.

"How can I help you?" the Chinese receptionist asks with a fake smile on her face. It's obvious she doesn't like black people past the money in their pockets.

"I'm here to see Ming," she points seeing her way into the back of the salon.

"Ming, busy. You wait right there!" she yells.

"Excuse me?" Yvonna says turning around to face her.

"You must wait like rest!"

Yvonna's lips pierce and she places her hand on her hip. She couldn't stand the bitch to begin with and was about to give her a piece of her mind until a lady walks behind the receptionist and whispers something into her ear. The woman looks at Yvonna as if she's Satan.

"Oh. Uh, you go back. It's fine," the woman recants after the woman whispers into her ear and walks off.

Yvonna didn't know that the lady told her that Yvonna was the one who was all over the news for killing so many people.

"You bitches stupid in here." She says before walking away.

The moment Yvonna walks up to Ming, a smile spreads across Ming's face. Unlike some, Ming liked Yvonna's devilish nature. In the country for only five years, 29-year-old Ming had grown bored with natives from her hometown in China, and in the busy salon. She traded them quickly for black culture and black men.

"Yvonna," she says standing up to hug her. Ming's short height doesn't take away from her beauty. Her hair is styled in a coal black shoulder length bob and she's sporting an old school black Adidas sweat suit. "Where you been, slut?"

Yvonna pushes her arm and says, "All ova." The girl whose nails she was doing sighs trying to win Ming's attention back.

"Just soak." Ming tells her. "I be one minute."

"But I been soakin' for five minutes! I need my nails did," the girl continues rolling her neck and smacking her lips together. "I got somewhere to go shit!"

"Oooooooo, biiiitch! You get my ass and kiss!" Ming slaps her flat ass using broken English. "Leave now!"

The girls pushes out of her seat and yells, "But I need my nails did!" Her nails dripping wet.

"You should think before you flap the mouth! Out!"

The girl takes a look at Yvonna blaming her for the entire scenario with her eyes. When she's gone, Ming focuses back on Yvonna who is laughing so hard a little piss escapes her body.

"What you laugh about? I tell you the same thing when I first met you!"

"I know, and I cursed your ass out for points in here!" They embrace again.

"I know…that's why I like you. Come my, friend. Tell me your problem."

"Ming, you got four customer waiting!" one of her coworkers warns when she sees her abandoning her station to walk further to the back of the store.

"They can wait," she swats her away like a fly.

"What's wrong with them bitches?"

"Just jealous," she tells Yvonna.

When they walk to the back, she and Yvonna sit down in the small lounge area.

"What's up?" Ming closes the door and locks it for privacy.

"I'm looking for Cream. You seen her?"

Ming leans back in her seat and says, "Oh...I see. You want to kill?"

"Ming don't be stupid. I just want to apologize for how I treated her."

"You lie. You lie real good."

"I'm serious. Have you seen her or not?"

"Yeah. She came by once last week. She move too," Ming looks up toward the ceiling. Yvonna catches a glimpse of her brown eyes and she thinks she's pretty. She'd definitely fuck her if she had to. "She gain much way also."

"Where does she live?"

"I don't know. But I find out for you my friend."

"Good. If you do, there's something in it for you."

"What?"

"Money."

"Take a look." She flashes her diamond rings. "Ming the richest bitch in Maryland." Yvonna laughs.

"I want something else." She continues.

"What, Ming?"

"I tell later. For now, let me work on your problem."

Yvonna smiles. She doesn't know what Ming has up her sleeve, but she has to admit, waiting to find out is very titillating.

# PUSSY JUICE

The inmates in the visiting room FCI Fairton prison in New Jersey were saints compared to the crazy mothafucka who was about to walk through the doors. After months of seducing Tree, the best friend of the man Bernice helped kill, she was finally able to meet him. She wrote to him on a major pen pal service.

When Yvonna walks through the door, the entire visiting room grows quiet. A blonde wig covers her natural hair and the bangs hang over her eyebrows. Wearing a pink fitted sweater and blue True Religion jeans, she struts seductively over to the man she'd been waiting to meet. In all of the pictures she sent him, the wig stayed on.

Her confidence was high and then when she walks into his presence, she's scared.

"You okay?" he asks sensing her fear.

"Oh…uh…yes. I…I don't know what's wrong with me."

"You sure?" She nods trying to win her confidence back.

He smiles and says, "Good. I'm glad you came. And your pictures don't do you justice!" Tree examines her small sexy frame and hugs her for as long as he's allowed to per *Visitation Policy*. "And you soft too!" He places his hand in the small of her back and the prisoners look on in envy.

"You wouldn't believe how soft I really am," she winks as they take their seats.

"I've seen you somewhere."

"I was thinking the same thing."

Although the initial meeting was not what she had in mind, she can't deny how handsome he is to be in his fifties. His pictures seemed so *prison-ness.*

His typical khaki uniform and unsightly black leather-like boots fail to drown out his appeal. His 6-foot frame hovers over her like a powerful oak tree. His complexion gives him a Hawaiian mystique and he favors the actor Dwayne "The Rock" Johnson.

"I don't know about you," Yvonna starts trying not to look into his eyes. "But I like to have a drink when I meet someone for the first time. You wanna drink?"

"Take a look around," he smiles. He is desperately trying to keep his cool because for real all he wants to do is stuff six inches of hard dick in her mouth and watch her swallow. "I'm in jail, baby. Ain't no bar in here."

"I know where we are, sweetie. But you don't need a bar if you dealin' with me. Where's the bathroom?"

"Over there," he points curiously.

Yvonna gets up and sashays to the restroom. She makes a sexy spectacle of herself as she moves. A small baby vying for his incarcerated father's attention can't steal his eyes off her as she swings her blond hair for show.

Once inside the bathroom, she goes into a stall, pulls her panties down, and removes a large cylinder bottle from inside her pussy. Before opening it, she puckers her lips, and runs the outside of the bottle over them and smiles.

"I know it's been a minute since you tasted pussy. The wait is over." She says to herself. She wants the scent of her pussy to remain on his lips long after she leaves him.

When she's done, she opens the squirt bottle, fills her mouth with the CIROC vodka and ecstasy pill concoction and holds it in the inside of her mouth. She's swallows a little to loosen up but not enough to cloud her judgment.

Afterwards she walks back outside. Realizing all eyes were on her, including the jealous-hating-ass-correctional officers, she waits three minutes before kissing Tree. When she thinks the attention is off of her she kisses him deeply. Tree's eyes widen when he smells the sweetness of her pussy mixed with the bitterness of the vodka.

"That's enough!" Dom Manchester, a CO, yells, breaking them up. He walks hurriedly over to him. "Green, open your mouth." He complies hoping the smell of the vodka doesn't seep out.

Dom looks inside his mouth. "Lift up your tongue!" He does and he's mad his discovery ends in vain. "Aight, but next time you try something like that, your visit is over!" he continues walking away.

"I can't stand that fake ass nigga!" he scoffs loud enough for him to hear.

"Are you gonna worry about him, or focus on me?"

Realizing he's a fool for allowing Dom to irritate he drops the subject.

"You wild! But I like you!" he compliments. "Not many chicks woulda snuck vodka inside their pussy."

"Well you gotta raise your standards."

"You right about that."

"Now that you've tasted my pussy…you owe me."

"I owe you huh?"

"That's what I said."

"So what you need, Treyana?"

"My name ain't…," she stops herself from making a mistake.

She almost forgot she gave him Treyana's name instead of her own. She knew one quick look at her records during the visitation approval process, and she would not be able to get inside. So without Treyana's knowledge, she stole her identity to get next to Tree. It hadn't been the first time she used her name and it wouldn't be the last.

"Yvonna, you ain't on a date bitch!" Gabriella shouts from the sidelines. "Hurry up and get to the point."

"Shut up! I got it!" Yvonna screams looking to her right.

"You aight?" Tree asks her. He looks where she was looking and saw no one.

"Y…yeah…uh…I'm sorry," she smiles trying to conceal the little bit of crazy that seeped out. "Tree…I'ma be real wit' you." She leans in. "I need you to kill somebody."

Tree looks around to see if anyone heard her. When he believes no one has, he says, "Fuck you talkin' 'bout?"

"Exactly what I said," Yvonna's tone is flat and the alcohol gives her power. "You not in here for your sunny disposition. You in here because you a criminal. A drug dealer…a *murderer*."

"Murderer?" he repeats. "What you think you know 'bout me little girl?"

"I know you killed your best friend for pussy. Is that enough?"

"Who are you?"

"Someone who knows more about you than you do about them."

"You betta be careful." He warns.

"Why? I'm simply asking you to do what you do best. So don't act all reformed on me just yet."

"Bitch, I just met you!" he scowls. "And outside of sendin' me a few sexy pictures, that's all you did for me. I don't owe you shit."

"We're about to become real acquainted, Tree. That's the bottom line. You got something in here I need. And don't worry, I'll make it worth your while and keep your little murder secret. I'll give you a gift so mind blowing, you'll want to pay me instead."

Tree looks around once more and then back at Yvonna. He couldn't believe someone so beautiful could waltz inside the prison and demand such an extraordinary request. What scares him the most was not what she wanted him to do, but how she asked.

"Let's say I'm interested…who is it you want handled?"

She smiles and says, "His name is Swoopes. You know him?"

"Yeah. I know him."

"Good. He'll be getting out soon so we have to move fast."

"Hold up," he says with his hands outstretched making contact with her body. "I didn't agree to do shit yet."

"Green, if I have to talk to you again about violating policy that's it!"

Everyone looks at Tree and laughs to them selves. Tree isn't laughing. Tree looks at Dom and secretly lusts over the moment he'd finally have a chance to crack his skull. Yvonna picking up on this says, "I'll even throw in his body as an added bonus."

Now she has his attention. "Why do you want this nigga gone?"

"That's my personal business, Tree. There's no need in understanding the why's as it is what's in it for you. Let's just say this, you'll receive a letter from me in a few weeks. In the letter I'll list what I want you to do to him."

"You already said what you want."

"I know but I want his life here to be miserable *before* it's over."

"You crazy," he laughs. He can't believe the gall of this bitch.

"Don't ever call me crazy again."

He laughs and her face remains as straight as an arrow. And for the first time in his life, he's horrified of another person. A woman at that.

"Now," she continues, "the letter will be coded to throw people off. The sentences themselves will make sense but put together they won't. It'll look like a poem. What you'll need to do is decode my real message by writing down the last word of each sentence. It'll tell you *exactly* what I want done." He sits back in his hard plastic seat and focuses on her.

"Why should I risk my life for you? I'm comin' home soon. All I have to do is stay outta trouble."

She moves closer to him so that he could feel the warmth from her body, then she looks into his eyes.

"You'll do it because I'll kill Bernice Santana. Your reason for being here."

The sly smile is wiped from his face. Not a day goes by that he doesn't think of Bernice. After they killed her boyfriend, and his best friend Dylan, Tree was later indicted on King Pin charges. And since he and Bernice got together sexually before he went in, she promised him that she'd stay by his side. It wasn't until later that he discovered that the only thing she cared about was the money. Because with Dylan dead, and Tree in prison, who was going to provide the lifestyle for her she was accustomed to?

Bernice gold-digging ass managed to think of a way when she convinced Tree to put her son Bilal on since he still had ties in the drug game despite being incarcerated. He did, and the moment young Bilal started to bring in the big bucks, Bernice cut Tree off as smoothly as the tip of a circumcised dick. Her betrayal enraged him and he had plans to kill her himself when he came home. And since he provided the DEA with a lead on a Columbian connect who was supplying dope to DC by using pregnant women's wombs, his time was cut in half. But now, Yvonna presented a new opportunity.

"How you find out about me?"

"Again…it doesn't matter. Just know that you can trust me."

"I trust no one," he tells her.

"Well you'll have to if you want her taken care of. I know all about how she did you. And I know where she lives."

He pauses and says, "Handle him first and I'll be waitin' on the letter."

She looks at the CO and says, "Great. And don't worry you'll be pleased with my work."

"Don't cross me." He reminds her with a raised eyebrow.

"And you betta not cross me. Those who do, never live to cross another person again. And you won't be any different."

# CRAZY NEVER DIES

Lily's small body is spread out in the middle of her living room floor. Empty bottles and trash from various carry-out's surround her. The sun peaking in her window causes her to stir before eventually bringing her to complete consciousness. Half drunk, and half sleep, she curses the rays for bringing light to what she hated most of all…the fact that she was still alive.

Lily pulls up her blue khaki pants, and pulls down her white t-shirt and closes the shades. Once the darkness from the thick curtains embraces her, she flops down on the brown couch; it was the only furniture in her one bedroom apartment in SW, Washington D.C. The ringing phone surprises her because it had been months since she'd paid any bills. She lost electricity the night before.

Grabbing the handset from the end table, she burps yesterday's liquor and says, "Who the fuck is this?"

"Uh…is this detective Lily Alverez-Martin?"

Since no one has called her detective since she went on disability two years earlier, she reasoned that the caller must've been connected to her job.

"What's this about? I'm busy right now," she lies.

"It's about Yvonna. Yvonna Harris."

Lily's heartbeat speeds and she feels faint. Although thoughts of Yvonna stay with her every second of the day, even after her partner Shonda Wright committed suicide, she still tries to forget the day she heard her name.

"Detective, Martin. Are you still there?"

"How did you get my number?"

"I know your ex-husband, Mitchell Martin. He gave it to me."

Her husband left her a year ago after she traded their vows for random sexual encounters during drunken bar escapades.

"Well what do you want with me?" she asks sitting up straight.

"I'm sorry to bother you. And I know you don't know me. It's just that…I need your help. My name's Jona Maxwell, the psychiatrist caring for Yvonna."

"Is that what you call it these days? *Caring?*"

"Excuse me?"

"That bitch can never be cured or cared for. And if you believe she can, you and the whore of a mother of yours are both fools."

Jona gasps and says, "Mrs. Martin, I'm not calling here to cause you any trouble, and I'd appreciate if you'd leave my mother out if it and give me the respect I'm trying to give to you," she pauses and waits for an apology that never comes. "Anyway, I agree with you. She can't be cured and I'm worried that she might not be taking our medication. Also, she claims her husband has left her and no one has heard from him."

"Her husband? Dave Walters?"

"Yes."

"Well if she did kill him that serves him right. The way he defended her in court."

"I understand that you may be angry, but not too long ago I caught her identifying with her personality again. And I'm concerned."

"I knew it!" Lily says as she hops up from the sofa. She feels invigorated. She'd been telling people that Yvonna would strike again and no one believed her. They all thought she was on a personal vendetta after her partner took her own life. "What are you people going to do? If you don't move now she'll get worse."

"We can't do anything right now. I need proof."

"Well you said you caught her *identifying.* Can't you make the decision to have her recommitted? Aren't you her doctor?"

"It's not that easy. I've tried to press the issue with the head doctors here and each time she passes their tests." Lily pours a cup of vodka, shaking the bottle a little to get a few drops of liquor from the sides. She downs the remnants in the cup and opens a new bottle. Lily is uninterested until she says, "I think it was a mistake to let Yvonna back out on the streets and if we put our heads together, we can get her back where she belongs. In a straight jacket."

For the first time in a year, Lily smiles.

"I like you. And because I like you, you can count on me to help."

# NASTY MATTERS

Earlier in the week Treyana told Yvonna that she overheard Bernice on the phone scheduling a doctor's appointment for today for her seven-year-old grandchild, Bilal Jr. She couldn't wait to execute the first part of her plan.

"They're coming now," Treyana says as she stands on the opposite end of the children's hallway out of Bernice's view. She was on the phone with Yvonna who was on the other end also hiding from view.

"Good, is the boy with her?"

Although Yvonna called herself being inconspicuous she stood out like the last chicken on the plate in a fat farm. She was wearing a fashionable short mini royal blue Duchess dress by Acne with her oversized black Chanel shades. And she was seriously depleting the nest egg she stole from Dave's house by spending so much money on fashion. As it stood now, she barely had enough money to stay in a hotel.

"Yes. He's with her. What are you going to do?" Treyana watches Bernice and Bilal Jr. sign in and sit in the chairs in the waiting area.

"Treyana the less you know the better. Just remember to do what I told you."

"Are you going to hurt him? He's just a child."

Treyana was worried because before arriving at the hospital, Yvonna had her running all around DC looking for the oldest buildings she could find. She ran into each one hopeful and came back out pissed the fuck off. She was specific about what she was looking for…housing made before 1976. What for, Treyana couldn't say. But it wasn't until she entered into the most run-down-decapitated building she could find that she came out with a smile on her face.

"Bitch, worry about them shit queens you gave birth to and let me worry about the rest. Now do the next step." Yvonna sees the back of Bernice's and Bilal Jr. heads as she waits. "You're holding up progress."

Treyana ends the call and walks to a nurse's station a few feet behind Bernice. It was in another section on the children's unit. Bernice could only see Treyana if she turned around but she still had to be careful.

"Excuse me," Treyana says to the young black nurse who was on the phone.

"One minute please?"

When Treyana sees her kind smile she's confident that she'd be able to get her because of her innocent look. When she's done she says, "How can I help you?"

Treyana put on her best *girlfriend-gossip* whisper and replies, "I ain't tryin' to be funny, but me and my friend was about to leave when we saw that little boy over there. Ain't he the one somebody took from some house in Hyattsville, Maryland? His face was all over the news."

"What little boy?" she asks as her eyebrows rise.

"Girl you ain't been watchin' TV?"

"I do, but I don't remember no little boy missing."

"What? Everybody heard about the lady who had her only child taken from her. Remember? The boy's father was killed in a drive by shooting on their wedding day."

"Which one?" the nurse asks walking from behind the counter.

"Right there," she points.

The nurse looks with a sad expression at Bilal Jr., "How do you know it's him?"

"Girl I remember a face like that anywhere. I'm surprised you don't."

The young nurse looks again and not wanting to appear stupid she says, "I do remember him. Oh my goodness!" Treyana can't believe her gullibility.

"So what do we do?"

"I think you should walk over there and get her to walk back with you. Tell her you need to see her. I'll have my friend walk over to the little boy to make sure it's him. If it is, we'll call the police. If not, I'll signal to you that he's not the one."

"I'm not sure. Shouldn't I call the police first?"

"Not right now!" Treyana yells, nervous about getting them involved. "Let's make sure it's him first."

"Okay. I'll do it."

"Okay. Let me tell my friend."

Treyana steps back and pretends to be calling her friend and the nurse walks over to Bernice. At first Bernice was going to bring her grandson with her until the nurse suggests he remains in case the doctor calls his name. Because Bernice is a slick bitch, she immediately smells a rat. She wonders what the nurse could possibly want with her in another unit. Still, she struts over to the station looking more like she's thirty-somethin' in her Gucci black romper than fifty-somethin'. When she disappears, Yvonna walks up to Bilal Jr, with a can of Coke in her hand.

The moment Bilal Jr.'s eyes look at her, her heart melts. He's older and looks so much like his father that for a moment, Yvonna wants to wrap her arms around him and tell him how much she misses him.

That is until Gabriella says, "Bitch, do what you came to do so we can go about our business. This little bastard is the reason you lost your baby. Remember? Had Sabrina not betrayed you, you would've never gotten into the car accident with Dave's bitch ass."

Yvonna pulls herself together and says, "Ain't your name, Bilal?"

Bilal, taken by Yvonna's beauty says, "Yeah. How you know me?"

"You go to school with my daughter. The doctor called her into the office and she had to leave but she asked me to talk to you."

"What's her name?"

"Paradise. I named her after me."

He smiles in the only way his father could and replies, "I don't know her."

"She said you wouldn't and she's shy. She's afraid you won't like her."

His head drops and he looks back into her eyes.

"She like me?"

"Yes," Yvonna says taking a look back at Bernice who is still occupied.

"Look…she asked me to say hi but I have to go inside with her now."

Yvonna looks at the nurse's station again and catches Bernice looking at them. She turns her head quickly before she sees her face. If Bernice catches her, she will call the cops immediately because Yvonna would be violating the restraining order. Yvonna could see Bernice moving toward them.

"Look, I have to go. We'll see each other again."

She kisses him on the lips and says, "I got an extra soda for Paradise but she's with the doctor. Want it?"

He nods and accepts the drink from her.

"I'll see you around."

"Okay," he smiles.

As she was leaving, Bernice walks over to Bilal missing Yvonna by seconds. She looks at the back of the woman's head and wonders what she was saying to her grandson

"Was she talking to you?"

"Yeah."

"What she say?"

"Her daughter goes to school with me. She's nice," he says as he sips the soda in the can.

"That's all she said?"

"Yep."

Although Yvonna wasn't there to see it, somehow she knew he'd keep her secret. In her mind, she knew he'd be just like his father…a no good ass liar.

 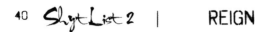

# ANCIENT CHINESE SECRET

Ming parks her silver Porsche on a side street in New Jersey. She and Yvonna had just followed Dom Manchester, the correctional officer from the prison to a grocery store. He walked into the store after leaving work, and now they were waiting for him to come out.

"You lookin' awfully sexy," Yvonna encourages nudging her leg. "Where you get this outfit from."

"Girl, please!" she says rolling her eyes. "Bitches, don't have shit on me! Including you."

"You never answer my questions. And for your information, your ass ain't got shit on me in the fashions department." Ming laughs.

"So, we going to get to do my little *fantasies* tonight?" Ming had found Cream for Yvonna and wanted her payoff.

"You are so disgusting. Most people have one but you have two," Yvonna says secretly loving her fetishes. "I would've never guessed that about you."

"There's lot about Ming you don't know."

"I believe you. One part of your fantasy I know we can do but you have to tell me if you like him first before we do the other part."

"I saw the back of his head and tight little ass when he walk in to the store. Ming already know me can do many nice things to his body."

She was still laughing until she sees him come out of the gro-

41

cers, "Quick, Ming. Get ready. Push your titties up." Yvonna tries to adjust the outfit to expose more of her breasts and a nipple pops out.

Ming slaps her hand and says, "They good." She covers her exposure. "But he's gonna be on my ass hard. Worry 'bout that."

"Your titties, Ming!" Yvonna ignores the attention she was giving to her flat ass. "If we have a chance to rope his ass it'll be on your titties. You don't have an ass."

"Ming, got more ass than you."

"Doubt it!" Yvonna yells before Ming places on her large black Gucci shades and grabs her black and gold Gucci purse.

She struts hurriedly in Dom's direction trying hard to appear in a rush instead of being on a mission. She was pulling it off and Yvonna is so impressed, she wants to knight her into *black sisterhood*. Although Ming doesn't have the body of a black girl, her titties are perky and bounce along with her runway walk. Yvonna was counting on him to be a titty man. But if he wasn't they had plans to "Go Hard".

Ming places her phone against her head and talks to Yvonna about nothing in particular.

"I don't care what he wants. If he can't fuck me good, he can't fuck me at all!" She was trying to appear in a deep conversation.

Dom hears her sexual words and is immediately aroused. But Ming struts her 5 foot 2 inch frame past him wearing a blue romper from Dolce & Gabana like he doesn't exists. Her large shades and diamond studded earrings glamour out an outfit that without them would give her a whorish appeal.

She was almost to the sliding doors of the grocers when he yells, "Can I go with you, sexy?" Ming smiles before turning around. Yvonna is still on the phone.

"Hold on, Yoy, someone talk to me."

Yvonna yells in the phone, "Get his ass, bitch!"

"You talk to me?" Ming says walking up on him. The phone in her hand drops a little to her side.

"Yeah. I couldn't let something as fine as you walk away from me. So get rid of whoever that is on the phone."

"You very confident." she says licking her lips. "What if me don't like that? What if you not my kind?"

Ming loves the attention and is pleased at his height and the way his body fills out his correctional officer's uniform. He's very handsome and she can't wait to fuck.

"We won't know unless we find out." He steps up closer and looks down on her. His mint breath seals the deal. "Now, will we?"

Ming is silent before she says, "Yoy, something came up. I have to go."

That was code word for, "We got his ass. Keep up with this car and don't lose him."

"I'm right behind you." Yvonna tells her.

# A NOT SO PERFECT WORLD

"Treyana what is going on with you?" Avante asks as they lay in bed together. "You're hiding something from me. Talk to me."

"Avante, please. I'm just not feeling well." She turns her back to him and pulls the covers over her shoulders.

"Is it something I did?"

"No."

"Well can we talk?" He places a concerned hand on her shoulder.

Treyana flips the switch on the lamp on the end table next to her side of the large king size bed, lays flat on her back and says, "Do we have to? I'm really tired."

"Yes we have to. Now what's up, Treyana? Ever since somebody harmed the kids, you been actin' different and I think you know something about it."

"Oh so now you're blaming me for hurting the kids?" She looks at him.

"I said you *know* something about it. I'm sure of it. I've been knowing you for over fifteen years and know when something's wrong."

"Avante, I'm not trying to hear this shit right now! I'm going through a lot of stuff I gotta work out on my own."

Irritated with his nagging, she turns to her side again preparing to cut off the lamp until he places his hand around her throat and squeezes. Then he straddles her body and stares down at her.

"Don't fuck with me, Treyana."

"You're hurting me," she manages to say clawing at his muscular arms. "Please stop."

This was *their* secret. A secret not even her mother, co-workers or friends knew about. When Treyana first got with him, he beat her religiously. He took his silent frustrations out on her, never telling her why. He beat her so much, that after a while, she became tough and immune to his blows. Only when she got pregnant, did he let up…a little and even married her. When the twins were born, the beatings returned. This is when she started acting out, fighting the world and everybody in it.

Before long, she stopped caring for her apartment, kids and body. He grew disgusted with the monster he created and when a pretty young lady showed interest, he left. She found solace in the street sleeping with random strangers. Keeping his secret even after he left her for her white neighbor Cream, she fought hard to win him back. With Yvonna's help, she did.

From the moment they remarried, he never touched her. She thought it was because of love. He knew it was for fear of losing his FBI position. On many occasions he wanted to strike her for running off at the mouth but what if she called the police and the word got out? It had been two years since he resisted the urge of hitting her and he could not take it any longer.

"Now you're my wife and I demand to know what's going on."

Only because he wants an answer does her release his hold. Treyana, nervous and afraid rubs her throat and looks up at him. A tear falls down the side of her face and onto the pillow.

"I don't know what's going on. I would never hurt our children, Avante. Ever."

"Then why have you been refusing me in the bedroom."

"Because I have a lot on my mind. I'm not trying to disrespect you."

"I don't believe you."

"It's true." He smacks her so hard in the face that she temporarily loses sight.

"You're lying."

"Avante if I knew something, anything, I would tell you. Please stop this," she says calmly. "You promised you wouldn't do this."

"Treyana, if I find out that you lying to me, I'll kill you. I'm still the same man you knew, just in a different packaging."

"I know, baby. I know." He throws the covers off her body, pushes her legs and scrutinizes her vagina for being shaved.

"Why you cut your pussy hair? You know I hate that shit."

"I'm sorry." He pushes the side of her face in anger. "You always fuckin' sorry."

Remembering the words he loved to hear when he beat her back in the day she says, "Please take me. I know I'm not worthy."

Disgusted with her for no good reasons, he moves in and out of her anyway. Treyana hates her world lately and lies motionless in the bed. Everything went from bad to great to worse than ever before. In that moment she made a decision, if her environment didn't kill her, she was going to kill herself.

# NASTY BITCHES

The moment Ming enters Dom's house, she's impressed with his taste of design. Two huge black leather couches sit on top of Italian grey rugs. And thick black curtains with green and burgundy chiffon layers underline them giving his home a cozy appeal.

"You have woman live here?" Ming asks walking inside throwing her purse next to the end of the couch.

"Naw, I live by myself."

He walks to the kitchen and removes a bottle of Vodka and two drinking glasses from the freezer. He joins Ming on the sofa. Filling their glasses he smiles at her beauty and sex appeal. She looks into his eyes, removes her shoes and wiggles her shiny black toes. "Cute feet," he says.

Ming takes the cup, swallows the liquid and replies, "Glad you like. Now suck them."

He laughs at her comment. "Sorry, I don't lick nobody's feet. Not even my mother's."

Why he would associate licking feet with his mother perplexes her. Not to mention Ming is angry that he refuses to do what she's asked. She looks at him like he's lost his mind, stands up, grabs her shoes, purse and walks toward the door.

"Open this door," she says holding her high heels in one hand and her purse in the other. "I don't fuck wit' no niggas who can't fuck me right. Don't have time." Her hand rests on the doorknob and she unlocks it without his knowing.

"Look, we can have a good time here tonight, but I ain't about to lick no feet."

He had never sucked a female's toes and never had plans on changing his mind. But there was something nasty about Ming that he had to have and he knew if he didn't comply, he'd regret this moment for the rest of his life.

"If you don't…I leave. I'm not playing. You never met a freakier bitch in all you life. Chinese women are the baddest."

He walks up to her, looks down at her pretty face and drops to his knees until he's lower than her original height. She steps back, leans against the door, lifts her tiny leg and allows her foot to rest comfortably on his shoulder.

"Suck."

He takes her small foot and starting with the smallest toe places each one in his mouth. Her feet smell like apples and suddenly it's not too bad.

"Your toes are sweet," he says in between placing three in his mouth.

"My toes sweet like my pussy. You suck that next cause I'm a nasty bitch."

The moment the words come out of her mouth, with her Chinese accent and broken sentences, he grows hard. Ming leads him away from the door so that he doesn't discover it's unlocked. Once she reaches the sofa, she wiggles out of the one-piece romper she's wearing and it drops to the floor. She isn't wearing any underwear.

"I'ma fuck you soooo good." He promises.

"Fuck me better."

He pulls the zipper down on his pants and allows them to drop to his knees. His boxers follow and he strokes his stiff penis. Using his free hand he pulls Ming toward him and she jumps on top of him like a mother carrying a child on her hip. He releases himself and pulls her around the front kissing him softly in the mouth. Next she suckles his bottom lip until she bites it.

"Oouuuuch!" he screams in her face.

"You soft? Me don't like soft men. Me like my men rough and tough like me."

Fearing she'd leave before he fucks the shit out of her, he says,

"Don't bite me so hard next time."

She ignores him and starts kissing him roughly again. He soon realizes that she's a handful and that he might have to fuck her ass up if she doesn't calm down. Still, her kisses arouse him and he eases into her tight pussy. Her head drops and her shiny black hair reveal a tattoo he didn't see on her neck. The tip of a leather whip touches the bottom of her left ear and in a snake like motion, extends to the crack of her ass. The tattoo is beyond sexy and he fucks her harder while looking at the intricate design.

Ming handles his strokes like a trooper. The harder he fucks her, the easier she handles him. She's riding him like he's a prized horse. His thighs tighten and he's about to release inside of her when Ming wiggles off of him and says, "Not yet. Not yet."

"Don't play games."

"I'm not. But don't cum so quickly. I hate one minute man."

While he's thinking how she could've possibly known he was ready to release, she turns him around so that his back faces the door, then she drops to her knees and places his stiff penis inside her mouth. "I want to taste."

Not expecting the treat, he smiles and palms her tiny head as she takes his entire dick into her mouth without stopping for air. In his entire life...he'd never...ever...came across a female whose head game was as thorough as hers. He heard of Chinese women being the truth but this was ridiculous.

"Oh my....oh my fuckin'....oh shit!" he cries out loud.

Just when he releases his cream into her mouth, Yvonna steps behind him and shoves the heel of Ming's shoe inside his ass. Once it's all the way inside, she turns it and Mings stands up in awe. He looks at Ming in horror and a vein forms into the middle of his forehead.

At first the agony mixed with his cumming confuses him but it's not long before he realizes he's in extreme pain. Ming steps away from him and he falls face first to the couch, his legs drip with his own blood. Before he could defend himself, Yvonna jumps on his back and whispers softly into his ear.

"How does it feel to be fucked with?"

He doesn't understand Yvonna's question and Ming stands quietly on the sidelines. This was not their plan. Yvonna told Ming that she'd come in and fuck him with her as a part of her fantasy.

Ming had two fantasies she wanted to carry out. First she wanted to inflict pain on another, than she wanted to have sex with a *black* woman. She'd wanted Yvonna since she laid eyes on her and after hearing the stories in the news, she wanted her even more. She figured someone crazy enough to inflict pain could take pain too. Yvonna promised that she'd allow her to slap, punch and hit her, while Yvonna licked her pussy but now it looked like it wouldn't happen. Ming never knew that she would be an accessory to a murder.

"What did I do to you?!" he yells still shocked at the turn of events. The pain is incapacitating and to move a little worsens the situation. Yvonna continues to press her weight on his back with a knife remaining firmly in her hands.

"You didn't mind your fuckin' business. It's too late now."

Not waiting on his response, she takes the knife and slices his throat. When his lifeless body lays face down on his sofa, Yvonna stands up and looks down at him. She doesn't care that she'd just killed a mother's only son. She thought about how pleased Tree would be once he got wind of her work.

Seeing his nut on the floor she says, "Damn, I was only out there for ten minutes. You good as shit Ming."

"Fuck that! I need you to make up to Ming. You lied."

Ming's response causes Yvonna to like her even more. She wasn't concerned about the corpse at her feet. She was concerned about not getting her rocks off and Yvonna deemed then that she was a girl after her own heart.

"Ming, when it's right, I'm gonna fuck you so good, I'm gonna have to make you my bitch."

Mings smiles and says, "Naw. You my bitch. There's only one boss in this relationship and that's Ming!"

They laugh clean up Ming's fingerprints and leave.

 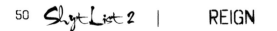

# A CHANCE
# ENCOUNTER

Yvonna sat in the waiting room on the phone talking to Treyana. She was early for her psychiatric appointment and decided to make a few phone calls. Patients who were incapable of caring for them selves sat next to their caregivers as they tended to their every need. Yvonna didn't consider herself anything like, *them*. Sure, she came to the realization that Gabriella couldn't be seen by other people. But in her mind, she was real and to date no doctor or pill could convince her otherwise.

"So what's going on? Did Bernice lose it when Bilal Jr. got sick?"

"Yeah. She was hurt pretty bad. He's her grandson, Yvonna. How would you feel if someone hurt your child?"

"Someone did. And I took care of that." She says referring to Dave who caused her to get into a car accident, which resulted in a miscarriage.

"What are you talking about?"

Not wanting to let Treyana on that she'd killed Dave she says, "It doesn't matter. The bitch is getting what she deserves. So what's going on now?"

Yvonna had turned Treyana to a personal spy and she loved every minute of it. Two days after Yvonna had been around Bilal Jr. he had suffered violent abdominal pains and was rushed to the hospital and had been there ever since. It turns out he had a terrible reaction to the lead paint chips Yvonna placed into his soda. It took doctors a day just to find out what was wrong with him.

"She's in the hospital with Bilal," Treyana says in a soft voice. "They're not sure if he's going to make it. He looks so bad, Yvonna. This is terrible."

While she loved the idea of Bernice suffering, for some reason, hearing that he was about to die caused her stomach to churn. Suddenly she feels as if speaking to him was a mistake because she liked him.

"Well…she should've never took Sabrina's side when she had that baby behind my back. And if something happens to him, well…I guess he'll be with his dead mother."

"He's just a baby, Yvonna. Are you sure you wanna do this?"

The question causes an ache in her heart. *Maybe I am going too far.* She thinks. The moment the question arises, Gabriella appears.

"If you buy in to that shit, you dumber than I thought. That kid wasn't going to make it anyway with Bernice's ass taking care of him. Might as well send him to be with his mother."

Yvonna immediately toughens up and says, "Bitch I know exactly what I'm doing. Bernice's *fish-puss smellin' ass* shoulda stayed outta my business, and this would've never happened. I'm not going to be satisfied until everybody gets what they deserve. Alive and hurt is good, but dead will work too."

"Okay," she sighs. "Well…I guess you should feel proud then because he may die. I can't take any of this anymore. I have too much going on in my personal life."

Treyana hangs up the phone before Yvonna can contest. Treyana was so disgusted by what was going on that it was becoming difficult to control how she felt.

Gabriella says, "Look at you putting your head down."

Yvonna looks around before she speaks to be sure know one hears her.

"What difference does it make?"

"It makes a lot of difference. You actin' like you forgot about everything everybody did to you." She shakes her head. "This is why I got to take over sometimes and push off for your weak ass. Man up, Yvonna."

In the past, when Gabriella killed it was always because she wasn't strong enough to do it. Those were the times Yvonna would black out and have no recollection of the events. But with Yvonna identifying more with her personality it wouldn't be long before Yvonna no longer exists. She wishes she had someone by her side to love and to lean on during the tough times. But how could she, when she killed everyone she loved and who loved her back?

"Yvonna?" a male voice says. Yvonna, upon hearing her name, gives the person her complete attention.

"Yes?" she looks up and sees Bradshaw Hughes.

Her heart thumps heavily in her chest. She hadn't seen him since she was released almost a year ago from Green Meadows mental institution. He'd been there for killing his wife's family but never discussed the reason he murdered or why. Yvonna was certain that it had something to do with his little girl. He talked about her all the time and felt that his absence placed her in immediate danger. When she was released, she never saw him again but he stayed in the back of her mind.

Bradshaw was beyond handsome. He stood about 5'11 with broad shoulders and dark eyes. He favored Idris Alba, the actor who played Stringer Bell from the show, *The Wire*.

"Bradshaw? Is that you?" she smiles and stands to greet him. "I can't believe it."

"How have you been?" he gives her a hug so strong and confident that when he releases her she feels weak. "It's feels like I haven't seen you in ages."

"About a year?" She says stepping away from him. Having the ability to see how financially stable a person was doing by their fashion, she quickly observed he was doing well.

Bradshaw looks fly in his expensive blue jeans and white button down shirt by Dsquared2. It was definitely a step up from the unfavorable blue cotton uniform at the institution. His energy draws her in like a magnet and she wants to fuck him on the spot.

"What have you been up to?" She asks unconsciously smoothing down the sides of her hair with her hand.

"Just makin' it. I have to come here for the rest of my life just to be able to see my daughter."

"You got her back?"

"No. I'll never have custody of her," he says with a sneer. Whenever he thinks about not being with his little girl, he becomes a monster. "For the rest of my life I'll have to see her with a police escort, or at least until she's eighteen."

"When are you going to tell me what happened?"

"Naw. I wanna leave that part of me behind."

"I understand. So how's she doing?" Yvonna asks surprised that she was genuinely concerned. The reaction…the sensitivity toward him was why Gabriella hated him. Anyone who could make Yvonna emotionally vulnerable, thereby opening herself up to disappointment, rejection and lost causes Gabriella to rise.

"She's good. I just feel bad that we'll never be able to be a real family. The way I figure it, once I make enough money, anything's possible. Shit, if I gotta pay for a full time police escort in my home to get her, I'll do what I gotta do. They said that might be an option."

"Yvonna, get this loser outta here," Gabriella yells from her right. "This dude is so fuckin' whack it's pathetic."

In that moment something unexpected happens. It was something that the psychiatrists or the medicine they made her take when she was institutionalized, could not do. For the first time ever, Yvonna totally ignored Gabriella. She didn't react physically or mentally to her words. She'd tried this in the past but could never pull it off. Something about Bradshaw causes her to react differently and this infuriates Gabriella.

"You think somebody who looks like him will want you? If you do you got another thing comin'. Men like him don't want losers. Look at yourself! You don't deserve love! You're not worthy of it."

"I'm so happy your daughter is doing well," Yvonna says keeping a straight face although Gabriella's words were growing tough to hear. "I know how much you care about her."

"She's my life." Yvonna remembers the last time someone loved her like that. And it was Dave. "Enough about my little girl, I'm trying to get me a woman in my life."

"I know you got somebody."

"I don't. I'm dead serious. So when you gonna let me take you out?"

"I can't do that," Yvonna disputes. She knew Gabriella would do everything in her power to sabotage their date only to eventually take his life.

He smiles, strokes his neatly trimmed goatee and says, "You funny."

"Why I got to be funny?"

"Because we've played this game before. I know what kind of man you want and I can be that."

"Have you forgotten that I'm married?"

"Naw…have you?"

Yvonna is silent as she tries to maintain the lie she's told everybody. That Dave, the man who would've given his life to be with her, in the end, did exactly that.

"Look…I gotta run." She says. "Uh…I'm glad to hear everything's working out for you."

"You sure?"

She smiles and says, "Positive. You and I are from two different worlds."

"Maybe that's what will make it work," he says. "Here, take my card. Call me," she takes the card and he walks away.

Yvonna takes her seat and tries to keep her eyes off of the shadow of his physique leaving. When he's gone, she lifts her head up and wonders if she'd ever be able to have love again. After all, it was love that sent her on a mission of vengeance. It was the need for love that caused her to unconsciously split her personalities, just to deal with life. Maybe love could reverse her pain too.

"There's no need in you worrying about him. He'll be no better than the rest. You did the right thing," Gabriella appears, in the seat next to her. "It'll be me and you for life."

*That's what I'm worried about.*

55

# A QUICK DECISION
# QUICKLY BECOMES A
# WRONG DECISION

"I don't think this will work. You don't know her condition. I've spent a lot of time with Yvonna, and she's smart. Smarter than most," Jona says as she watches Lily fuss over wires.

"If she was so smart she wouldn't have to see you," Lily says as she is readjusting the hidden microphone under the armrest of the chair in which Yvonna will be sitting in within thirty minutes. "You *so-called* professionals," she says sarcastically. "Give this freak-job too much credit. She's no more human than an ape running around in the wild. She just needs to be caged."

Jona frowns and wonders if she just through her a racist comment.

"And you cops don't give her *enough* credit. Yvonna Harris is far from an ape. But the longer she's out there, the more she's evolving. Now I want to catch her as much as you do. But we *must* remember, she hid two personalities and killed two people before she was old enough to buy liquor."

Lily doesn't want to hear Jona's wise words. As far as she was concerned, had everyone took her and her partner seriously, a lot of people would be alive.

"We'll see how smart she is." Lily places the microphone in the perfect position and steps back to look at it. "Have you gotten in contact with Terrell?"

"He won't answer my call."

"You should go see him."

"I don't think he wants a part of this. Think about it, you didn't either."

"Try harder. With the information he has on her, these taped recording and my surveillance tapes we should be fine. Question, how are you going to get this accepted in court?"

"I got the hospital Yvonna to sign a document agreeing to taped sessions when I first took her case. It's standard for my patients and is used for situations like this."

"Doesn't the recorder have to be visible?"

"No. Not as long as she signed my document. With you doing surveillance my case will be easier to prove."

"I got you. Just don't fuck this up. And remember, you have to get her mad. The madder she get's the easier it will be to bring Gabriella out. She's like her bodyguard or some bullshit. She shows up only when she needs protection physically or mentally."

"Wow…I have to give you credit. You know more about her than I realized."

"I know *everything* about her. I was in the courtroom during her trial everyday. And I still say she's not smart. She's a snake so she's able to hide in more places."

"I hear you."

"So…are you going to let me in on what you're going to say to her? Maybe we can rehearse a little." Lily grabs the black leather book bag and packs her equipment inside of it. Afterwards, she zips it up and places it on her back. Her small frame and short haircut makes her look like a young boy.

"I'm sorry I can't do that. She's still my patient and her case is still confidential." She says waving Yvonna's file.

"Don't you think you're breeching that policy by asking for my help in the first place? And you already told me that you think she's identifying again with her personality."

"I did but I told you nothing specific," Jona says sitting behind her desk. "It's public information that Yvonna was hospitalized for her disorder." Remembering she wants to ask Lily something private she says, "How did your partner take her life?"

"You know how," Lily's face is distorted and she immediately gets on the defensive. Trying to avoid the question, she fusses with the bag, readjusting it over and over. "Yvonna was released after all of the hard work we put into this fuckin' case! And she couldn't take it anymore. She felt betrayed by a system she loved. That's what happened!" She pauses and looks at Jona with narrow eyes feeling as if she's on trial. "I'm not going over this again! I've told the department everything I know! This is not my fault! It's theirs! A great cop took her life because of a fucked up legal system. Now if you don't believe me, I don't give a fuck! I did nothing wrong! Nothing!"

"Lily, are you okay?" Jona asks softly after witnessing her tangent.

The conversation is interrupted when there's a knock on the door. She walks from around her desk and answers it. When they both see it is Yvonna, their mouths drop.

# FUNNY DAY SMARTER PLAN

"Yvonna…what are you doing here? Your appointment is in fifteen minutes."

Yvonna pushes past her and struts inside. Her eyes are fixed on Lily's. She hated her. In her mind, it was Lily and her partner Shonda who caused her only sister to turn on her. When Yvonna saw Jesse on the tape discussing their family secrets she felt betrayed.

"I'm here *and* on time. Isn't that what you told me to do?" she sits in the seat and crosses her legs. "Anyway, I come early all the time after you requested it of me.

"Uh…yes. I just didn't think you would be *this* early."

Yvonna laughs and replies, "Jona cut the bullshit. You're just embarrassed because you got caught conspiring with Mr. Mullet over here."

"Yvonna, please! Don't be rude."

"It's true. Even her dead partner can see what's going on here."

"And what's that?" Jona asks. She is surprised at how quiet Lily is even after Yvonna's harsh comments. Just minutes earlier she appeared confident and now that it is time to fight, she was cowering and she seems terrified.

"Let's see how you would put it. You're trying to *catch* me in something. You two bitches can't fight alone, so you have to jump me. But I'm from southeast DC. I know how to handle both of you at the same time."

"That's not true. No one is trying to jump you."

"It most certainly is, Jona," she laughs. "And since I ruined this cunt-juice drinker's life which caused her partner to tap out and burn in hell, she's deciding to help you."

"I don't know what you're talking about, Detective Martin is a patient of mine."

"She needs to be but I'm sure she isn't."

Yvonna loving the fear in Lily's face decides to fuck with her. She hadn't seen her since she stood up in court years earlier ranting and raving saying, 'Yvonna Harris must be taken off the streets! And if America's court system is worth its weight it will take her life like she took the lives of so many innocent people'.

And now, here in Yvonna's presence she can't cope. The thunder she presented on the stand is now reduced to a faint echo.

"You know exactly what I'm talking about, Lily," Yvonna says breathing in her face. "So…here I am…*Live* and in living color. What are you going to do now? Kill me, Officer Lily? Because I'd like to see you try. I'll beat your ass faster than you can change your mind."

"I…I…I…didn't…say that."

"Sure you did, officer."

"Yvonna sit down!" Jona demands hitting her desk with her balled up fist. "You better compose yourself!"

Yvonna laughs, looks at her and then back at Lily. "You bitches never in life came face to face with somebody like me and you don't know what to do."

When she says that, a foul odor so strong fills the room that it causes Yvonna's stomach to churn.

Lily stutters, "Uh…Jona, I'll call you later. I have to go." She runs out of the room without waiting on a response.

Yvonna looks down where she stood and sees a small pile of brown loose matter on the floor.

"Wow…that bitch shit on herself! Are you serious?!"

Jona looks at the mound and says, "That's not funny, Yvonna."

"Why isn't it? She was scared shitless!"

"Yvonna we're going to have to reschedule this appointment." Jona picks up her phone. "Dawn, please send somebody upstairs immediately to clean my office. There's been a mistake."

Yvonna laughs and says, "A mistake. That's what you call it huh?"

Jona hangs up. "Yvonna, I'll call you when it's time for us to reschedule."

With a smile on her face as bright as the sun she says, "Yes...*let's* reschedule." She stands up, leans on her desk and replies, "You'll have to get a partner stronger than her if you wanna fuck wit' us."

"Us?" Jona repeats surprised at her admission.

"You heard me. Be careful, Jona. Be *extremely* careful," she walks toward the door and says, "Oh...let me put this with the rest of the shit." With that she drops the microphone that was on the seat in the feces. "You're right. I *am* smart, Jona. And I'm smarter than you too. Remember that."

She strolls out of the door. Although Jona was clueless, Lily's body reaction knew what Jona did not. Lily had stood face to face with Yvonna before. But since her involvement in the case she'd never...*ever* been in the company of Gabriella until today. And the moment Yvonna walked through the door, the look in her eyes told her that she finally had. And as long as she lived, she hoped she wouldn't have to again.

# LET'S GET IT OVER WITH

"Treyana don't start no shit this time. Say exactly what I told you to say. When you get into her house, place this bag in one of her cabinets. Do you understand?" She hands her a plastic sandwich bag filled with the paint chips used to poison Bilal.

"Yes. I understand," she says as they sit in a rented black Honda outside of Bernice's house.

Yvonna made an anonymous call to the Department of Child Protective Services. She wanted them to think Bernice was trying to kill her own blood. She did almost the same thing to Sabrina when she called the cops to report that she'd left him in the house by himself, even though she was the one who convinced Sabrina to do it.

Bilal Jr. survived and for some reason, a part of her was relieved. She wanted Bernice hurt more than she wanted him harmed. Her ultimate plan was to get the child removed so that she'd feel hurt and all alone. And when the time was right, she'd kill her.

"Don't mess up and don't try to be slick and take off the microphone either. I'm not playing with you. Remember our plan."

Yvonna wants her to wear the microphone to monitor what she says.

"Yvonna, please stop threatening me! I'm sick of this shit! You've taken me through hell and back and right about now...I don't care if you fuckin' kill me or not!"

Yvonna sits back in the drivers seat and says, "Well...well....well," she looks her over like she'd been gone a long time and had finally returned. "I guess you not a desperate housewife after all. You're the hood rat I knew from D.C."

"I'm serious, Yvonna. I don't know how much more of this I'll be able to take. Sometimes I feel death is better than living like this."

"I understand what you're saying, death would better. But you're forgetting one main point."

"What?"

"You aren't the one I have intentions on killing if you fuck up. Oh no sweet, Treyana," she says as she wipes her cheek with the back of her hand. She squeezes her chin and positions her face so that they're eye to eye. "I need you alive so that you can die slowly, knowing all the while that you're the cause of your family's death. So let me ask you now, is death really better than living?"

Treyana snatches the bag from Yvonna, storms out of the car and runs up to Bernice's door. She takes a deep breath, before knocking. She knows if she seems too rattled, Bernice will be on full alert and suspect something.

Bernice opens the door. "Treyana?" she says looking her over. "So let me guess...you're in the neighborhood *again* and decided to just stop by?"

"No, I heard about what happened with Bilal Jr., and I wanted to see how you were doing. And if you needed anything."

"I'm doing fine." She opens the door wider. "Come inside. I was just watering my plants."

"Where's Bilal?"

"He's still at the hospital but he comes home later on today."

She closes the door behind herself.

She walks inside and sits down feeling like a phony for her part in Yvonna's plan. Treyana looks at Bernice. Normally she'd be wearing fly designer labels in an attempt to maintain her youth. Now she was looking closer to her natural age of fifty-somethin'. Yvonna had been back for only a few months and already she was causing problems in people's lives.

"Did they say what happened?"

"Treyana, they told me but I don't understand." She sits next to her. "I keep thinking over and over how he could come in the way of lead poisoning."

"Lead poisoning? How is that possible?"

"Who knows," she says hunching her shoulders. "I've been out all week retracing the places he's been. I've been everywhere. The school, the store, his friend's houses and nothing makes sense."

"What about here?"

"My house was made way after 1976, the year they made lead paint." She stands up grabs a large yellow cup to water her plants.

"Any long term problems?"

"They say it's too early to tell. He's still young. But if it impacted him that bad, there's a possibility that it will cause memory issues. He may even have problems in school."

She places the cup down and flops down on the sofa in defeat and Treyana scoots next to her rubbing her leg. Bernice places her face in her hands and cries.

"Things will be okay, Bernice. You're strong. I know you can handle anything that comes your way."

"I don't know, Treyana. Not this time. I've wronged so many people. I've done so much dirt. God has taken my son, Bilal Jr's mother and maybe even my grandson. I prayed all night begging God for forgiveness. I hope he hears me. I pray he hears me."

"You're doing good by your grandson and God isn't doing this to you. Bilal and Sabrina were dealt tough blows but it wasn't your fault. I know they're smiling down from heaven. Trust me. They're proud of you and they love you."

"Look at you," Bernice says rising up from her tear soaked palms. "You're all grown up. You look good."

"Not really. I'm not as together as you think."

"Well you hide it well."

"We're women," she says looking at her. "We have to."

"You know what, I'm glad you came over." She rubs her knee.

"Me too." She places her hand over Bernice's.

"I wish we could've been close."

"Don't worry, Bernice."

"I'm serious. It's just me and you so tell me something, why don't you want people to know that," Treyana cuts her off in mid-sentence.

"Bernice, I came for *you*, not me. So please don't talk about that."

"I have too. You have my grandbabies and you don't allow me to see them. How come? Those twins mean so much to me, Treyana. And I hate that we can't all be together especially after Bilal died. I've kept your secret for so long. Please let me be a part of their lives."

"Bernice, please stop!"

"I'm serious. That bitch, Yvonna has gone on with her life and there's no reason why you can't sneak them over here for me to see them. Bilal Jr's their brother and they don't even know him. I hate that you and Bilal chose to keep such a major secret from everybody, Treyana. But if you would allow me just to see the children, my grandbabies, I promise that I will never tell your husband about this. I just want to be around my grand kids. I need to keep Bilal's spirit near me and his kids are the only way I know how."

There is a silence so thick in the room that it was difficult to move without feeling weighed down by its presence.

"You really should not have said that," Treyana sobs. "I begged you never to *ever* mention our secret and you just couldn't do it. Now everything's going to be messed up."

"No…it won't. Nobody will know! I promise!"

"I wish it was that simple, Bernice," Treyana says as she stands. Tears fall out of her eyes by the pounds.

"What…what do you mean?"

When Bernice asks the question, a loud bang sounds off on the front door.

"Who is that?" she asks looking at Treyana feeling she'd have the answer. She stands up and looks at the door, which moves slightly due to the heavy banging.

"I'm sorry, Bernice. I never wanted any of this to happen. I hope you believe me."

# SHE KNEW LESS THAN SHE THOUGHT

Bernice opens the door and covers her mouth when she sees Yvonna standing in the doorway with a gun in her hand. She looks demonic. But how can she not, she was Gabriella, the devil herself. She walks slowly inside closing and locking the door behind her.

Treyana passes out cold. The moment is too much for her to bear. On the table next to Treyana, Gabriella dumps the water from the large yellow cup Bernice was using to water her plants. She dumps all of it on her. Treyana comes to coughing and gagging loudly. The moment she moves, Gabriella kicks her in the stomach.

"You fuckin', slut! You slept with Bilal and had kids by him?! Behind her back!"

"Yvonna, please!"

"All this time she thought she knew you. You ain't nothin' but a scandalous ass bitch!"

She's so scared that she doesn't recognize that Gabriella is referring to Yvonna as a separate person.

"I'm so…sorry, Yvonna!" she tries to sit up straight, her entire body drenched from the water. "Please, forgive me. It happened one time. We never saw each other after that! I wasn't in love with him!"

"You a fuckin' liarrrrrrrrrrrrrrrrrrrrrrrrrrr!" she screams.

Bernice knew her fate,…death. After all, this would make the second time she kept a secret from Yvonna about her son's infidelities.

It was one thing to sleep with a bitch, but Bilal was running around town fucking anything with a hole.

Thinking she could exit before Gabriella takes the rest of her rage out on her, she moves for the door. It was a fatal mistake. As if she had eyes on the back of her head, she whips around, aims her 9mm Ruger equipped with a silencer, and shoots her once in the right arm.

"Awwwww!" Bernice screams falling against the wall. Red blood splatters everywhere.

"I'm not hardly done with you yet, bitch!" Gabriella says shooting her in the right leg next. "Please...stoop! I'm sorry, Yvonna!" she drops to the floor.

"You'll never be sorry enough for me you dusty, bitch. Both of you gonna pay for this shit."

Gabriella picks up the phone and calls the one man she knew she could count on when she wanted something done. It was the same worthless degenerate who tattooed Treyana's sons for cash.

"Ya'll, fucked up this time."

---

"That's good, Drew. I don't think the knots can get any tighter than that."

Andrew Whinston, a fuck up, a crack head, and a heartless bastard, could always be counted on to do the most horrible things for enough money to feed his dope habit. He'd been stabbed, jumped and shot multiple times for wronging people in the pursuit of his habit and had a record thicker than a phone book. Two of the bullet wounds he suffered were by Yvonna's gun when he tried to take her money and not finish a job he started. He learned quickly that it was better to steal from his own mother and burn in hell than it was to get on her bad side. His large build, scarred face, and curved back, which broke after he was beaten and never healed properly, earned him the nickname Igor.

"Well, well, well," Gabriella says. "Let me take a look at them."

She made them strip naked earlier upstairs while Drew watched to be sure they stayed in line. She went downstairs to prepare her torture scheme.

And now they were on their knees in the basement of Bernice's house. Their arms were tied behind their backs and another rope connected their lower bodies. It was long enough around their waists to allow their backs to touch. Hot water was in the basement sink and they wondered what she had planned.

"Yvonna, I have to tell you something about," Drew stops after she throws her hand up at him.

"Not now." She says thinking he wanted the high she promised him for helping her. "Tell me," Gabriella says smoking a cigarette while looking at Treyana. "How did you come to fuck Yvonna's man?" She sits in a chair looking down on them.

There bodies tremble as they realize that the personality they'd heard of during Yvonna's case was taking over. And Bernice's blood from the bullet wounds spill onto the floor beneath them.

"Yvonna, please," Treyana cries. "It was only once. You know I use to buy smoke from Bilal. We was cool. We got to smokin' and one thing led to another. My husband had just left me and I was lonely. I promise we never tried to be together again. Ever."

"Lift them up, Drew," she is frustrated with her pleading. Drew lifts them up and leads them to the narrow sink.

"This is how it's gonna work. We're going to put both of your upper bodies in the sink. Now if you *both* stay under, you'll *both* die. But…if you try to fight, only one of you will be able to come up for air by leaning on the back of the other forcing them deeper into the water." She began laughing loving her plan. "But if you do, the other person will drown."

"Please," Bernice cries continuing to loose blood. "Don't do this! I'm gonna die."

Drew places them in the water, and surprisingly, Bernice raises her head first, and leans on Treyana's back gasping for air. Gabriella sits back in her seat eager to watch a good fight. But when Treyana doesn't fight back, her eyes widen. *Fuck is this chic doin'?* Treyana remains under water as Bernice's old ass leans on her for support. Treyana moves a little in the beginning, but soon the muscles in Treyana's legs began to relax. It was obvious. She'd given up.

"Oh no you don't, bitch!" Gabriella says leaping from her seat knocking the chair to the floor. She grabs a fist full of Treyana's hair, pulls her up and knocks Bernice into the water. She's finished with Bernice but not Treyana.

"Let...m...me die, Yvonna. I don't care." She says as water escapes her eyes, mouth and nose.

"Not yet. Drew, cut this bitch's throat and bag her when you're done," she says referring to Bernice.

"You got it. But...you got somethin' for me? I'm feelin' real bad right now." He rubs his arms.

"Boy!!! You's a worrisome ass, junkie," she says reaching into her pants throwing him a sack. It bounces off of his nose and hits the floor and scrambles to pick it up. "Slice this bitch throat first and smoke that shit later."

Gabriella unties Treyana's hands and Drew slices Bernice's throat. Her feet kick in swift jerking motions before stopping altogether. She was as dead as dead could be.

Gabriella returns her focus to Treyana. First she pulls her by her hair and drags her along the floor until her back is up against the wall. The smell of Drew smoking dope sickens her stomach and she wonders how the fuck he set up lab so quickly.

"Why you tryin' to die?" She asks Treyana.

"Yvonna, please. Let me die! Because, you gonna do what you want to anyway. And ain't nothin' I can do about it," she says weakly.

She stoops down and looks into her eyes. She knew something else was up. "What the fuck is up with you?!"

"Yvonna..." she laughs weakly. "You not as smart as you think you are."

"And why is that, bitch?!"

"Check my pants. Upstairs," her laughter is now hysterical.

"For what?"

"Because your wire wasn't the only one I was wearing."

# LEAVE ME OUT OF THIS SHIT

Jona holds the phone in her hand and it shakes uncontrollably. She has asked Yvonna everyday to bring her husband along to participate in her sessions. First she'd say work wouldn't allow him, so Jona contacted Each One Teach One, his non-profit organization to verify her truth, and discovered she was lying. Next she'd say he left her. Believing Yvonna had something to do with him missing, she decides to tilt the scales to beat Yvonna at her own game.

"Mam, has he been missing for more than 48 hours?" the officer asks.

"Yes."

"Where was he last seen?"

"At his home."

"Have you gone to check on him?"

"Yes. And his car is there, but he's not."

"What's his full name?"

"Dave Walters."

What Jona was really trying to do was stir up controversy around him being missing. The only problem is, with Lily no longer answering her calls, she has to fight alone. So it was time to fight dirty.

TWO
LONG...LONG...WEEKS
LATER

# A PENNY FOR YOUR THOUGHTS

Penny placed the hot tea on the red dinner trey next to a bologna sandwich with cheese. Time was not kind to Penny's posture or her face. Although she exuded love to all those she cared for as a nurse and in her personal life, she never found anyone…not one single soul, to show her love in return. Still, the selfishness of others never stopped her from loving them all the same.

Lifting the trey off of her spotless cream kitchen counter, she carefully walks toward the basement, where Yvonna had stayed for the past few weeks. She loved caring for her and kept the promise she made to her the first time she saw her, that if she needed her, she'd always be there. Just Yvonna being in the house, gave her purpose and a reason to get up in the morning. Yvonna had ran out of money and quickly turned to Penny for help by crying to her that Dave had left her for another woman. Penny trusting her, allowed her into her home.

"Yvonna, I's got your food, girly. I knows if you have it your way, you'd stay down there all day doin' nothin', but if you gonna stay wit' me, old Penny gots to make sure you eats!" she says before knocking on the door.

Right before she twists the knob and enters the basement, something Yvonna had begged her not to do, Yvonna burst out of the door causing Penny to spill the tea over the shiny hardwood floor.

"I'm sorry," Yvonna says. She locks the door behind herself

with the tiny key Penny gave her. "I didn't know you were there."

Penny sits the trey on a small wooden counter and wipes the tea from the floor with the napkins on the trey.

"Don't you go worryin' yourself about it. I came to the door afta you asked me to keep your privacy. So I got exactly what I deserved. Bumped," she laughs.

"I don't know why you so nice to me."

"'Cause I'm supposed to take care of you."

Yvonna smiles and helps her clean up the mess before sitting in the beige living room sofa that was covered with plastic. Penny's entire home looked like a page out of a 1975 magazine. Beads covered almost every doorway, and all of the couches and chairs, including the ones in the dining room, were covered with plastic. Beige, cream and green were the dominating colors. Her place was warm and cozy but lonely.

On the walls framed pictures of her son, Baker were everywhere. In every one of them, he looked unhappy, like life wasn't kind to him.

"What happened to your son?" Yvonna asks, nibbling on her sandwich and looking at his pictures.

Penny who was in the kitchen making Yvonna another cup of tea, stops in her tracks and looks down at the floor. Hearing the question causes her more discomfort than she wants. But the unconditional love she has for Yvonna, causes her to answer the question anyway.

"He...he got tired of livin'," she says as she walks into the living room. She places a fresh cup of Lemon tea on the table next to Yvonna. "And trust me when I tell you...I knows it was my fault," she looks at one of his pictures on the wall, takes a deep breath and pauses. "I guess I neva could understand how a man so young could be so tired. Wit everything." She sat on the recliner in front of Yvonna.

"What do you mean?"

"Yvonna, when yous grow up. It's ya parents responsibility to take care of you. To make sure your life is one worth livin'. At least until you can finds a way on your own."

Yvonna thinks about the abuse she endured at the hands of her father and how her mother took his side. Her heart starts to ache and she desperately tries to gain control of her pain.

"I'm sure it wasn't your fault."

"Yes it was. I failed him."

"How?" Yvonna places her sandwich down and focuses on Penny. "You seem like you care so much about people. I can't see you being anything but wonderful to him. I only wish my mother treated me half as good as you treat me."

"Don't hands me a reward just yet," Penny says softly. "My actions today come from years of experience in heartache and pain."

Yvonna laughs. "Well...what happened?"

"When he was younga, much, much younga than you, he told me he wasn't happy...and that he was scared all the time. I...I neva understood it. I gave him as much love as I could hold in one day, includin' the love I shoulda had for myself. But...but it was neva enough. No matta what I did, he neva had the smile a child should have when they wakes up in the mornin' to witness life. Neva," she shakes her head and tears escape her eyes.

"He always seemed to carry the burden of fifty mens on his shouldas. And lil' by lil', he started gettin' worse in school. He would-n't do his work. And if somebody said somethin' to him, he'd start a fight. So I'd talk to him, and he'd seem to do betta. He always tried to do what I wanted, even when he couldn't.

"So when the calls from school stopped comin', I thought he was okay. Turns out he just isolated himself. He stayed alone so he wouldn't have to deals wit' people. His grades dropped all the way down. And it started to be hard just to get him out of bed.

"Well one day, I decided to stop bein' scared. I had to be a parent. So I sat him down and asked him what was wrong. I guess I shoul-da asked before, 'cept I don't think I wanted to know the answa." She gets up and starts dusting the old mahogany dining room table and Yvonna stands, following behind her like a lost child. Her son's story seemed eerily like hers.

"Well, I came to his room early one morning. I figured if some-thin' was wrong wit my baby, I had to know, to deal wit it, best I could!" she punches the table and dents it slightly. Yvonna glances at the table and see other craters and figures she's relived the story many times before. "I woke him up and he was angry at first. Until I said, 'Baby what is wrong wit' you? Why is you so angry wit' life?' And when I asked him," she smiles. "His eyes lit up and my heart softened. I knew then that all he wanted was somebody to ask what he needed. I hadn't seen him smile since he was five. I guess just me askin'…just me havin' the courage to want to know what could be holdin' his mind hostage so long, gave him a sense of relief. And then…he turns around to me and says, 'Ma, I hear voices. All the time. Day and night and telling me to kill myself. I don't know why. I'm scared because I think people are talkin' to me, that ain't here. Can you help? Can you make them stop, mama?'"

Yvonna backs out of the dining room and flops on the couch. She is shocked at Penny's admission. But Penny continues, not noticing Yvonna's detachment.

"And…I…I…said, 'Stop lyin'! If you don't stop makin' up stories like those, people gonna think you serious! They gonna think you crazy and take you away from me! Do you want that?' And when I did that, when I said those hateful words to him, I took the lil' life he managed to use to just walk around this world, away. He was left wit' nothin'." When she turns around and looks at Yvonna, her eyes are bloodshot red and filled with tears. "I didn't believe my son, and I killed him. If I had believed him, he'da neva placed the barrel of my gun to his head and kill himself."

"That bitch is fucking crazy! And you're stupid as shit if you listen to her. She's probably some lesbian tryin' to get you to fuck her old ass or somethin'. And don't think for one minute I'm going to stay around and watch that nasty shit either." Gabriella appears on Yvonna's right.

"Shut up!" Yvonna yells.

"You shut up and look at yourself. If you believe that old slut, I'll hurt her. Don't make me do it, Yvonna. You know I'm not playin'!"

"You leave her alone! If you hurt her I'll kill you!" Yvonna yells fearful of what her mental condition might make her do.

Looking at Penny she says, "Penny. I have to talk to you. I...don't think it's a good idea for me to stay here. I don't want to hurt you." Yvonna surprises herself by caring for Penny.

"She can't hurt me," Penny says softly. "She can't hurt me because she's you and I know you want to get better. And yous don't have to go through none of dis alone. I've studied your case. Them white folks gots medicine for stuff like this. But you gots to take it," Penny disappears into the kitchen, opens the top of a blue cookie jar and removes a pill bottle. She walks back to the couch. "I gots this from the hospital, the day you called me and told me you needed a place to stay. I'm not 'sposed to have it, and I'll answa to God for my sins for stealin', but I know if you take it, you'll be betta. And you'll be able to live your life. Ain't that what you want?"

Penny looks into Yvonna's eyes and sees sorrow. The energy she shows matches her son's exactly when he asked for help and she denied him.

And suddenly, as if Penny had said the most hateful thing imaginable to Yvonna, her face changes.

"Bitch, you don't know who you're fuckin' wit!"

Penny unmoved by the presence of Yvonna's multiple personality syndrome, straightens her spine and lifts her head.

"Yvonna, you're still wit' me, baby," she grabs her hand forcefully to take control of the situation. "This is you. You're one person. Not two. And you're still wit' me right now."

Gabriella snatches her hand away and says, "Bitch you betta stay out of my life! I'm warnin' you."

With that she gets up and storms out of the house. Little does she know, staying out of her life was the last thing Penny planned to do.

# SOMEBODY ELSE
# OUTSIDE OF HERSELF

Yvonna's mind rushes. She always felt close to Penny but after hearing her son's story, she felt even closer to her. She realizes she must talk to Penny to warn her that caring for her might place her life in danger. It was as if her soul was divided in half. One part loved Penny and the other part hated her for making her trust anyone outside of herself.

Yvonna hops out of a cab in front of Duke Ellington's campus. The sun shines brightly. "Stay right here, I won't be long." She tells the cab driver.

Slowly, she moves past the other students keeping her distance from her intended target, her 14-year-old sister, Jesse. Although Jhane moves Jesse from place to place to keep Yvonna away from her, it didn't work. Jesse was the one person nobody could keep her away from.

Yvonna walks closer to Jesse's locker and smiles. She'd been there many times before and knew Jesse's routine perfectly. Although Jesse had lost a limb, she's happy when she sees her new prosthetic arm. Yvonna found out a year earlier that John Hopkins had developed a procedure to create prosthesis that could listen to the brain to provide patients with more fluid motions. She sent the clip to Jhane anonymously so that Jesse could know about the procedure. It pleases her that the masculine bitch took her advice.

Jesse is surrounded by a bunch of girls and it's apparent that she was popular in school. Her confidence had grown and she was now so beautiful that it was hard not spotting her in a crowded room. When the bell rang, Jesse and her friends focus on their lockers grabbing what they need for class. The other kids scatter everywhere to make their classes on time.

But Jesse isn't speeding. She stops and looks directly at Yvonna. Jesse's eyes widen but this time, she doesn't run. Instead she walks up to Yvonna.

"You haven't been here in a few days. I thought you finally left me alone," she says softly. "I guess I was wrong."

"You know I've been watching you?"

"Yvonna, it's hard not to see you. Looked how you're dressed," she points out.

Yvonna takes notice to the silk black Robert Cavalli dress, with the embedded silk scarf belt she is wearing.

"I guess the dress is a bit much huh?"

"The Cavalli? I'm talking about the red sequin Nina Ricci shoes!" she laughs.

At that moment Yvonna's heart skips. She was actually having a conversation with her baby sister and she wasn't running.

"Wait a minute, what do you know about fashion?"

"After running from you all my life, I had to learn something about you," she says with disappointment. Her head drops, she readjusts her book bag and says, "look...please don't follow me. I like it here, Yvonna. I have friends and I'm really good at singing. My life has changed."

"You sing? I didn't know."

"I'm working on an album and everything."

"That's great! I'm happy for you."

"Thank you. But are you *really* happy for me?"

"Yes, Jesse. I am."

"Good. So please don't come back. If Jhane finds out you've been following me again, she'll move me. I'll lose everything."

Yvonna's face becomes angry.

"Please don't hurt her, Yvonna. I love her. She's taken care of me and I feel happy with her. Okay?"

All Yvonna wants to do is murder the beastly woman known as *Aunt Jhane*. In fact, she had plans to see her later that week.

"I'm not like that anymore, Jesse. I just came to see you."

"Good," she smiles. Jesse turns around to walk away but she stops and turns around to look at her sister. "How are you?"

Yvonna's stomach flutters and one tear forms in the wells of her eye. Her sister actually cared enough to ask how she was.

"Uh...I'm fine. Thanks for asking."

"Good." She smiles. "I'm happy to hear you're doing good."

Without another word, Jesse walks away leaving Yvonna alone. Yvonna is tempted to run behind her, to convince her to play hooky from school. There is so much that she wants to know. Like does she have a boyfriend? Was she in any trouble she could help her with? And did she miss her a little?

Just speaking to Jesse causes her to think about being a better person. But when she walks out of the building, and toward her cab, hate consumes her all over again. Because outside of the school sat five police cars. And they all had one goal, to take one crazy ass bitch into police custody.

# NOT THIS SHIT AGAIN

The interrogating room in Washington DC is hot but Yvonna remains cool. She'd learned along time ago that if you're under investigation, your interview starts the moment you walk through the door.

The two officers on the other hand were losing their cool. It had been over an hour and still, Yvonna stuck to her guns. They tried to break her down using old methods and all failed. Someone should have told them that Yvonna Harris was not the normal suspect.

"So let me get this straight, you expect us to believe that you don't know where your husband is? You expect us to believe he just fell off of the face of the earth?" Officer Jenson asks. Peter Jensen's white complexion flush red and his large nose was dripping with sweat giving him a glossy glow. Although he wasn't all that attractive, compared to his partner Guy Peterson, he was a male model. If nothing else, Peter's body was in supreme shape.

"Peter, if you're going to ask me a question over and over again, at least change it up a little," she says crossing her legs. "'cause to tell you the truth, I'm getting bored with it all."

"I don't care if you're getting bored or not! I want answers."

"And I gave you one. I'm sorry if it's not to your liking. I have not seen him since he left me."

"You expect us to believe that?" Officer Jensen says sitting in a seat directly on the left of her. He is overweight and breathing heavily. His dark skin was ashy and he looks dusty. It didn't help that his thick mustache makes it almost difficult to understand what he was saying.

"I know you look at me and say to yourself, 'if I ever got a chance to sleep with her dirty panties under my nose, I'd rather cut my dick off than leave'. But what you have to realize is this…a man like you didn't leave me because a man like you never had a chance with me. Dave was different," she smirks.

"*Was*? You sound like he's gone forever," Samuels says.

"Yes. He *was* with me now he's *not*."

"You think you're smart don't you?"

"Officer…what do you want? You're wastin' my time."

Officer Samuels opens another folder and says, "What do you know about the disappearance of Bernice Santana and Treyana Piler?"

"I'm not interested in either one of them. I thought you were questioning me on my husband so why are you still bringing that up? I don't know anything about them."

"So you want us to believe you haven't been in Treyana's presence?" Jensen asks.

"I didn't say that. I said I'm not interested in either one of them. And I don't know anything about their disappearances and it's obvious you don't either. Now look…if you fellas are not going to charge me, I have a beer to drink and a dick to fuck and would like to go about my business."

"With your husband?"

"I just said we're not together, mister."

"No you didn't. You said you hadn't heard from him." Jensen continues thinking he's on to something.

Yvonna laughs, shakes her head and says, "You do the worse job of trying to entrap somebody I've ever seen in my life. Let me give you a few pointers, before you can began to entrap someone, you must ask the right questions at the right times."

"Lady I don't know what you're talking about. I'm not trying to entrap you. I'm simply doing my job. And that is, trying to find the whereabouts of three missing people. And you're sitting here lying saying that you didn't hear from them."

Yvonna leand in toward him, licks her lips and says, "Now when did I say I didn't hear from them?"

"You said it when we…,"

"When we what? Do you even know what you're saying?" She

interrupts him.

"Yes, you said it earlier when we…no…you just said it right before I asked you the initial question."

"So I said it when you asked me the initial question? What was your initial question?"

"I asked you, uh…did you hear from Pliers. And you said you hadn't heard from her."

"Are you sure I said I didn't hear from her…or did I say I'm not interested in her? Which one is it officer?"

"It was when…wait…I asked you after you said…,"

"After I said what officer?" she interrupts. She leans back in her seat and smiles at how unraveled he has become.

"Look…I said I hadn't talked or asked you the initial question before you came in."

"Do you even know what you're sayin?"

"I know what I'm saying, you're just trying to mess me…"

"I'm trying to mess you what," she interjects."

"I know what you're doing young lady. And although my partner might be tripping over his own feet a little, I know *exactly* what I want to know. And what I want to know is this…where the fuck is Dave Walters, Bernice Santana and Treyana Pliers?"

Yvonna smiles at how Samuels stops her from making his partner look like an idiot.

"Like I said, I won't be able to help you because I'm not interested in either one of them. And as a contingency of my release, I'm not even allowed to be around Bernice Santana."

"Breaking the law never stopped you before."

"You don't know me. So don't believe everything you read in the papers."

Officer Samuels was just about to dig deeper into his investigation when an older black man opens the door and says, "Samuels, I have to talk to you for a minute."

"Not now, man. I'm in a meeting."

"This is serious," he says lowering his voice. "You told me to let you know right away when we got a break. We have one."

Officer Samuels pushes his chair back, stands up and says, "Think about what I said, young lady. This is serious. And we can't help you if you don't help us."

Samuels meets the other man at the door. The man's face is bunched up and he obviously has something urgent to tell him that can't wait.

"They found her." He tries his best to whisper but Yvonna's ear hustling skills are impeccable and she hears everything.

"What do you mean they found her?" he asks moving in closer.

"They found her. In her house. In a makeshift storm shelter below the house."

"But we tore her house upside down! It's impossible for her to be inside!" he yells. Spit escapes his mouth and he looks like a wild animal about to attack.

"Apparently you didn't tare it up too good. The man said they found her." Yvonna interrupts. He turns around and looks at Yvonna who wears a smirk on her face.

"I wouldn't laugh just yet," he says before focusing back on the officer. "Was anybody with her?"

"Yes."

"Who? Plier?"

"No. It was a man." Samuels's holds up the wall for support. He felt foolish that his investigators not only missed Bernice's body, but also another victim. His head is spinning so fast that he is afraid to ask another question for fear he'd get the answer. "Who is he?"

"We don't know. They're trying to get his identity. But there's more."

Jensen walks over to the commotion and listens.

"What else is it?" Samuels asks.

"Her head…uh…was…chopped off, and," the bearer of bad news turns away from the men. He is about to vomit and wants to spare them if he can. "He was on the floor, completely nude. With his penis in the victim's mouth. He looked like he suffered a drug overdose. There was a lot of blood under his nose."

Both men look at Yvonna who is laughing so hard she almost

falls out of her seat. They know she has everything to do with it but with the way the murder scene was set up, it places her in the clear.

"I'm glad you think it's funny," Jensen says angrily. "But don't forget, we still haven't found Plier."

"That sounds like a problem that belongs to you, not me, officer. But unless you have a case against me, I suggest you let me go before you have a problem you won't be able to afford."

The men look at each other knowing what they have to do. Neither of them wants to admit it, but she is right. Without evidence, there is nothing they could do. So they do the inevitable and let her go.

# HERE I AM AGAIN

Yvonna sits in the large leather recliner as her feet rests in the bowl that was full of warm soap water. Ming is busy mixing a special purple nail color just for Yvonna. She didn't want anybody in the world having shades like hers.

"Ming, hurry up and bring your chinky-eyed ass over here! My water's getting cold!"

"Shut up! You ask me to do something and than fuss! I'm coming you impatient, heffa!"

Yvonna laughs at the way Ming curses. She was teaching her the proper way to lay a bitch out but she still wasn't getting it.

"You gettin' better, bitch. Still need work though."

Ming laughs. "Fuck you!"

Yvonna tunes her out and focuses back on her letter. She finally finished composing it and wanted to make sure it was perfect. After all, she was planning a murder and torture. With Bernice dead, she could move on to Swoopes. *You gonna wish you ain't fuck wit me!* She thinks to herself.

Ming sits in front of her and says, "Give your feet! But don't wet up my outfit."

"I'm not thinking about your outfit."

"So, Yvonna. I give to you information. What are you going to do now?"

"You don't wanna know all of that."

"I do. I'm very interested."

"I got my ideas."

"So when you give to me my fantasy?"

"Soon, Ming."

"How soon?"

"Soon! Look, I hope you don't think we together or know shit like that just because of our arrangement."

"I'm not thinkin' about you. I just want you to make good on deal."

"I got you." Yvonna focuses on the letter again. "Ming, let me read something to you. Tell me what you think."

"Go 'head," she says as she carves the cuticles around her toenails.

She clears her throat and reads the poem.

*You are I.*
*And you are what I want.*
*I am her who can't live without him.*
*You are my heart beat.*
*I'd rather be raped*
*And*
*I'd rather be tortured.*
*Until I say when.*
*Because it's*
*Not going to do me any good at all*
*To be without you. I said*
*That until it's all said and*
*Done*
*That you are what I*
*Want.*
*You…not him*
*When you left I felt killed.*

Ming stops working on her feet and says, "That's it?"

"Yeah. What you think?"

"That's no poem! That's stupid! That means nothin'!"

Yvonna laughs. "It ain't hardly stupid. And trust me, it definitely means something."

Sure the poem was not her best work, but she was sure that if Tree listened and followed her instructions by reading the last word of each sentence it would read, *"I want him beat, raped, and tortured. When it's all said and done, I want him killed"*.

After she is done with the letter she folds it, places it in an envelope and licks it shut. A smile comes across her face because Swoopes is one of the main people she wants to kill personally. She still remembered how he and his friends raped and beat her only to leave her for dead in an abandoned house. So, she desired nothing more than for the same fate to happen to him. Had it not been for her deceased husband Dave, she would not be alive.

When Dave enters her mind, she is overwhelmed with loneliness and horniness. Murder always does arouse her. It tugs at her even more when she sees Ming kissing one of her jump off dudes she fucked from time to time, at the sink

"Ming hurry the fuck up! I got somewhere to be!" she hates looking at the fine ass nigga she's face sucking.

Ming put her middle finger up in the air.

"If I listen to that weak ass poem, you can give to me five minutes."

"Flat ass bitch!"

Yvonna sighs and throws her head in the headrest. It had been so long since she had a man's company. A man's companionship. A man's dick. And then she remembered…Bradshaw. She pulls out his card and decides to give him a call.

The phone rings twice before he says, "Yvonna, I was waiting on you to call."

She smiles and says, "And how did you know it was me?"

"Because I gave you a number I just got the day we met. I hadn't even given it to anyone yet. When it rang for the first time, I wanted you to be the first to call."

Yvonna takes notice at his tone and conversation. He sounds a little too soft for her liking. She was used to rough necks and Bradshaw put her in the mind of the good doctor Terrell she lived with in Baltimore who she couldn't stand.

"Are you at work or somethin'?" she asks turned off by him already.

"Yeah. Why you ask?"

"It figures," she says rolling her eyes.

"Where are you? Let me take you out."

"I'm in the nail salon in Hyattsville."

"Cool. Meet me at the book store in Eastover Shopping center."

*Did this nigga just say, Cool and Book Store in the same sentence?* She thinks.

"Book store? That's not my idea of a first date."

He laughs and said, "I know but trust me, they have a nice set up in there. We'll be able to drink some coffee, sit back and relax. What do you say?"

Although she wasn't the reading or talking type, she did have to admit that his idea was original.

"I'll be there in thirty minutes. You did say Eastover right?"

"Yeah. It's Cartel Café & Books in Oxon Hill, Maryland. I'll see you in a minute."

She hangs up the phone and looks at Ming. For some reason, she was growing jealous of the attention she was giving her male friend. It wasn't that she was in to her, she just hated that Ming wasn't focused on her.

"Ming! Come on!" she yells.

Both the fine ass nigga and Ming look at her. You can tell he doesn't like that she keeps calling her despite Ming being at work. She decides to fuck with him also.

"Wait. Two more minutes."

"If you come now, I'll give you what you've been asking for."

Ming looks at the guy, says one word to him and walks away. He looks at Yvonna shakes his head and walks out of the nail salon.

"You not play are you?"

"There's only one way to find out."

Yvonna laughs and sinks into her seat having claimed defeat when she realizes she hadn't split into Gabriella in a day. This is odd because whenever she expresses deep emotion, or concern for anybody her personal hater Gabriella appears. Something was definitely going on.

She looks at her watch and notices it was 4:30. That means she'd have about two hours to spend with him before she had to rush home and take caution to keep her little secret…Treyana, in Penny's basement. She couldn't risk Penny finding out that she was in her home.

She had been with her ever since they left Bernice's. It made her angry to discover that Treyana was recording Yvonna's conversations with a recorder. The only problem was when Gabriella drenched her with the water from the yellow cup, the cheap recorder broke immediately It was far from the wire Treyana bragged about. And for her consistent betrayal, she made her pay greatly.

---

"When are you due, Pretty eyes?" the cashier says to one of her customers. The pretty dark skin woman had eyes as shiny as marbles and was nine months pregnant.

"In a month, girl. But let me get out of here and read my books, I'll check you later. I'll probably be finished these in a day."

Yvonna sighs irritated with both of them bitches. "I wish the fuck she takes them home and read 'em then!" she says to Bradshaw who doesn't cosign.

When the pretty pregnant lady leaves, the cashier rings up Brad's purchase.

"You want anything?" he asks as Yvonna as pays for his.

"No I'm good."

He pays for his purchases and they walk to the back of the store to sit in one of the large black leather sofas.

"So, tell me, what have you been up to?"

"Nothin'," she says hating the *getting to know* process. "Look…haven't we gone through all this at the clinic?"

"All what?"

"You know…the short talk bullshit."

Bradshaw's eyebrows rise.

"Come again."

She sighs and says, "Bradshaw, I'ma be real with you. I'm trying to fuck. Now this book store is cute and all, but unless these people gonna let me jump on your dick back here, I'm trying to leave. So what's up?"

He almost spills the coffee over the floor when he hears her comment."

"Come again."

"I said I'm trying to fuck."

"Uh…Yvonna, I wasn't trying to disrespect you. I was trying to…," he stops after she rolls her eyes. "Look. I'm use to a thug as nigga and if you gonna be Mr. Romeo, you need one of them meek-lookin' bitches at the register. Because trust me, I'm not gonna be able to bump wit' you."

Bradshaw looks at her with confusion at first. But as if someone changes the channel, his entire personality flips. Without saying a word he suddenly seems as if he'd been possessed with Swag.

Bradshaw stands up, adjusts his pants and says, "Fuck you sittin' down for? Get up."

His shoulders drop and his black Armani slacks move as comfortably as a new pair of fresh sweatpants as he walks toward the door.

"I knew the nigga I remembered in the institute was in there some where. You been out here too long if you think I like that soft shit was gonna work for me."

"Shawty you aint' seen shit yet."

---

They didn't get halfway inside the elevator at the Super 8 hotel off of Indian Head highway in Maryland before he stuffs Yvonna with nine inches of dick. Grabbing her around her waist, he pulls her toward the back of the elevator and her body rests against his chest. To the naked eye they look like a loving couple. When two people get on from the next floor, and stand in front of them, they smile. The couple doesn't see her skirt hiked up with his dick inside her.

"Bitch I'm about to rip that pussy up when we get in that mothafucka," he whispers in her ear.

"Nigga, don't talk shit," she smiles when they look at them suspiciously. "Show and prove!"

She wouldn't dare tell him that he was already ripping her pussy up due to his thickness. When the elevator opens, he pulls his dick out of her wet pussy, adjusts his pants and straightens her skirt.

"Have fun," Yvonna tells them.

He snatches her and the violence he is exhibiting is doing nothing but turning her on even more. Bradshaw was clearly the right man for the job and he reminds her of Bilal.

Once they get to the room door, he opens it and she walks in first. When the door closes he smacks her so hard, that for a moment, she gets intimidated. She falls on the floor and feels the sting from her rug burnt scratched knees. She rolls over and licks the blood from the corner of her mouth. Lying flat on her back, she wiggles out of the black skirt she's wearing.

"That's how the fuck I like it," she says. When her skirt is off, she removes her panties and opens her legs wide. Then she spreads her soft pussy lips apart so that he can see her already wet pink center. "You made it slick now come get it."

"I got this shit," he takes his pants off. They dropped to the floor and he removes his boxers. There before her, stood not necessarily the longest but certainly the widest dick she'd ever seen in her life. He strokes his already rock hardness in his hand. "I guess your husband ain't hittin' that thing right after all."

"What husband, nigga?" she says as she moves around erotically.

"The husband you supposedly married," he gets down on the floor and is about to plunge into her. His muscles buckle as he prepares to dive into her.

"I ain't married. And even if I was, I wouldn't give a fuck right now."

He laughs at her defiance and eases into her slowly before going deeper.

"Awwwwww! That's right, daddy! Now you hittin' that shit!

How you know I like it like that, huh?"

"So you like cheatin' on your husband?" he says with one hand on her throat and the other on the floor for support.

In her mind it was weird that he chose to mention Dave. And for a second, it turned her off. But she got herself aroused again and moved into his sexual dives.

"Yeah, I'm cheatin' on his whack ass. And if you don't fuck me harder than this…you 'bout to get the fuck up."

He hit her again. *And again.* She was on the verge of cumming and is so aroused by his violence that she isn't going to be able to control her orgasm. Feeling as if he is about to release, he places his fingers in her mouth and she slowly runs her tongue up and down his fingers.

"Awww…fuuuuuckkkk!" he yells. "This shit too fuckin' good!"

"I'm cummin' too," her screams join his.

In seconds, he releases himself into her and she gladly accepts. Afterwards, he smiles at her rubbing her cheek.

"You wild as shit," he tells her looking into her eyes.

"Apparently not wilder than you," she says, her face and body a little sore from the violence.

He picks her up, and places her gently on the bed. Then he places the covers over her partially nude body.

"You're different," she tells him as he scoots under the covers with her.

"Why's that?"

"One minute you're kickin' my ass, next minute you're caring about me."

"That's what you like ain't it?"

She giggles and says, "What you think?"

"Okay…so I gave you what you wanted. Nothing more and nothing less."

She was silent before she says, "Am I going to see you again?"

"Now you wanna see a nigga again, huh? After he kick ya ass."

"Yeah. I like a real nigga."

"I'm a real whether I hit you or not."

"That might be true, but you wouldn't be real enough for me."

"I wonder how real you really are?"

"You wanna find out?"

"Yeah. I got a promise I got to keep. You gonna help me?"

"Yes."

"You say yes before knowing what it is?"

"I trust you're not gonna give me nothin' I can't handle. And judgin' by the look in your eyes, I think I might like it."

Yvonna hops out of bed, her ass jiggles a little sending Bradshaw on another sexual frenzy. She picks up her purse from the floor and removes her phone. She was perfectly confident in her nakedness and this was another attraction to him.

"Ming, meet me at the hotel I texted you earlier," she says looking at him.

"He's with it."

"Ming?" he smiles at the idea of having two women at the same time.

"Ming." She assures him with her eyes, already knowing he's in for a treat.

His eyes sparkle and he licks his lips. She is still smiling when she realizes Penny will be coming home soon. And if she didn't hurry, it might be too late to prevent her from going downstairs. Although she didn't peg her as the nosey type, she couldn't be sure. Penny's cell rings twice before she picks up.

"Hey, sweetheart. Are you okay?"

"Yeah. I'm good. I was wondering when you're going to be home from work. I was going to wait up for you."

"Awww, you so sweet sometimes I think I don't deserve ya!"

Yvonna laughs until she sees Bradshaw in the bed, at full thickness again. Her pussy pulsates and she wants to jump on top of him for the ride. Ming being only around the corner, knocks on the door. Bradshaw opens it, naked. The moment she steps inside, she drops the red short raincoat she's wearing and greets him with a kiss. All without saying not even hello.

Bradshaw places his hand behind her head and kisses her back.

The tattoo on Ming's back turns Yvonna on as she looks at the interaction between two strangers. Bradshaw picks her up and carry her to the bed. With her shoes still on Ming hops on top of him and rides his dick letting her head drop behind her. At this point, Yvonna doesn't know what the fuck Penny's old ass is talking about on the phone.

"Get ova, here," Bradshaw says to Yvonna as he pumps into Ming.

"Are ya there baby?" Penny asks.

"Oh…uh…yeah."

"Oh, I thought I lost you. Did you hear what I said?"

"Fuck no," she blurts out.

"Yvonna?" Penny says her name wondering if she was splitting personalities again. "Are you okay?"

Now Bradshaw has facilitated a 69 and Yvonna's pussy is dripping wet. She doesn't know if she should join them or get her rocks off by watching.

"Yeah, I'm fine. "

"Okay. Well I'll I'm not gonna make it home 'til 5 this mornin'. They asked old Penny to help out in the maternity unit. And we got some lady's who 'bout to pop any minute now."

"Aw…that's messed up," she says trying to hide her excitement. She's taking note at how Ming has the entire shaft of his dick in her mouth. Balls and all. "Well, wake me up when you get home."

"Naw. I want you to gets your rest. Now I left you the tea you like in that microwave oven you likes so much. I tell you I don't understand why you young kids be messin' wit them microwave things. Anyhow, alls you got to do is hit enter and drink ya tea. Okay, sweetie?"

"I will."

"Good cause I,"

Yvonna hangs up in Penny's face before she can finish her sentence when she sees Bradshaw's toes curl. He's about to cum and she doesn't want to miss the fun.

They spent the next six months hooking up to fuck, suck and beat the hell out of each other. They'd even established and understanding and Yvonna never mind Bradshaw fucking Ming on the side from time to time as long as he broke her off. Some how, during these months, Yvonna had grown closer to Penny too.

Yvonna's only problem with Penny was that she seemed to flip out when Yvonna didn't come straight home. And since that was about three times a week, they were often at odds. Still she had to say, with her new man, and new best friend, she was having the time of her life.

# THERE'S NO PAIN LIKE NOT KNOWING

It was after midnight and like he had every day for the past six months since his wife was missing, he roams around their home waiting on word of her return. Still, he hears nothing. The lights flicker on and off and he looks up thinking the bulbs need to be changed. He does nothing, because flickering lights are the least of his worries.

Guilt took him when she initially didn't come home. He wondered if his abuse caused her to leave. Then he grew angry. How dare she leave him? If their marriage failed, he would be the one to make the call it was over not her. When neither guilt or anger made him feel better, he settled on the overwhelming sense of loss.

Deciding to check on their children, he walks to their rooms and slowly open their door. The light from the hallway shines against their small sleeping faces without waking them. He smiles, leans up against the doorway and stares. How he wishes he could close his eyes for one moment. Sleep deprivation has claimed him. And although he wanted rest, his mind wouldn't.

He quietly closes the door and walks to the living room. Grabbing the Remy bottle off the table, he pours him a drink on the rocks.

"Where are you, Treyana? Where are you?" the empty glass rests in his hand.

When she doesn't answer, he swallows the entire drink and

pours another. He does this four times before the effects finally take hold of him.

He looks at the mail accumulating on the table. Treyana took care of the bills so leaving them was his way of defying the obvious, that Treyana may never come home.

Under the mound of mail circulars and bills, he sees the edge of a red envelope. He pushes the others aside and examine the envelope fully. There is no return address and his name was written with penmanship so perfect, it looks like it isn't be real. Curious, he opens it at once and pulls out a purple card with the same handwriting. It read,

*Losing a love brings a pain you can't deny. But have you ever looked in your sons' eyes? If you do I'm sure you'll see. That the life you live is full of deceit. I'm sure you think I don't speak truth. But a small blood test brings with it proof.*

The letter falls out his hand and floats to the floor. His right leg shakes violently and he bears down on it with unusual force to get it to stop. Like the letter said, he can't deny that his sons don't have his eyes. He never told Treyana how he felt and he blamed himself for being skeptical. But the years brought time and still they looked more and more unlike him. *Familiar* no doubt, but unlike him.

Slowly he rises and walks back toward his children's' room. And as if they knew it was time for their mother's secret to be revealed, they stir in their beds and look at him in the doorway.

Tears roll down his eyes as he realizes that the children in the room, the ones he cared for all their lives, were not of his blood and not worthy of baring his last name. Their eyes said it all. Sure they were his wife's children, but he could not say with uncertainty, that they were *his* sons. Now he needed answers more than anything, and he was willing to do what he had to, to get them.

# FEELS TOO GOOD

Yvonna wakes up to a peaceful view of the morning sky from Bradshaw's bedroom window. The sun shines brightly and she smiles at its view. She is at peace. The heat from Bradshaw's body feels like a warm electric blanket against her bare skin. She has to give it to herself…she always could pull a top-notch nigga, crazy or not.

When she backs up a little into Bradshaw, he pulls her closer. Her body had gotten fuller and she went from a size six to twelve although it seemed to be all in the right places. Loving how his hands move over her body, she decides to turn around to get a better view of her man, although they hadn't made it official.

When she turns around, she sees a leg draped over his waist with a red pump wiggling. Gabriella rises from behind him and rests her head on his shoulder. She smiles. Yvonna doesn't.

"You didn't think you could get rid of me, did you?" It had been weeks since she'd seen her.

Yvonna hops out of bed and stares at the scene as if she's pushed into a horror movie. Missing the warmth of Yvonna's body, he opens his eyes and says, "What's wrong, shawty?" He looks behind him and back at her. "Everything okay?"

"Yeah, what's wrong, bitch? Tell this nigga yo ass certified so he can leave you like the rest of them. Go 'head!"

Yvonna looks at Gabriella instead of Bradshaw. And since she sees her resting on his arm, this is where her attention goes. To him it looks like she's looking at his shoulder

"Yvonna! You aight?" he asks sitting up. Gabriella stands up, and Yvonna sees her wearing a red bra and panty set.

"The man is talking to you and here you are staring into space like a dumb ass." She places her hands on her hips.

"It's happening again?" Bradshaw asks. For the first time since she sees Gabriella in the room, she acknowledges him by looking into his eyes. "You wanna talk about it, baby?"

A tear runs down her face, "I just want this to stop. I don't want to be like this."

"Then make it stop. Take the medicine they give you."

"You don't understand. I'm scared."

"Scared of what? Of makin' this shit stop?"

"No. Of being alone. I'm scared that I won't be strong enough without her." She looks at him with pleading eyes.

"You are strong enough. She is you."

Bradshaw stands up and walks toward her. She has forgotten that with him she didn't have to lie. They were in the mental institution together. And because she could be herself with him, this made her more vulnerable to heartache. And vulnerability is the one emotion she tries to block by protecting herself through creating the Gabriella personality. Bradshaw pulls Yvonna into his chest and holds her strongly.

"I got you, Yvonna. You better than this shit. You been through this already and you came through. You are strong."

Yvonna tries to listen but all she can think about is that once he releases her Gabriella will be still there and that he'd be wrong. She needed him to be right. She needed to trust someone. Bradshaw was the kind of man she needed. He is strong…kinky…and willing to stick by her despite her disorder.

"You stupid if you fall in love with this nigga! You know the games men play!"

Yvonna sobs harder and Bradshaw holds her tighter rocking her in his arms. "You bigger than this shit! You can control it, Yvonna. Stay with me. Tell me you bigger! Tell me!"

"I can't."

"Yes you can! You control this shit not the other way around! Now let me hear you say it, baby! Let me hear you be what I know you can. Will this shit!"

He maintains the hold he has on her until the words he needs to hear exit her soft lips.

"I…uh…am stronger…than this." She says in a lowly voice.

"I can't hear you! The woman I met got this shit under control. Now say it again, and when I let you go she gonna be gone. Okay?" she doesn't' respond and he grips her arms tighter altering the ease of the blood flowing through her arms. With stern eyes he says, "Do you hear me?"

"Y…yes."

Bradshaw takes his hands off of her and backs up slowly. Her view is partially blocked because of his muscular chest and broad shoulders. The further he steps back, the better her view becomes until finally, she can confirm that there are no signs of Gabriella.

"She here?" he asks hopefully.

"No," she says looking behind her and around the room. "She's not here."

In this moment she isn't the tough girl she usually was. But out of the darkness, she gains light. Bradshaw was right. She went against everything she knew and trusted him and he was right.

He smiles. "See, you got this shit."

She's falling for him and decides to talk to him seriously about her disorder. She wants to be open about everything before putting the rest of her heart into him. Because history showed that love was not her friend and unless he was *Father Time*, she didn't see how now would be any different. The vibration of her phone in her purse breaks her attention. She walks toward it and picks it up. Bradshaw jumps back in bed.

"Who is it?"

"Penny. She callin' from the house."

"Why so many times?"

"I don't know.'

She presses ignore. And with the screen clear, she's able to scroll through twenty missed numbers from Penny. It made no sense. Had she found Treyana in the basement of her home? One thing was certain, she couldn't wait around there to find out.

# I'M NOT TRYING TO BE

Yvonna creeps up the steps of Penny's home carefully. She wants to avoid her until she finds out much she knows. She loved Penny. In fact, they spent many days talking about Penny's life and the details Yvonna felt comfortable sharing about her past. Penny was quickly becoming the mother she always wanted despite not baring one physical resemblance. But when it came to her privacy, and the protection of it, Yvonna didn't fuck around.

*Fuck does this greasy black bitch want anyway?* She thinks. *"Calling my phone like she lost her mind!"*

After peeking into the front window briefly she decides to go inside when she doesn't see her anywhere. It is important that she remains as silent as possible. Once inside, she looks around again.

*Penny, please don't say you went downstairs after I asked you not to.* She says to herself. *Please. I don't want to hurt you.*

She moves cautiously toward the basement. Once she arrives at the basement door, she removes the small key to unlock it. She opens the door and is about to go downstairs until she sees Penny in the kitchen. She is so preoccupied with chopping a small object that she doesn't notice Yvonna about ten feet away from her.

Taking one more step, Yvonna can see the object is a pill. *What are you doing?* She says to herself. When the item is small enough, she scoops it off the counter with her hand and dusts it into the teacup that Yvonna uses regularly. Her mouth drops. *You wretched bitch.* She thinks. When the powder makes it within the cup, Penny stirs the potion.

Yvonna's conflicted. The tea Penny told her was made with

love was made with poison. Not wanting Penny to know she was on to her black ass, she backs up carefully and makes her way to the basement. She is hurt and tears roll down her face. She loves Penny and here she is betraying her. She'd deal with her later and in her own way. For sure.

---

"When are you going to let me go? I been here for months." Treyana asks as she sits on the floor with her arms tied behind her back against an old radiator. She is wearing a red shirt and is naked from the waist down. Her hair is all over her head and she looks like the dusty bitch she was before Yvonna cleaned her up years earlier. "My husband is going to come looking for me. Please let me go."

"I can't do that. So don't ask me, sweetheart." Yvonna stands over her and looks down at her. "And don't worry about your husband coming for you. I sent him a little message on your behalf. If anything, you'll be lucky if he doesn't come through that door and help me kill you. Seeing as though you cheated on him with my dead boyfriend and all. It seems Bilal had a thing for nasty bitches."

"What did you tell Avante?" Treyana tries to sit up straight.

"I told him to look into the eyes of his children," Yvonna sits on her bed. "I'm sure he'll realize after reading it, that they look nothing like him. He probably already knows. I can't even believe I missed it."

Treyana's head drops. "Why are you doing this to me? And my family? Why don't you just leave us alone?"

"Because I warned you about messing with me, and you didn't listen."

She is quiet before saying, "You're so unhappy you don't even realize it. But I know one day, things are going to change for you. And when they do, they're going to be for the worst. One day you'll get exactly what you deserve."

"I have no doubt I will. But…you're first."

Yvonna changes into her comfortable clothing and walks back upstairs, locking the door behind her. She must deal with Penny and her actions would depend on Penny's response.

"Yvonna. How are you sweetheart?"

Yvonna sits on the couch angry with Penny for putting her in this situation.

"I'm fine," Penny places a hot cup of tea next to her.

"That's good, sweetheart. 'Cause when I knocked on your door, and you aint' ansa this morning old Penny got worried."

"And why would *old ass Penny* worry and call my phone twenty million times?"

"I wasn't trying to be a bother. Just worried about you that's all."

Yvonna lifts the tea and holds it to her mouth like she is about to drink it. She sees her bushy eyebrows rise in the hope that she'd down the poison so she decides to fuck with her a little bit.

"So, you worry about me, huh?" she places the cup down and Penny's breath releases from her body in disappointment. She wants Yvonna to drink the tea so badly it's showing in her actions.

"Drink your tea, baby. It's good for you."

"I will. But what's wrong? Are you okay?"

"Oh…uh…yes. I am."

"You don't look it. Have some tea."

"I can't!" she yells standing up.

"Why not? I'll just make myself another cup."

"That's okay. I'll make some later."

"If you let this bitch get by without handling her, I'm gonna take care of her myself tonight."

Yvonna tries to ignore Gabriella's voice. And because it is more difficult now to block her out than it was the night before, she is starting to realize that the medicine Penny gave her might have been working and she wondered how long she'd been giving it to her. It was also evident that without it, she became more emotional causing the Gabriella personality to take over totally.

"I know you hear me, Yvonna. Don't fuck wit' me! I'm not going to allow you to ignore me much longer. I'm the only one who cares about you."

"Are you okay?" Penny asks witnessing the blank expression

on Yvonna's face. "You don't look to good, chile."

"Yvonna, kill this bitch right now! She been druggin' you and you gonna let her get away with it?"

Yvonna trying to protect Penny, gets up from the sofa and moves hurriedly toward the basement.

"Yvonna, are you okay?" she asks walking behind her.

Silence.

"Yvonna, …talk to me."

Yvonna felt around in her pockets for the key to unlock the door. She is nervous and sweat begoms to form on her forehead. She has to get away. If she doesn't she will most certainly hurt her.

"Yvonna, you don't have to do this. You don't have to deal wit' this kinda pressha alone. I'm here for you. But you got to let me do for you what I can."

"Kill her, Yvonna! Kill her now! She's violating. She's in to our space! Take care of her! I don't trust her!"

"Baby," Penny says touching her shoulder.

Yvonna grabs Penny's hand and squeezes it so hard, her knuckles sound as if they would crack.

"Keep your hands off me bitch," she tells her before opening the door and closing the door behind her. "Stay the fuck away from me!"

When Yvonna makes it downstairs, she muscles up for another problem when she doesn't see Treyana tied against the rusted radiator anymore. Panic immediately sets in and she hustles toward the back of the basement, toward the back entrance.

"Where are you, bitch?" she asks looking everywhere.

Silence.

"I know you in here somewhere. If I have to come get you, I'm not going to be nice. I'm serious. Don't fuck with me."

Yvonna picks up the rusted weed clippers from a worktable and walks softly toward the back door. Once at the door, she sees the red shirt. Treyana is on the floor crawling until Yvonna grabs her back into the house closing the door locking the door behind her.

"You thought you were gonna get away from me that easy? She asks pulling her hair.

"Let me go! I wanna see my kids. I miss my family!"

"You gonna miss more than that! I told you I couldn't let you go until my plan was done. But you just had to be a busy body, bitch. Now you're going to pay. Big time for this shit! You hear me?"

Treyana turns around kicking and swinging wildly. She stands up and is about to run when Yvonna runs after her. The edge of a metal worktable digs into her stomach because Treyana is not in her grip. When Treyana stumbles and falls, Yvonna dives after her. Then she grabs her right hand, and jabs the clippers into her fingers over and over again.

"Awwwwww!!!! You're hurting me! Please stop! Somebody help me!!!!"

*Boom! Boom! Boom!*

Penny hears the commotion from upstairs and bangs on the door with the force of six men. *Still,* the reinforced door she built about five years earlier doesn't budge. She made it secure in case she ever had to live there for shelter in an emergency situation. Now she wishes she hadn't.

"Now you did it! Now I'm gonna fuck you up for this!"

Yvonna digs the weed clippers deeper into Treyana's hand. Blood splatters everywhere and all kinds of thoughts enter her mind. What was she going to do with her now? How was she going to explain to Penny where the commotion came from? And most of all, how was she going to dispose of the body?

After the fifth stab Treyana appears to be going out of consciousness and for some reason, Yvonna is growing weaker also. Perhaps it was all the energy she exerted into restraining and assaulting her.

No…something else was definitely going on. Treyana passes out, and Yvonna is suddenly consumed with pain. She believes Treyana must've stabbed her and she didn't realize it.

"What did you do to me?" Yvonna asks weakly.

Right before she gets her answer, Penny kicks in the back door and sees Yvonna laying in a puddle of her own blood, with her fingers mutilated. And most importantly, she was all *alone.*

105

# A PACKED DECISION

The cafeteria at FCI Fairton Federal Prison was crowded with hungry inmates. Everybody is either talking about the jail time they had left, or what they'd do as free men. Tree sits at the table with four others, while Swoopes talked about his life prior to being incarcerated.

Tree knew Swoopes from the past but Swoopes didn't recognize him. Tree was glad he didn't. Their past was not worth remembering. And it wouldn't prevent Tree from doing what needed to be done. At first he wasn't going to carry out his part of the deal even after she murdered the Correctional officer. But after she murdered Bernice, he knew not following through on the plan would cause him more problems than one body was worth. Especially after learning that the woman he thought was Treyana, was actually Yvonna Harris, the woman he'd read about in the paper years earlier.

The discovery came while looking at some old photos Swoopes had in his room of Bilal and his friends. Although Swoopes was not happy about her being in any of his photos, he didn't trash them because a few of the pictures were taken during parties he wanted to remember.

It was easy for Tree to be fooled by Yvonna's disguise because she always wore a wig in the pictures she sent. But what Yvonna didn't know was that he was also famiiar with her.

"Yo, Swoopes, tell me about that crazy bitch you were talking about again."

"Who? Yvonna?" he asks. His left eye is still covered by a black eye patch and his right hand is missing three fingers the men he owed money chopped off for a debt he paid late.

"Yeah. You neva got through tellin' me cuz that bitch ass nigga Jake started talkin' bout that broad and shit."

"Oh yeah," he says remembering their conversation in the TV room earlier. "So look, this bitch was crazy as shit. She was slicin' niggas dicks off, cuttin' up people's kids and rapin' other girls and shit." He lies.

"Man how the fuck did she do all that and it took them all that time to catch her?"

"You actin' like the police are smart or somethin'. It's easy to get ova on them mothafuckas."

"Well if it's so easy, how come you in here?" Corn, another inmate asks after laughing. Inmates at the table chuckle. Corn has huge arms and large knuckles but most thought his bark was worse than his bite. He sees Swoopes' eye patch and missing fingers as weaknesses.

"Dis nigga crazy," he responds pointing at him while looking at Tree. "First off, do you even know me?" The question is rhetorical because he knew he didn't. "I didn't think so, so stay the fuck out of my business."

"I don't need to know you. If you talkin' at the table, you talkin' to everybody." Corn cracks his knuckles and looks at him. He is clearly mad about something and decides to take it out on who he perceives to be the weakest man in the room.

Swoopes gives him a once over and ignores him. This embarrasses Corn and induces a surge of anger through his body. "And like I said before I was interrupted by this sucka ass nigga. So this broad runnin' around the city merkin' niggas left and right. I think some of the cops knew and was lettin' her get away wit' that shit." As Swoopes continues with his conversation, Corn is breathing in and out heavily. He is building himself up to take some kind of action. "She killed 'bout two of the niggas I use to roll wit'," he is in midsentence when Corn takes his milk carton and smacks it up against his face. *Splash!*

Swoopes' patch moves and exposes his damaged eye. He moves it back in place and hits him with blow after blow. Corn quickly finds out that Swoopes' handicap, is not a handicap after all. Finally with one last blow, Corn is knocked to the floor. His legs fly up in the air and his black boot comes off his foot smacking him in the face. Niggas are heckling his ass and making the situation worse.

"Damn, that nigga fuckin' his shit up!" someone yells.

"Dude ain't get one in since he smacked him in the face with the carton."

The CO's don't see what was going on at first because their attention is drawn to another argument that happens across the way. Swoopes is just about to punish his ass for more points until he sees two inmates rush toward him. Tree decides to give him a hand when he hits the first dude up to bat fracturing his nose on impact.

When Babble Mouth Johnson, a snitching ass white inmate, decides to increase his kiss ass points by alerting the Co's of the fight, Swoopes and Tree take their seats.Everyone at the table sits down to avoid being pointed out and asked to give an account on what happened. Swoopes grabs his food and acts natural while Tree tosses his meal around in his trey. The inmates look like a well-behaved group of punk bitches.

"What happened?" An officer asks Tree.

"I don't know," Tree tells him, swallowing his food. "You gotta ask them niggas down there."

"What happened, Roberts?" He asks Corn who was now on his feet.

He wipes the blood off the corner of his mouth, grabs his boot and looks at Swoopes. "Nothin'. I fell."

"You fell huh?" he asks with an inquisitors glare. He nods. "Well fall your ass out of here before you get locked down."

Corn walks away but not without looking at Swoopes and Tree again. The CO's looked at everyone at the table and follow Corn away from the scene. When they are gone, Swoopes and Tree laugh.

"Fuck was wrong wit' that nigga?"

"He mad 'cause that bitch he dealin' wit' fuckin' wit' his roommate. He took pictures of that nigga's girl and her address and started writing her. That slut wrote back."

"Are you serious?"

"Fuck yeah! She used to visit Corn and his roommate would

find somebody to see him on the same day. The whole time they'd be in each otha's face and shit."

"Conversatin'?!"

"Naw. Just lookin' at each otha 'cross the room and shit. But a week later the broad sends a letter and forgets who she was sendin' it to. She meant to send it to his roommate but Corn got it instead and flipped. They locked his ass down for 90 days because he went crazy. Tearin' shit down in his room," Tree laughs. "He did all that shit and that nigga that took his bitch was right in his cell with him. They said this nigga was cryin' and askin' him why he broke his heart." Everyone chuckles. "I'm surprised you ain't hear that shit."

"Man I neva even looked at that nigga in my life."

"I feel you. But anyway his roommate got out a day later. He went on parole and my man Shawn D from northwest, said he moved in wit' that bitch and they getting' married."

"Damn…that's some foul shit!"

"That's how niggas be. You gotta watch what's yours."

"On that note, I'm out. I got some shit to take care of back in the cell," he gives Tree a pound. "One."

"One." Tree responds.

When he leaves, Stevie who is sitting right next to him, as if they aren't in cahoots, speaks through tightened lips.

"So when you want me to do that?" he asks grabbing a milk carton to cover his lips.

"Tonight. His celly in the infirmary so he'll be by himself."

Stevie grabs his dick just thinking about fucking Swoopes. Unlike other down low brothers, he admitted to fucking other men. And if somebody challenged him on it, he'd have no problems standing up for what he believes in. And in this case, he believes in tight ass buttholes.

"Cool. Don't worry. I got that shit. I'll take the smokes but I'da did it for free."

Tree is silent because Stevie is talking too much.

"You neva did tell me why you want me to do this though."

"Cuz it's none of your business. Just remember the plan."

"Trust me. It will be my pleasure."

---

Swoopes is in his room doing pushups with his head away from the door. He is just about to do his last set, when someone enters.

"Not now, Jo. I'm not done," he says preparing to finish his exercise.

He thinks it was Jo Cramer coming for the tenth time that day to borrow his magazines. He is about to cuss his pressed ass out. But he doesn't get the chance to when he feels the body weight of another man against his back. His face is smashed against the grungy cold floor. And when he tries to speak, his tooth breaks and lodges underneath his tongue. The harder he fights, the more pressure is placed on top of him. His voice can not rise because a large callus hand is placed against his lips. This is the worse thing that could've happened to him.

When he was younger his father, who was a part of an underground child sex ring, use to make him give oral sex every night when his wife Bernice, went to bed. Bernice had married him when she left her ex-boyfriend Dylan during one of their fights. She was initially attracted to him because of how well she thought he took care of his adopted son. It didn't take her long to realize that what she thought was a lie. And truthfully, Bernice didn't know a lot about Poris or Dylan for that matter.

Poris Mitchell, Swoopes' father, was a tall man with very light skin. He wasn't very attractive and had it not been for his large home and money, and her need to make Dylan jealous, Bernice would have never dealt with him. A major characteristic about him was that whenever he showed emotion of any kind, his face would turn flush red.

It wasn't until his father tried to sexually abuse Bilal, his stepbrother, that things changed in his life. To this day, Swoopes has nightmares and it has impacted his relationships with men and women.

---

"Hi, boys. I just came to bring ya'll some cookies and milk." Poris said after he entered the boy's bedroom.

"Where's my mother?" Bilal asked. His eyes lit up but he knew eating food in the bed went against his mother's rules.

"She's sleep. Who wants chocolate chip and who wants raisin?"

Taylor Mitchell aka Swoopes, sat on his bed with the covers raised over his mouth, barely showing his eyes. He saw his father's complexion and knew what he really wanted. Sex.

"I'll take chocolate!" Bilal, who was only ten at the time yelled. Poris smiled having won him over and sat on the edge of his bed.

"What about you, son? You want oatmeal raisin or chocolate?"

"I don't want any," he shook his head repeatedly.

"You sure? They're really good."

"I'm sure."

"Yes you do. Why don't you come on over here, and sit next to me and Bilal."

"Daddy, I don't want to."

"Taylor Mitchell you get over here this instant!" he demanded.

Bilal feeling uncomfortable with Poris's change of attitude decided to defend his stepbrother.

"On second thought, I don't want any cookies."

Poris whipped his head around and looked at Bilal.

"Yes you do," he told him with a treacherous stare. "And so you don't get any cookies on your pajamas, why don't you take off your shirt. You don't want me to tell your mother you're eating in the bed do you?"

Bilal, who was still young and confused, did as he was told. And before long, Swoopes sat on the edge of the bed next to them.

"Look at you," Poris said to Bilal in a caring tone. "You have such a beautiful chest. Doesn't he have a beautiful chest, Taylor?" Swoopes couldn't face Bilal. He was unnerved. "Don't be rude! Look at him, Taylor!"

Swoopes raised his eyes a little and saw the confusion on Bilal's face.

"What's going on?" Bilal asked.

"Nothin'. We're all friends here and we like to touch one another," Poris said after placing his hand on his immature chest. "Touch your brother, Taylor."

"No…please," he said shaking his head. "I don't want to."

"Do it!"

Bilal finally saw what was happening. His mother warned him of freak ass niggas like this and most importantly, she told him what to do if something like this ever happened. And he remembered everything she said.

"I'm gonna tell my mother!" he yelled in a strong firm voice. "Don't put your fuckin' hands!"

Taylor for the first time raised his head and kept his eyes on Bilal. After Bilal challenged him, he ran out of the room and toward Poris and Bernice's bedroom. When she found out what happened, she felt helpless and hurt that she placed her only son in so much danger. Immediately she got on the phone and called the police. Afterwards she made mental notes to divorce her husband of five months and take a heap of his money with her.

When the cops arrived that night, they asked Swoopes was what Bilal saying true. Poris, who stood out of view of everyone else in the living room, gave Swoopes a dark stare. He told him many times before that if he ever told anybody about what he made him do sexually, he'd kill him. But something about Bilal's strength made him strong and he wasn't as afraid as he usually was.

"Well, son? Is what your brother saying true or not?"

"Yes. It is."

Poris was locked up for child molestation and Swoopes was placed in foster home after foster home. He ran away so much, stealing people's possessions in the process, that he earned the nickname Swoopes. It would take him only a minute to swoop your shit right out from up under you.

The system, and life had turned him into a cold, selfish person. Eventually Swoopes ran into Bilal many years later. Bilal was with the YBM (Young Black Millionarez) and Swoopes after running away from people he owed money, sought refuge with his stepbrother by joining the same gang.

Bilal never told anyone of their *mutual* friends how Poris tried

 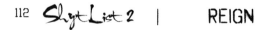

to violate both of them. Anyway, the topic was too embarrassing. But Swoopes always thought he did. He always felt like someone was judging him or wanted something from him. What Swoopes didn't know was that he was on to something. Because although Bilal didn't tell any of their *mutual* friends their secret, he did tell the bitch he hated most of all, Yvonna. And when it was time, she decided to use his deep dark secret against him.

---

The man moaned deeply in Swoopes' ear as he took his self-respect. Swoopes thought he was about to die when he felt another man's penis being rammed in and out of him. For five minutes, he was put into the worse physical and emotional pain of his entire life. And when the rape was over, he was hit with one swift motion on his right temple rendering him unconscious.

---

"Where you goin' man?" Stevie asks passing Tree in the hall-way.

"'Bout to go to sleep. I'ma get up wit you later."

"Aight. I wanted to rap to you about that. Can we talk now? It's important."

Tree looks at him and says in a deep voice, "I said, lada, nigga."

Stevie walks away confused at his response.

Once Tree arrived in his room, he rushes to the sink. Looking behind him once to be sure no one was coming in his cell, he takes a cloth and wipes his soiled penis mixed with semen and sperm as best as he could. He decided to do the honors of raping Swoopes himself. It wasn't like he didn't have experience.

Taking one look at himself in the mirror, he's disgusted. Tree had been a closeted homosexual all his life. When his best friend was alive, they shared their compulsion together. Sometimes he missed Dylan, Bernice's ex-boyfriend...*and* his lover.

# A NEW CHAPTER
# A NEW STORY

"So how is she? I mean…has she regained her concha-ness?"

"Penny, you know I'm not supposed to be talking to you about a patient's case."

She stares at her weary. Lately she hadn't been home and when she does come back, she's hurt. "I know docta. But you see, I'm the only family she got."

Penny looks down at Yvonna who is in bed connected to several monitors and machines. "Penny, you are not related to her. So why the interference?"

"Cause she needs me. Everybody needs somebody."

"Oh well," he says after a heavy breath. "Have it your way." She smiles. "I still don't understand how her fingers got mutilated though. It doesn't make much sense."

"Like I said, someone was tryin' to break in my home and she fought 'em and they stabbed her. I caught 'em runnin' away."

Doctor June looks at her over his red rim glasses. "You're lying. But there's nothing I can do. For your sake I hope you know what you're doing."

Before he leaves she says, "Docta, do you think it's possible to ever fully get over Multiple Personality Disorder? Not that she is havin' a problem. I just wanna know."

"Why?"

"Just curious, docta. Really."

"Well, for starters it's not called Multiple Personality disorder anymore. It's referred to as Dissociative Identity Disorder, or DID. Usually the ego or personality will take control of the individual's behavior, which results in memory loss. Now if I remember her case correctly, Yvonna not only experienced routine takeovers by other personalities, but she also was able to talk and see them."

"I'm not talkin' 'bout her." Penny corrects him. "This is *just* a general question."

"Well it's an odd general question."

"It's general all the same."

He clears his throat and says, "Normally only auditory hallucinations exists. And because of these vast differences, Yvonna's case, even though we aren't referring to her, is different."

"But can DID be cured?"

"Not unless they're able to reconnect the identities to make them one functioning individuals."

"Thank you, docta."

"Good luck, Penny."

When he leaves the room, she looks down at Yvonna's soft face. Penny had been placing antidepressants in her tea faithfully and she was aware that when she didn't come home, missing dosages could cause the disorder to resurface. That's why she lied to the authorities and the hospital staff about what happened to her fingers. She didn't know what caused her to hurt herself but she had a feeling DID was to blame.

"Get well, honey. I love you."

With that she rubs her rough hand slowly across Yvonna's forehead and walks out of the room. And when she does, her eyes open. But Yvonna is not the same.

# INTRODUCING GABRIELLA

## THE CRAZIEST BITCH ALIVE

# NOW SHYT HAS GOTTEN SERIOUS

The beeping of the monitors and the fashion-less white robes were making her sick. She needed out. She needed to get away. And most of all, she needed revenge. But when Yvonna opens her eyes, she isn't herself. She is Gabriella, the dominant, the heartless and cruelest soul on the planet.

Yvonna duplicated personalities in an attempt to make the people in her life do, think and act the way she thought they should be. This was why she'd often hold on to other personalities, like her father and then Treyana long after their deaths. Yvonna was the ruthless and Gabriella was the heartless.

Gabriela committed the murders when Yvonna lost control of people and situations although most of the time the murders occurred without Yvonna's recollection. But when Yvonna regained consciousness and identified with their personalities, despite them being dead, she was usually in control. Before long violence becomes second nature. Sure, she had other personalities prior to Gabriella. But when she came along, she forgot about them all. In fact it was during the most confusing times of her life, that Gabriella came to her.

---

"Yvonna what are you doing up here?"

Yvonna sat on a worn out blue recliner in the corner of her dark living room, looking out a window. She loved staring at the huge letter "t" as she thought of another place, far, *far* away. She imagined she had loving parents and that they would somehow come back to take her away from a fucked up reality. But these make-believe parent's, never came.

"I wanna stay up here." Yvonna looked at her with the pleading eyes of a child. Her red dress was too small for her, and the red strawberries that were on the front of it, were missing thread and lacking color. "I don't want to go downstairs."

"Well you have to." Diane's tall linky body looked worn out and abused. The dirty jeans that she wore were so thin in the knee and buttock area, that they were developing holes. And her large tough black wig made her look much older than thirty-five. Still, there was beauty on her caramel colored face, but not in her eyes. "You're being rude to your father and his company. They love to see you dance and they have guests."

"Mama, please. They don't make me dance. They make me," Yvonna was cut off in midsentence by her mother's boisterous tone.

"Stop lyin' to me! Your father loves you! Now get downstairs!"

"But I'm scared, mamma. I don't like it down there. They hurt me."

"Yvonna Harris, get down them fuckin' stairs now!" When Yvonna doesn't move she grabs her fragile shoulders roughly, meshing them together in an awkward motion. "You messin' shit up for me! Them men pay good money to see you dance. Besides, there are other kids down there. Don't you want to be with other kids?"

"No, mamma. I want to stay here with you." She held on to Diane's leg and she kicked her off. This was the most rebellious Yvonna had ever been.

"If I have to tell you again, you won't eat for a whole week! Now go!"

She released Yvonna. She was supposed to be her protector yet she was the furthest thing from it. Diane couldn't safeguard anyone if she wanted to because she was the keeper of many secrets.

"Okay, mama. I'm going." She backs away from her.

"Good. And when you get back, I'll let you eat the cereal you like to eat for dinner. Okay?"

Yvonna nodded her head and walked to the basement. Her body trembled because she knew *they'd* be waiting. *They* always were and there were *always* new ones. They were united by their sins. Once a month they'd come with their liquor, loud mouths and video cameras to abuse children and Yvonna's parents hosted the event, but why?

Although she remembered most of the predators' faces prior to splitting into the Gabriella personality, after some time she forgot most of them. Instead of dwelling on such despair, she created Charmaine and Shelby to keep her company. Charmaine was the first personality she ever had and Shelby followed sometime after that. They were with her during the worse years of abuse. The personalities, although distinct in their appearances, appeared to come from nowhere.

Yvonna bended the corner in the basement and looked at the five men present.

"What took you so long?" one asked.

"Yeah. You had us waiting." Another one said.

Their eyes followed her until she stood before them while Yvonna's father sat on the chair looking at her with lust. The strangers were seated in a circle with three naked young boys standing in the middle. Jo and Diane were respected in their group because of their *access* to children. No one asked where they got the children from and no one cared.

The five men present were Joe Harris, Dylan Merrick, Tamal "Tree" Green, Poris Mitchell and Derrick Knight. And they all had three things in common. They all enjoyed having sex with young children, they all paid for it and they all deserved to burn in hell. It was Dylan and Tamal's first time attending, but it wouldn't be their last. It took them forever to win Jo and Diane's trust and their hard work had finally paid off.

"You hear them, girl?" Jo continued. "What took you so long?"

"I was talking to mama. Upstairs." She said in a weak voice.

"Don't be sorry, get over here."

Yvonna walked slowly in the middle and suddenly she saw Charmaine and Shelby in a corner. Although most of the men preferred boys, Tamal and Dylan liked both. They were the ones who requested Yvonna.

"Get on top of her," Tamal told one of the young boys once she was in the middle. Her red dress sat at her feet. "And put your mouth on her young pussy. She like that. Don't you, Yvonna?"

Yvonna started to cry and her personalities, Charmaine and Shelby began shaking in the corner. They were duplicates of her current mental state…innocent, young and helpless.

"Na…na…now, I like that," Tree said looking at the boy stoop down. He had a weird speech impediment when it came to saying the word, *now*. He would stutter a few times before getting the word out.

"Please," Yvonna sobbed. "I don't like this."

"Shut up! You do like it you young bitch!" Jo said. He got up and smacked her in the face. "Stop acting like you don't!"

"Man, I paid my money to see this," Dylan disputed. "If she don't do it, I'ma take my money elsewhere."

"She gonna do it," Tamal stopped him. "Ain't you?"

Dylan wasn't *that* into women. In fact the only women he ever cared about was Bernice, and that was only because she bore him a son. Their heterosexual relationship concealed his sexuality. At first he had thoughts of sexually abusing Bilal also and he even grew excited the closer the day came to his birth. But when he was born and he looked into his eyes, he realized he couldn't bring himself to do it. He decided to stick to abusing other people's children. Not feeling totally satisfied behind closed doors he managed to create a new fantasy with Bernice.

It consisted of placing foreign objects in and out of his ass. Although it soothed some of his urges, it wasn't until he met Tamal "Tree" Green that he was totally complete. With Tamal he could play the closeted homosexual game. This worked for a while until Tamal wanted something Dylan wasn't able to give him, a public gay relationship. This enraged Tamal who wanted him to leave Bernice. So naturally when Bernice, who knew nothing about her boyfriend's sexuality approached Tree with an idea to make some money, he accepted in the name of revenge.

Realizing pleading with the adults would not stop anything from happening; she complied and endured the sexual abuse as they coached the children along.

"Charmaine and Shelby please," she begged during the violation of her body. "Help me."

"Who you talking to?" Derrick, a short man who was abused himself as a child asked. "Why are you always talking to yourself?"

"Please, Charmaine and Shelby. Help me."

They didn't help her because they couldn't. They cowered in the corner and turned their backs on her. And after fifteen minutes of abuse and taping, the men tired of her.

"Now you can leave," Joe told her. "Come give daddy a kiss first."

She did as she was told and looked back at the boys feeling sorrow for them. One of the children was Swoopes. He kept his head down and covered his privates with his hands. He seemed detached and angry. Yvonna grabbed her dress and looked at Charmaine and Shelby once more. She felt they left her dejected and all alone and before long she hated them.

With her clothing partially on, Yvonna ran back up the stairs broken inside. Right before she took solace in her bedroom, she saw her mother sitting in the recliner with a *new* child in her arms. Jhane, the woman she'd grown to know as her aunt was standing above Diane. Her face had traces of dried tears upon it. She was thin and the years of drug abuse had taken its toll on her body. When Yvonna looked at Jhane, a woman she saw no more than three times, Jhane turned away from her. And for some reason, Yvonna longed to have a relationship with her. It never happened.

Diane handed Jhane some money and after tucking it in her worn out jean pocket, she watched her leave. Once she was gone, Diane rocked the baby lovingly in her arms. Yvonna would have given anything for her mother to hold her with such care.

"Who is that?" Yvonna asked in a soft tone.

"Why?"

"Just wanna know," she said walking closer.

"Did you finish dancing for the men downstairs?"

Yvonna's mother always referred to what went on downstairs as dancing and Yvonna wondered if she really knew what they were doing to her.

"Yes, mama. I did. Who's that?" she repeated.

Diane's eyes look at the ceiling as she thought of a lie. When she found an appropriate answer she said, "Stop being dumb. You know this is your baby sister."

"Baby sister?" Yvonna asked focusing on the baby's features.

She'd been living there alone with her mother and father and never had a sister.

"But I don't have a sister."

Diane gripped her up by her dress again with one hand and yelled, "You betta not eva tell nobody that shit! If you do, I'll give you away." Yvonna didn't have a great life anyway, but she certainly didn't want to go somewhere that could be worse. "You do have a baby sister! Do you hear me?" Diane's breasts pressed against the baby's small head and Yvonna is worried she'd smother her.

"Yes…Yes…I know, mama." She looked back at the baby with concern.

Diane let Yvonna go and focused on the child in her arms.

"That's right. Now if anybody asks you, her name is Jesse. Jesse is gonna make me a lot of money."

"Okay, mama."

"What's her name, Yvonna?" She asked giving her an on the spot test.

"Jesse. Jesse Harris."

"Now get out of my face and wash up. You stink."

Yvonna didn't realize but in that moment, something changed inside of her. She'd developed a strength she never knew existed. And most of all, she developed a strong unconditional love for another. She made up in her mind that she'd always protect her, even if her life depended on it. She did not want the same dangers to come to baby Jesse that she endured.

Once in her room, she was still thinking about baby Jesse when she saw someone inside. "Who are you?!" she said loudly. The girl startled her.

"Yvonna are you talkin' to yourself again?!!!"

Yvonna who knew she'd suffer a severe beating if she were caught talking to herself, body began to tremble. "No, mama! I'm not talking to myself."

"Good! Now take a bath and clean that room!" Yvonna breathed a little easier and closed the door.

"How did you get in here?"

"I let myself in. You don't remember me? I'm your new friend."

"But I don't have a best friend."

"Yes you do. Do you wanna be friends with me?" She seemed confident and Yvonna wish she was the same way.

"What's your name?" she asked.

"Gabriella." She smiles. "And don't worry 'bout nothin', I'm going to protect you from now on. Whenever you're sad, or hurt, I'll be by your side. Forever and ever."

Yvonna developed Gabreilla to protect her baby sister. And although Shelby and Charmaine would show up every now and again, it was Gabriella she favored and before long the others were completely gone.

---

Gabriella opens her eyes in her hospital room and looks around. She'd been pretending to be out of it all day. She remained still as the nurses, doctors and staff members tried to determine how her fingers got mutilated. To them the wounds looked self-inflicted. And all she thought about was finishing what Yvonna started, whether she wanted to or not.

"About time she's gone," she says to herself referring to Penny. "I can't take one more day of Man Hands Penny touchin' me."

Gabriella eases out of bed. Her clothes were so soaked with blood that they destroyed them immediately after tearing them off her body. On a mission, she moves toward the door. When she doesn't see lurking hospital officials staring at her she quickly dips back into the room and places on a pair of hospital slippers.

"I gotta get outta here before these no good ass doctors try to drug me up again. That's all the fuck they know how to do. Drug a bitch up and shit."

Once the slippers are on, she snatches the needles out of her arm. Her right hand throbs with pain but before long she feels nothing. Crazy bastards are known for having a strong threshold for pain. And there was no one crazier than this bitch. Although the bandages do make it harder for her to move around, she walks hurriedly through the hallway. Dipping into each room, she manages to steal enough clothing to conceal her body. The only problem is, she looks the worse she'd ever did in her life.

"Yvonna, I sure hope you know what I'm doing for us. I'd never be caught dead in this bullshit if it wasn't for you."

Yvonna can't respond because Gabriella has totally taken over and now all hell is about to break loose. Before leaving she manages to steal a syringe. Wearing a run down old brown cap with the word moose stitched on the front and an oversized black shirt and oversized jeans, she exits the hospital in a frenzy.

"Now where can I go?" The sun is bright and cars whiz up and down the street. Everyone was in a rush and so was she. With the money fund being spent entirely on fashion, she's broke. She needed a sucka to take her in. And then it dawns on her. "I feel like seein' me some old ass Penny today!"

# THERE'S NO STOPPING HER NOW

Gabriella is in Chevy Chase on the side of the building looking for the perfect prey. It doesn't take her long to find one. With her plan embedded firmly in her mind, she decides to execute it. The pretty target with almond colored skin that she spots is thin, pretty and fly. She takes notice of the designer jeans she wears along with her stylish red Prada jacket.

Gabriella walks hurriedly toward her and she is carrying five or six shopping bags in her hands. When the girl deactivates her alarm, Gabriella sees the silver Range Rover and is proud of her choice.

"I swear I be knowin' how to pick 'em."

The license plates reads, Crystal. *I hate bitches name Crystal.* She thinks. The woman was opening her trunk when Gabriella yells, "So you still gonna fuck wit' my man, huh?" She has her hands on her hips and the girl's pretty green eyes widen believing she must be talking to someone else.

"Are you talkin' to me?"

"Don't play games wit' me. Keep that shit up and I'll stomp you every-which-a-way."

"I'm serious. I think you got the wrong person."

"Bitch, you know who I am! I'm sick of you sneakin' behind my back and sleepin' wit' what's mine!" Gabriella points to herself.

"Are you kidding me?" she says as she accidentally drops her bags. Gabriella notices a brown shoebox with white lettering and knew it could be none other than Christian Louboutin's signature atop of it. "James still messin' wit' you?"

She can't believe how gullible the girl is. Not only was she buying the story, she is name-dropping.

"Yes, I'm talkin' about James' bitch ass." Gabriella steps closer. "My fuckin' husband, James! And since you don't know how to listen, I'ma have to make you!"

The girl looks like she is about to shit herself when Gabriella balls up her fist.

"Please don't hurt me. I'm sorry! I really am." She begins to cry. "I knew he was married but he told me he didn't want to be with her because she had let herself go. Not saying that you let yourself go," she offers as an apology, looking at Gabriella's drab clothing. "He's supposed to be moving in with me next week and everything. If I knew you were still in the picture, I wouldn't have ever continued to sleep with him."

"Well that's not good enough, bitch. I'm 'bout to kick your ass so you will know better in the future."

Gabriella was preparing to hit her square in the face to set the tone, when she says, "What if we go approach him together? I'll tell him to his face it's over. Just please don't hit me. If I fight, my father won't let me be in his fashion show next month."

What the fuck? Gabriella thinks. "You just might've saved yourself from an ass whoopin'." She jumps inside the truck. "Let's go then, I gotta make a stop first."

---

Gabriella makes the unsuspecting girl run her all around town. It was nice being chauffeured. First they stopped at Target where she picked up a few items. And when Crystal tried to stay in the car, Gabriella forced her to get out. There was no way on earth she was letting her money-bag-car-driving-ass get away. Besides, she had credit cards and cash and Gabriella realized she suddenly hit the jackpot!

After getting all she needed, compliments of her hostage, they get back in the truck. Gabriella allows her to talk as she writes a letter sealing the envelope. Now all she needed was a mailbox. While she looks around for one she occasionally sizes the girl up.

What Gabriella wasn't sure of was her shoe size so she decides to ask.

"What happened to your hand?" Crystal asks turning left and right on the streets leading to James' barber shop in DC.

"None of your business. Look, pull over up the street I gotta fart and I don't wanna blow you away in here."

The girl looks at her and wrinkles up her face. "Did you just say fart?"

"Yes and you might be rich but I know you know what the fuck a fart is. So unless you want me to blow this mothafucka out, I suggest you pull over."

The girl pulls over and the moment she does Gabriella says, "Cute shoes! What size are they?"

"8 ½," she smiles.

"Perfect." Gabriella lunges the butcher knife she just bought into her stomach. Her eyes bulge and turn a shade of red. She touches the knife's handle like it will go away and Gabriella pushes it deeper and twists it into her abdomen.

"Don't fight it. Just let it go. It's over. You had a nice life and I'm sure your family will give you a rock star funeral."

The girl looks at her and tears stream down her face. Why had she trusted a stranger? She looks back down at the knife and back at Gabriella again. And Gabriella, being the impatient bitch that she is says, "Damn, slut would you die already! I got shit to do!"

So she pushes it deeper inside of her and pounds the end of the handle with her fist for added measure. And finally the girl falls back into her plush cream-colored leather seat and closes her eyes. "Thank you! I was so not feeling the drawn out ass death scene."

Gabriella jumps out of the car and runs to the driver's side and opens her door. The girl's body drops halfway out and she pulls her completely into the street. She was just about to leave until she remembers the knife has her fingerprints on it and she is still wearing the shoes she wants.

But when she attempts to take the knife out, it doesn't move easily. So she places a foot, which is covered with a blue hospital slipper on her chest, balances herself and with her good hand, yanks it out.

"Got it!" she cheers raising the knife in the air, which is dripping with blood.

Realizing there's nothing to cheer about, she puts her arm down and wipes the blood onto the girl's jacket. And then she takes her shoes off her feet and jumps back into the truck. A ten-year old girl stands in shock witnessing the entire scene.

"Oh don't worry. She's just drunk. She'll be okay."

With that she slams the car door shut and peels into traffic. Being the multi-tasker that she is, she runs over and over in her mind what she plans to do and to who she plans to do it to. She sees her plans so clear in her mind that she smiles with delight.

"I'll have my way in not much longer."

Once she gets far enough away from the scene, she rummages through the girl's shopping bags. She is disappointed when she realizes her taste isn't as grand as she hoped.

"Damn. I didn't take you for a mediocre type bitch," she sighs. "I woulda neva picked this brown dress with your skin tone." She shakes her head in outrage.

With her clothing choices limited, she wiggles into the best of the worse settling upon the grim brown dress. The dress is not as comfortable as the hospital clothes even though it was her size. *What the fuck did you do to our body, Yvonna? Eating out all the time and shit!* She decides to keep the dress on despite slight discomfort and eases into the stolen pair of shoes.

"I'll give you credit for these," she says looking at the pumps against her toned legs. "You most definitely know how to pick a fly pair of shoes." She throws the hospital gear out the window and searches for good theme music.

"Damn! Not the Carter 3." She says excitedly moving in her seat. She loves Lil' Wayne "Who knew you fucked with Weezie?"

She places the CD in and allows his mellow voice to run through her body. Then she looks through the Target bag to be sure she has everything she needs to carry out her plans.

"Okay...let's see. One syringe, one bottle of liquid Drano, one comb, one brush, two paper bags." Then she digs into the girl's purse and pulls out some credit cards and cash. "Okay, a little bit of money and some plastic." She places the truck into drive. "I got everything I need. Now lets get down to business!"

# THE START OF SOMETHIN' VENGEFUL

"Yeah, this look likes the perfect place!" It was late in the evening and the sky had turned to a purple hue. Gabriella places the stolen Range Rover, which she was cruising around in like she owned the bitch in park and jumps out. She stands out as she struts down the small block that she happened upon in southeast DC. Crack heads and dope fiends were plenty in this area and they were exactly who she was looking for.

"Now which one of you funky bastards do I want?"

She scans the crowd for the *thickest-nappy-est-bushiest-headed mothafucka* she could find. "Ah ha!" She smiles quickly identifying her match. "Excuse me."

The crack head who is about 6 foot tall, dark skinned and thin fixes the old black dress coat he's wearing, smooth's out his crusted beard with his hands and says, "No, excuse me! And we can excuse each other for the whole night if you want to." He is stunting like he was straight out of an old Colt 45 commercial.

Gabriella laughs and says, "Honey I wouldn't give you the time of day, if I were driving eighty miles an hour and you were standing in front of my car."

"Well excuuuusssse, me." His breath stank of infection and alcohol.

"Great, you a drunk too," she backs up and places her bandaged hand on her hip. "Look, *Pookie*, you wanna make some cash or what?"

"Hell yeah! What you want me to do to you?" He claps his rusty hands together and licks what's left of his dried up lips.

"For starters you can stop thinkin' about this pussy cause it ain't gonna happen, Mr. Roach." He's offended but remains silent. "Now, I want you to brush and comb that nest of a head of yours over this bag," she pulls out the comb and brush and hands it to him. "Then I want you to give it to me when you're done. Capeesh?"

"What kind of freaky shit is this?"

"None of your damn business." Gabriella tares the brown paper bag open and moves toward a small patch of grass. She places the bag on the ground and says, "Now get over here." The man follows although slightly confused.

"You sure you not gonna tell me what's going on?"

Gabriella smacks him in the face so hard, for a second he's sober. He rubs his bruised face and looks like a child who got punished for disrespecting his mother.

"Now are you gonna stop actin' like Sherlock Holmes or are you going to be the crack head I'm paying you for?" The man sees something crazed in her eyes and gets on his knees.

"I knew you had some sense in that fucked up body of yours."

As requested, he bends over so that his head is directly above the ripped bag, and combs and brushes his hair over top of it. His eyes meet hers in between the strokes and the fear stricken man is afraid she'll hit him again. Dandruff, tiny hair follicles, and even small bugs fall on top of the bag.

"That's so yuck-a-licous!" She proclaims.

"Is that's enough?" She examines the mess.

"Comb that knot a few more times." He does. "Good. Now fold it up in a ball and put it in here." After he folds the bag closed, keeping its contents in tact, she holds another bag open and he drops it inside. Then she folds that bag several times shut.

"Here is your comb and brush," he says handing it to her.

She frowns at the filthy articles. "Honey you couldn't pay me to take that shit back. Keep it, you need it more than me."

Gabriella rummages through the Target bag she's holding and says, "Now let me pay you." She pulls out a few items including the blood-stained butcher knife and says, "Oh...can you hold this for me for a second? It's in the way and I'm looking for your money."

"What the fuck?" he grabs the knife by the handle, looking at it from side to side. "What were you cooking?"

"Nothing," she says accepting the weapon back with a napkin to avoid getting new fingerprints on it after just recently wiping *hers* off. She places it carefully in the bag. "I'm so silly. Your money is right here in my pocket. Take this one hundred dollar bill. I'm paying you for your silence and your trifling ways. But you betta neva, *eva*, tell anybody you saw me. Understand?" she points at him. He nods in agreement. "Great! Get your high on. I'm outta here. Oh yeah, do you know where I can buy a gun?"

Reluctantly he directs her down the street and she leaves the lowly man exactly where she met him. She adjusts the rearview mirror so that she can see herself inside of it and says, "I love when shit comes together!"

# OLD BITCHES
# OLD TRICKS

Gabriella parks the stolen Range Rover a few blocks down and walks to Penny's house with her Target bag in hand. She doesn't knock right away. She was trying to get herself in mode to be meek and humble like Yvonna and was finding it very difficult to pull off. Taking a deep breath she says, "I'm just gonna have to do the best I can."

She knocks twice and looks like a sad puppy.

"Yvonna? What are you doin' here?" she doesn't seem that happy to see her.

"You not happy to see me?" she asks softly.

"Oh…yeah." She stares at her body as if something's wrong and than focuses on her eyes. They look different to Penny. "Of course I am. But you're 'spose to be in the hospital. I just left you."

"Yeah well I hate hospitals. Can I come in or not?"

"Of course, chile." She opens the door wider and Gabriella strolls inside.

When the door closes, she sees Bradshaw sitting on the sofa. She squints her eyes and wonders how long it will take her to rip his throat out until she remembers that she just might need his ass.

"Bradshaw? What you doing here?" He stands and walks up to her looking at her hand.

"He was worried 'bout ya. And decided to stop on by to check on ya. He says he hadn't heard from ya in a while. I told him you hurt yourself and was in the hospital."

"I guess."

"I didn't know you had a boyfriend."

"I didn't know I had one either?" Gabriella examines his fashionable white long sleeve dress shirt, pink cashmere vest and blue jean.

"How did you get my address?"

"I drop you off all the time. What are you talking about?" She doesn't answer. "Anyway, you always told me if I hadn't heard from you in a couple of days, I should come looking for you. So I'm here."

*That damn, Yvonna!* She thinks. "Oh yeah. I remember." She lies.

He places his hands on her shoulders. She despises the way he made Yvonna lose to reason and she was determined not to be easily seduced. She is in control not him.

Gabriella snatches herself away and says, "Well, I'm fine. You can leave now."

"Can I talk to you before I leave? Alone?" he asks. They both look at Penny. "It's kind of private."

"Oh...I'm sorry...I have a prayer circle that'll be startin' in 'bout fifteen minutes. But ya welcome to take him downstairs though. I cleaned up for you." She walks up to Gabriella and looks into her eyes again but Gabriella looks away. "How's your hand?"

"Doesn't hurt one bit." Gabriella focuses on the multicolored housecoat.

"That's good. Real good. I'm glad you're home," Penny continues looking at her. "Oh, and some movie company folks stopped by wantin' my input on your story. I chased 'em out of here. They wanted to offer me a lot of money and I just wanted you to know."

"Doesn't matter. Well, I guess we'll go downstairs now."

Right before she opens the door to the basement Penny says, "And, Yvonna. Does the box need to be dropped off today?"

"What box?"

"The box you told me to keep."

Gabriella not knowing what she means says, "Oh. That box. No, it's fine."

She has no idea what the old fool is saying but decides to give it no more attention than she already has. Penny on the other hand, watches her until she is completely out of sight.

---

"So what was so important?" she asks him as they sit on the foot of the bed.

"I wanted to check on you. But what's up wit' your hand?"

"A long story."

"Aight. At first I thought you were fucked up with me for being distant when we were together. I got a lot on my mind and you know I'm tryin' to get some extra cash to get my daughter. They tellin' me if I can afford 24-hour in home that they may never let her stay with me. She's in the foster care system now."

"Look, I'm not tryin' to be rude but I don't care." His face tightens up and he takes a deep breath. "It doesn't matter. It's not that deep."

"What does that mean?"

"What does it sound like?" she says as she stands up to get undressed. When she's naked she turns around and looks at him. "You wanna fuck or what?"

It wasn't what he had planned but they spent the next thirty minutes having passionate sex. There was something about the way her body moved that he liked.

"You were different tonight. And did I tell you how that I love the weight you gained?" He adjusts the covers and his pants hang at the end of the bed.

"I don't remember but I move different 'cause you used to fuckin' Yvonna's cornball ass not me."

"Yvonna?" He asks separating his body from hers to look into her eyes. "You saying that you not Yvonna?"

"What you think? Yvonna ain't got shit on my fuck game."

Bradshaw sits up in the bed and leans against the headboard. "Then tell me 'bout you."

"Oh, you not scared?"

"Scared of what?"

"Of all the things people say I did. And all the people they say I hurt."

"Naw. I'm interested. I wanna know what makes you tick. You're different."

"We are. And personally I don't think there's anything wrong with us."

"Us?"

"Yeah, me and Yvonna. I think people just need to let us be. We might not be like everyone thinks we should be, but we're real. I'm real. And we don't need no medicine to change us."

"Are you her protector?"

"Something like that. I think I'm more into protecting me than anything. If I don't, Yvonna's gullible ass would kill us both. She'll let them doctors tell her all kinds of shit and before we know it we'll be crazy."

Bradshaw couldn't believe his ears and Gabriella loves the attention she was getting from him. So many times the doctors and professionals spent time trying to get rid of her. It felt good being.

"I like you. And I hope you stay around."

"It doesn't bother you that I've hurt so many people?"

"I like you just the way you are." She smiles until she notices something in his eyes isn't right.

"Are you playing games wit' me? Are you fuckin' wit' me?" She shoots daggers at him with her eyes. "'Cause it's not a good idea to fuck wit' me."

"I'm not…fuckin' wit' you." If he wasn't scared before he is now. "I'm bein' honest."

There is a long pause of silence between them. He reaches for his pants which were on the bed the entire time they made love, and pulls out another condom.

"You tryin' to go another round?"

She smiles and says, "You just try and keep up."

 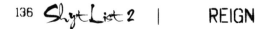

# ZONED OUT

Swoopes was in the cafeteria eating for the first time in three days. He hadn't been out of his room since he was raped. And he didn't know who the fuck assaulted him. When he looks around, anybody within a few feet of him could've been a suspect. He imagined them talking behind his back and most importantly, he reasons that unless he finds out soon who took his respect, they would most certainly try to get some boy ass again.

"Damn, where you been at, homie?" Tree asks walking up behind him. On edge and not recognizing his voice yet, Swoopes reaches under the table, lifts his pants and touches the homemade shank taped to his leg. But when he realizes who it is, he lets it fall back down to position. "You been missin' in action."

"Yeah, I wasn't feelin' well." Swoopes says faking a cough.

"That shit ain't contagious is it?" he jokes.

"I can't call it," Swoopes laughs.

"I'm just fuckin' wit' you young, blood. Everything cool?"

Swoopes moves his food around his plate. "Yeah, I'm good. What's up wit' you, though?"

"Ain't shit. You know they shipped Corn's ass to another prison last night."

Swoopes looks up from his plate and at Tree to be sure he heard him correctly.

"They shipped him to another prison? For what?"

"I don't know. Somebody said he turned FEDS and they had to get him outta here for protection. I couldn't stand that nigga no way."

Swoopes doesn't have an appetite but after hearing about

Corn's transfer, he wasn't sure he'd ever be able to eat again.

"You aight, Swoo?"

Swoopes moves around in the hard plastic chair trying to get comfortable . It wasn't working. He swallows hard and opens another button on his shirt so that the heat rising from his skin can escape. "Oh…uh…yeah. I'm fine."

"You don't look like it. You look like you about to past out and shit."

He never, *ever*, considered Corn. He didn't peg him for the raping type. And now that his name was mentioned, he wonders why he hadn't. Even though rape was a fowl ass way to get a nigga back, if it were his method, it certainly worked.

"Look, man. I'm 'bout to roll. You want the rest of my food?"

"Hell, yeah," Tree says reaching for his bread.

When Tree extends his hand and reaches for Swoopes' meal, he recognizes his large knuckles and how rough they look. He hadn't expected to remember exact details about that day because what he wanted to forget. But there was no denying that after noticing Tree's hands, he was sure Tree was the one who had violated him.

"Hey, you still comin' by my cell tonight right?" Tree tares off the bread he got from Swoope's plate. "Na…Na…now, I got some smoke and drink in my room."

Swoopes body feels light and his knees buckle. He'd heard that speech defect before, when he was younger. And just like the memory of Tree's hands were recalled to mind, so was his impediment. It was both unique and stupid so how could he not remember?

Now there were men who were considered tough, rough and strong. But there was no man, in the *entire* prison, who possessed the strength that Swoopes had in that moment. Because it took everything in his power not to rip him a part right where he sat. But he was smart. He had to be. If he wanted him like he wanted him, he had no choice but to fall back and wait. Swoopes inhales and keeps his chest filled with the oxygen he needs to handle the situation.

"If you got smoke and drink, you know I'm there." He smirks.

"I'm serious, Swoo." He continues eating the bread. The fucking pet name he gave him pissed Swoopes off.

"Swoopes, man. My name is Swoopes."

"What?" Tree laughs looking up at him.

"I ain't tryin' to be funny, but my name is Swoopes. Not Swoo." It was bad enough that he took his ass, and even worse that he had to wait to knock his block off. But he had no intentions on letting this bitch ass nigga continue to call him by a personal pet name he'd created.

"Oh…no doubt. I meant Swoopes." Tree senses something wrong but doesn't think things through. "I gotta rap to you 'bout somethin' later too."

"Don't worry. I'll be there. You can count on that."

---

Tree's eyes can barely open because bandages appear to be covering his lids. And from what he could see through the cracks, he wasn't in his room. Not to mention that the mattress was much softer than the one in his cell. And when he tries to move, pain shoots through every limb in his body.

"Don't move," a woman's voice advises. "You are not the same as you were yesterday." *Not the same man I was yesterday? Fuck does she mean?* He thinks.

"Wha…what's goin' on?"

"You've been badly hurt. We found you in your cell on the floor in a puddle of your own blood and liquor."

A flash of Swoopes coming into his room, drinking liquor was the last thing he could remember. He called himself about to finish Yvonna's request and he ended up getting dealt with. Everything else was a blur. He had been placed himself in a cage with a lion was tore to pieces.

"So, what's wrong wit' me?"

"It appears you got intoxicated and got into a fight. You know it's a violation to have liquor in prison, Mr. Green."

"I ain't tryin' to hear that shit right now! I need details on my condition!"

"Well you betta be trying to hear it because your life has changed forever." Her voice lost all concern and was replaced with contempt. "Do you know who did this?"

"No! I…I don't," he lies.

"Are you sure?"

"Yes I am! Now tell me what the fuck is up."

"Your spine is fractured. The skin over your eyes are almost completely gone, you have severe cuts on your face and…and…," she hesitates.

"What? What is it?"

"And your penis has been completely severed from your body. We couldn't find it, so it could not be reattached."

"Awwwwwwwwwwwwwwwwwwwwwwwwwww!" he screams.

"Let me get the counselor."

---

### Three weeks Later

The prison was on lock after the attack on Tree and as usual no one knew shit. And because Swoopes was considered a *friend*, no one suspected him.

He made a decision earlier in the morning to kill members of his family when he was free in 14 months but he needed addresses first. He could have handed this duty to members of the YBM but he did not want them knowing he was fucked. It wasn't enough that he forced Tree into an alcoholic stupor, before beating him over and over, finally cutting his penis off with his shank and flushing it down the toilet. He needed and wanted more to be done.

The only reason he left him alive was because he knew that it was next to impossible for a man to go about the world without a dick. Anyway he felt people gave *death* too much credit as a form of punishment. And since he'd never died, he couldn't vouch that it would be good enough for Tree. For all he knew death could bring a reward that Tree's slum ass didn't deserve. *But*…he could vouch that life, if fucked up enough, could be a living hell.

While rummaging through his personal mail, he happens upon a stack of letters. Most of them came from a PO address and for a moment, he's discouraged. *I need a fuckin' address. Where does your fam live mothafucka?* He thinks.

As he skims through the letters, he notices a girl's name on the envelope says Treyana. *What you got to do with this shit?* He knew her from his hometown and was trying to add things up. He opens a few of the letters and reads briefly through them. But when he sees one of the pictures sent, he stumbles. *Yvonna? What the fuck!* He doesn't understand why the letters were from Treyana but the pictures were of Yvonna. Wanting time to quarterback the whole situation, he takes the letters and walks to his cell.

He's happy he still doesn't have a celly because he needed extreme privacy. As he lies down, he reads them all one by one. *None of these make any sense!* Jo Cramer enters into the room right before he answers his own question.

"Is it a good time now?" he asks referring to his magazines.

"Yo! Fuck is you so pressed for?!" Swoopes yells tucking the letters behind him.

Jo is so startled that he temporarily forgets what he came for. "I…I just wanted something to read the…uh…you told me I could…read the magazines. So I came by to…uh…see…if I could get them now."

"You know what," Swoopes leaps off his bunk opens his locker and grabs the magazines. Next he slams him so hard in the face with them that Jo's bottom lip cracks open and bleeds. "Now get the fuck outta here before I break ya jaw!"

Jo runs down the hall with the magazines in tote. *Thirsty ass nigga.* Now alone, he holds the letter that originally caught his attention. He sits down and his feet remain planted on the floor. His muscles buckle involuntarily due to how angry he is.

Opening the letter once more, he reads the poem and again it makes no sense.

"Fuck does this mean you crazy bitch?"

This time he pushes his anger aside and focuses on the words, not necessarily their meaning.

*You are I. And you are what I want. I am her who can't live without him. You are my heart beat. I'd rather be raped. And. I'd rather be tortured. Until I say when. Because it's. Not going to do me any good at all. To be without you. I said. That until it's all said and. Done. That you are what I. Want.You...not him. When you left I felt killed.*

He stands up and holds the paper so tightly in his hand it crumbles. She used the same code they used when he was a member of the YBM.

"Bilal must've taught her." He says to himself shaking his head.

He reads it out loud the way it should be read; *"I want him beat, raped, and tortured. When it's all said and done, I want him killed".*

He balls the letter up and looks out before him. Now shit just got serious. Did she know about his involvement in her case? *Naw. It's impossible.* He tears down the pictures he has of sexy women on his wall. Even the pictures of his celly's children got taken down. He replaces them all with one picture of Yvonna. From the moment Bilal introduced him to her he didn't like her. He didn't even know why and had no memory of them meeting as children. But he did know that he hated the air she breathed.

He decides to chill out in prison. He'd play by the rules and play their little games, something he never considered before. If he felt himself slipping, he would refocus on his goal by looking at her face. He didn't want anything to interfere with his release. She'd be the first person he'd see when his feet hit the pavement. Swoopes smiles. For the first time in life, he has inspiration, and her name is Yvonna Harris.

"I hope you ready for me, bitch."

# EVERYTHING COMES
# TO THE LIGHT

"I can't tell you no more than I already have." Avante sits on the couch with his pants unbuttoned and his shirt half open.

"Maybe there's something or somebody you left out," Jensen says. "Think."

"Avante looks up at the officers with disgust. And again, the lights flicker on and off like they did earlier. They ignore it.

"There has to be something else," Jensen persists. "One detail overlooked."

He stands up and his clothes fail to cover his body securely, exposing his white cotton boxers a little around the waist. "You're starting to make me think I'm a suspect."

"Not yet but you act like it. And why didn't you tell the FBI?" Samuels asks.

He looks at them, "Because I wasn't looking for special consideration."

"Special consideration? To find your wife?" The lights flicker again but this time they take a little longer to come back on. "Do you need to change your bulbs or something?" Officer Jensen inquires as he looks up again, the large hairs in his beefy nose showing.

Intoxicated he says, "Maybe it's her ghost or somethin'." He laughs in bad taste.

"That's not funny, Mr. Plier."

"It is to me. And anyway it can't be a single bulb problem because all the lights in the house go out." He says with an attitude.

"You need to relax." Jensen is sick of his mouth.

"That's easier said than done."

When the lights flicker off this time, they are unable to continue with their conversation because they are in complete darkness.

"Where is your electric box?" Officer Samuels asks. "Something must be wrong."

"It's outside." He swallows his liquor. "In the back of the house."

They all walk into the darkness of the night and around back.

"Got a flash light?" Jensen asks stepping up to the extra large panel.

Avante in a drunken stupor pats his pockets. "Naw, not on me." The cops shake their heads tiring of him quickly.

"Well do you have a key to open the box at least?" Samuels asks using the light on his phone to see a little. "Wait! It's open. But hold up! What the fuck is that smell?"

He moves away from it. Because truth be told, there is only one smell on earth that is fouler than any smell imaginable.

"I don't know but I'm about to find out." Jensen pulls the handle.

Avante stops and turns around just in time to see Treyana's head roll out, followed by other parts of her body. The blood had soaked into the panel causing the circuits to trip and the lights to flicker. She'd been in their the day after she was murdered.

"OH MY GOOOOOODDDDD!" Avante cries seeing his wife's dismembered body. "PLLLLEASE HELP MEEEEE!!!"

He rushes toward the scene and the officers stop him. After all, she's not his wife any more. She is now homicide evidence.

# ALL CLOSED EYES DON'T SLEEP

Penny is snoring for points until in between a heavy breath she feels pressure against her body. She opens her eyes and is horrified to see Yvonna lying directly on top of her, with her head resting upon her breasts as if she were a child.

"What are you doin'?[" Penny is scared to make a sudden move.

"Listening."

"To what?!"

"Your breaths. You're a hard sleeper. I've been here for almost ten minutes." She says looking up at her before resting her head comfortably. "You really shouldn't sleep that hard. Someone could take full advantage of you if they wanted."

"What are ya doin' in my room, chile?"

Coldly she says, "I wanted to see how fast a heart beats, before it stops."

"You betta be tellin' me somethin' cause I don't understand what you sayin'."

"Cut the bullshit. You know exactly what I'm sayin'."

"I don't know!"

Gabriella places a gun barrel to her head all while maintaining her position on Penny's body. *Click.* She cocks the hammer.

"Do you understand now?"

"Gabriella?"

"In the flesh."

"Why are you doin' this?"

"Because you a meddlin' bitch who won't go away."

"Don't do this. I care about ya."

"You don't care about anybody but yourself."

"I *do* love ya. And I'm askin' you to spare my life."

"It's too late." Gabriella laughs. She is about to pull the trigger when Penny jerks her body roughly and the gun falls out of her hands and onto the floor. Gabriella tries to reach for it until she feels cold steel against the side of her waist.

"Get up, bitch before I blow your ass to the future!" Penny turns on the lamp.

"I'm not...," she is cut off due to Penny firing into the wall before placing the gun back on her waist.

BOOM! "The next one's goin' in your body. Now get the fuck up!"

Gabriella's eases off of Penny. When she does, Penny stands up and looks into her eyes. She maintains her aim at Gabriella who backs against the wall. Gabriella feels a little lightheaded and her stomach feels queasy the moment she stands and she wonders why. Penny squints her eyes to look at her. Something is different about her but in the dark of the night it's too hard to tell.

"I'm smarter than you thought, huh?" Gabriella thinks she talks like a runaway slave so how could she possibly be intelligent? "Yvonna gaves me a code phrase. She said if I ever doubted it was her I should ask, 'Does the box need to be dropped off today'?"

Recalling the question a few days ago she says, "That's what that dumb shit was about."

"If that's what you choose to calls it. Alls I know is if yous were my Yvonna ya woulda said, 'I already mailed it.' But you didn't know the ansa."

Gabriella didn't want to admit it, but Yvonna played it smart.

"If you thought I *wasn't* Yvonna why would you let me in your house?"

"Because you use ta go away afta some time. But…I see she's gettin' worse. I talked to Terrell Shines and Jona though. They told me what I gotta do to help, but ya gets the best treatment if you recommit yaself. Jona says she tried but you won't consent. They gonna keep you safe and cure ya, but you gots to let 'em."

It pissed Gabriella the fuck off that Terrell and Jona couldn't stay the fuck out of her business and she couldn't wait to get at them.

"And just what the fuck did they tell you to do to help me?" she asks making the universal quotation signs with her fingers.

"I already started. I been puttin' medicine in the food."

Gabriella laughs. "I already know about the tea." Penny is surprised and wonders how she knows. "And I don't eat anything else here."

"You ate *packaged* foods." Gabriella figures that's what caused the queasiness.

"You's a dumb bitch."

"I'm doin' it 'cause I love you. And placing the medicine in the bottled water was one of the only ways I knew how."

*The water?* She thinks. *I ain't been drinking the water.* "You're a liar!"

"I don't lie, 'specially 'bout peoples I care about. Anyway, you gonna get on out my house right now, and I'ma be prayin' for you from a far. 'Til I think of somethin' else. And, the cops been callin' me. I ain't met with 'em yet, but I gots plans to meet with 'em tomorrow." Gabriella clenches her fist and takes one step toward Penny thinking she could take her.

"Do you really want to test my aim?"

"Them fuckin' pig cops gonna get what they deserve too."

Gabriella was getting angrier and even though Penny had the gun, she was slightly frightened.

"Get out of my house!" She stiffens her arms and refreshes her aim. "Now I loves Yvonna, but I loves myself mo and won't hesitate to put one in ya and pray to the good Lord above lada." Gabriella's eyes narrow.

"Okay, I'm leavin'," Gabriella smirks.

"Now that I *already* know for show! So we gonna do it like this. You gonna back up all the way out of my house. If you don't make no sudden moves, you'll live. Are we clear, chile?"

Penny lifts Gabriella's weapon off the floor and tucks in the back of her cotton black pajama pants like a thug off a D.C., corner. For a woman of God she sure handled her weapons like a pro. "I need to get a few things downstairs. Can I?"

"Out!"

"Well can I have my gun?"

"Get out of here now!" Penny yells cutting her off.

Gabriella backs all the way out of Penny's house like she was told and when she was completely gone Penny made a call. Yvonna would not be safe in her condition and she wanted her to have help.

"911 how may I help you?"

"Yes, I need the police. Please send them right away."

# WHEN CRAZIES ATTACK

Gabriella looks through the window of Jona's house. She's contemplating on how to get inside so she can kill her. She had her address for a while and only planned to use it if she threatened to take her freedom again and by speaking to Penny she felt she did just that.

Jona works busily on her computer and Gabriella wonders if whatever held her attention, had something to do with her. She holds the names of the additional people she plans to exact revenge on in her hands. She didn't include the names of the people Yvonna hated because she already had their names etched firmly in her mind and on her body. This was Gabriella's personal list and because of it, it was the most dangerous of all. Staring at the list, her hands shake with rage.

*Jona*
*Terrell*
*Samuels*
*Jensen*
*Lily*

She was still staring at the list when a Rottweiler, who's head was so large it bends the corner of the small brick house before the rest of his body, runs toward her. She mistakenly drops the list on the ground and runs for her life.

Jona looks up from her computer when she hears her dog barking and walks toward the window. She sees no one. Wanting to know what caused Titan to bark, she decides to go outside. Before leaving she grabs her loaded 12-gauge shotgun that stayed by the door. She opens it walking carefully outside.

"Titan!" she calls. He runs to her.

"What happened?" she asks although she knows he can't answer.

The dog's heavy panting plays in the background. Squinting her eyes, she sees someone staring at her up the street but she can't see his or her face. She looks at her dog and back up the street but the person is gone. Patting Titan on top of his massive cranium she says, "Good boy. Good boy."

Whoever it was, Titan clearly ran them away. While the dog licks her hand, she looks down on her green lawn and notices a white piece of paper. She bends down and picks it up, her dog still beside her. Opening it fully she sees a typed sheet of paper with a group of names, including hers. Loosing her balance, she stumbles against her house and rests against it for support.

"It was, Yvonna." She says to herself. "Oh my gawd it was Yvonna!"

# THE STATION

The Forensic department is spotless as clerks move about trying to provide the evidence necessary to solve cases. Officer Jensen and Samuels stand in front of Cheryl Hanks, a beautiful white clerk with blonde hair.

"So how soon can we get the prints from the electrical panel? And the Bernice Santana case?" Jensen asks her as Cheryl sits in front of her computer scanning through millions of fingerprints.

"I'm going to work on it as quickly as possible, but I can't make any promises or provide you with a firm date. You know we're backed up around here."

"But this is the Yvonna Harris case." Samuels chimes in. "And we need this back ASAP."

"I know what and who it's about Samuels."

"Well what's the problem?" Samuels persists.

She sighs. "Nothing."

"Make this one special," Peter says placing his hand on her back.

"I'll do what I can."

"Thanks, love."

When they walk away Jensen asks, "You fuckin' her ain't you?"

"What do you think?"

They laugh on the way to their next destination.

---

"What do you guys want with me?" Lily asks sitting on the only available space on her couch. Her place as trashy as ever.

"Lily, what are you doing to yourself?" Jensen looks around. Coming from Sir Funks-a-lot that carried a lot of weight. Literally.

"Yeah, Lily. This has gotten out of control." He walks to her window and opens it. Cool fresh air rushes inside. "It smells like pussy that ain't been washed in twenty days in here." Samuels adds.

"You've had pussy that ain't been washed in twenty days?" Jensen asks.

"You haven't?"

They laugh and focus their attention back on Lily. "I just want to be left alone."

"You know if you want to kill yourself, there's a better way." Jensen knocks a bunch of trash out of a recliner to sit down. "You don't have to take the long route."

"Yeah. Cause ever since you're partner died, you've been going down hill."

"I don't want to talk about it."

"Well you need to do somethin' and you need to do it soon," Says Samuels. "Because we need your help." He sits down on the other end of the sofa.

"I'm not interested in following Yvonna if that's what you want. I want no parts of that shit. I gave my entire life to the police department and it hasn't been worth it."

"DAMN IT, LILY! STOP FEELIN' SORRY FOR YOURSELF AND TELL ME WHAT THE FUCK IS GOING ON!" Samuels's boisterous voice booms.

Instead of being angry, Lily drops her head and sobs. She's an emotional mess.

"I didn't know...I swear I didn't know! But when I found out, I was afraid!"

"You didn't know what?" Samuels pries. "And what were you afraid of?"

"I didn't know Shonda did what she did," she continues crying heavily. "And when I found out, I never told anyone."

"Start from the beginning, Lily. Just start from the beginning."

## The Day Crazy Dave Caught Up With Yvonna At The Hotel

"Yvonna! Yvonna!" a male voice yelled from an undetermined location.

When she didn't look due to examining the car, the person became persistent. Turning toward the voice, she saw Swoopes in the passenger seat of a White Yukon Denali with a black eye patch over his left eye. She hadn't planned on seeing him and was quite aware of how he felt about her. She almost dropped her shopping bags due to being so frightened.

*What the fuck is going on around here?* She thought. When Dave got out of the driver seat and walked up on her, she was a little relieved they came together. She thought Swoopes was there to kill her.

"I got to talk to you!" he said frantically.

"For what? And how you know I was here?"

"Sabrina told me you weren't staying with her no more," he advised as a look of urgency came over his face. "So I asked Cream and she told me where to find you."

"Well I can't talk now," she responded as she briefly looked him up and down. He looked so much like the rapper "Young Buck" without the corn rolls that it was scary.

She turned to walk away but he grabbed her wrist. He let her go remembering the last time he held her against her will.

"Look," he said looking around to be sure no one was listening. "The police been round the way askin' questions 'bout you. Somebody said you were in town."

"What they want from me?" she questioned looking over at Swoopes who was frowning.

"Dave, come on man," Swoopes hollered. "We gotta be at the shop by 7:00! Ain't nobody got time for that bitch!"

"Fuck you!" Yvonna yelled.

"Nigga hold up," he said turning around irritated at his outburst. "Look," he turned back to Yvonna. "Call me here." He handed her a card which read, *"Dave Walters, Each One Teach One. Children's advocate."*

"Whatever," she responded taking the card from him and tossing it in one of her bags. "I'll call you when I can. And what happened to his eye?"

"It's a long story." With that he dipped off. Her eyes met Swoope's once more before they sped off. He hated her and she felt it.

Later on that day Swoopes met up with Shonda in a rundown arcade center in Southeast DC.

"Shonda, what you gonna do? You wastin' time when I need this bitch dead."

"I gotta be honest, I'm not feelin' the murder thing. I'm a cop Swoopes."

"Well you betta start feelin' it, cop!" he says getting in her face.

"Why do you hate her so much?"

"I got my reasons."

His mind was made up and she knew it. "What if I set her up instead?"

"Set her up how?"

"I'll frame her for a murder or somethin'."

"How the fuck you gonna do that?"

"I don't know. But I do know this girl from southwest who's a sharp shooter. And, on a camera she'll look just like Yvonna just as long as she doesn't show her entire face. We'll tail Yvonna and when it's the right time, we'll make a move. I'll press the issue to everybody in my department that Yvonna's involved somehow and before you know it, she'll be a suspected murderer."

"She's one now."

"And that's why it'll work." Silence.

"This shit betta work!"

"It will. But look…when it's done, how much longer will you blackmail me?"

"Come on, Shonda! We go way back. You one of my favorite customers. I'll stop when I get what I want." He laughed. "You can trust me."

"What about the tape of me smokin' and buyin' from you? You

gonna get rid of that too?"

"Not before I see this bitch locked up for whatever scheme you got hatched."

Swoopes walked off and left her alone. The next day she and hit woman Katrina Carber followed Yvonna all day. And when they saw her in the Friday's restaurant, they found the perfect person and the perfect situation to carry out Shonda's plan.

---

### At Friday's Restaurant

She placed both plates on Yvonna's side of the table.

"Bitch I had enough of your shit!" Gabriella responded. "One of them plates belong to me."

The waitress rolled her eyes at Yvonna and walked off.

"She must've heard you cuss her out earlier," Yvonna replied. "Don't even trip!"

"I got somethin' for that bitch later," she responded as the waitress walked off.

"You heard that?" Shonda asked Katrina. They were seated at a nearby table and saw the interaction between Yvonna and the waitress.

"Yeah."

"But why is she talking to herself?" Shonda said out loud. "That bitch is crazy."

"I know. But fuck all that, I need you to pull this off. Now I paid you twenty five hundred and you'll get five thousand when you finished."

"Where did you get that kind of money from?"

"Don't worry about it." She was not about to tell her that she stole the money from evidence at the precinct. And if she did she feared she'd want more. "Meet the waitress when she get's off of work. Just don't forget to dress like her as much as possible. You already wear a similar hairstyle but don't let the camera see your face. Side profiles are okay because we need those shots. You got it?!"

"How do I know you won't frame me for it?"

"Katrina I got enough evidence on you to put you away for the rest of your life. I still have the weapon you used when you accidently shot that pastor when he came out of the church cause you was trying to get somebody else. Trust me. If I wanted you behind bars I could have you."

"Not if I kill you instead." She said raising her head and looking her square in the eyes. Silence.

"You *could* kill me. But I gave your name to my people, and if you don't carry this shit through, they'll kill you instead. We're in this together now. You may know who I am, but you haven't the slightest idea who *they* are."

Katrina released the air from her chest and said, "Why you doin' this anyway? Ain't you a cop?"

"I don't know what I am anymore. But if you fuck this up, you won't be alive long enough to find out."

---

### The Night Of The Verdict

Shonda stood outside on the court steps. The day was beautiful yet everything going on around her world felt grey. Katrina had done as she was paid to and Jasmine McDonald had been murdered. Still, unless Yvonna was found guilty and sentenced to jail, Swoopes wouldn't find her work satisfactory. She pressed the button to accept the call from the prison. Her hand shook as she held the cell phone to her ear.

"Swoopes?"

"Who else bitch?!"

"Everything looks good. We don't think she'll get away with this."

"Well I hope for your sake it sticks! 'Cause if it don't, your boys in blue gonna get that tape. My own brother set me up and I shouldn't even be in here. Choosin' females before family. I want that nigga's world ROCKED."

"I've done all I can. Please don't ruin my career." She knew it

didn't look promising that Yvonna would get locked up even though she told him otherwise. Her doctors had managed to provide the jury with enough evidence to deem her crazy.

"It betta stick," he said before hanging up.

"Who was that?" Lily asked walking up behind her.

Shonda turned around and faced her. "Oh…uh, it was no one." She placed the phone in her pocket.

"But what could be taken from you, Shonda? Are you gonna talk to me? I'm your partner."

"I said nothing! Now leave me alone!!"

Lily and Shonda ran up the steps leading to the court building. Once inside, they both took their seats in the jammed packed courtroom. Had it not been for other officers saving them seats, they would have not had one. They got there right before the jury gave their verdict.

"Jury have you reached a verdict?" Judge Tyland asked.

Yvonna looked worried and innocent as she awaited their decision.

"Yes, we the people find Yvonna Harris not guilty by reason of insanity." An older black woman said. The courtroom erupted in noise.

Yvonna hugged her attorney and smiled at Dave who had been supporting her the entire time.

"Order in the court!" Judge Tyland yelled.

The jury was so taken aback by what they saw on the hypnotism tapes, that they felt she didn't deserve jail and needed help. The way she spoke of the rape when she was a child, and how her mother didn't believe her, tugged at their hearts.

Shonda dropped her head in defeat. She knew everything she ever loved and everybody she ever cared about was about to be taken away. To make matters worse, now killing Yvonna was no longer an option because she was in custody. She sobbed heavily, and from that point on she considered her life over.

---

## Back at Lily's Apartment

Officer Jensen and Samuels are in a trance. They can't believe their ears.

"Let me get this straight, Yvonna Harris did not commit the Friday's Restaurant murder?" Officer Samuels asks. Lily with a drink in her hand shakes her head no.

"But, she never fought the murder in court. I think she took the blame for it."

Lily laughs at both of them. "You two are so damn special! This is why this bitch won't rest until she ruins us. You're too busy thinking in terms of her being sane! Of course she believed she did it! She believes she sees people and talks to them in public. She doesn't know who the fuck she murdered! Wake up!"

"Where are you goin' with this?" Jensen asks insulted by her comment.

"Think! It's called autosuggestion. She thought she did it because she'd killed so many people, she could no longer tell the difference. Hell," she gets up and pours herself another drink. "How many times have we used it to get suspects to confess? In the end, she really thought she murdered Jasmine Mcdonald."

The men look at each other and say, "Hey, can you pour us two drinks please?"

She laughs and rinses off two dirty cups. "Sorry, I don't have any clean glasses."

"The dirtier the better," Jensen rubs his forehead to reduce his headache.

"So what happened to Shonda? What made her kill herself?"

She hands them their drinks and sits down. "I was hoping you'd forget to ask me about that."

---

### The Day Shonda Took Her life

Lily walked into Shonda's apartment after receiving a desperate phone call. She told her she was sorry for everything and hung up. But Lily couldn't rest until she found out what was happening. But when

she opened the door to her apartment using the key Shonda had given her, she saw Shonda was not alone. Shonda was seated on a stool crying while two men circled her. They had YBM jackets on and it was apparent that they were there for business.

"I thought you said you lived alone?" one of them asked Shonda.

"I do. She's my partner."

"You really shouldn'tve came here," one of them told Lily. "It was the worse decision in your life. Lock the door, Rook," he told the other man.

Lily was angry with herself now for leaving her weapon at home. "W…What's going on?"

"Your partner here didn't come through on a deal. We were gonna show the tape of her smokin' dope to the cops, but a few members of the YBM were also in the tape." He smacked her in the back of her head. "So Swoopes came up with a better idea."

"Please don't do that again." Lily requested although she's disgusted by her partner's actions.

"Just what the fuck you goin' do?" Lily was at a disadvantage. "Just what I thought. Well look, I'd like to draw this out but we have something to do."

The other man grabbed Lily and was about to shoot her. She said, "Don't kill me."

"That's not possible." The leader said.

"Please. Don't kill me. If you don't, I'll kill her myself."

Shonda raised her head and looked at her partner. "What did you say?"

"You heard me!" Heavy laughter filled the room.

"Hold fast, did you just say you'd kill her yourself?"

Lily looked at Shonda and said, "Yes. If you let me go. You'll know if I didn't go through with it and I'm sure you also know where to find me. This way you'll avoid a murder rap for killing a cop. I know you don't want that on your hands."

She was right, killing a cop was serious and if they were caught by other cops, they might not live to make it to trial.

"How do I know you won't snitch?" the leader walked over to Lily and looked down on her. Lily's eyes remained on Shonda's. The betrayal Shonda felt was unbearable.

"Because I know they can't protect me," she responded looking up at him. "They never could." She focused back on Shonda.

"You smarter than I gave you credit for. Because you right, no one can protect you now." He walked away. "Rook, let's let the officers get down to business."

"You serious? What if Swoopes asks us what happened?"

The leader looked at the man and said, "We'll tell him it's all been taken care of."

They moved toward the door. Right before he left he looked back at Lily.

"I don't have to tell you to keep this between us. Because I know you know betta than to cross us." With that they walked out and Lily and Shonda stared at each other.

"So you gonna kill me?" Shonda asked dropping her head again.

"No. You gonna kill yourself. You dead anyway. You made a decision without consulting me. And worse of all, I know what you did. It's the least you can do for me. It's the least you can do to make this right and not make me kill you by my own hands."

"You know about what I did?"

"I knew all along you had the waitress Jasmine killed. I overheard you talking on the phone to Katrina at Feeny's retirement party. What I didn't know was why. At first I thought it was because you believed that Yvonna deserved to be off the street so bad, that you were willing to do whatever you could to make it happen. But I caught up with Now I'm finding out that you're nothing more than a washed up ass dopehead."

"I'm not using anymore. When I was they found out I was a cop and taped me buying drugs from them. I don't even know how they found out. That shit was over five years ago and one day I come home to a letter telling me to meet him somewhere. He showed me the tape and blackmailed me. I guess they were waiting for the right time to use their card, and they did. But I've been clean for five years, Lily. I swear."

Lily was frustrated and wanted to get down to business. "Where's your gun?"

"On the couch." Lily walked toward the couch grabbed the gun and handed it to her.

"Now do it."

Shonda cried heavily. "I'm so sorry. Please forgive me."

After five more minutes of crying, and a prayer, Shonda placed the gun to her head and pulled the trigger. Prior to killing herself, Lily felt for dishonoring her badge Shonda deserved to die but it didn't make her feel any better.

She had to live with feeling like Yvonna *really* should be punished. She had to live with members of the YBM knowing their agreement and the possibility of them using it against her in the future. And she had to live with not being strong enough to fight against the YBM to save her partner's life. And then she realized that a system that would let a certified person go free could do nothing to protect her.

---

### Back At Lily's

The officers were on their fourth glass. "Wow. I can't believe it," Samuels says.

"It's all true."

"Well, we certainly have to tell someone," Jensen decides.

Lily looks at him and laughs. "You won't do that."

"Why wouldn't we? I want no parts of this bullshit."

"Because if you do, she'll get away with everything else you're trying to book her for. They'll comb through this case so much you won't have one."

"We can't just let this information sit!" Jensen says yelling.

"We can and we *will*. It's the only way," Lily laughs hysterically.

"What's so damn funny?" Jensen asks.

"Because I've just invited you boys into my private hell. How does it feel?"

They look at each other. "So what's the plan?"

"If we're gonna do this, we have to do it smart."

"We?"

"Yes. I've decided to help you. I got this shit off my chest."

"So now what?"

"We have to be smarter than her and believe me, she's smart. You haven't been in the presence of evil until you've been around her." They look at each other and silently agree, having met her before. "And we'll need more people to help us.

"Who would get involved in this bullshit?" Samuels asks.

"You'd be surprised."

"Since you know so much, we're told that she kills people she seeks revenge on." Jensen starts. "So who do you think she's after next?"

"Since Bernice Santana and Treyana are dead, I'd say Jhane because Swoopes is in jail. And to tell you the truth for his part in this shit, I wouldn't mind if she killed his ass." She's angry. "And you might want to offer Jhane protection until this blows over."

"We offered Jhane protection and she refused."

"That's mighty dumb." She pauses. "But I feel like I'm missing somebody else."

"Well you said you testified against her. How you know she isn't after you?" Samuels asks.

"I don't know. And I don't know that she isn't after you either."

Both men swallow hard. "Well who else?" Lily paces her filthy floor in circles.

"Who am I missing?" she taps her chin. "Who is it?!" She stops in her place. "Oh…oh…Cream Justice! Where is Cream Justice?!"

# CATCH A DEAD MAN BY HIS TOES

It had been a warm night when Gabriella crept inside of Jhane's home a few days back in Washington, DC. She let herself in through the garage door she left opened. Once inside, she carefully removed ten tampons from the opened box, and pierced a tiny whole through the plastic using a syringe, dampening the cotton with the liquid Drano. She hoped she'd be around to see her ass scream when it was time to use them.

Now Gabriella sits impatiently outside of Jhane's house in a rental car. It was Thursday and Jhane always ate at Olive Garden, her favorite restaurant. But where was she now? She needed to follow her to carry out another part of her nasty plan.

"How's the trip?" Jhane asks Jesse as she plops down into her favorite green recliner. The chair rocks back and forth making a squeaky sound. "Is Mexico beautiful?"

"Oh, auntie Jhane! I can't explain how pretty it is here. I wish you were here with me." Her voice echoes from the speakerphone.

"I'm just happy you're there."

"Thank you for sending me. I really didn't think we'd be able to afford it. I mean, I know you've been struggling with me going to Duke and all the lessons."

"You deserve the best. Owwwww," she says softly rubbing her chest.

"Is everything okay auntie, Jhane?"

"Oh…yeah. Everything's fine." She falls back into the softness of the recliner and tries to place the pain she's feeling in her body out of her mind. It's so unbearable that she doesn't think she'll be able to do conceal it from Jesse. "Well, let me go grab a bite. Anyway you should be enjoying Mexico, not wasting time talking to me."

"Where are you going? To Olive Garden?"

She laughs. "You know me too well!"

"Hey, auntie," she pauses. "Have you seen her?"

"No. The police wanted me to have security here, but I refused. I'm not afraid of her anymore."

"Are you sure?"

"Yes. I'm sure. Now stop worrying about me and enjoy the rest of your trip."

"Okay, auntie. I love you."

"And I love you more than you could ever know."

When Jhane ends the call, she allows her weight to fall deeply into the soft recliner. After all these years, Jhane had allowed Jessse to think that the blood they shared didn't extend past niece and aunt ship. They were so much more. They were mother and daughter. But Jesse wasn't her only child. She also gave birth to Yvonna and a very deep dark secret surrounded their births. In the past Jhane used drugs to. She'd seen so many things and did much more and enjoyed medicating her pain away.

Jhane reaches down in the corner of her recliner, and feels for her blue leather heroine kit. She places it in her lap and looks up at the ceiling out in front of her.

"I'm trying to be a better person. I hope you know that."

After she lies to herself, she inserts the needle into her arm and sits back allowing the heroine to control her. She feels a wave of euphoria and suddenly she could care less about her niece, daughter or any other relative for that matter.

She sits in that chair for thirty minutes, without moving. And when her high disintegrates, she's dropped back into her pitiful world. In an unbalanced state, she stands up and moves to the bathroom. Once inside she flops down on top of the toilet and spreads her beefy legs. Yellow urine escapes her body before turning red soon after. She got her period. Opening the cabinet under the sink she removes a tampon and pushes the poison deeply inside.

---

"No problem, mam. I'll take care of that for you right away!"

The small waitress walks away to fill Jhane's usual order at the Olive Garden. But little did she know, extra parmesan wasn't the only thing she'd be eating. When the waitress leaves the kitchen fifteen minutes later with Jhane's meal in hand, she's stopped by Gabriella. Dressed in a form fitting one-piece jean outfit, she was far from being inconspicuous.

"Excuse me," Gabriella says placing a hand on her shoulder. "That isn't for the woman over there is it?"

The young white waitress with red hair says. "Yes it is."

"Great! Let me take that for you. She's a good friend of mine."

"I'm sorry I can't do that." She looks Gabriella up and down and smiles looking at her body. "You're beautiful and glowing." She changes the subject.

Picking up the wrong meaning of her inquisitive stare she says, "This is Versace, honey! And trust me it'll take more than slinging sauce rings around here before you'll ever be able to afford something as fly as this."

"I was only giving you a compliment!"

"And I'm giving you some advice."

"Mam I have to get back to work," her lips stop flapping when she sees the one hundred dollar bill Gabriella is waving.

"Mr. Benjamin does seem to have that effect on them." She snatches the plate and gives her the money. "Now be gone." When she doesn't move fast enough she stomps her Prada pump and yells, "Shooo! Shoooo! I've got work to do."

When the scrawny waitress leaves her sight, she walks to a table in the back that is out of view from the business of the restaurant. Then she removes the paper bag from her purse. Next she pours the dandruff, dirt and hair pile she collected from the dope head on the DC into Jhane's meal. Next she grabs the oregano and parmesan cheese jars from the table and shakes them like two maracas over her food to disguise the mess. Realizing she can't bring her the food and expect her to eat it, she stops a male waiter.

"Hey, handsome."

"Hello. Are you okay? Do you need anything?"

"Actually I do," she says holding the plate like it is a pizza. "Do you mind taking this plate to my friend over there? I have to rush to the restroom."

"Of course not!" he says blushing. He is extra considerate and she doesn't know why. In fact, everyone had been so nice to her lately it bugged the hell out of her. He was just about to walk the plate over to her when he sees a small hair that wasn't concealed with enough oregano and parmesan. "I'm gonna take this back there's a hair in it."

"Don't worry about it. She doesn't mind."

He laughs and said, "You're kidding right?"

She leans in and whispers heavily so that he can hear and read her lips. "Listen, Fuck-boy. I said she doesn't mind. Now go take the fuckin' plate!"

He hesitantly takes the plate and looks at her in horror. Arriving at the table, he places the food down saying something to her before running off. Gabriella hides in case he was ratting her out. But when Jhane takes heaping spoon after heaping of the spaghetti and swallows, a smile spreads across her face.

When her phone vibrates she looks at it and sees it's a text message from Ming.

*I come back from China next week. I have great news! Will share when I return. And yes, you can stay with me as long as you need.*

Gabriella is irritated because she's running out of money and can no longer use the credit cards because they are stolen and the hotels she likes are expensive.

Focusing back on Jhane she says, "Eat up! You greedy, fat bitch!" Placing nastiness in her food and poison in her tampons were just small ways of getting revenge. The real prize would come once she killed her.

The moment thoughts of Jhane dying enter her mind, Jhane moves around uncomfortably in her chair. *Did you get your period?* She hopes. *Did you use them toxic filled tampons?* Jhane attempts to readjust herself by tugging at the seat of her pants. She even takes a few more bites of her spaghetti. That is until her face bares a grimacing stare. She's in excruciating pain.

"Are you okay, mam?" a lady asks next to her.

"I…uh…don't know. I…I feel hot. My skin burns."

"Want me to call 911?" She stands behind her placing a hand on her back.

"I…don't think so," She stands and then doubles over. "I have to go."

Jhane runs outside and Gabriella is laughing so hard that she feels a fluttering sensation in her stomach. Gabriella follows, trying to maintain at least a ten feet distance. Jhane can't stand up straight the entire walk to her car.

"You are so beautiful," A white woman says to looking at her body.

"I know, bitch, now move. You in my way."

The woman holds her open mouth in shock and walks off. She decides that she must see where she's going. But she changes her mind when she sees the two cops she can't fucking stand walking toward the restaurant. She backs up, spots a wooden phone booth and hides inside. The male waiter she punked earlier, sees her hurrying away seconds before the officers approach him.

"Excuse me son," Officer Jensen says. "Can we talk to you for a minute?"

"Am I in trouble?"

"I don't know. It depends on what you tell us." His face turns red.

"O…okay," he swallows hard.

"Have you seen this woman? Someone said they saw someone fitting her description come in here."

The man looks at the picture and looks behind him in

Gabriella's direction. Out of view of the officers, she runs her finger across her neck in a slicing motion.

The terrified young waiter swallows hard again, turns back around and looks at the officers. "No sir, I haven't seen her."

"Are you sure son? You seem out of it."

"Yes, sir. I'm sure. I haven't seen her before."

"Well if you do, take this card and call me." The officer hands it to him. "It's really important, son. This woman is dangerous."

When they leave the restaurant Gabriella hangs back awhile. She knows now that it would be difficult finishing her list, but she had no intentions of stopping until she was done. "It's gonna take more than that to stop me, bitches. Way more."

# SCARY KINDA LOVE

Peter and Guy are at their desks waiting for Cheryl's call. When the phone doesn't ring after two hours of waiting, Peter decides to call her instead.

"Have you gotten any of the fingerprints back?" Jensen asks.

"You have to be patient." Irritation is heavy in her voice.

"And I told you that case is important and that I need it now! A lot of people have been showing up missing and her doctor says she hasn't been to any of her appointments or taking her medicine." Silence.

"Please don't call me bothering me at work. I'm tired of this little game and you have to wait just like the others."

He clears his throat and walks away from his desk in case Guy overheard the conversation and became aware of his lies. In front of his partner he portrayed himself to be the man when he was far from it.

"What do you mean?"

"You have been harassing me ever since I left you and I'm tired of it, Peter. Now I will show you respect, but only as it relates to our business relationship."

The phone produces wetness from his body temperature raising. When he first met her she was timid and afraid of him and now she's acting like he never beat her a day in her life. "Peter. Peter. Are you there?"

"Listen slut! I'm still the man you knew and don't for one moment think you left me. I let you go because if I wanted you dead, you would be. Now...I sucked your pussy dry every night we were together for over a year. Whether I wanted to or not and most nights I didn't. Now I'm asking for your help. Are you going to help me or not?" Silence.

"Peter Jensen, I want you in my office first thing in the morning," a male voice demands.

Peter is so shocked from hearing her boss's voice that he almost drops the phone. Although he doesn't report to him directly, he outranked Peter and a complaint from him carried weight.

"Yes…sir."

"Good! And just so you know, I ran the fingerprints personally. We'll deal with both matters tomorrow." Peter hangs up and stares into space.

"Peter…what she say?" Guy asks walking over to him. "Are the results back or not?"

Peter can't speak. He is realizing that this case was already taking more from him than he was willing to give.

# TAXI CAB CONFESSIONS

"Where are you going young, lady?" the taxi driver asks Gabriella in the rear view mirror. His Jamaican accent is thick despite speaking very clear English.

"I'm going to 6745 Old Marlboro Pike." She gave and address in the vicinity but not the exact one.

"You got it." He says taking a look at her beauty again.

"How was your night?"

"Well, let's see. I tried to kill somebody today but the cops came so I couldn't finish her off. And now it's going to put a dent in everything else."

"Oh…really?" His eyebrows rise and he thinks she's joking. "You too pretty to be a murderer."

"Trust me," she says crossing her legs and leaning back into her seat. She adjusts her shirt a little to get more comfortable. "There are a lot of pretty killers out there."

"And why do you kill?"

"Because I can. Why do you drive people around like a slave?" She says looking into the mirror at him. "Cause you can." He frowns and she smiles.

"You can't find anything better to do with your time?"

"No. There's nothing more liberating than taking a life."

"You sound serious."

"Who said I wasn't?" He looks at her and then back at the road.

"We're here." He can't wait to get her crazy ass out of his car.

She opens the door and eases out. "If you wait, I'll let you set your own tip."

"Sure." The moment her feet hit the curb he pulls off. SCCCCCUUUURRRRRRRRRRRR!

Gabriella looks behind her and laughs before hiking the two long blocks up the dark street leading to Bradshaw's house. Her stomach flutters again and it's starting to irritate her. She rubs it a little and keeps walking. She hated depending on others and needing somewhere to stay. But what else could she do? All her money was gone and Penny would send her up the long road if she stepped foot back on her property. Bradshaw was her only hope.

Once at Bradshaw's house, she walks up the large stairs of his townhome. And when she is one step away from his front door, she glances into the window and sees the movie company officials who had tried to get her story.

"Tim and Mora!" She says out loud.

They were sitting on the couch listening to a small tape recorder they had connected to speakers. And then…she hears her own voice.

*"Yeah, me and Yvonna. I think people just need to let us be. We might not be like everyone thinks we should be, but we're real. I'm real. And we don't need no medicine to change us."*

He had a tape recorder in his jean pockets when he came to visit her and she didn't know it. Bradshaw was careful about making sure that his jeans remained on the bed the entire time they spoke and made love. From the moment he met her in the doctor's office he had ulterior motives and they were to gain information on her story that the court reports couldn't provide.

They really wanted the details from her but after they propositioned Yvonna and she refused, they sent Bradshaw. In fact, the phone number he gave her was provided by the movie company. It was a set up. Everything.

Bradshaw was so dead set on doing whatever he had to do to get the money necessary to get his daughter back that he didn't take time to realize who he was fucking with. He thought Yvonna was *faking* crazy like, he did to dodge murder charges. Behind her back, to the movie representatives, he praised how great her acting skills were and commented on how she even had him participate in overcoming the Gabriella personality. Perhaps if he'd realize the severity of her situation, he would've rather pack up and move out of town than to cross her. Bradshaw was making a grave mistake and he didn't even know it. Seeing and hearing his treachery causes her to stumble backwards, grabbing the rail before falling to the ground.

"I shoulda known you were nothin' more than a fuckin' liar!" she curses the night air. "You better be glad I don't have my gun."

Feeling like she needed to do something now, she picks up one of the large grey stones in his yard and throws it against his living room window. *CRASH!*

She runs down the stairs and hides. "What was that?" Bradshaw asks as the crew follows him.

"I don't know," he looks around.

"Have any enemies?" they joke.

"Not that I know of."

"Well let's get back in and finish this story. You're about to become a rich man."

They go inside but he remains outside scanning the grounds. When Gabriella sees he's alone, she steps out and shows herself.

"You're a dead man." She tells him in a calm voice. "I told you not to fuck with me but you didn't get it." He is so stunned that he doesn't move for two minutes. "You should've checked my rep cause you fucked with the wrong bitch."

After that, she walks away. Her steps go from walking to running. She's angry for allowing herself to feel something for another human being. But, she makes a promise to never let it happen again.

Ever.

# CHANGE OF HEART

"We know you heard from her by now. She didn't just disappear off the face of the earth." Peter says.

"Are you sure? I mean...ya said you haven't found her."

"Don't be smart!"

"Well it's true. And I ain't gotta tell you shit even if I *did* know where she was. So unless you chargin' me with somethin', I suggest ya leave me a lone" Penny yells to the top of her lungs on the steps of her house.

Peter is quiet and observes what she *isn't* saying more than what she *is* saying. Her eyes told him she cared about Yvonna.

"Penny, why are you protecting her?" he looks upon her dark wrinkled face.

"I'm not protectin' nobody."

"I think you are. You called the police a while back saying someone was in your house. Who was it? Was it Yvonna?"

"If I knew 'em dey wouldn't have been strangers now would dey?"

"Look, we're here to solve a case." Guy intrudes. "We don't mean to be rude and if we are, I apologize." The anger is wiped clean from her face.

"You said she stayed here a while. Do you mind if we see the room where she stayed? We won't be long." Guy asks.

Peter looks at him as if he's stupid. In his mind if the woman wasn't willing to help, why would she allow them into her home? "Sure," she says opening the door wide. "Come on inside."

They didn't know that Penny cleaned the basement from top to bottom and was not concerned about them finding anything anyway. Although she didn't believe in murder of innocent people, she also didn't believe Yvonna was of her right frame of mind and still wanted to help her.

"Wow," Guy says looking around. "Smells real clean doesn't it?"

"Yeah, *too* clean." Peter adds looking over the neat basement.

They move around a few items, pictures and shoes Yvonna still had inside. They even look under the bed and around Penny's workbench. Still they find nothing.

"Let's go. She's cleaned this place spotless. We won't find anything here."

"That's why she let us in. Well, let me go drop off the kids in the pool," Peter says moving into the tiny pink bathroom where he plans on taking a shit.

Plopping down on the toilet, he pulls out his cell phone and looks at the screen. He was supposed to go to meet Chief Walker earlier that morning but didn't go. He figured the damage was done and he should focus on bringing Yvonna into custody. He reasons he doesn't need to see the fingerprint results to know Yvonna is guilty. He's not even looking for other suspects even though Yvonna has not been formally charged. As it stands now, the only thing she was wanted for, was missing her court ordered doctor appointments with Jona and he was using this as a means to break the law.

After straining and releasing shit into the bowl, he exhales, flushes and stands up. He is just about to leave without washing his hands or his ass until he turns around and looks at the small commode.

"I wonder." He says to himself balls dangling and shit spinning in the toilet.

He lifts the top off the toilet tank and removes a plastic bag with a black journal inside. "I knew it!"

After getting himself together, which doesn't include flushing the toilet or washing his hands, he rushes outside eager to show his partner his revelation. If she wrote anything incriminating in the journal he knew he'd have a case. The only problem is, he doesn't have a warrant.

# MUST KNOW

Gabriella sits in a wheel chair wearing a big ugly black wig, and large glasses. She'd gotten her hands on some oversized jeans and a large grey shirt that she placed wet stains throughout it. Leaned to the side, she looks like she is suffering from a body debilitating disease and that was her intent. The more docile she appeared, the less harmless she appeared. And the less harmless, the greater chance she had that they'd leave her the fuck alone. She even had a clear cup in her hand, which she filled with soapy water to represent spit.

"Hello, mam. Do you need any help?" a nurse asks. Gabriella is only a few feet from Jhane's door. To prevent her voice from being detected, she shakes her head no.

"You're sure?" she asks bending down and placing her hand gently on her knee.

Again she nods yes, a little more roughly this time.

"'Cause I don't mind taking you to where you have to go."

Gabriella sits up and says, "Look bitch! I said I'm fine! Now beat it!"

The nurse backs into the wall, looks down at Gabriella and walks hurriedly down the hallway. "Damn! How many times do a bitch got to shake her head no?!"

When the nurse is out of sight, Gabriella goes back into meek mode and rolls herself inside Jhane's room. It did her heart good to see Jhane hooked up to all types of machines and shit. Although she had to admit, she didn't think soaking Jhane's tampon with liquid Drano would cause such a major problem. Once she was fully inside the room, she pulls the curtain to conceal them.

"Look at you. You're a pitiful looking, bitch," Gabriella laughs.

Jhane's eyes are closed and her head is turned in the opposite direction. Gabriella walks around the bed and looks at her face. When she gets closer, she stoops down and smacks her so hard, her lips tremble. Loving the way her skin feels under her fingers, she smacks her again. And again. And again until her lips bleed.

When she stops Jhane opens her eyes and say, "Are you done?"

Gabriella is shocked at her response and that she took blow after blow without flinching. "You were up the entire time?"

"Are…you…done?" she repeats pronouncing each word clearly.

Gabriella steps back.

"I don't know if I'm done, bitch," she says getting her gumption back. "Give me a second and I might hit your ass again."

"The officers told me someone spotted you following me in the restaurant. Is it true?"

"What do you think?"

"Yvonna, I'm sorry." She looks at her. "I'm sorry for hurting you. I really am. I know you don't believe me. And to be honest, I don't expect you too. But…I was young when I got pregnant with you. And there are many things…many, many things that you don't know about."

"Pregnant with me? Fuck are you talking about?"

"You are my child. And because of circumstances which I can't explain in detail. I hated *THEM*. I hated all of *THEM* for forcing me to give you up. I fought them so *hard*, Yvonna." Tears roll out of her eyes and unto the pillow behind her head. She looks at the ceiling. "But they are heartless. They have control over everything, even my sister. I know you don't believe me but I really did fight to get you back and even was going to tell someone about them, and they promised if I did, they'd make my life a living hell. I didn't know how to get over the pain, but they showed me. They introduced me to drugs," she looks back at Gabriella. "And I loved it. Before long, they managed to convince me that you were evil and that everything I experienced was your fault. After awhile, I was happy to give you up and hated you everyday in the process."

"I'm don't understand what the fuck your telling us! This doesn't make any fucking sense!" Gabriella grows loud not thinking about who might hear her.

"I'm your mother. You're my daughter. You and Jesse both and we were born into something, we couldn't get out of. The pain I felt whenever looking at you cut me so deep that I bailed out on you and I was wrong."

Gabriella takes four steps back until her legs give out and her body drops into a yellow chair against the wall, by the windowsill.

"I was so wrong and I'm finally realizing it now. I was a coward."

Gabriella is suddenly gone and it is Yvonna who sits in the room alone. Her mind wanders over what was just said. She remembers it all. She immediately goes back to the day Jesse was shot and taken to the hospital.

---

### The Day Jesse Was Shot

Thirty minutes later Jhane rushed into the hospital to speak to the doctors. When Yvonna stood up to greet her, Jhane looked at her coldly.

"Get the fuck away from me, bitch!" Jhane told her with her fist balled up. "When Jesse pulls through, she's staying with me. I don't care what you say or that deadbeat father of yours says." She walked off to talk to the doctors.

"Don't worry about her." Sabrina gripped her.

"Yeah! She's just upset at what's happening with Jesse." Cream added.

Yvonna didn't want to say anything, but Jhane's attitude toward her hurt but she was going to play it off. *Fuck my family.* Yvonna thought. *I got my girls and they got me! And when my sister gets betta, the three of dem will be all I care about.*

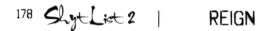

## Current Moment

Yvonna, looks up at Jhane and says, "If I'm your daughter, why would you hurt me so badly?"

"Because you reminded me of my failures. You reminded me of *THEM* and at that point in my life, I had escaped and couldn't risk going back. *THEY* warned me to be careful and they watched my every move. *THEY* still do."

"Who are *THEY*? And what do *THEY* go to do with me?"

"Yvonna, I can't say a lot. It's for your own protection. I just want you to know that I was an awful mother. And trust me, I'm getting everything I deserve."

Yvonna's very confused and can't seem to wrap her tortured mind around everything that Jhane is saying so she focuses on what she wants to know most of all.

"Who are the people, who raised me?"

"She isn't your mother and he isn't your father."

Yvonna feels like she's on the verge of a nervous break down and she drinks the water in Jhane's cup. "Well who were they? I need to know what's going on!"

"I'm sorry, I can't say much more."

"Well why fuckin' tell me if you won't tell me everything?" she asks as tears fall down her face.

"Because I'm dying from breast cancer. It's progressing rapidly and they don't think I'll make it past a few days." Yvonna is quiet and for some reason she's hurt. "Yvonna. Please come here," Jhane reaches out to her.

Yvonna stands and walks up to her. "Before I die, I want you to know that I've always loved you. Even when I felt I didn't. The more I hated you, the more I realized my love. Hate and love are closely related, Yvonna. And when you have your baby, you'll understand that sometimes you don't make the right decisions although you mean to. And, I made the worse mistakes in my life and most of them before I was old enough to know what was going on. Your health problem, is my fault." Yvonna looks away and Jhane pulls her hand. "Look at me, Yvonna." She does. "It's all my fault. Jesse loves you and if she sees you trying, she'll be by your side. You two need each other but she's scared and got to know she's safe around you. Let the hospital help."

In that moment Jhane gives something to Yvonna she always wanted, a mother's love. Although there were still many, many unanswered questions, for the second Jhane recognizes her wrongs, Yvonna feels euphoric. And then she realizes she won't have her in her life. She realizes that she'll die soon and again she'll be alone. She doesn't understand why everybody she cares about, everyone she ever loved, is taken from her. She hates life and curses God for bringing her into the world.

Now she's angry and feels motions in her stomach. Her head is spinning and like it had many times before, hate consumes her. She snatches her hand away.

"I hope you rot in hell you fat, ugly bitch. And because I don't trust your fate to Cancer, I'm gonna make sure death happens to you now."

Yvonna snatches the pillow from up under her neck, takes the finger monitor of Jhane's hand that the doctor used to check the pressure, and places it on her own to prevent the nurses from detecting something is wrong. Next she presses the shallow pillow over her face. Jhane's legs and arms kick and jerk, but Yvonna maintains her pressure pushing harder and harder into the bed.

"Die bitch! Die!" She cries. "Fucking die!"

And when Jhane stops moving, Yvonna removes the pillow from her face and places it back up under her head. She looks down at her lifeless body. This was the first time she'd been so close to her and she immediately recognizes their resemblance. *You were my mother.* Now she hates herself and Jhane even more. Not to mention she left her with so many unanswered questions. "Death looks good on you."

Yvonna slides the pressure monitor off of her finger, hops back in the wheelchair, and pushes herself out the door. The nurses and hospital aides rush toward Jhane's room missing Yvonna by seconds. It was the happy ending she always wanted.

# NO INVOLVEMENT

"Do you mind if I have a seat?"

"What is this about?" Terrell Shines asks as he looks at Jona Maxwell from behind his desk.

"I've been calling you, but you stopped answering my calls. Is there a reason?"

"Jona Maxwell?" It was the first time they'd met in person.

"Yes." She sits down without waiting for him to offer.

"Look…I have an appointment in a few minutes. I'm gonna need you to leave."

"Sir, we really need your help. Please. Just a few moments."

Terrell walks around his desk and sits on the edge of it. Folding his arms against his muscular chest, he looks down at her and she's intimidated. Now she understands how her patients feel. Not only was she taken by how attractive he was, she was also taken by his elusiveness. She was trained to read minds but failed when it came to reading men. She was so bad at it that she hadn't fucked in over two years.

"What do you need?"

"Yvonna has gotten worse. And I don't know if you've been looking at the news, but there are several people dead who had contact with her in the past and several others missing. Now I know you two had a relationship and you might feel uncomfortable helping us, but we need you."

"We?"

"Yes, there are quite a few of us."

He laughs. "What is this? A task force?"

"Sort of. Right now she's really only wanted for questioning and for missing her appointments with me. The last information we had on her she was in the hospital for an injury to her hand. No one has been able to reach her since."

"I've given up trying to help Yvonna. And to be honest, I'm not sure why whenever her name comes up, people come to me. She was my fiancé not my patient. I only helped her out when she needed me and then she ran off with that Dave person." He sounds bitter like he's still in love and Jona is slightly jealous.

When he sits down she observes the pictures against his wall. In all of them he is alone, and for some reason, she is pleased because she thinks he's single. She was angry with herself for choosing such a modest looking outfit. She looks like someone's mother instead of a single horny woman.

"Terrell, I beg you to reconsider."

"Leave now."

Jona drops her head, pushes her chair back and stands up. Walking over to his desk, she reaches in her purse, removes the list Yvonna created and places it on his desk. Then she jots down an address on his notepad and puts it down.

"That's a list she created recently." She closes her purse and places it on her arm. "And we're all going to be there tomorrow night if you want to come. Enjoy the rest of your day," she says looking up for a minute to see his face.

"Good bye, Ms. Maxwell." For some reason his shortness she takes personally.

"Good bye." She turns around and walks hurriedly toward the door. It looks like their plan would have to be worked out minus one doctor.

# TIME IS NOW

"What is your problem, Peter! Your GOT DAMN ASS OUT THERE THREATENIN' FEMALE OFFICERS AND SHIT" Lieutenant Michael Cronnell yells.

"Sir, I'm trying to solve this case."

"I want this case solved too but you're out there on some GOT DAMN personal bullshit! I suggest you back off! Cause you're five seconds from findin' yourself in the unemployment line. And about that red-head, it's over. Don't go within two feet of her or the only thing you gonna be fuckin' is me! Am I clear?!"

"Yes, sir." He says embarrassed at his outburst.

Without waiting on a response, Cronnell picks up a manila folder and slides it across his desk. "This came for you!" Cronnell storms away.

"Peter, what's goin' on?" Guy finally asks. He didn't dare speak while his boss was there for fear he'd receive some of the backlash.

Peter ignores him and opens the results. When he does the wind is knocked out of his body.

"What is it, Peter?" Guy asks standing up. "What the fuck is it?"

# LIGHT JOGGING

Bradshaw was jogging on down his street for his daily five-mile run. With the money he was getting from the movie company, he was on top of the world. And, he'd already made arrangements to get the in house security necessary to get custody of his daughter. Thoughts of betraying Yvonna did cross his mind but he couldn't take her seriously. Because if his daughter's social workers found out that he was dealing with someone like Yvonna, he would have been deemed unfit and risked losing her for the rest of his life. It would have never worked.

"Looking good, Mr. Shaw." Yells a white woman who has been sweet on him ever since he moved to the Upper Marlboro area earlier in the year. "Need help with that tight little bun of yours?"

"How 'bout I join you for some coffee later," he tells her.

Coffee meant joining her like he often did for a morning fuck session. "I'll get a pot brewing."

He winks and jogs on his way. The moment he reaches a group of trees at the bottom of the hill, he sees a woman smiling at him in an old red Ford Forerunner. He recognizes her immediately.

"There he goes!" Gabriella says to her.

Realizing the only person she had in her life was Gabriella, she stopped trying to fight what *was* and just let things *be*. Gabriella would always be a part of her life and she liked it because it made her stronger.

"I see his fucking ass!"

He quickly scans his surroundings to see where he can run. But it's too late. She already presses the gas pedal running smack dab into his body knocking him to the ground. It's difficult to run over him at first, but she builds up enough momentum to push the large stolen truck over his limbs. His body trails under her truck for about a half of mile before eventually falling off.

"Dead men speak no tales." Yvonna says.

"Not even for a movie deal." Gabriella laughs.

# SICK & FUCKING TIRED

Using the money she'd stolen from an elderly man she carjacked for his truck, she checked into a hotel in DC. She knew she couldn't stay long because her cash was low and she knew Ming would be coming back to America soon. Ming was happy to make a space for her in her large eight-bedroom house in Bowie.

Lately Yvonna had been suffering from depression so badly that all she wanted to do was eat, sleep and cry. Revenge was always great, but at this point she needed more. She needed love.

Sitting on the bed, she pulls out a large sweater from her shopping bag, which is three sizes too big for her and swallows her body. She'd gained so much weight around her stomach, ass and thighs, that she'd begun to hate her body. Easing into the sweater, she through some sweat pants on ready to watch TV when Ming knocks on the door.

She opens it. "Oh my goodness!" Yvonna yells looking at her friend. She missed her a lot.

"Don't act like you miss me bitch. Who you got in here fucking?" Ming looks around in a long fur coat. Her face is full.

"It's not even that kind of party."

Ming takes her coat off revealing a large protruding belly and Yvonna's mouth drops.

"Ming, you're fat!"

"No! I'm pregnant you're fat!" she says looking at the large sweater. "You don't dress same. Why?" She asks pointing at her body. "Fuck you been doing?"

"Long story," Yvonna says depressed. "But who is the father?"

"You not believe," Ming continues in her broken English. Her breasts are larger and she even has a nice ass. Pregnancy becomes her.

"I don't know....Choy...Ho...Hung? Who? Just tell me, bitch!"

"Bradshaw, the man we fucked threesome with when I in town." She says excitedly.

Yvonna can't believe she got pregnant by him, especially after she left his body earlier for dead. "And you kept it?"

"Why not? Me want black baby, me keep black baby." She rubs her stomach and speaks as if it's some kind of nigger doll or something.

Suddenly Yvonna is jealous because she realizes that for the rest of Ming's life she'd always have someone to care for her and she couldn't say the same about her self.

"What's wrong my friend?"

"Nothing." She lies.

"You sure?"

"Yes."

"Wanna get high?" Ming asks retrieving a joint from her purse.

"I thought you weren't supposed to smoke while you're pregnant."

"Girl, please! This baby might as well know early that Ming gets fucked up!"

They laugh and enjoy each other's company and for the first time in a long time, Yvonna smiles.

# NOW WHAT

Jona Maxwell, Lily Alvarez-Martin, Guy Samuels and Peter Jensen sit in a quiet conference room in a Hyatt hotel.

"I don't understand. How could Cream's fingerprints be on the electric panel instead of Yvonna's?" Jona continues.

"I don't know either, but we probably won't find out for a while." Peter says.

"Where is Cream? She just seemed to drop off the face of the earth!" Guy adds.

"If Yvonna had anything to do with it, she probably did." Lily adds. She gained a little weight since sharing her secret about her partner.

"Did they get a match on the fingerprints from the Bernice Santana case?" Jona asks having nothing much to contribute other than random questions.

"Yes. Bernice Santana was murdered by the victim they found her with. His name was Andrew Whinston, and they're saying he killed himself and her."

"What about Crystal Baisley? A witness saw a woman fitting Yvonna's description taking a knife out of her body on the side of the road. In broad daylight." Jona continues trying her best to be sure no stones are left unturned.

"I know. But they found the knife not too far from the crime scene and tested the prints. They belonged to a Cole Warren. They caught up with him and he was in a drug induced daze and for days couldn't even remember his own name."

"And Jhane?" she hesitates.

"She had cancer and died of natural causes."

Jona frantically looks around the room. It finally sank in. Yvonna could do whatever she wanted, to whomever she wanted. "She's getting away with it. She's killing everybody she wants to and is getting away with it! We're next!" Jona suddenly cries.

The room is silent. They all saw the list Jona had shown them not too long ago with their names on it and they knew their fate was coming soon.

"I don't know why ya'll thought we could kill this bitch by conventional means. We'll never get her if we try to do things the *right* way." Lily adds. Once the weaker one, she had quickly become one of the strongest out of the group.

"She's right. But we don't have to become victims. I have someone I want you all to meet." Peter says getting up to open the door. But when he does, instead of seeing his surprised guest, in walks Terrell. After seeing his name on the list, and being aware of Yvonna's capabilities, he decides to join the group.

"Thanks for coming." Jona says.

He doesn't respond and finds a seat amongst the other walking dead. Not wanting him to feel uncomfortable just yet, Peter's continues.

"We have to fight back if we wanna survive." He goes to the door and motions for someone to come in. In walks a man whose 6 feet 5 and clearly in disguise. "Here is our answer. He's going to make our problem go away."

Lily cheers. "About time! Now we're talking."

Everyone but Peter's looks at her as if she's crazy. "Are you suggesting we participate in murder?" Terrell questions.

"I'm suggesting that we survive."

Terrell grabs his keys and is preparing to leave when Peter opens Yvonna's journal he stole from Penny's house. He reads a passage.

"*And Terrell, that no good ass limp dick mothafucka is goin' pay for gett in' my fuckin' business. He can't last a minute in the bedroom. Maybe when he's a stiff, his dick will stay hard and last.*" He closes the book when he's done.

Gary laughs a little and Peter looks at Terrell. His desire to live overcomes his embarrassment and he takes a seat.

"There's a passage in here about each one of you. Including me. We have to kill this crazy bitch. She has chronicled most her of her life in here and I haven't been able to sleep since reading this thing. I couldn't enter this into evidence because I took it without a warrant. I'm playing her game now."

"And her doctors and lawyers would probably find some way to get it thrown out of court anyway." Lily adds.

"So what do you wanna do?" the guest asks. He was so still and quiet they forgot he was in there.

"He'll murder her for ten grand. That's two thousand a piece and by paying him, we seal our pact and take back our lives. He'll even make it look like a murder/rape. What do you wanna do?" He looks around the room and sees everyone mentally weighing their options.

It was evident that it must've taken a super crazy bitch to make two doctors and three cops conspire together in murder. But they had no other options having tried everything they could. At the end of the day, their names were on her list and lately she had won every game played. One by one they all agreed, and they left the rest in God's hands.

# BONE CRUSHER

"Sir, sir...can you hear me?" a nurse asks Bradshaw as he lies in the bed paralyzed from the neck down. "If you can hear me, blink your eyes." He blinks.

"Sir, you've been hurt very badly and we're going to need you to help us help you." There were two cops present. "We're going to bring over a letter board. When you see the first letter you want to use to help us, blink." She brings over the letter board. "Blink now if you understand what I'm saying."

*Blink.*

"Do you know who did this?"

*Blink.*

"Great. Let's get started."

The nurse points at letter after letter and the process seems to take twenty minutes. But one by one he blinks and the nurse's expression changes from hopefulness, to disappointment as each word is formed.

"Sir, are you sure?"

*Blink.*

"So you're going to let whoever did this just get away?"

*Blink.*

The officers exhale and throw their hands up in the air. "Well, if you change your mind, I'm sure you'll find a way to *blink* and let us know. We're out of here."

When they are gone the nurse looks at what is spelled. It reads, *'She will kill me and I don't want to die.'*

"Whoever she is can't hurt you now." A tear runs down his face hearing her lies.

# DATE WITH DEATH

Yvonna was removing her clothes after just recently leaving the free clinic in southeast DC. She had a lot of information to absorb and wanted to get in the tub and relax to let everything soak in. If she had a mother to explain her body, visiting the clinic would not have been necessary. Looking at her phone, she saw that Ming texted her to say she'd be picking her up in the morning. And as promised, she agreed to let her live with her.

Every step she takes around the room weighs on her both mentally and physically.

She had just removed her sweat pants and was wearing nothing outside of a large comfortable black sweater and her panties. When she hears a knock at the door she yells, "Who is it?"

When she doesn't get an answer, she continues about the room, unpacking clothes and preparing for her bath. She was hoping whoever it was got the message and just went away. They don't and she hears the knock again.

"Who is it?!" she yells, her face contorted.

Feeling frustrated, she walks to the door and swings it open. When she does she's met with a blow to her face and falls to the floor. Who are you?!" she screams as the tall masked man rushes toward her. "Why are you hurting me?!"

He hits her over and over and she begs for mercy. He had orders to make her case look personal using assault and battery.

"Please. You're hurting us," she says. "Please stop."

Out of all the people she'd killed, here she was begging for the mercy she never gave her victims. And just as she'd ignored their requests, the stranger was ignoring hers.

She manages to get and runs for the door. He catches her and pulls her backward by her sweater sending her feet and legs up in the air before she drops back to the floor again. He tries to grab her to finish his work but she's using legs, arms, toes, knees and every other body part she could. Yvonna is strong and he's surprised.

It looks as if she might get away again until he hits her so hard in her eye, she see's stars. Over and over he beats her in the face with brute force. Yvonna's life and crimes suddenly flash before her eyes and she sees some of their faces. She was a killer and quickly comes to the realization that like her victims, she must die.

When she has nothing left to fight him with anyway, the man places his large hands around her throat, tightens and squeezes. Her head turns to her left and she see's Gabriella beside her, lying face up. She also looks weak. He squeezes tighter and tears roll off her face.

"I don't wanna die," Gabriella says softly. "I don't wanna die."

"It'll be okay." Yvonna smiles and the man notices her calmness and squeezes her throat harder.

In all of his life he never fought so hard to kill someone. There was a first for everything but it isn't long before Yvonna sees a bright calming light and closes her eyes.

## WE NOT FUCKING AROUND THIS TIME!
### IF YOU LIKE THE WAY THE STORY ENDED, DON'T READ THE NEXT PAGE!

# YOU JUST HAD TO DO IT!
## FUCK IT! READ AT YOUR OWN DAMN RISK!

# I AIN'T GOIN' BE ABLE TO DO IT

The hit man was still choking her until she closes her eyes.

"Finally," he says wiping the sweat off of his head with the back of his hand.

But when he stands up, he maneuvers her sweater by mistake and her nine-month-old belly is exposed. He's overcome with immediate grief.

Fifty-year-old Charles Bank had been killing for over twenty years and had three rules. *Never kill a child. Never kill an elderly person. And never kill a pregnant woman.* He'd just broken his own rule and was angry believing he'd have bad luck.

He knows it's just a matter of seconds before she dies. So he picks her body up and places her carefully on the bed. He's angry at Peter who he knows personally for not telling him. He had no idea that Peter hadn't seen her in months.

Charles spent a few minutes conducting mouth-to-mouth resuscitation and is discouraged until she coughs. She's alive. Yvonna looks at him and is too weak to be afraid. Still not sure she's out of the darkness, he leaves her there, drives a mile up the road and calls the ambulance.

Thanks to Charles, Yvonna Harris, was alive and kicking.

 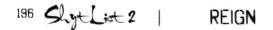

# CHANGED?

## 1 YEAR LATER

"What made her commit to your program?" Penny who is accompanied with Jesse and Yvonna's one-year-old daughter Delilah, asks. They sit in comfortable cloth chairs in front of her desk. And Delilah tries repeatedly to grab a crystal baby bird off the desk.

"Excuse me," Penny says cutting the doctor off before she speaks. "No, Delilah. Ya can't have that." She takes it from the baby's hands.

Yvonna had reached out to Penny last week and begged her to care for her daughter Delilah because she knew Penny would love her like her own, especially if Yvonna was trying to get help. Something Penny had always wanted.

Penny gladly agreed to care for Delilah until she finished the program in 6 months. She committed for many reasons including not wanting the system to take her baby. After all, she had missed appointments with Jona and risked jail time. But, no one but Penny ever *really* knew that Yvonna was still suffering from DID. And no one at all, knew she had killed again.

Ming, Yvonna's best friend, had an attitude when she committed herself and gave Delilah to Penny. She wanted to care for Delilah. But Yvonna didn't think it was a good idea because she didn't even take great care of Boy, her own son, not to mention she was always going back and forth to China. Delilah's beautiful brown skin and rosy cheeks got attention wherever she roamed. Just like her mother, she was strikingly beautiful and to be a baby, extremely smart.

"She says she committed herself for her own reasons."

"Can she leave at anytime now?" Jesse asks.

"Unfortunately not. Once they commit to our program, they must continue."

As the adults speak amongst themselves, Delilah continues to reach for the crystal bird. "No, Delilah." Penny says firmly and lovingly removing the bird again from her hands. "It's not yours so ya can't have it." Delilah cries and she looks so cute, Penny is immediately remorseful.

"She's been doing really well and this program is one of the best in the country for Dissociative Identity Disorder." The doctor continues ignoring the baby altogether. "We had to design a special program for Yvonna since her symptoms don't necessarily fit perfectly into the DID category." Doctor Connie Griswald advises.

"So who's payin' for this?"

"Her case is so unique that we were able to get funding and her friend Ming picks up most of the other costs."

Penny and Jesse look at one another because they met Ming a month back and neither of them cared for her because they thought she was a bad influence.

"You seem optimistic doctor," Jesse starts. "And I don't mean to be rude but they said my sister was cured before. And since you accepted her as a patient, despite her having relapses, how can you be sure?" she'd grown into a beautiful young woman with a thriving career as a local singing artist. At the end of the day, unlike her sister, she was mostly boring.

"Well we've been studying her thoroughly and we think we've managed to combine the personalities into one. We also know why she splits into personalities. She's been very cooperative and it makes the process easier."

"Wait you want to keep Gabriella?" Jesse questions.

"Not necessarily keep Gabriella. But, there are some good qualities that Gabriella possesses. For instance she's strong, vocal and...,"

"Evil." Penny interrupts. She looks at the doctor and then at Jesse. "Oh, I'm sorry."

They laugh. "Don't be sorry," Jesse says. "You and I both know how dangerous Gabriella can be."

"I understand why you're concerned, but it is important to remember that Gabriella is not real."

"Try tellin' her that when she in ya face," Penny adds.

"I understand. I really do. But we're finally getting to the root of the problem. Still, Yvonna has been through a lot and we haven't fully scratched the surface yet. And with this movie coming out about her life, she needs support."

"We're going to be here for her," Jesse adds. "We just need to be sure."

The doctor stands up from her desk and says, "Do you want to see her?"

"I don't want her to know that we're here. I just want to lay my eyes on her, to make sure she's okay."

"Yeah. I think we wants her to stay focused." Penny offers.

Penny picks up baby Delilah and they all walk down a long bright hallway to Yvonna's room. They come upon a cream door with a large vertical window. Yvonna is inside reading a book and never looks up to see them there.

"She looks good," Jesse smiles. Ever since she was told her aunt died from cancer, she really wanted to make things work with her sister. She was her only family. "She looks peaceful."

The proud doctor beams. "I knew you'd be pleased."

Baby Delilah coos and they're worried she can hear them in the hallway.

"Don't worry, the room is sound proof. We made it that way so that they can have peace against the distractions other patients bring."

Penny looks at Yvonna again and wants to cry. She can also tell by looking at her that she's changed. "It looks like ya program is workin'." Penny says, rocking Delilah lightly.

"It is. Well, let's go over a few more items and I'll let you all go." The doctor says walking away. Jesse follows and Penny hangs back a little longer to catch another glimpse of Yvonna through the window. But when she does, Yvonna looks at her. Penny smiles at first but there's something in Yvonna's eyes that's evilly familiar and Penny is frightened.

Not being able to look at her any longer she rushes to catch up with the doctor with Baby Delilah in her arms. Penny is so panicky, that she doesn't see the stolen crystal bird in Delilah's hands.

# ON THE OTHER SIDE
# OF TOWN

Terrell, Peter, Guy, Jona and Lily were in a quiet restaurant twenty miles outside of DC. Their plan to kill Yvonna was foiled after discovering she was pregnant. The hit man couldn't bring himself to pull the trigger or for that matter, give their money back. He said they needed to count it as a lost considering they didn't provide him with enough information. It didn't matter that they hadn't seen her in months and was surprised that he even found her so quickly.

Their plan to commit murder and save themselves had changed, but it still would be carried out. The only difference now was that they needed to do it themselves.

"So what's this about?" Jona asks Terrell, who she'd been seeing lately.

"As you all know Yvonna committed herself into a new facility in Virginia. Well, I managed to get a hold of something you all might be interested in."

He picks up a large cylinder poster holder and removes a sketch but does not show the drawing just yet.

"Part of the program for DID is to have the patients describe who they see in their minds physically. I thought this method was particularly groundbreaking especially for Yvonna since she'd taken on her father's personality. So how do we know every personality she sees, isn't coming from a real person?"

"We don't." Jona adds.

Everyone is interested because they know it's going somewhere big.

"Well?" Lily says eying the rolled up sketch. She had gained twenty pounds and everyone was amazed at how beautiful she was. She grew her hair out and favored Eva Mendez a lot. "Show us!"

"One second," he says with his hand out. "Well…when they finished with Yvonna, and she gave the artist the details necessary to create a composite drawing of Gabriella, this is what they came up with." He unrolls the sketch and lays it down flat on the table. They all look at it and then back at one another.

"It can't be," Guy says looking at the sketch and than back at Terrell.

"So you remember this case?" Terrell inquires.

"Remember it, it was all over the fucking news!"

"I don't remember this," Jona says.

"If you gonna hang out with cops you got to know the cases," Lily starts. "This little girl wandered into a Baptist church in DC on a Sunday morning about twenty somethin' years ago. The congregation referred to her as an angel because she seemed to have come from the sky. She was there every Sunday for six months faithfully and would always be hungry and dirty."

"Where were her parents?" Jona persists.

"Whenever they would ask her," Guy picks up. "She'd tell them she'd get in trouble if she told them their names. So they kept her secret, fed and took care of her until one Sunday she didn't show up."

Jona eyes sadden. "So what they do?"

"They were devastated." Lily continues. "They had gotten so use to taking care of her that they'd built a room in the basement of their church for her and everything. She was the church's daughter. They'd bought clothes for her and would send her off with packaged snacks. They said she always took two of everything when she left. It was like she was looking out for somebody else.

"Anyway, they reported her missing and the media went mad. They hired a forensic artist and with Pastor Robinson's help, they drew the little girl's picture." She points at the drawing on the table. "It looked awfully like this and it was put up everywhere. They raised a million dollar reward to find her."

"Oh my God." Jona says. "What happened?"

"Nothing," Terrell says. "They never found her and the church was never the same."

Jona looks at the picture trying to remember something. "What was her name?"

Chill bumps run through their spines when they realized that even the name was the same. "G…Gabriella." Terrell manages. "They called her Gabriella."

Silence. "But she looks older in this picture." Peter says. "The same eyes, and even the same face but just older. How is this possible?"

"Maybe she knew her. All I know is we have to find out." Terrell ends.

---

## In A Ritzy Maryland Home Development

"Did you feed, Spike?" Lavera Aniston, a 26-year-old African American woman asks her son, as she turns over steaks on the grill in their backyard. She knows if they don't feed their dog, he'll want theirs.

"No, mommy," Quentin says, playing with his portable game. "He's eating."

Lavera walks to the dog's house and screams when she see's him chewing a white female's hand.

**MAJOR SPOILER! DON'T READ UNLESS YOU READ THE BOOK!**

## Shyt List Two Questions

Do you think Dave was the man for Yvonna?

Do you think Treyana was wrong for sleeping with Bilal and getting pregnant by him?

Are you angry that Bernice knew about the children and didn't tell?

Do you think Avante will still love the twins?

What do you think will become of Bilal Jr?

Where do you think Cream is?

In all honesty, did you think Ming was a figment of Yvonna's imagination?

Where do you think Diane and Jo got the children they used to molest from?

Having known much more of Yvonna's story, do you think she is the victim or a villain?

Do you think Yvonna should appreciate Penny's love or do you want Penny to stay out of her business? Do you think Penny has ulterior motives?

When did you know Yvonna was pregnant and what areas can you point out in the story, where clues were given?

Do you love or hate Gabriella?

Why do you think Jhane was afraid to tell Yvonna about "Them" and who do you think "They" are?

Do you think Yvonna will ever find and keep true love with a man?

Do you think Delilah will suffer from mental illness?

What do you think Swoopes real motive is for wanting to kill Yvonna?

Do you think Yvonna will be a good mother?

What do you believe is the most shocking twist in the story?

# COMING SOON

**ShytList 3**

AND A CHILD SHALL LEAD THEM

Cartel Publications Order Form
www.thecartelpublications.com
*Inmates ONLY get novels for $10.00 per book!*

| Titles | | Fee |
|---|---|---|
| Shyt List | _____ | $15.00 |
| Shyt List 2 | _____ | $15.00 |
| Pitbulls In A Skirt | _____ | $15.00 |
| Pitbulls In A Skirt 2 | _____ | $15.00 |
| Victoria's Secret | _____ | $15.00 |
| Poison | _____ | $15.00 |
| Poison 2 | _____ | $15.00 |
| Hell Razor Honeys | _____ | $15.00 |
| Hell Razor Honeys 2 | _____ | $15.00 |
| A Hustler's Son 2 | _____ | $15.00 |
| Black And Ugly As Ever | _____ | $15.00 |
| Year of The Crack Mom | _____ | $15.00 |
| The Face That Launched A Thousand Bullets | _____ | $15.00 |
| The Unusual Suspects | _____ | $15.00 |
| Miss Wayne & The Queens of DC | _____ | $15.00 |

**Please allow 5-7 business days for delivery. The Cartel is not responsible for prison orders rejected.**

**(CARTEL CAFÉ AND BOOKS STORE REQUESTS)**
**Inmates we are now accepting order requests for ANY PAPER-BACK BOOK you want outside of the Cartel Titles. Books will be shipped directly from our bookstore. <u>If it's in print, we can get it!</u> We are NOT responsible for books out of print. For Special Order Requests, Please send $15.00 and the name of book below. To prevent refund if 1st special request novel is out of print, please include 2nd requested novel in case the other is unavailable. SORRY, NO STAMPS ACCEPTED WITH SPECIAL ORDERS!**

Special Order Book 1. _____

Special Order Book 2. _____

*Please add $4.00 per book for shipping and handling. NO PERSONAL CHECKS ACCEPTED!*

The Cartel Publications * P.O. Box 486 * Owings Mills * MD * 21117

Name: _____

Address: _____

_____

Contact#/Email: _____

# CARTEL PUBLICATIONS TITLES

NO ONE ON THE SHELVES
HAS SWAGGER LIKE US
CARTEL PUBLICATIONS
WWW.THECARTELPUBLICATIONS.COM

# Toujours
# Provence

## Peter Mayle

VINTAGE DEPARTURES

VINTAGE BOOKS

A DIVISION OF RANDOM HOUSE, INC.

NEW YORK

FIRST VINTAGE DEPARTURES EDITION, JUNE 1992

Library of Congress Cataloging-in-Publication Data
Mayle, Peter.
Toujours Provence/Peter Mayle ; drawings by Judith Clancy.
—1st Vintage Books ed.
p.     cm.
"Originally published...in Great Britain by Hamish Hamilton,
Inc., London in 1991"—T.p. verso.
ISBN 0-679-73604-2 (pbk.)
1. Provence (France)—Social life and customs.    2. Mayle, Peter—
Homes and haunts—France—Provence.    I. Title.
[DC611.P961M36    1992]
944′.9—dc20        91-50719
CIP

Manufactured in the United States of America

579D86

# Toujours Provence

Drawings by Judith Clancy

# Peter Mayle

# Toujours Provence

Peter Mayle spent fifteen years in advertising, first as a copywriter and then as a reluctant executive, before leaving the business in 1975 to write books. His work has been translated into seventeen languages, and he has contributed to the London *Sunday Times,* the *Financial Times,* and the *Independent,* as well as *Gentlemen's Quarterly* and *Esquire.*

*A Year in Provence* won the British Book Awards' "Best Travel Book of the Year" in 1989. Mr. Mayle's most recent book is *Chasing Cézanne.* He and his wife live in Provence.

To Jennie, as always,
and to the friends and partners in research
who have been so generous in so many ways:
Michel from Châteauneuf, Michel from Cabrières,
Henriette and Faustin, Alain the truffle hunter,
Christopher, Catherine, and Bernard

*Mille mercis*

# Contents

*Les Invalides*   3

The English *Écrevisse*   15

Boy   27

Passing 50 Without Breaking the Speed Limit   37

The Singing Toads of St. Pantaléon   49

No Spitting in Châteauneuf-du-Pape   59

Buying Truffles from Monsieur X   73

*Napoléons* at the Bottom of the Garden   87

As Advertised in *Vogue*   101

Mainly Dry Periods, with Scattered Fires   117

Dinner with Pavarotti   129

A *Pastis* Lesson   139

The *Flic*   151

Mouthful for Mouthful with the Athlete Gourmet   163

Fashion and Sporting Notes from the
Ménerbes Dog Show   183

Inside the Belly of Avignon   193

Postcards from Summer   203

Arrest That Dog!   219

Life Through Rosé-Tinted Spectacles   231

# Toujours Provence

# Les Invalides

I had been to a pharmacy in Apt for toothpaste and suntan oil, two innocent and perfectly healthy purchases. When I arrived home and took them out of the bag, I found that the girl who served me had included an instructive but puzzling gift. It was an expensively printed leaflet in full color. On the front was a picture of a snail sitting on the toilet. He looked doleful, as if he'd been there for some time without achieving anything worthwhile. His horns drooped. His eye was lackluster. Above this sad picture was printed *La Constipation*.

What had I done to deserve this? Did I look constipated? Or was the fact that I bought toothpaste and suntan oil somehow significant to the expert pharmacist's eye—a hint that all was not well in my digestive system? Maybe the girl knew something I didn't. I started to read the leaflet.

"Nothing," it said, "is more banal and more frequent than constipation." About 20 percent of the French population, so the writer claimed, suffered from the horrors of *ballonnement* and *gêne abdominale*. And yet, to a casual observer like myself,

3

there were no obvious signs of discomfort among the people on the streets, in the bars and cafés, or even in the restaurants—where presumably 20 percent of the clientele tucking into two substantial meals a day were doing so in spite of their *ballonnements*. What fortitude in the face of adversity!

I had always thought of Provence as one of the healthier places in the world. The air is clean, the climate is dry, fresh fruit and vegetables are abundantly available, cooking is done with olive oil, stress doesn't seem to exist—there could hardly be a more wholesome set of circumstances. And everybody looks very well. But if 20 percent of those ruddy faces and hearty appetites were concealing the suffering caused by a traffic jam in the *transit intestinal*, what else might they be concealing? I decided to pay closer attention to Provençal complaints and remedies, and gradually became aware that there is indeed a local affliction, which I think extends to the entire country. It is hypochondria.

A Frenchman never feels out of sorts; he has a *crise*. The most popular of these is a *crise de foie*, when the liver finally rebels against the punishment inflicted by *pastis*, five-course meals, and the tots of *marc* and the *vin d'honneur* served at everything from the opening of a car showroom to the annual meeting of the village Communist Party. The simple cure is no alcohol and plenty of mineral water, but a much more satisfactory solution—because it supports the idea of illness rather than admitting self-indulgence—is a trip to the pharmacy and a consultation with the sympathetic white-coated lady behind the counter.

I used to wonder why most pharmacies have chairs arranged between the surgical trusses and the *cellulite* treatment kits, and now I know. It is so that one can wait more comfortably while Monsieur Machin explains, in great whispered detail and with considerable massaging of the engorged throat, the tender kidney, the reluctant intestine, or whatever else ails him, how he came to this painful state. The pharmacist, who is trained in patience and diagnosis, listens carefully, asks a few questions, and then proposes a number of possible solutions. Packets and jars and ampoules are produced. More discussion. A choice is finally made, and Monsieur Machin carefully folds up the vital pieces of paper that will enable him to claim back most of the cost of his medication from Social Security. Fifteen or twenty minutes have passed, and everyone moves up a chair.

These trips to the pharmacy are only for the more robust invalids. For serious illness, or imaginary serious illness, there is, even in relatively remote country areas like ours, a network of first aid specialists that amazes visitors from cities, where you need to be a millionaire before you can be sick in comfort. All the towns, and many of the villages, have their own ambulance services, on call 24 hours a day. Registered nurses will come to the house. *Doctors* will come to the house, a practice I'm told is almost extinct in London.

We had a brief but intense experience with the French medical system early last summer. The guinea pig was Benson, a young American visitor on his first trip to Europe. When I picked him up at the Avignon railroad station, he croaked hello, coughed, and clapped a handkerchief to his mouth. I asked him what was the matter.

He pointed to his throat and made wheezing noises.

"Mono," he said.

Mono? I had no idea what that was, but I did know that Americans have much more sophisticated ailments than we do—hematomas instead of bruises, migraine instead of a headache, postnasal drip—and so I muttered something about fresh air soon clearing it up and helped him into the car. On the way home, I learned that mono was the intimate form of address for mononucleosis, a viral infection causing considerable soreness of the throat. "Like broken glass," said Benson, huddled behind his sunglasses and his handkerchief. "We have to call my brother in Brooklyn. He's a doctor."

We got back to the house to find the phone out of order. It was the beginning of a long holiday weekend, and so we would be without it for three days, normally a blessing. But Brooklyn had to be called. There was one particular antibiotic, a *state of the art* antibiotic, that Benson said would overcome all known forms of mono. I went down to the phone booth at Les Baumettes and fed it with five-franc pieces while Brooklyn Hospital searched for Benson's brother. He gave me the name of the wonder drug. I called a doctor and asked him if he could come to the house.

He arrived within an hour and inspected the invalid, who was resting behind his sunglasses in a darkened room.

"*Alors, monsieur . . .*" the doctor began, but Benson cut him short.

"Mono," he said, pointing at his throat.

"*Comment?*"

"Mono, man. Mononucleosis."

"*Ah, mononucléose. Peut-être, peut-être.*"

The doctor looked into Benson's angry throat and took a swab. He wanted to run a laboratory test on the virus. And now, would Monsieur lower his trousers? He took out a syringe, which Benson peered at suspiciously over his shoulder as he slowly dropped his Calvin Klein jeans to half-mast.

"Tell him I'm allergic to most antibiotics. He should call my brother in Brooklyn."

*"Comment?"*

I explained the problem. Did the doctor by any chance have the wonder drug in his bag? *Non*. We looked at each other around Benson's bare buttocks. They jerked as Benson coughed painfully. The doctor said he must be given something to reduce the inflammation, and that side effects from this particular shot were extremely rare. I passed the news on to Benson.

"Well . . . OK." He bent over, and the doctor injected with a flourish, like a matador going in over the horns. *"Voilà!"*

While Benson waited for allergic reactions to send him reeling, the doctor told me that he would arrange for a nurse to come twice a day to give further injections, and that the test results would be in on Saturday. As soon as he had them, he would make out the necessary prescriptions. He wished us a *bonne soirée*. Benson communed noisily with his handkerchief. I thought a *bonne soirée* was unlikely.

The nurse came and went, the test results came through, and the doctor reappeared on Saturday evening as promised. The young Monsieur had been correct. It was *mononucléose*, but we would conquer it with the resources of French medicine. The doctor began to scribble like a poet in heat. As prescription after prescription flowed from his pen, it seemed as though every single resource was going to be called into action. He passed over a wad of hieroglyphics, and wished us a *bon weekend*. That too was unlikely.

The Sunday of a holiday weekend in rural France is not the easiest time to find a pharmacy open for business, and the only one for miles around was the *pharmacie de garde* on the outskirts of Cavaillon. I was there at 8:30, and joined a man clutching a wad of prescriptions almost as thick as mine.

Together we read the notice taped to the glass door: Opening time was not until 10:00.

The man sighed, and looked me up and down.

"Are you an emergency?"

No. It was for a friend.

He nodded. He himself had an important *arthrose* in his shoulder, and also some malign fungus of the feet. He was not going to stand for an hour and a half in the sun to wait for the pharmacy to open. He sat down on the pavement next to the door and started to read chapter one of his prescriptions. I decided to go and have breakfast.

"Come back well before ten," he said. "There will be many people today."

How did he know? Was a Sunday morning visit to the pharmacy a regular prelunch treat? I thanked him and ignored his advice, killing time with an old copy of *Le Provençal* in a café.

When I returned to the pharmacy just before ten, it looked as though *le tout Cavaillon* had gathered outside. There were dozens of them standing with their voluminous prescriptions, swapping symptoms in the manner of an angler describing a prize fish. Monsieur *Angine* boasted about his sore throat. Madame *Varices* countered with the history of her varicose veins. The halt and the maimed chattered away cheerfully, consulting their watches and pressing ever closer to the still-locked door. At last, to a murmured accompaniment of *enfin* and *elle arrive*, a girl appeared from the back of the pharmacy, opened up, and stepped smartly aside as the stampede jostled through. Not for the first time, I realized that the Anglo-Saxon custom of the orderly queue has no place in French life.

I must have been there for half an hour before I was able

8

to take advantage of a gap in the mêlée and give my documents to the pharmacist. She produced a plastic shopping bag and started to fill it with boxes and bottles, rubber-stamping each prescription as she worked her way through the pile, a copy for her, a copy for me. With the bag at bursting point, one prescription remained. After disappearing for five minutes, the pharmacist admitted defeat; she was out of stock of whatever it was, and I would have to get it from another pharmacy. However, it was not grave, because the important medication was all there in the bag. Enough, it seemed to me, to bring a regiment back from the dead.

Benson sucked and gargled and inhaled his way through the menu. By the next morning he had emerged from the shadow of the grave and was feeling sufficiently recovered to join us on a trip to the Ménerbes pharmacy in search of the last prescription.

One of the village elders was there when we arrived, perched on a stool while his shopping bag was being stuffed full of nostrums. Curious about what exotic disease the foreigners might have, he remained seated while our prescription was being filled, leaning forward to see what was in the packet as it was put on the counter.

The pharmacist opened the packet and took out a foil-wrapped object the size of a fat Alka-Seltzer tablet. She held it up to Benson.

"*Deux fois par jour*," she said.

Benson shook his head and put his hand to his throat.

"Too big," he said. "I couldn't swallow anything that size."

We translated for the pharmacist, but before she could reply the old man collapsed with laughter, rocking perilously on his stool and wiping his eyes with the back of a knobbly hand.

The pharmacist smiled, and made delicate upward motions with the foil-wrapped lump. *"C'est un suppositoire."*

Benson looked bewildered. The old man, still laughing, hopped down from his stool and took the suppository from the pharmacist.

*"Regardez,"* he said to Benson. *"On fait comme ça."*

He moved away from the counter to give himself space, bent forward, holding the suppository above his head, and then, with a flowing backwards swoop of his arm, applied the suppository firmly to the seat of his trousers. *"Tok!"* said the old man. He looked up at Benson. *"Vous voyez?"*

"Up the *ass*?" Benson shook his head again. "Hey, that's weird. Jesus." He put on his sunglasses and moved a couple of paces backwards. "We don't do that where I come from."

We tried to explain that it was a very efficient method of getting medication into the bloodstream, but he wasn't convinced. And when we said that it wouldn't give him a sore throat either, he wasn't amused. I often wonder what he told his brother the doctor back in Brooklyn.

Shortly afterward, I met my neighbor Massot in the forest and told him about the suppository lesson. It was droll, he thought, but for a truly *dramatique* episode there was nothing to touch the story of the man who had gone into the hospital to have his appendix out and had woken up with his left leg amputated. *Beh oui.*

I said it couldn't be true, but Massot insisted that it was.

"If I am ever ill," he said, "I go to the vet. You know where you are with vets. I don't trust doctors."

Fortunately, Massot's view of the French medical profession is as unlikely to reflect reality as most of his views. There may be doctors with a taste for amputation in Provence, but we have never met them. In fact, apart from our brush with mononucleosis, we've only seen the doctor once, and that was to combat an attack of bureaucracy.

It was the climax of months of paper shuffling that we had gone through in order to get our *cartes de séjour*—the identity cards that are issued to foreign residents of France. We had been to the *Mairie*, to the *Préfecture*, to the *Bureau des Impôts*, and back again to the *Mairie*. Everywhere we went, we were told that another form was required which, *naturellement*, could only be obtained somewhere else. In the end, when we were convinced that we had a full set of certificates, attestations, declarations, photographs, and vital statistics, we made what we thought would be our last triumphal visit to the *Mairie*.

Our dossiers were examined carefully. Everything seemed to be in order. We were not going to be a drain on the state. We had no criminal record. We were not seeking to steal employment from French workers. *Bon.* The dossiers were closed. At last we were going to be official.

The secretary of the *Mairie* smiled nicely and passed over two more forms. It was necessary, she said, to have a medical examination to prove that we were of sound mind and body. Doctor Fenelon in Bonnieux would be pleased to examine us. Off to Bonnieux we went.

Doctor Fenelon was charming and brisk as he X-rayed us and took us through the fine print of a short questionnaire. Were we mad? No. Epileptic? No. Addicted to drugs? Alcoholic? Prone to fainting? I was half-expecting to be interrogated about bowel movements in case we might be adding to the constipated sector of the French population, but that didn't seem to be a concern of the immigration authorities. We signed the forms. Doctor Fenelon signed the forms. Then he opened a drawer and produced two more forms.

He was apologetic. *"Bien sûr, vous n'avez pas le problème, mais . . ."* he shrugged, and explained that we must take the forms into Cavaillon and have a blood test before he could give us our *certificats sanitaires*.

Was there anything special that we were being tested for?

*"Ah, oui."* He looked even more apologetic. *"La syphilis."*

# The English *Écrevisse*

"Writing is a dog's life, but the only life worth living." That was Flaubert's opinion, and it is a fair expression of the way it feels if you choose to spend your working days putting words down on pieces of paper.

For most of the time, it's a solitary, monotonous business. There is the occasional reward of a good sentence—or rather, what you think is a good sentence, since there's nobody else to tell you. There are long, unproductive stretches when you consider taking up some form of regular and useful employment like chartered accountancy. There is constant doubt that anyone will want to read what you're writing, panic at missing deadlines that you have imposed on yourself, and the deflating realization that those deadlines couldn't matter less to the rest of the world. A thousand words a day, or nothing; it makes no difference to anyone else but you. That part of writing is undoubtedly a dog's life.

What makes it worth living is the happy shock of discovering that you have managed to give a few hours of entertainment to people you've never met. And if some of them should write to tell you, the pleasure of receiving their letters is like applause. It makes up for all the grind. You abandon thoughts of a career in accountancy and make tentative plans for another book.

My first letter arrived shortly after the publication in April of *A Year in Provence*. It came from Luxembourg, polite and complimentary, and I kept looking at it all day. The next week a man wrote asking how to grow truffles in New Zealand. Then the letters began to arrive in a steady trickle—from London, from Beijing, from Queensland, from Her Majesty's Prison at Wormwood Scrubs, from the expatriate community on the Riviera, from the wilds of Wiltshire and the Surrey hills—some on embossed, true-blue, toff's writing paper, others on pages torn from exercise books, one on the back of a map of the London Underground. The addresses were often so vague that the Post Office had to perform small marvels of deduction: "*Les Anglais*, Bonnieux" found us, despite the fact that we don't live in Bonnieux. So did my favorite: "*L'Écrevisse Anglais*, Ménerbes, Provence."

The letters were friendly and encouraging, and whenever there was an address to reply to, I replied, thinking that would be the end of it. But often it wasn't. Before long we found ourselves in the undeserved position of resident advisers on every aspect of Provençal life from buying a house to finding a baby-sitter. A woman telephoned from Memphis to ask about the burglary rate in the Vaucluse. A photographer from Essex wanted to know if he could make a living taking pictures in the Lubéron. Couples thinking about moving to Provence wrote pages of questions. Would their children fit in in the local schools? How high was the cost of living? What about doctors? What about income tax? Was it lonely? Would they be happy? We answered as best we could, but it was slightly uncomfortable to be involved in the personal decisions of total strangers.

And then, as summer set in, what had been dropping through the mailbox started coming up the drive. Letters turned into people.

It was hot and dry, and I was doing some Provençal weeding in the bone-hard ground with a pickax when a car arrived and the driver emerged with a broad smile, waving a copy of my book at me.

"Tracked you down!" he said. "Did a little detective work in the village. No trouble at all."

I signed the book and felt like a real author, and when my wife came back from Cavaillon she was properly impressed. "A fan," she said. "You should have taken a photograph. How amazing that someone should bother."

She was less impressed a few days later when we were leaving the house to go out to dinner and found a pretty blonde lurking behind the cypress tree in the front garden.

"Are you him?" asked the blonde.

"Yes," said my wife. "What a pity. We're just going out." Blondes are probably used to reactions like that from wives. She left.

"That might have been a fan," I said to my wife.

"She can go and be a fan somewhere else," she said. "And you can take that smirk off your face."

During July and August we became used to finding unfamiliar faces at the front door. Most of them were apologetic and well-mannered, just wanting their books signed, grateful for a glass of wine and a few minutes sitting in the courtyard out of the heat of the sun. They all seemed to be fascinated by the stone table we had finally managed to install with such difficulty.

"So *this* is The Table," they'd say, walking around it and running their fingers over the surface as if it was one of Henry Moore's best efforts. It was a very curious sensation to have ourselves, our dogs (who loved it), and our house inspected with such interest. And, I suppose inevitably, there were times when it wasn't curious but irritating, when a visit felt more like an invasion.

Unseen by us one afternoon when the temperature was over 100 degrees, the husband, the wife, and the wife's friend, noses and knees sunburned to a matching angry red, had parked at the end of the drive and walked up to the house. The dogs were asleep and hadn't heard them. When I went indoors to get a beer, I found them in the sitting room, chatting to each other as they examined the books and the furniture. I was startled. They weren't.

"Ah, there you are," said the husband. "We read the bits in the Sunday *Times*, so we decided to pop in."

That was it. No excuses, no hint of awkwardness, no thought that I might not be thrilled to see them. They didn't even have a copy of the book. Waiting for the paperback to come out, they said. Hardcover books are so expensive these days. They oozed an unfortunate mixture of familiarity and condescension.

It is not often that I take against people on sight, but I took against them. I asked them to leave.

The husband's red wattles turned even redder, and he puffed up like an aggrieved turkey who had just been told the bad news about Christmas.

"But we've driven all the way over from Saint-Rémy." I asked him to drive all the way back, and they left in a cloud of muttering. That's *one* book we won't be buying, only wanted to *look*, anyone would think it was Buckingham Palace. I watched them march down the drive to their Volvo, shoulders rigid with indignation, and thought about getting a Rottweiler.

After that, the sight of a car slowing down and stopping on the road in front of the house was the signal for what came to be known as a crawler alert. "Make yourself decent," my wife would say, "I think they're coming up the drive. No—they've stopped at the mailbox." And later on, when I went down to collect the post, there was a copy of the book in a plastic bag, to be signed and left under a stone on top of the well. The next day it was gone; taken, I hoped, by the considerate people who had delivered it without wanting to disturb us.

By the end of summer, we were not the only ones to have received some attention from the public. Our neighbour Faustin had been asked to autograph a book, which had puzzled him since, as he said, he was not an *écrivang*. When I told him that people had been reading about him in England, he took off his cap and smoothed his hair and said *Ah bon?* twice, sounding rather pleased.

Maurice the chef had also done his share of signing, and said he'd never had so many English customers in his restaurant. Some of them had been surprised to find that he actually existed; they thought I'd made him up. Others had arrived with copies of the book and had ordered, down to the final glass of *marc*, a meal that they had read about.

And then there was the celebrity plumber, Monsieur Menicucci, who drops in from time to time between his *oeuvres* to share with us his thoughts on politics, wild mushrooms, climatic irregularities, the prospects for the French rugby team, the genius of Mozart, and any exciting developments in the world of sanitary fittings. I gave him a copy of the book and showed him passages in which he had starred, and told him that some of our visitors had expressed a desire to meet him.

He adjusted his woollen bonnet and straightened the collar of his old check shirt. *"C'est vrai?"*

Yes, I said, absolutely true. His name had even appeared in the Sunday *Times*. Perhaps I should organize a signing session for him.

*"Ah, Monsieur Peter, vous rigolez."* But I could see that he was not displeased at the idea, and he went off holding his book as carefully as if he were carrying a fragile and expensive bidet.

The voice on the other end of the phone could have come all the way from Sydney, cheerful and twangy.

"G'day. Wally Storer here, from the English Bookshop in Cannes. Plenty of Brits down here, and your book's going nicely. How about coming along to sign a few copies one day during the Film Festival?"

I have always had doubts about the literary appetite of people in the film business. An old friend who works in Hollywood confessed that he had read one book in six years, and he was considered a borderline intellectual. If you mention Rimbaud in Bel Air it is assumed that you're talking about Sylvester Stallone. I didn't hold out much hope for writer's cramp and mammoth sales. Even so, I thought it would be fun. Maybe I'd see a star, or a topless sensation on the Croisette, or—the rarest sight in town—a smiling waiter on the Carlton Hotel terrace. I said I'd be happy to come.

It was hot and sunny, bad weather for bookshops, as I joined the traffic crawling into town. Bright new signs on the lampposts announced that Cannes was twinned with Beverly Hills, and I could imagine the mayors finding endless excuses to exchange visits in the cause of municipal friendship and the shared interest of taking free holidays.

Outside the Palais des Festivals, what seemed to be the entire Cannes police force, equipped with revolvers, walkie-talkies, and sunglasses, was busy creating a series of traffic jams and making sure Clint Eastwood didn't get kidnapped. With the skill that comes from many years of practice, they directed cars into snarling knots and then whistled at them furiously, sending the drivers off to the next snarling knot with irritated jerks of the head. It took me 10 minutes to cover 50 yards. When I finally reached the vast underground car park, I saw that an earlier victim of the chaos had scrawled on the wall: "Cannes is a great place to visit, but I wouldn't want to spend the day here."

I went to a café on the Croisette to have breakfast and look for stars. Everyone else was doing the same thing. Never have so many unknowns inspected each other so carefully. All the girls were wearing pouts and trying to look bored. All the men carried listings of the films to be shown that day and made important notes in the margins. One or two cordless phones were placed with casual prominence next to the croissants, and everyone displayed plastic delegates' badges and the obligatory Festival bag, with *Le Film Français/Cannes 90* printed on it. There was no mention of *Le Film Américain* or *Le Film Anglais*, but I suppose that's one of the advantages of being the host on these occasions; you get to choose the bags.

The Croisette was planted with a forest of posters carrying the names of actors, directors, producers, and, for all I knew, hairdressers. They were positioned directly opposite the big hotels, presumably so that the hero of each poster could see his name every morning from his bedroom window before having the traditional Cannes breakfast of ham and ego. A feeling of hustle was in the air, of big deals and big bucks, and the groups of hustlers walking along the Croisette were oblivious to the old beggar sitting on the pavement outside the Hotel Majestic with a lonely 20-centime piece in his upturned, tattered hat.

Fortified by my dose of glamour, I left the moguls to it and went down the narrow Rue Bivouac-Napoléon to the English Bookshop, preparing for the odd experience of sitting in a shop window hoping for someone—anyone—to ask me to sign a book. I'd done one or two signings before. They were unnerving occasions when I had been stared at from a safe distance by people who were unwilling to venture within talking range. Perhaps they thought I'd bite. Little did they know the relief authors feel when a brave spirit approaches the table. After a few minutes of sitting on your own, you're ready to clutch at any straw and sign anything from books and photographs to old copies of *Nice-Matin* and checks.

Fortunately, Wally Storer and his wife had anticipated author's funk and had stocked the shop with friends and customers. What inducements they had used to drag them off the beach I didn't know, but I was grateful to be kept busy, and I even started to wish I'd brought Monsieur Menicucci along. He could have answered much better than I why French drains behave and smell the way they do, which I found to be a topic of common curiosity among English expatriates. Isn't it strange, they said, that the French are so good at sophisticated technology like high-speed trains and electronic telephone systems and the Concorde, and yet revert to the 18th century in their bathrooms. Only the other day, an elderly lady informed me, she had flushed her toilet and the remains of a mixed salad had surfaced in the bowl. Really, it was *too bad*. That sort of thing would never happen in Cheltenham.

The signing came to an end, and we went round the corner to a bar. Americans and English outnumbered the natives, but natives in Cannes are few and far between. Even many of the police, I was told, are imported from Corsica.

They were still patrolling the Croisette when I left, toying with the traffic and eyeing the girls who sauntered by in varying stages of undress. The old beggar hadn't moved from his pitch in front of the Majestic, and his 20-centime piece was as lonely as ever. I dropped some coins in his hat and he told me, in English, to have a nice day. I wondered if he was practicing for Beverly Hills.

# Boy

My wife first saw him on the road into Ménerbes. He was walking along beside a man whose neat, clean clothes contrasted sharply with his own disreputable appearance, a filthy rug hung over a framework of bones. And yet, despite the matted coat and burr-encrusted head, it was obvious that this dog was one of a breed peculiar to France, a species of rough-haired pointer known officially as the Griffon Korthals. Beneath that shabby exterior lurked a *chien de race*.

One of our dogs was a Korthals, but they are not often seen in Provence, and so my wife stopped the car to talk to a fellow owner. What a coincidence it was, she said, that she had one of the same unusual breed.

The man looked down at the dog, who had paused to take a dust bath, and stepped backwards to distance himself from the tangle of legs and ears that was squirming in the ditch.

"*Madame*," he said, "he accompanies me, but he is not my dog. We met on the road. I don't know who he belongs to."

When my wife returned from the village and told me about

27

the dog, I should have seen trouble coming. Dogs are to her what mink coats are to other women; she would like a house full of them. We already had two, and I thought that was quite enough. She agreed, although without conviction, and during the next few days I noticed that she kept looking hopefully down to the road to see if the apparition was still in the neighborhood.

It would probably have ended there if a friend hadn't called from the village to tell us that a dog just like one of ours was spending every day outside the *épicerie*, drawn by the scent of hams and homemade *pâtés*. Each night he disappeared. Nobody in the village knew his owner. Perhaps he was lost.

My wife had a *crise de chien*. She had found out that lost or abandoned dogs are kept by the *Société Protectrice des Animaux* (the French ASPCA) for less than a week. If unclaimed, they are put down. How could we let this happen to any dog, let alone a nobly born creature of undoubted pedigree?

I telephoned the SPA and drew a blank. My wife began to spend several hours a day in the village on the pretext of buying a loaf of bread, but the dog had vanished. When I said that he had obviously gone back home, my wife looked at me as though I had suggested roasting a baby for dinner. I telephoned the SPA again.

Two weeks passed without sight of the dog. My wife moped, and the man at the SPA became bored with our daily calls. And then our contact at the *épicerie* came up with some hard news: the dog was living in the forest outside the house of one of her customers, who was giving him scraps and letting him sleep on the terrace.

I have rarely seen a woman move so quickly. Within half an hour my wife was coming back up the drive with a smile visible from fifty yards away. Next to her in the car I could see the enormous shaggy head of her passenger. She got out of the car, still beaming.

"He must be starving," she said. "He's eaten his seat belt. Isn't he wonderful?"

The dog was coaxed from his seat and stood there wagging everything. He looked frightful—an unsanitary furball the size of an Alsatian, with a garnish of twigs and leaves entwined in his knotted coat, bones protruding from his body, and an immense brown nose poking through the undergrowth of his moustache. He lifted his leg against the side of the car and kicked up the gravel with his paws before lying down on his stomach, back legs stretched out behind him and six inches of pink tongue, speckled with fragments of seat belt, lolling from his mouth.

"Isn't he wonderful?" my wife said again.

I held out my hand to him. He got up, took my wrist in his jaws, and started to pull me into the courtyard. He had very impressive teeth.

"There you are. He likes you."

I asked if we could offer him something else to eat, and retrieved my dented wrist. He emptied a large bowl of dog food in three gulps, drank noisily from a bucket of water, and wiped his whiskers by hurling himself on the grass. Our two bitches didn't know what to make of him, and neither did I.

"Poor thing," said my wife. "We'll have to take him to the vet, and get him clipped."

There are moments in every marriage when it is futile to argue. I made an appointment with Madame Hélène, *toilettage de chiens*, for that afternoon, since no respectable vet would touch him in his current state. Madame Hélène, I hoped, would be used to the grooming problems of country dogs.

She was very brave about it after her initial shock. Her other client, a miniature apricot-colored poodle, whimpered and tried to hide in a magazine rack.

"Perhaps it would be best," she said, "if I attended to him first. He is very highly perfumed, *n'est-ce pas?* Where has he been?"

"I think in the forest."

"Mmm." Madame Hélène wrinkled her nose, and put on a pair of rubber gloves. "Can you come back in an hour?"

I bought a flea collar, and stopped for a beer in the café at Robion while I tried to come to terms with the prospect of being a three-dog family. There was, of course, always the chance that the previous owner could be found, and then I would have only two dogs and a distraught wife. But in any case, it was not a choice I could make. If there was a canine guardian angel, he would decide. I hoped he was paying attention.

The dog was tethered to a tree in Madame Hélène's garden when I got back, wriggling with pleasure as I came through the gate. He had been clipped down to stubble, making his head look even bigger and his bones even more prominent. The only part of him that had escaped severe pruning was his stumpy tail, which had a whiskery fringe trimmed to a modified pom-pom. He looked mad and extraordinary, like a child's drawing of a stick dog, but at least he smelled clean.

He was thrilled to be back in the car and sat bolt upright on the seat, leaning over from time to time for a tentative nibble at my wrist and making small humming noises that I assumed were signs of contentment.

In fact, they must have been hunger, because he fell on the meal that was waiting for him at home, putting one foot on the empty bowl to keep it still while he tried to lick off the enamel. My wife watched him with the expression that most women reserve for well-behaved and intelligent children. I steeled myself, and said that we must start thinking about finding his owner.

The discussion continued over dinner, with the dog asleep under the table on my wife's feet, snoring loudly. We agreed that he should spend the night in an outbuilding, with the door left open so that he could leave if he wanted to. If he was still there in the morning, we would call the only other man we knew in the region who had a Korthals and ask his advice.

My wife was up at dawn, and shortly afterward I was woken by a hairy face thrust into mine; the dog was still with us. It soon became clear that he was determined to stay, and that he knew exactly how he was going to convince us that life without him would be unthinkable. He was a shameless flatterer. One look from us was enough to set his whole bony body quivering with evident delight, and a pat sent him into ecstasy. Two or three days of this and I knew we would be lost. With mixed feelings, I called Monsieur Grégoire, the man we had met one day in Apt with his Korthals.

He and his wife came over the next day to inspect our lodger. Monsieur Grégoire looked inside his ears to see if he had been tattooed with the number that identifies pedigreed dogs in case they should stray. All serious owners, he said, do this. The numbers are stored in a computer in Paris, and if you find a tattooed dog the central office will put you in touch with the owner.

Monsieur Grégoire shook his head. No number. "*Alors,*" he said, "he has not been *tatoué*, and he has not been fed correctly. I think he is abandoned—probably a Christmas present that grew too big. It happens often. He will be better living with you." The dog flapped his ears and wagged himself vigorously. He wasn't about to argue.

"*Comme il est beau,*" said Madame Grégoire, and then made a suggestion that might easily have increased the dog population in our house to double figures. What did we think, she asked, about a marriage between the foundling and their young bitch?

I knew what one of us thought, but by then the two women were planning the whole romantic episode.

"You must come up to our house," said Madame Grégoire, "and we can drink champagne while the two of them are . . ." she searched for a sufficiently delicate word ". . . outside."

Fortunately, her husband was made of more practical stuff. "First," he said, "we must see if they are sympathetic. Then, perhaps . . ." He looked at the dog with the appraising eye of a prospective father-in-law. The dog put a meaty paw on his knee. Madame cooed. If ever I had seen a *fait accompli*, this was it.

"But we have forgotten something," said Madame after another bout of cooing. "What is his name? Something heroic would be suitable, no? With that head." She patted the dog's skull, and he rolled his eyes at her. "Something like Victor, or Achille."

The dog sprawled on his back with his legs in the air. By no stretch of the imagination could he be described as heroic, but he was conspicuously masculine, and there and then we decided on his name.

"We thought we'd call him Boy. *Ça veut dire 'garçon' en Anglais.*"

"Boy? *Oui, c'est génial,*" said Madame. So Boy he was.

We arranged to take him up to meet his fiancée, as Madame called her, in two or three weeks, after he'd been inoculated, tattooed, fed decently, and generally made into as presentable a suitor as possible. In between his trips to the vet and his enormous meals, he spent his time insinuating himself into the household. Every morning he would be waiting outside the courtyard door, squeaking with excitement at the thought of the day ahead and grabbing the first wrist that came within range. Within a week, he was promoted from a blanket in the outbuilding to a basket in the courtyard. Within ten days, he was sleeping in the house, under the dining table. Our two bitches deferred to him. My wife bought him tennis balls to play with, which he ate. He chased lizards, and discovered the cooling delights of sitting on the steps leading into the swimming pool. He was in dog heaven.

The day arrived for what Madame Grégoire described as the *rendez-vous d'amour*, and we drove up to the spectacular rolling countryside above Saignon where Monsieur Grégoire had converted an old stone stable block into a long, low house overlooking the valley and the village of St. Martin-de-Castillon in the far distance.

Boy had gained weight and a thicker coat, but he was still lacking in social polish. He bounded from the car and lifted his leg on a newly planted sapling, churning up a patch of young lawn with his back paws. Madame found him charming. Monsieur, it seemed, was not so sure; I noticed him looking at Boy with a slightly critical eye. Their bitch ignored him, concentrating instead on a series of ambushes mounted against our other two dogs. Boy climbed a hillock at the end of the house and jumped onto the roof. We went inside for tea and cherries marinated in *eau-de-vie*.

"He is looking well, Boy," said Monsieur Grégoire.

"*Magnifique*," said Madame.

"*Oui, mais* . . ." There was something worrying Monsieur. He got up and fetched a magazine. It was the latest issue of the official organ of the *Club Korthals de France*, page after page of photographs showing dogs at the pointing position, dogs with birds in their mouths, dogs swimming, dogs sitting obediently by their masters.

"*Vous voyez*," said Monsieur, "all these dogs have the classic coat, the *poil dur*. It is a characteristic of the breed."

I looked at the pictures. The dogs all had flat, rough coats. I looked at Boy, who was now pressing his great brown nose against the window. His coat had grown after clipping into a mass of grey and brown ringlets that we thought rather distinguished. Not Monsieur Grégoire.

"Unfortunately," he said, "he has grown to resemble a *mouton*. From the neck up, he is a Korthals. From the neck down, he is a sheep. I am desolated, but this would be a *mésalliance*."

My wife almost choked on her cherries. Madame looked dismayed. Monsieur was apologetic. I was relieved. Two dogs and a sheep would do for the time being.

Boy is still, as far as we know, a bachelor.

# Passing 50 Without
# Breaking the
# Speed Limit

I have never paid any great attention to my birthdays, even
those that marked the accomplishment of having tottered
through another ten years of life. I was working on the day
I turned 30, I was working on the day I turned 40, and I
was quite happy at the thought of working on my 50th birthday. But it was not to be. Madame my wife had different
ideas.

"You're going to be half a hundred," she said. "Considering
the amount of wine you drink, that is some kind of achievement. We should celebrate."

There is no arguing with her when she has a certain set
to her chin, and so we talked about how and where the deed
should be done. I might have known that my wife had already
arranged it; she was listening to my suggestions—a trip to
Aix, a *déjeuner flottant* in the pool, a day by the sea at Cassis
—out of politeness. When I ran out of inspiration, she moved
in. A picnic in the Lubéron, she said, with a few close friends.
That was the way to celebrate a birthday in Provence. She

painted lyrical pictures of a sun-dappled glade in the forest. I wouldn't even have to wear long trousers. I'd love it.

I couldn't imagine loving a picnic. My picnic experiences, limited as they had been to England, had left memories of rising damp creeping up the spine from permanently moist earth, of ants disputing with me over the food, of tepid white wine, and of scuttling for shelter when the inevitable cloud arrived overhead and burst on top of us. I loathed picnics. Rather ungraciously, I said so.

This one, said my wife, would be different. She had it all worked out. In fact, she was in deep consultation with Maurice, and what she had in mind would be not only civilized but highly picturesque, an occasion to rival Glyndebourne on a dry day.

Maurice, the chef and owner of the Auberge de la Loube in Buoux and a serious horse fancier, had over the years collected and restored two or three 19th-century *calèches*, or open carriages, and a horse-drawn limousine, a stagecoach, *une vraie diligence*. He was now offering his more adventurous clients the chance to trot to lunch. I would *love* it.

I recognize inevitability when it stares me in the face, and it was settled. We invited eight friends and kept our fingers crossed, less tightly than we would have done in England, for fine weather. Although it had only rained once since early April, two months before, June in Provence is unpredictable and sometimes wet.

But when I woke and went out into the courtyard, the seven o'clock sky was a never-ending blue, the color of a Gauloise packet. The flagstones were warm under my bare feet, and our resident lizards had already taken up their sunbathing positions, flattened and motionless against the wall of the house. Just to get up to a morning like this was enough of a birthday present.

The beginning of a hot summer day in the Lubéron, sitting on the terrace with a bowl of *café crème*, the bees rummaging in the lavender, and the light turning the forest to a dark burnished green, is better than waking up suddenly rich. Warmth gives me a sense of physical well-being and optimism; I didn't feel a day older than 49, and looking down at ten brown toes I hoped I'd be doing exactly the same thing on my 60th birthday.

A little later, as warmth was turning into heat, the hum-buzz of the bees was blotted out by the clatter of a diesel engine, and I watched as a venerable open-top Land Rover, painted camouflage green, panted up the drive and stopped in a cloud of dust. It was Bennett, looking like the recon-naissance scout from a Long Range Desert Group—shorts and shirt of military cut, tank commander sunglasses, vehicle festooned with jerricans and kitbags, face deeply tanned. Only the headgear, a Louis Vuitton baseball cap, would have been out of place at El Alamein. He had crossed enemy lines on the main N100 road, successfully invaded Ménerbes, and was now ready for the final push into the mountains.

"My God, you're looking old," he said. "Do you mind if I make a quick call? I left my swimming trunks at the house where I was staying last night. They're khaki, like General Noriega's underpants. Very unusual. I'd hate to lose them."

While Bennett was on the phone, we rounded up our two houseguests and three dogs and packed them in the car for the drive up to Buoux, where we were meeting the others. Bennett came out of the house and adjusted his baseball cap against the glare, and we set off in convoy, the Land Rover and its chauffeur attracting considerable interest from the peasants, waist-deep in the vines on either side of the road.

After Bonnieux, the scenery became wilder and harsher, vines giving way to rock and scrub oak and purple-striped lavender fields. There were no cars and no houses. We could have been a hundred miles away from the chic villages of the Lubéron, and it pleased me to think that so much savage, empty country still existed. It would be a long time before there was a boutique or a real estate agent's office up here.

We turned down into the deep valley. Buoux dozed. The dog who lives on the woodpile just past the *Mairie* opened one eye and barked perfunctorily, and a child holding a kitten looked up, small white saucers in a round brown face, at the unusual sight of traffic.

The area around the Auberge resembled a casting session for a film that had not quite decided on plot, characters, wardrobe, or period. There was a white suit and a wide-brimmed Panama; there were shorts and espadrilles, a silk dress, a Mexican peon's outfit, scarves and bright shawls, hats of various colors and ages, one immaculately turned out baby, and, leaping from his Land Rover to supervise kit inspection, our man from the desert.

Maurice appeared from the horses' parking area, smiling at us and the glorious weather. He was dressed in his Provençal Sunday best—white shirt and trousers, black bootlace tie, plum red waistcoat, and an old flat straw hat. His friend, who was to drive the second carriage, was also in white, set off by thick crimson braces and a magnificent salt-and-pepper moustache, a dead ringer for Yves Montand in *Jean de Florette*.

"*Venez!*" said Maurice. "Come and see the horses." He led us through the garden, asking about the state of our appetites. The advance party had just left by van to set up the picnic, and there was a feast on board, enough to feed the whole of Buoux.

The horses were tethered in the shade, coats glossy, manes and tails coiffed. One of them whinnied and nosed at Maurice's waistcoat, looking for a sugar lump. The youngest guest, perched on her father's shoulders, gurgled at the sight of such a monster and leaned forward to poke one tentative pink finger into its shining chestnut flank. The horse mistook her for a fly and whisked a long tail.

We watched as Maurice and Yves Montand hitched up the horses to the open *calèche*, black trimmed with red, and the seven-seater *diligence*, red trimmed with black—both of them oiled and waxed and buffed to a state of showroom finish. Maurice had spent all winter working on them and they were, as he said, "*impecc.*" The only modern addition was a vintage car horn the size and shape of a bugle, for use when overtaking less highly tuned carriages, and to *éclater* any chickens who were thinking of crossing the road. "*Allez! Montez!*"

We climbed in and moved off, observing the speed limit through the village. The dog on the woodpile barked good-bye, and we headed out into open country.

To travel in this way is to make you regret the invention of the car. There is a different view of everything, more commanding and somehow more interesting. There is a comfortable, swaying rhythm as the suspension adjusts to the gait of the horse and the changes of camber and surface. There is a pleasant background of old-fashioned noises as the harness creaks and the hooves clop and the steel rims of the wheels crunch the grit on the road. There is the *parfum*—a blend of warm horse, saddle soap, wood varnish, and the smells of the fields that come to the nose unobstructed by windows. And there is the speed, or lack of it, which allows you time to *look*. In a car you're in a fast room. You see a blur, an impression; you're insulated from the countryside. In a carriage, you're part of it.

"*Trottez!*" Maurice flicked the horse's rump with the whip and we changed into second gear. "She's lazy, this one," he said, "and greedy. She goes more quickly on the way back, when she knows she will eat." A long scarlet field, dense with poppies, unrolled slowly in the valley below us, and in the sky a buzzard wheeled and dipped, wings outstretched and still, balancing on air. As I watched it, a cloud covered the sun for a few moments and I could see the rays coming out behind it in dark, almost black spokes.

We turned off the road and followed a narrow track that twisted through the trees, and the sound of the horse's hooves was muffled by ragged, fragrant carpets of wild thyme. I asked Maurice how he found his picnic spots, and he told me that every week, on his day off, he had been exploring on horseback, sometimes riding for hours without meeting anyone. "We're only twenty minutes from Apt," he said, "but nobody comes up here. Just me and the rabbits."

The forest became thicker and the track narrower, barely wide enough for the carriage. Then we turned past an outcrop of rock, ducked through a tunnel of branches, and there it was, spread out before us. Lunch.

"*Voilà!*" said Maurice. "*Le restaurant est ouvert.*"

At the end of a flat, grassy clearing, a table for ten had been set in the shade of a sprawling scrub oak—a table with a crisp white cloth, with ice buckets, with starched cotton napkins, with bowls of fresh flowers, with proper cutlery and proper chairs. Behind the table, a long-empty dry stone *borie*, originally a shepherd's hut, had been turned into a rustic bar, and I heard the pop of corks and clink of glasses. All my misgivings about picnics vanished. This was as far away from a damp bottom and ant sandwiches as one could possibly imagine.

Maurice roped off an area of the clearing and unhitched the horses, who rolled on their backs in the grass with the relief of two elderly ladies released from their corsets. The blinds of the *diligence* were drawn, and the youngest guest retired for a nap while the rest of us had a restorative glass of chilled peach champagne in the tiny open courtyard of the *borie*.

There is nothing like a comfortable adventure to put people in a good humor, and Maurice could hardly have hoped for a more appreciative audience. He deserved it. He had thought of everything, from an abundance of ice to toothpicks, and, as he had said, there was no danger of us going hungry. He called us to sit down and gave us a guided tour of the first course: melon, quails' eggs, creamy *brandade* of cod, game *pâté*, stuffed tomatoes, marinated mushrooms—on and on it went, stretching from one end of the table to the other, looking, under the filtered sunlight, like an implausibly perfect still life from the pages of one of those art cookbooks that never sees the kitchen.

There was a short pause while I was presented with the heaviest and most accurate birthday card I had ever received—a round metal road sign, two feet in diameter, with a blunt reminder of the passing years in large black numerals: 50. *Bon anniversaire* and *bon appétit*.

We ate and drank like heroes, getting up in between courses, glasses in hand, to take recuperative strolls before coming back to the table for more. Lunch lasted nearly four hours, and by the time coffee and the birthday *gâteau* were served we had reached that state of contented inertia where

43

even conversation is conducted in slow motion. The world was a rosy place. Fifty was a wonderful age.

The horses must have noticed the increased weight of their loads as they pulled out of the clearing toward the road that led back to Buoux, but they seemed more frisky than they had been in the morning, tossing their heads and testing the air through twitching nostrils. Sudden gusts of wind plucked at straw hats, and there was a growl of thunder. Within minutes, the blue sky turned black.

We had just reached the road when the hail started—pea-sized and painful, stinging the tops of our heads in the open *calèche* and bouncing off the broad wet back of the horse. She needed no encouragement from the whip. She was going full tilt, head down, body steaming. The brim of Maurice's straw hat had collapsed into bedraggled ears, and his red waistcoat was bleeding onto his trousers. He laughed, and shouted into the wind, "*Oh là là, le pique-nique Anglais!*"

My wife and I made a tent out of a travel blanket, and looked back to see how the *diligence* was dealing with the downpour. The top was obviously less weatherproof than it looked. Hands appeared from the side, tipping hatfuls of water overboard.

We came down into Buoux with Maurice braced, stiff-legged, hauling the reins tight against the headlong enthusiasm of the horse. She had scented home and food. To hell with humans and their picnics.

The sodden but cheerful storm victims gathered in the restaurant to be revived with tea and coffee and *marc*. Gone were the elegant picnickers of the morning, replaced by dripping, lank-haired figures dressed in varying degrees of transparency. Showing through a pair of once-white, once-opaque trousers, red-lettered knickers wished us all Merry Xmas.

Clothes that had billowed now clung, and the straw hats looked like plates of congealed cornflakes. We each stood in our own private pools of water.

Madame and Marcel, the waiter, who had driven back in the van, served an assortment of dry clothes along with the *marc*, and the restaurant was transformed into a changing room. Bennett, pensive under his baseball cap, wondered if he might borrow a pair of swimming trunks for the drive home; the Land Rover was awash, and the driver's seat a puddle. But at least, he said, looking out the window, the storm was over.

If it was over in Buoux, it had never happened in Ménerbes. The drive up to the house was still dusty, the grass was still brown, the courtyard was still hot. We watched the sun as it balanced for a moment in the notch of the twin peaks to the west of the house before disappearing beneath a flushed sky.

"Well," said my wife, "now do you like picnics?"

What a question. Of course I like picnics. I love picnics.

clancy

# The Singing Toads
# of St. Pantaléon

Of all the bizarre events organized to celebrate the mass decapitation of the French aristocracy 200 years ago, one of the most bizarre has so far gone unreported. Not even our local paper, which frequently makes front-page stories out of incidents as minor as the theft of a van from the Coustellet market or an intervillage *boules* contest—not even the newshounds of *Le Provençal* were sufficiently well informed to pick it up. This is a world exclusive.

I first heard about it toward the end of winter. Two men in the café opposite the *boulangerie* at Lumières were discussing a question that had never occurred to me: Could toads sing?

The larger of the two men, a stonemason from the look of his powerful, scarred hands and the fine coating of dust that covered his blue *combinaisons*, clearly didn't think so.

"If toads can sing," he said, "then I'm the President of France." He took a deep pull from his glass of red wine. "Eh, madame," he bellowed at the woman behind the bar, "what do you think?"

Madame looked up from sweeping the floor and rested her hands on the broom handle while she gave the matter her attention.

"It is evident that you're not the President of France," she said. "But as for toads . . . ?" She shrugged. "I know nothing of toads. It's possible. Life is strange. I once had a Siamese cat who always used the *toilette*. I have color photographs of it."

The smaller man leaned back in his chair as if a point had just been proved.

"You see? Anything is possible. My brother-in-law told me there is a man in St. Pantaléon with many toads. He is training them for the *Bicentenaire*."

"*Ah bon?*" said the big man. "And what will they do? Wave flags? Dance?"

"They will sing." The smaller man finished his wine and pushed back his chair. "By the 14th July, I am assured that they will be able to perform the '*Marseillaise*.'"

The two of them left, still arguing, and I tried to imagine how one could teach creatures with a limited vocal range to reproduce the stirring strains that make every patriotic Frenchman tingle with pride at the thought of noble severed heads dropping into baskets. Maybe it could be done. I had only heard untrained frogs croaking around the house in the summer. The larger and perhaps more gifted toad might easily be able to span more octaves and hold the long notes. But how were toads trained, and what kind of man would devote his time to such a challenge? I was fascinated.

Before trying to find the man in St. Pantaléon, I decided to get a second opinion. My neighbor Massot would know about toads. He knew, so he frequently told me, everything there was to know about nature, the weather, and any living creature that walked or flew or crawled across Provence. He was a little shaky on politics and property prices, but there was nobody to touch him on wildlife.

I walked along the track at the edge of the forest to the clammy little hollow where Massot's house was huddled into the side of a steep bank. His three dogs hurled themselves toward me until their chains jerked them up on their hind legs. I stayed out of range and whistled. There was the sound of something falling to the floor and a curse—*putain!*—and Massot appeared at the door with dripping orange-colored hands.

He came up the drive and kicked his dogs into silence, and gave me his elbow to shake. He had been decorating, he said, to make his property even more desirable when he resumed his efforts to sell it in the spring. Did I not think the orange was very gay?

After admiring his artistic judgment, I asked him what he could tell me about toads. He plucked at his moustache, turning half of it orange before remembering the paint on his fingers.

"*Merde.*" He rubbed his moustache with a rag, spreading paint over his already garish complexion, which the wind and cheap wine had seasoned to the color of a new brick.

He looked pensive, and then shook his head.

"I have never eaten toads," he said. "Frogs, yes. But toads, never. Doubtless there is an English recipe. No?"

I decided not to attempt describing the English delicacy called toad-in-the-hole. "I don't want to eat them. I want to know if they can sing."

Massot peered at me for a moment, trying to make up his mind whether I was serious. He bared his dreadful teeth. "Dogs can sing," he said. "You just kick them in the *couilles* and then . . ." He lifted his head and howled. "Toads might sing. Who knows? It is all a question of training with animals. My uncle in Forcalquier had a goat that danced whenever it heard an accordion. It was very droll, that goat, although in my opinion not as graceful as a pig I once saw with some gypsies—now *there* was a dancer. *Très délicat*, despite the size."

I told Massot what I had overheard in the café. Did he, by any chance, know the man who trained toads?

"*Non. Il n'est pas du coin.*" St. Pantaléon, although only a few kilometers away, was on the other side of the main N100 road and was therefore regarded as foreign territory.

Massot was starting to tell me an improbable story about a tame lizard when he remembered his painting, proferred his elbow once again, and went back to his orange walls. On the way home, I came to the conclusion that it was no use asking any of our other neighbors about events taking place so far away. I would have to go to St. Pantaléon and continue my research there.

St. Pantaléon is not large, even by village standards. There might be a hundred inhabitants, there is an *auberge*, and there is a tiny 12th-century church with a graveyard cut out of rock. The graves have been empty for years, but the shapes remain, some of them baby-sized. It was eerie and cold that day, with the *mistral* rattling the branches of trees, bare as bones.

An old woman was sweeping her doorstep with the wind at her back, helping the dust and empty Gauloise packets on their way to her neighbor's doorstep. I asked her if she could direct me to the house of the gentleman with the singing toads. She rolled her eyes and disappeared into the house, slamming the door behind her. As I walked on, I could see the curtain twitch at her window. At lunchtime, she would tell her husband about a mad foreigner roaming the streets.

Just before the bend in the road that leads to Monsieur Aude's workshop—*the Ferronerie d'Art*—a man was crouched over his Mobylette, poking it with a screwdriver. I asked him.

"*Beh oui*," he said. "It is Monsieur Salques. They say he is an *amateur* of toads, but I have never met him. He lives outside the village."

I followed his directions until I came to a small stone house set back from the road. The gravel on the drive looked as though it had been combed, the mailbox was freshly painted, and a business card, protected by Perspex, announced in copperplate script, HONORÉ SALQUES, *ÉTUDES DIVERSES*. That seemed to cover almost any field of study. I wondered what else he did in between supervising choir practice with his toads.

He opened the door as I was walking up the drive and watched me, his head thrust forward and his eyes bright behind gold-rimmed glasses. He radiated neatness, from his precisely parted black hair down to his noticeably clean small shoes. His trousers had sharp creases and he wore a tie. I could hear the sound of flute music coming from inside the house.

"At last," he said. "The telephone has been *en panne* for three days. It is a disgrace." He pecked his head toward me. "Where are your tools?"

I explained that I hadn't come to repair his phone, but to learn about his interesting work with toads. He preened, smoothing his already smooth tie with a neat white hand.

"You're English. I can tell. How pleasing to hear that news of my little celebration has reached England."

I didn't like to tell him that it had been the cause of

considerable disbelief as close as Lumières, and since he was now in a good humor I asked if I could perhaps visit the choir. He made little clucking noises and wagged a finger under my nose. "It is clear you know nothing about toads. They do not become active until spring. But if you wish, I will show you where they are. Wait there."

He went into the house, and reappeared wearing a thick cardigan against the chill, carrying a flashlight and a large old key labeled, in copperplate script, STUDIO. I followed him through the garden until we came to a beehive-shaped building made from dry, flat stones—one of the *bories* that were typical of Vaucluse architecture a thousand years ago.

Salques opened the door and shone the flashlight into the *borie*. Against the walls were banks of sandy soil, sloping down to an inflatable plastic paddling pool in the middle. Hanging from the ceiling above the pool was a microphone, but there was no sign of any of the *artistes*.

"They are asleep in the sand," said Salques, gesturing with his flashlight. "Here"—he shone the flashlight along the bank at the foot of the left wall—"I have the species *Bufo viridis*. The sound it makes resembles a canary." He puckered up his mouth and trilled for me. "And over here"—the torch swept across to the opposite bank of soil—"the *Bufo calamita*. It has a vocal sac capable of enormous expansion, and the call is *très, très fort*." He sunk his chin into his chest and croaked. "You see? There is a great contrast between the two sounds."

Monsieur Salques then explained how he was going to produce music from what seemed to me to be unpromising material. In the spring, when a bufo's fancy lightly turns to thoughts of mating, the inhabitants of the sandy banks were going to emerge and frolic in the paddling pool, singing their songs of love. For reasons of genetic modesty, this would only take place at night, but—*pas de problème*—every birdlike squeak and manly croak would be passed via a microphone to a tape recorder in Monsieur Salques's study. From there, it would be edited, remixed, leveled, synthesized, and generally transformed through the magic of electronics until it became recognizable as the "*Marseillaise.*"

And that was only the beginning. With 1992 soon to be upon us, Monsieur Salques was composing a completely original opus—a national anthem for the countries of the Common Market. Did I not find that an exciting concept?

Far from being excited, my reaction was deep disappointment. I had been hoping for live performances, massed bands of toads with their enormous vocal sacs swelling in unison, Salques conducting from his podium, the star contralto toad delivering a poignant solo, the audience hanging on to every squeak and gribbet. That would have been a musical experience to treasure.

But electronically processed croaking? It was eccentric, certainly, but it lacked the fine untrammeled lunacy of the living toad choir. As for a Common Market anthem, I had serious doubts. If the bureaucrats in Brussels could take years to reach agreement on simple matters like the color of a passport and the acceptable bacteria count in yogurt, what hope was there of consensus on a tune, let alone a tune sung by toads? What would Mrs. Thatcher say?

In fact, I knew what Mrs. Thatcher would say—"They must be *British* toads"—but I didn't want to mingle politics with art, so I just asked the obvious question.

Why use toads?

Monsieur Salques looked at me as though I was being deliberately obtuse. "Because," he said, "it has never been done."

Of course.

During the months of spring and early summer, I often thought of going back to see how Monsieur Salques and his toads were getting on, but I decided to wait until July, when the *concerto Bufo* would have been recorded. With luck, I might also hear the anthem of the Common Market.

But when I arrived at the house, there was no Monsieur Salques. A woman with a face like a walnut opened the door, clutching the business end of a vacuum cleaner in her other hand.

Was Monsieur at home? The woman backed into the house and turned off the vacuum cleaner.

*Non.* He has departed for Paris. After a pause, she added: For the celebrations of the *Bicentenaire*.

Then he will have taken his music?

That I cannot say. I am the housekeeper.

I didn't want to waste the trip entirely, so I asked if I could see the toads.

*Non.* They are tired. Monsieur Salques has said they must not be disturbed.

Thank you, *Madame.*

*De rien, Monsieur.*

In the days leading up to July 14th, the papers were filled with news of the preparations in Paris—the floats, the fireworks, the visiting heads of state, Catherine Deneuve's wardrobe—but nowhere could I find any mention, even in the culture sections, of the singing toads. Bastille Day came and went without a single croak. I knew he should have done it live.

clancy

# No Spitting in
# Châteauneuf-du-Pape

August in Provence is a time to lie low, to seek shade, to move slowly, and to limit your excursions to very short distances. Lizards know best, and I should have known better.

It was in the high eighties by 9:30, and when I got into the car I immediately felt like a piece of chicken about to be *sautéed*. I looked at the map to find roads that would keep me away from the tourist traffic and heat-maddened truck drivers, and a bead of sweat dropped from my nose to score a direct hit on my destination—Châteauneuf-du-Pape, the small town with the big wine.

Months before, in the winter, I had met a man called Michel at a dinner to celebrate the engagement of two friends of ours. The first bottles of wine came. Toasts were proposed. But I noticed that while the rest of us were merely drinking, Michel was conducting a personal, very intense ritual.

He stared into his glass before picking it up, then cupped it in the palm of his hand and swirled it gently three or four times. Raising the glass to eye level, he peered at the traces of wine that his swirling had caused to trickle down the inner sides. His nose, with nostrils alert and flared, was presented to the wine and made a thorough investigation. Deep sniffing. One final swirl, and he took the first mouthful, but only on trial.

It obviously had to pass several tests before being allowed down the throat. Michel chewed it for a few reflective seconds. He pursed his lips and took a little air into his mouth and made discreet rinsing noises. Lifting his eyes to heaven, he flexed his cheeks in and out to encourage a free flow around tongue and molars and then, apparently satisfied with the wine's ability to withstand an oral assault, he swallowed.

He noticed that I had been watching the performance, and grinned. *"Pas mal, pas mal."* He took another, less elaborate swallow, and saluted the glass with raised eyebrows. "It was a good year, '85."

As I found out during dinner, Michel was a *négociant*, a professional wine drinker, a buyer of grapes and a seller of nectar. He specialized in the wines of the south, from Tavel *rosé* (the favorite wine, so he said, of Louis XIV) through the gold-tinged whites to the heavy, heady reds of Gigondas. But of all the wines in his extensive collection, his *merveille*, the one he would like to die drinking, was the Châteauneuf-du-Pape.

He described it as though he were talking about a woman. His hands caressed the air. Delicate kisses dusted his fingertips, and there was much talk of body and bouquet and *puissance*. It was not unknown, he said, for a Châteauneuf to reach fifteen percent of alcoholic content. And these days, when Bordeaux seems to get thinner every year and the price of Burgundy is only possible for the Japanese, the wines of Châteauneuf are nothing less than bargains. I must come up to his *caves* and see for myself. He would arrange a *dégustation*.

The time that elapses in Provence between planning a rendezvous and keeping it can often stretch into months, and sometimes years, and so I wasn't expecting an immediate invitation. Winter turned to spring, spring turned to summer, and summer melted into August, the most lethal month of the year to be toying with a fifteen-degree wine, and then Michel called.

"Tomorrow morning at eleven," he said. "In the *caves* at Châteauneuf. Eat plenty of bread at breakfast."

I had done what he suggested and, as an extra precaution, taken a soupspoonful of neat olive oil, which one of the local gourmets had told me was an excellent way to coat the stomach and cushion the system against repeated assaults by younger powerful wines. In any case, I thought as I drove down the twisting, baked country roads, I wouldn't be swallowing much. I would do as the experts do, rinse and spit.

Châteauneuf came into view, trembling in the heat haze, just before eleven o'clock. It is a place entirely dedicated to wine. Seductive invitations are everywhere, on sun-bleached, peeling boards, on freshly painted posters, hand-lettered on monster bottles, fixed to the wall, propped at the side of vineyards, stuck on pillars at the end of driveways. *Dégustez! Dégustez!*

I drove through the gateway in the high stone wall that protects the *Caves Bessac* from the outside world, parked in the shade, and unstuck myself from the car. I felt the sun come down on the top of my head like a close-fitting hat of hot air. In front of me was a long building, crenellated along the top, its façade blind except for huge double doors. A group of people, outlined against the black interior, were standing in the doorway, holding large bowls that glinted in the sun.

The *cave* felt almost cold, and the glass that Michel gave

me was pleasantly cool in my hand. It was one of the biggest glasses I had ever seen, a crystal bucket on a stem, with a bulbous belly narrowing at the top to the circumference of a goldfish bowl. Michel said it could hold three-quarters of a bottle of wine.

My eyes adjusted to the gloom after the glare outside, and I began to realize that this was not a modest *cave*. Twenty-five thousand bottles would have been lost in the murk of one of the distant corners. In fact, there were no bottles to be seen, just boulevards of barrels—enormous barrels lying on their sides supported by waist-high platforms, their upper curves twelve or fifteen feet above the ground. Scrawled in chalk on the flat face of each barrel were descriptions of the contents, and for the first time in my life I was able to walk through a wine list: Côtes-du-Rhône-Villages, Lirac, Vac-queyras, Saint-Joseph, Crozes-Hermitage, Tavel, Gigondas —thousands of liters of each, arranged in vintages and dozing silently toward maturity.

"*Alors*," said Michel, "you can't walk around with an empty glass. What are you going to have?"

There was too much choice. I didn't know where to start. Would Michel guide me through the barrels? I could see that the others had something in their goldfish bowls; I'd have the same.

Michel nodded. That would be best, he said, because we only had two hours, and he didn't want to waste our time on the very young wines when there were so many treasures that were ready to drink. I was glad I'd had the olive oil. Anything that qualified as a treasure was hardly spitting ma-terial. But two hours of swallowing would have me as supine as one of the barrels, and I asked if one was permitted to spit.

Michel waved his glass at a small drain that marked the entrance of the *Boulevard Côtes-du-Rhône.* "*Crachez si vous voulez, mais . . .*" It was clear that he thought it would be tragic to deny oneself the pleasure of the swallow, the bursting forth of flavors, the well-rounded finish, and the profound satisfaction that comes from drinking a work of art.

The *maître de chai*, a wiry old man in a cotton jacket the color of faded blue sky, appeared with a device that reminded me of a giant eye-dropper—three feet of glass tubing with a fist-sized rubber globe at one end. He aimed the nozzle and squeezed a generous measure of white wine into my glass, muttering a prayer as he squeezed: "*Hermitage '86, bouquet aux aromes de fleurs d'accacia. Sec, mais sans trop d'acidité.*"

I swirled and sniffed and rinsed and swallowed. Delicious. Michel was quite right. It would be a sin to consign this to the drain. With some relief, I saw that the others were tipping what they didn't drink into a large jug that stood on a nearby trestle table. Later, this would be transferred into a jar containing a *mère vinaigre*, and the result would be four-star vinegar.

Slowly, we worked our way down the boulevards. At each stop, the *maître de chai* climbed up his portable ladder to the top of the barrel, knocked out the bung, and inserted his thirsty nozzle, returning down the ladder as carefully as if he were carrying a loaded weapon—which, as the tasting progressed, it began to resemble.

The first few shots had been confined to the whites, the *rosés*, and the lighter reds. But as we moved into the deeper gloom at the back of the *cave*, the wines too became darker. And heavier. And noticeably stronger. Each of them was served to the accompaniment of its own short but reverent litany. The red Hermitage, with its nose of violets, raspberries, and mulberries, was a *vin viril*. The Côtes-du-Rhône *"Grande Cuvée"* was an elegant thoroughbred, fine and *étoffé*. I was impressed almost as much by the inventive vocabulary as by the wines themselves—fleshy, animal, muscular, well-built, voluptuous, sinewy—and the *maître* never repeated himself. I wondered whether he had been born with lyrical descriptive powers or whether he took a thesaurus to bed with him every night.

We finally arrived at Michel's *merveille*, the 1981 Châteauneuf-du-Pape. Although it would keep for several years to come, it was already a masterpiece, with its *robe profonde*, its hints of spice and truffle, its warmth, its balance—not to mention its alcoholic content, which was nudging fifteen percent. I thought Michel was going to take a header into his glass. It's nice to see a man who loves his work.

With some reluctance, he put down his glass and looked at his watch. "We must go," he said. "I'll get something to drink with lunch." He went to an office at the front of the *cave*, and came out carrying a crate of a dozen bottles. He was followed by a colleague, carrying another dozen. Eight of us were going to lunch. How many would survive?

We left the *cave* and winced under the force of the sun. I had restrained myself to sips rather than mouthfuls; nevertheless, my head gave one sharp throb in warning as I walked to the car. Water. I must have water before even sniffing any more wine.

Michel thumped me on the back. "There's nothing like a *dégustation* to give you a thirst," he said. "Don't worry. We have a sufficiency." Good grief.

The restaurant Michel had chosen was half an hour away, in the country outside Cavaillon. It was a *ferme auberge*, serving what he described as correct Provençal food in rustic surroundings. It was tucked away and hard to find, so I should stick closely to his car.

Easier said than done. So far as I know, there are no statistics to support my theory, but observation and heart-stopping personal experience have convinced me that a Frenchman with an empty stomach drives twice as fast as a Frenchman with a full stomach (which is already too fast for sanity and speed limits). And so it was with Michel. One minute he was there; the next he was a dust-smudged blur on the shimmering horizon, clipping the dry grass verges on the bends, booming through the narrow streets of villages in their midday coma, his gastronomic juices in overdrive. By the time we reached the restaurant, all pious thoughts of water were gone. I needed a drink.

The dining room of the farm was cool and noisy. A large television set in the corner, ignored by the clientele, jabbered to itself. The other customers, mostly men, were darkened by the sun and dressed for outdoor work in old shirts and sleeveless vests, with the flattened hair and white foreheads that come from wearing a cap. A nondescript dog whiffled in the corner, nose twitching sleepily at the spicy smell of cook-ing meat coming from the kitchen. I realized that I was ravenous.

We were introduced to André, the *patron*, whose appear-ance, dark and full-bodied, fitted the description of some of the wines we'd been tasting. There were undertones of garlic, Gauloises, and *pastis* present in his bouquet. He wore a loose shirt, short shorts, rubber sandals, and an emphatic black moustache. He had a voice that transcended the hubbub of the room.

*"Eh, Michel! Qu'est-ce que c'est? Orangina? Coca-Cola?"* He started to unpack the crates of wine and reached in the back

pocket of his shorts for a corkscrew. *"M'amour! Un seau, des glaçons, s'il te plaît."*

His wife, sturdy and smiling, came out of the kitchen carrying a tray and unloaded it on the table: two ice buckets, plates of pink *saucisson* dotted with tiny peppercorns, a dish of vivid radishes, and a deep bowl of thick *tapenade*, the olive and anchovy paste that is sometimes called the black butter of Provence. André was uncorking bottles like a machine, sniffing each cork as he drew it and arranging the bottles in a double line down the center of the table. Michel explained that these were some of the wines we hadn't had time to try in the *cave*, young Côtes-du-Rhône for the most part, with half a dozen older and more serious reinforcements from Gigondas to help when the cheese arrived.

There is something about lunch in France that never fails to overcome any small reserves of willpower that I possess. I can sit down, resolved to be moderate, determined to eat and drink lightly, and be there three hours later, nursing my wine and still open to temptation. I don't think it's greed. I think it's the atmosphere generated by a roomful of people who are totally intent on eating and drinking. And while they do it, they talk about it; not about politics or sport or business, but about what is on the plate and in the glass. Sauces are compared, recipes argued over, past meals remembered, and future meals planned. The world and its problems can be dealt with later on, but for the moment, *la bouffe* takes priority and contentment hangs in the air. I find it irresistible.

We eased into lunch like athletes limbering up. A radish, its top split open to hold a sliver of almost white butter and flecked with a pinch of coarse salt; a slice of *saucisson*, prickly with pepper on the tongue; rounds of toast made from yesterday's bread, shining with *tapenade*. Cool pink and white wines. Michel leaned across the table. "No spitting."

The *patron*, who was nipping away at a glass of red in between his duties, presented the first course with as much ceremony as a man in shorts and rubber sandals can muster, placing a deep *terrine*, its sides burnt almost black, on the table. He stuck an old kitchen knife into the *pâté*, then came back with a tall glass pot of *cornichons* and a dish of onion jam. *"Voilà, mes enfants. Bon appétit."*

The wine changed color as Michel dealt out his young reds, and the *terrine* was passed around the table for second slices. André came over from his card game to refill his glass. *"Ça va? Ça vous plaît?"* I told him how much I liked his onion jam. He told me to save some room for the next course, which was—he kissed his fingertips loudly—a triumph, *alouettes sans tête*, prepared specially for us by the hands of his adorable Monique.

Despite the rather grisly name (literally, larks without heads), it is a dish made from thin slices of beef rolled around slivers of salt pork, seasoned with chopped garlic and parsley, bathed in olive oil, dry white wine, stock, and tomato *coulis* and served neatly trussed with kitchen twine. It looks nothing like a lark—more like an opulent sausage—but some creative Provençal cook must have thought that larks sounded more appetizing than rolled beef, and the name has survived.

Monique brought in the *alouettes*, which André said he had shot that morning. He was a man who found it difficult to make a joke without delivering the punch line physically, and the nudge he delivered with his forearm almost knocked me into a vast tub of *ratatouille*.

The headless larks were hot and humming with garlic, and

Michel decided that they deserved a more solid wine. The Gigondas was promoted from the cheese course, and the collection of dead bottles at the end of the table was by now well into double figures. I asked Michel if he had any plans to work in the afternoon. He looked surprised. "I *am* working," he said. "This is how I like to sell wine. Have another glass."

Salad came, and then a basketwork tray of cheeses—fat white discs of fresh goat cheese, some mild Cantal, and a wheel of creamy St. Nectaire from the Auvergne. This inspired André, now installed at the head of the table, to produce another joke. There was this little boy in the Auvergne who was asked which he liked best, his mother or his father. The little boy thought for a moment. "I like bacon best," he said. André heaved with laughter. I was relieved to be out of nudging distance.

Scoops of sorbet were offered, and an apple tart, sleek with glaze, but I was defeated. When André saw me shake my head, he bellowed down the table, "You must eat. You need your strength. We're going to have a game of *boules*."

After coffee, he led us outside to show us the goats that he kept in a pen at the side of the restaurant. They were huddled in the shade of an outbuilding, and I envied them; they weren't being asked to play *boules* under a sun that was drilling lasers into the top of my head. It was no good. My eyes were aching from the glare and my stomach wanted desperately to lie down and digest in peace. I made my excuses, found a patch of grass under a plane tree, and lowered my lunch to the ground.

André woke me some time after six and asked if I was staying for dinner. There were *pieds et paquets*, he said, and

68

by some happy chance two or three bottles of the Gigondas had survived. With some difficulty, I escaped and drove home.

My wife had spent a sensible day in the shade and by the pool. She looked at me, a rumpled apparition, and asked if I had enjoyed myself.

"I hope they gave you something to eat," she said.

# Buying Truffles from Monsieur X

The whole furtive business began with a phone call from London. It was my friend Frank, who had been described once in a glossy magazine as a reclusive magnate. I knew him better as a gourmet of championship standard, a man who takes dinner as seriously as other men take politics. Frank in the kitchen is like a hound on the scent, sniffing, peering into bubbling saucepans, quivering with expectation. The smell of a rich *cassoulet* puts him in a trance. My wife says that he is one of the most rewarding eaters she has ever cooked for.

There was a hint of alarm in his voice when he explained why he was calling.

"It's March," he said, "and I'm worried about the truffles. Are there still some left?"

March is the end of the truffle season, and in the markets around us, as close as we were to the truffle country in the foothills of Mont Ventoux, the dealers seemed to have disappeared. I told Frank that he might have left it too late.

There was a horrified silence while he considered the gastronomic deprivation that stared him in the face—no truffle omelets, no truffles *en croûte*, no truffle-studded roast pork. The telephone line was heavy with disappointment.

"There's one man," I said, "who might have a few. I could try him."

Frank purred. "Excellent, excellent. Just a couple of kilos. I'm going to put them in egg boxes and keep them in the deep freeze. Truffles in the spring, truffles in the summer. Just a couple of kilos."

Two kilos of fresh truffles, at current Paris prices, would have cost more than a thousand pounds. Even down in Provence, bypassing the chain of middlemen and buying direct from the hunters with their muddy boots and leather hands, the investment would be impressive. I asked Frank if he was sure he wanted as much as two kilos.

"It wouldn't do to run short," he said. "Anyway, see what you can manage."

My only contact with the truffle business consisted of a telephone number scribbled on the back of a bill by the chef of one of our local restaurants. He had told us that this was *un homme sérieux* as far as truffles were concerned, a man of irreproachable honesty, which is not always the case in the murky world of truffle dealing, where petty swindles are rumored to be as common as sunny days in Aix. I had heard tales of truffles loaded with buckshot and caked with mud to increase their weight and, even worse, inferior specimens smuggled in from Italy and sold as native French truffles. Without a reliable supplier, one could get into some expensive trouble.

I called the number the chef had given me and mentioned

74

his name to the man who answered. *Ah, oui.* The credentials were accepted. What could he do for me?

Some truffles? Maybe two kilos?

"*Oh là là,*" said the voice. "Are you a restaurant?"

No, I said, I was buying on behalf of a friend in England.

"An Englishman? *Mon Dieu.*"

After a few minutes of sucking his teeth and explaining the considerable problems involved in finding so many truffles so late in the season, Monsieur X (his *nom de truffe*) promised to take his dogs into the hills and see what he could find. He would let me know, but it would not be a rapid affair. I must stay by the phone and be patient.

A week passed, nearly two, and then one evening the phone rang.

A voice said, "I have what you want. We can have a rendez-vous tomorrow evening."

He told me to be waiting by a telephone *cabine* on the Carpentras road at 6:00. What make and color was my car? And one important point: checks were not accepted. Cash, he said, was more agreeable. (This, as I later discovered, is standard practice in the truffle trade. Dealers don't believe in paperwork, don't issue receipts, and regard with disdain the ridiculous notion of income tax.)

I arrived at the phone box just before 6:00. The road was deserted, and I was uncomfortably conscious of the large wad of cash in my pocket. The papers had been full of reports of robberies and other unpleasantness on the back roads of the Vaucluse. Gangs of *voyous*, according to the crime reporter of *Le Provençal*, were out and about, and prudent citizens should stay at home.

What was I doing out here in the dark with a salami-sized

roll of 500-franc notes, a sitting and well-stuffed duck? I searched the car for a defensive weapon, but the best I could find was a shopping basket and an old copy of the *Guide Michelin*.

Ten slow minutes went by before I saw a set of headlights. A dented Citroën van wheezed up and stopped on the other side of the phone box. The driver and I looked at each other surreptitiously from the safety of our cars. He was alone. I got out.

I'd been expecting to meet an old peasant with black teeth, canvas boots, and a villainous sideways glance, but Monsieur X was young, with cropped black hair and a neat moustache. He looked pleasant. He even grinned as he shook my hand.

"You'd never have found my house in the dark," he said. "Follow me."

We drove off, leaving the main road for a twisting stony track that led deeper and deeper into the hills, Monsieur X driving as if he were on the *autoroute* with me bouncing and clattering behind. Eventually he turned through a narrow gateway and parked in front of an unlit house surrounded by clumps of scrub oak. As I opened the car door, a large Alsatian appeared from the shadows and inspected my leg thoughtfully. I hoped he'd been fed.

I could smell truffles as soon as I went through the front door—that ripe, faintly rotten smell that can find its way through everything except glass and tin. Even eggs, when stored in a box with a truffle, will taste of truffles.

And there they were on the kitchen table, piled in an old basket, black, knobbly, ugly, delicious, and expensive.

"*Voilà.*" Monsieur X held the basket up to my nose. "I've brushed off the mud. Don't wash them until just before you eat them."

He went to a cupboard and took out an ancient pair of scales, which he hung from a hook in the beam above the table. One by one, testing the truffles with a squeeze of his fingers to make sure they were still firm, he placed them on the blackened weighing dish, talking as he weighed them about his new experiment. He had bought a miniature Vietnamese pig, which he hoped to train into a truffle-finder *extraordinaire*. Pigs had a keener sense of smell than dogs, he said, but since the normal pig was the size of a small tractor he was not a convenient travelling companion on trips to the truffle grounds below Mont Ventoux.

The needles on the scales hovered and then settled on two kilos, and Monsieur X packed the truffles into two linen bags. He licked his thumb and counted the cash I gave him.

"*C'est bieng.*" He brought out a bottle of *marc* and two glasses, and we drank to the success of his pig-training scheme. Next season, he said, I must come with him one day to see the pig in action. It would be a major advance in detection technique—*le super-cochon*. As I was leaving, he gave me a handful of tiny truffles and his omelet recipe, and wished me bon voyage to London.

The scent of the truffles stayed with me in the car on the way home. The following day, my carry-on luggage smelt of truffles, and when the plane landed at Heathrow a heady whiff came out of the overhead locker as I prepared to take my bag past the X-ray eyes of British Customs. Other passengers looked at me curiously and edged away, as if I had terminal halitosis.

It was the time of Edwina Currie's salmonella alert, and I had visions of being cornered by a pack of sniffer dogs and thrown into quarantine for importing exotic substances that might endanger the nation's health. I walked tentatively

through Customs. Not a nostril twitched. The taxi driver,
however, was deeply suspicious.

"Blimey," he said, "what you got there?"

"Truffles."

"Oh, right. Truffles. Been dead long, have they?"

He closed the partition between us, and I was spared the
usual cab driver's monologue. When he dropped me at Frank's
house, he made a point of getting out and opening the back
windows.

The reclusive magnate himself greeted me, and pounced
on the truffles. He passed one of the linen bags around among
his dinner guests, some of whom were not at all sure what
they were sniffing, and then summoned from the kitchen his
domestic commander-in-chief, a Scotsman of such statuesque
demeanor that I always think of him as a General-Domo.

"I think we need to deal with these at once, Vaughan,"
said Frank.

Vaughan raised his eyebrows and sniffed delicately. He
knew what they were.

"Ah," he said, "the bonny truffle. This will do very well
with the *foie gras* tomorrow."

Monsieur X would have approved.

It was strange to be in London again after an absence of
nearly two years. I felt out of place and foreign, and I was
surprised at how much I had changed. Or maybe it was
London. There was endless talk about money, property
prices, the stock market, and corporate acrobatics of one sort
or another. The weather, once a traditional English complaint, was never mentioned, which was just as well. That

at least hadn't changed, and the days passed in a blur of grey drizzle, with people on the streets hunched up against the continuous dripping from above. Traffic barely moved, but most drivers didn't seem to notice; they were busy talking, presumably about money and property prices, on their car phones. I missed the light and the space and the huge open skies of Provence, and I realized that I would never willingly come back to live in a city again.

On the way out to the airport, the cab driver asked where I was going, and when I told him, he nodded knowingly.

"I was down there once," he said. "Fréjus, it was, in the caravan. Bloody expensive."

He charged me £25 for the ride, wished me a happy holiday, and warned me about the drinking water that had been his downfall in Fréjus. Three days on the khazi, he said. The wife had been well pleased.

I flew out of winter and into spring, and went through the informalities of arriving at Marignane, which I never understand. Marseille is reputed to be the center of half the drug business in Europe, and yet passengers carrying hand baggage stuffed with hashish, cocaine, heroin, English cheddar, or any other form of contraband can walk out of the airport without going through customs. It was, like the weather, a complete contrast to Heathrow.


Monsieur X was pleased to hear how welcome his two kilos had been.

"He is an *amateur*, your friend? A true lover of truffles?"

Yes he is, I said, but some of his friends were not too sure about the smell.

I could almost hear him shrug over the phone. It is a little special. Not everyone likes it. *Tant mieux* for those who do. He laughed, and his voice became confidential.

"I have something to show you," he said. "A film I made. We could drink some *marc* and watch it if you like."

When I finally found his house, the Alsatian greeted me like a long-lost bone, and Monsieur X called him off, hissing at him in the way that I had heard hunters use in the forest.

"He's just playful," he said. I'd heard that before too.

I followed him indoors to the cool, truffle-scented kitchen, and he poured *marc* into two thick tumblers. I must call him Alain, he said, pronouncing it with a good Provencal twang: *Alang*. We went into the sitting room, where the shutters had been closed against the sunlight, and he squatted in front of the television set to put a cassette into the video machine.

"*Voilà*," said Alain. "It is not Truffaut, but I have a friend with a camera. Now I want to make another one, but more *professionnel*."

The theme music from *Jean de Florette* started, and an image came up on the screen: Alain, seen from the back, and two dogs walking up a rocky hill, Mont Ventoux and its white crest in the far background. A title appeared—*Rabasses de Ma Colline*—and Alain explained that *rabasses* was the Provençal word for truffles.

Despite the slightly shaky hand of the camera operator and a certain abruptness in the editing, it was fascinating. It showed the dogs scenting tentatively, then scrabbling, then digging hard until Alain nudged them aside and, with enormous care, felt under the loosened soil. Every time he came up with a truffle, the dogs were rewarded with a biscuit or a scrap of sausage and the camera would zoom jerkily in to a close-up of an earth-covered hand holding an earth-covered lump. There was no recorded commentary, but Alain talked over the pictures.

"She works well, the little one," he said, as the picture showed a small, nondescript dog studying the base of a truffle oak, "but she's getting old." She began to dig, and Alain came into the shot. There was a close-up of a muddy nose, and Alain's hands pushing the dog's head away. His fingers probed the earth, picking out stones, scooping patiently until he had made a hole about six inches deep.

The film cut suddenly to show the sharp, alert face of a ferret, and Alain got up and pushed the fast forward button on the video machine. "That's just rabbit hunting," he said, "but there is something else here which is good, and not often to be seen today. It will soon be history."

He slowed the film down as the ferret was being put, somewhat unwillingly, into a rucksack. There was another sudden cut, this time to a clump of oak trees. A Citroën 2CV van lurched into the picture and stopped, and a very old man in a cloth cap and shapeless blue jacket got out, beamed at the camera, and went slowly to the back of the van. He opened the door and took out a crude wooden ramp. He looked to the camera and beamed again before reaching into the back of the van. He straightened up, holding the end of a piece of rope, beamed once more, and began to tug.

The van shuddered, and then, inch by inch, the dirty pink profile of a pig's head emerged. The old man tugged again, harder, and the monstrous creature swayed unsteadily down the ramp, twitching its ears and blinking. I half-expected it to follow its master's example and leer at the camera, but it just stood in the sun, vast, placid, unaffected by stardom.

"Last year," said Alain, "that pig found nearly three hundred kilos of truffles. *Un bon paquet.*"

I could hardly believe it. I was looking at an animal that earned more last year than most of those executives in London, and all without the benefit of a car phone.

The old man and the pig wandered off into the trees as though they were taking an aimless stroll, two rotund figures dappled by the winter sunshine. The screen went dark as the camera swooped down to a close-up of a pair of boots and across to a patch of earth. A muddy snout the size of a drainpipe poked into the shot, and the pig got down to work, its snout moving rhythmically back and forth, ears flopping over its eyes, a single-minded earth-moving machine.

The pig's head jerked, and the camera drew back to show the old man pulling on the rope. The pig was reluctant to leave what was obviously a highly desirable smell.

"The scent of truffles to a pig," said Alain, "is sexual. That is why one sometimes has difficulty persuading him to move."

The old man was having no luck with the rope. He bent down and put his shoulder against the pig's flank, and the two of them heaved against each other until the pig grudgingly gave way. The old man reached into his pocket and palmed something into the pig's mouth. Surely he wasn't feeding it truffles at 50 francs a bite?

"Acorns," said Alain. "Now watch."

The kneeling figure straightened up from the earth and turned to the camera, one hand outstretched. In it was a truffle slightly bigger than a golf ball, and in the background was the old peasant's smiling face, sun glinting on his gold fillings. The truffle went into a stained canvas satchel, and pig and peasant moved on to the next tree. The sequence finished with a shot of the old man holding out both hands, which were piled high with muddy lumps. A good morning's work.

I was looking forward to seeing the pig being loaded back into the van, which I imagined would require cunning, dexterity, and many acorns, but instead the film finished with a long shot of Mont Ventoux and some more *Jean de Florette* music.

"You see the problem with the normal pig," said Alain. I did indeed. "I am hoping that mine will have the nose without the . . ." he spread his arms wide to indicate bulk. "Come and see her. She has an English name. She is called Peegy."

Peegy lived inside a fenced enclosure next to Alain's two dogs. She was scarcely bigger than a fat Corgi, black, potbellied, and shy. We leaned on the fence and looked at her. She grunted, turned her back, and curled up in the corner. Alain said she was very amiable, and that he would start training her now that the season was finished and he had more time. I asked him how.

"With patience," he said. "I have trained the Alsatian to be a *chien truffier*, although it is not his instinct. I think the same is possible with the pig."

I said that I would love to see it in action, and Alain invited me to come with him in the winter for a day of hunting among the truffle oaks. He was the complete opposite of the suspicious, secretive peasants who were said to control the truffle trade in the Vaucluse; Alain was an enthusiast, happy to share his enthusiasm.

As I was leaving, he gave me a copy of a poster advertising a milestone in truffle history. In the village of Bédoin, at the foot of Mont Ventoux, there was to be an attempt on a world record: the biggest truffle omelet ever made, to be *"enregistrée comme record mondial au Guinness Book."* The statistics were astonishing—70,000 eggs, 100 kilos of truffles, 100 liters of oil, 11 kilos of salt, and 6 kilos of pepper were to be tossed, presumably by a team of Provençal giants, in an omelet pan with a diameter of ten meters. The proceeds were to go to charity. It would be a day to remember, said Alain. Even now, negotiations were in progress to purchase a fleet of brand new concrete mixers, which would churn the ingredients into the correct consistency, under the supervision of some of the most distinguished chefs in the Vaucluse.

I said that this was not the kind of event that one normally associated with the truffle business. It was too open, too public, not at all like the shady dealings that were rumored to take place in the back streets and markets.

"Ah, those," said Alain. "It is true there are some people who are a little . . ." he made a wriggling motion with his hand ". . . *serpentin.*" He looked at me and grinned. "Next time, I'll tell you some stories."

He waved me off, and I drove home wondering if I could persuade Frank to come over from London to witness the attempt on the omelet world record. It was the kind of gas-tronomic oddity he would enjoy, and of course Vaughan the General-Domo must come too. I could see him, impeccably turned out in his truffling outfit, directing operations as the concrete mixers swallowed the ingredients: "Another bucket of pepper in there, *mon bonhomme*, if you please." Maybe we could find a chef's hat for him, in his clan tartan, with matching trews. I came to the conclusion that I shouldn't drink *marc* in the afternoon. It does funny things to the brain.

# *Napoléons*
# at the Bottom
# of the Garden

At one end of the swimming pool, arranged in a long, low pile, our builders had left an assortment of souvenirs of their work on the house. Rubble and cracked flagstones, old light switches and chewed wiring, beer bottles and broken tiles. It was understood that one day Didier and Claude would come back with an empty truck and take the debris away. The strip of land would be *impeccable*, and we could plant the alley of rosebushes we had planned.

But somehow the truck was never empty, or Claude had broken a toe, or Didier was busy knocking down some distant ruin in the Basses-Alpes, and the souvenir pile remained at the end of the pool. In time it began to look quite pretty, an informal rockery softened by a healthy covering of weeds and splashed with poppies. I told my wife that it had a certain unplanned charm. She wasn't convinced. Roses, she said, were generally considered more attractive than rubble and beer bottles. I started to clear the pile.

In fact, I enjoy manual labor, the rhythm of it and the satisfaction of seeing order emerge from a neglected mess.

After a couple of weeks, I reached bare earth and retired in triumph with my blisters. My wife was very pleased. Now, she said, all we need are two deep trenches and 50 kilos of manure, and then we can plant. She got to work with the rose catalogues, and I patched up my blisters and bought a new pickax.

I had loosened about three yards of hard-packed earth when I saw a gleam of dirty yellow among the weed roots. Some long-dead farmer had obviously thrown away a *pastis* bottle one hot afternoon many years ago. But when I cleared away the earth, it wasn't a vintage bottle cap; it was a coin. I rinsed it under the hose, and it shone gold in the sun, the drops of water sliding down a bearded profile.

It was a 20-franc piece, dated 1857. On one side was the head of Napoléon III with his neat goatee and his position in society—*Empereur*—stamped in heroic type opposite his name. On the reverse, a laurel wreath, crowned with more heroic type proclaiming the *Empire Français*. Around the rim of the coin was the comforting statement that every Frenchman knows is true: *Dieu protège la France*.

My wife was as excited as I was. "There might be more of them," she said. "Keep digging."

Ten minutes later, I found a second coin, another 20-franc piece. This one was dated 1869, and the passing years had left no mark on Napoléon's profile except that he had sprouted a wreath on his head. I stood in the hole that I'd made and did some rough calculations. There were twenty more yards of trench to dig. At the current rate of one gold coin every yard, we could end up with a pocketful of *napoléons* and might even be able to afford lunch at the *Beaumanière* at Les Baux. I swung the pickax until my hands were raw, going deeper and deeper into the ground, watching through the beads of sweat for another wink from Napoléon.

I ended the day no richer, but with a hole deep enough to plant a fully grown tree, and the conviction that tomorrow would produce more treasure. Nobody would bury two miserable coins; these had obviously spilled out of the bulging sack that was still lying within pickax range, a fortune for the reluctant gardener.

To help us estimate the size of the fortune, we consulted the financial section of *Le Provençal*. In a country that traditionally keeps its savings in gold and under the mattress, there was bound to be a listing of current values. And there it was, in between the one-kilo gold ingot and the Mexican 50-peso piece: Napoléon's 20 francs were now worth 396 francs, and maybe more if the old boy's profile was in mint condition.

Never has a pickax been taken up with more enthusiasm, and it inevitably attracted Faustin's attention. He stopped on his way to do battle with the mildew that he was convinced was about to attack the vines, and asked what I was doing. Planting roses, I said.

"*Ah bon?* They must be large roses to need such an important hole. Rose trees, perhaps? From England? It is difficult here for roses. *Tache noire* is everywhere."

He shook his head, and I could tell he was going to give me the benefit of his pessimism. Faustin is on close terms with every kind of natural disaster, and he is happy to share this extensive knowledge with anyone foolish enough to hope for the best. To cheer him up, I told him about the gold *napoléons*.

He squatted at the side of the trench and pushed his cap,

stained blue with antimildew spray, onto the back of his head so that he could give the news his full attention.

"*Normalement*," he said, "Where there are one or two *napoléons*, it signifies that there are others. But this is not a good place to hide them." He waved his large brown paw in the direction of the house. "The well would be more safe. Or behind a *cheminée*."

I said that they might have been hidden in a hurry. Faustin shook his head again, and I realized that hurry was not an intellectual concept that he accepted, particularly when it came to hiding sacks of gold. "A peasant is never as *pressé* as that. Not with the *napoléons*. It is just bad luck that they dropped here."

I said it was good luck for me, and with that depressing thought he went off to look for catastrophe in the vineyard.

The days passed. The blisters flourished. The trench grew longer and deeper. The tally of *napoléons* remained at two. And yet it didn't make sense. No peasant would go out to work in the fields with gold coins in his pocket. A *cache* was there somewhere, I was sure of it, within feet of where I was standing.

I decided to ask for a second opinion from the self-appointed expert of the valley, the man from whom Provence held no secrets, the wise, venal, and congenitally crafty Massot. If anyone could guess, merely by sniffing the wind and spitting on the ground, where a sly old peasant had hidden his life savings, it was Massot.

I walked through the forest to his house and heard his dogs baying with frustrated blood lust as they picked up my scent. One day, I knew, they would break their chains and maul every living thing in the valley; I hoped that he would sell his house before they did.

Massot ambled across what he liked to call his front garden, an expanse of bare, trodden earth decorated with dog droppings and clumps of determined weeds. He looked up at me, squinting against the sun and the smoke from his fat yellow cigarette, and grunted.

*"On se promène?"*

No, I said. Today I had come to ask his advice. He grunted again and kicked his dogs into silence. We stood on either side of the rusty chain that separated his property from the forest path, close enough for me to catch his gamey smell of garlic and black tobacco. I told him about the two coins, and he unstuck the cigarette from his lower lip, inspecting the damp stub while his dogs padded back and forth on their chains, growling under their breath.

He found a home for his cigarette under one end of his stained moustache, and leaned toward me.

"Who have you told about this?" He looked over my shoulder, as if making sure that we were alone.

"My wife. And Faustin. That's all."

"Tell nobody else," he said, tapping the side of his nose with a grimy finger. "It is possible that there are more coins. This must be kept *entre nous*."

We walked back along the path so that Massot could see where the two coins had been found, and he gave me his explanation of the national passion for gold. Politicians, he said, were the cause of it, starting with the Revolution. After that, there were emperors, wars, countless presidents—most of them cretins, he said, and spat for emphasis—and devaluations that could turn a hundred francs into a hundred centimes overnight. No wonder the simple peasant didn't trust scraps of paper printed by those *salauds* in Paris. But gold—Massot held his hands in front of him and wriggled his fingers in an imaginary pile of *napoléons*—gold was always good, and in times of trouble it was even better. And the best gold of all was dead man's gold, because dead men don't argue. How fortunate we are, you and I, said Massot, to come across such an uncomplicated opportunity. It seemed that I had a partner.

We stood in the trench, Massot tugging on his moustache while he looked around him. The ground was flat, some of it planted with lavender, some covered in grass. There was no obvious spot for a hiding place, which Massot took to be an encouraging sign; an obvious place would have been discovered fifty years ago, and "our" gold removed. He climbed out of the trench, and paced off the distance to the well, then perched on the stone wall.

"It could be anywhere here," he said, and waved his arm over 50 square yards of ground. "*Évidemment*, that is too much for you to dig." Our partnership clearly didn't extend to a sharing of physical labor. "What we need is a *machin* for detecting metal." He turned his arm into a metal detector and passed it in sweeps over the grass, making clicking sounds. "*Beh oui*. That will find it."

"*Alors, qu'est-ce qu'on fait?*" Massot made the universal money gesture, rubbing his fingers and thumb together. It was time for a business meeting.

We agreed that I would finish digging the trench, and that Massot would take care of the high technology by renting a metal detector. All that remained to be decided was the financial participation of the partners. I suggested that 10 percent would be a reasonable price to pay for some undemanding work with a metal detector; Massot, however, said he would be more comfortable with 50 percent. There was the drive into Cavaillon to pick up the metal detector, the digging involved when we struck gold, and, most important, the confidence I could feel in having a completely trustworthy partner who would not broadcast the details of our new wealth throughout the neighborhood. Everything, said Massot, must be kept behind the teeth.

I looked at him as he smiled and nodded, and thought that it would be difficult to imagine a more untrustworthy old rogue this side of the bars of Marseille prison. Twenty percent, I said. He winced, sighed, accused me of being a *grippe-sou*, and settled for 25 percent. We shook hands on it, and he spat in the trench for luck as he left.

That was the last I saw of him for several days. I finished the trench, laced it with manure, and ordered the roses. The man who delivered them told me that I'd dug far too deep, and asked me why, but I kept the reason behind my teeth.

There is a widespread aversion in Provence to anything that resembles social planning. The Provençal prefers to drop in and surprise you rather than call first to make sure you're free. When he arrives, he expects you to have time for the pleasantries of a drink and a roundabout conversation before getting down to the purpose of the visit, and if you tell him you have to go out he is puzzled. Why rush? Half an hour is nothing. You'll only be late, and that's normal.

It was almost twilight, the time of day *entre chien et loup*, when we heard a van rattle to a stop outside the house. We were going over to see some friends for dinner in Goult, and so I went out to head off the visitor before he reached the bar and became impossible to dislodge.

The van had its back doors wide open, and was rocking from side to side. There was a thud as something hit the floor, followed by a curse. *Putaing!* It was my business partner, wrestling with a pickax that was stuck in the metal grill of the dog guard behind the driver's seat. With a final convulsion the pickax was wrenched free and Massot emerged backwards, slightly faster than he'd intended.

He was wearing camouflage trousers, a dun sweater, and a jungle-green army surplus hat, all well past their youth. He looked like a badly paid mercenary as he unloaded his equipment and laid it on the ground—the pickax, a long-handled mason's shovel, and an object wrapped in old sacking. Glancing round to see if anyone was watching, he removed the sacking and held up the metal detector.

"*Voilà!* This is *haut de gamme*, top of the range. It is efficacious to a depth of three meters."

He switched it on, and waved it over his tools. Sure enough, it detected a shovel and a pickax, chattering away like a set of agitated false teeth. Massot was delighted. "*Vous voyez?* When he finds metal, he talks. Better than digging, eh?"

I said that it was very impressive, and that I'd keep it safely locked up in the house until tomorrow.

"Tomorrow?" said Massot. "But we must start now."

I said it would be dark in half an hour, and Massot nodded patiently, as though I had finally grasped a very complex theory.

"Exactly!" He put down the metal detector and took hold of my arm. "We don't want the world watching us, do we? This kind of work is best done at night. It is more *discret*. *Allez!* You bring the tools."

There is another difficulty, I said. My wife and I are going out.

Massot stopped dead and stared at me, his eyebrows drawing themselves up to their full height in astonishment.

"Out? Tonight? *Now?*"

My wife called from the house. We were already late. Massot shrugged at the curious hours we kept, but insisted that tonight was the night. He would have to do it all, he said plaintively, himself. Could I lend him a flashlight? I showed him how to switch on the spotlight behind the well, which he adjusted so that it lit the area by the rose bed, muttering in irritation at being left *tout seul*.

We stopped halfway down the drive and looked back at Massot's elongated shadow moving through the trees, which were bathed in the glow of the spotlight. The ticking of the metal detector carried clearly in the evening air, and I had misgivings about the secrecy of the enterprise. We might as well have put up a sign at the end of the drive saying MAN LOOKING FOR GOLD.

We told our friends over dinner about the treasure hunt that was going on more or less under the cover of darkness. The husband, who had been born and raised in the Lubéron, was not optimistic. He told us that when metal detectors had first become available they were more popular with the peasants than hunting dogs. It was true that some gold had been found. But now, he said, the area had been combed so thoroughly that Massot would be lucky to find an old horseshoe.

Even so, he couldn't deny the existence of our two *napoléons*. There they were, on the table in front of him. He picked them up and chinked them in his hand. Who knows? Maybe we'd be lucky. Or maybe Massot would be lucky and we'd never hear about it. Was he someone who could be trusted? My wife and I looked at each other and decided it was time to go.

It was just after midnight when we got home, and Massot's van had gone. The spotlight had been switched off, but there was enough of a moon for us to see large mounds of earth scattered haphazardly across what we were trying to turn into a lawn. We decided to face the full extent of the damage in the morning.

It was as if a giant mole, maddened by claustrophobia, had been coming up for air and spitting out mouthfuls of metal. There were nails, fragments of a cartwheel rim, an ancient screwdriver, half a sickle, a dungeon-sized key, a brass rifle shell, bolts, bottle tops, the crumbling remains of a hoe, knife blades, the bottom of a sieve, birds' nests of baling wire, unidentifiable blobs of pure rust. But no gold.

Most of the newly planted rosebushes had survived, and the lavender bed was intact. Massot must have run out of enthusiasm.

I left him to sleep until the afternoon before going over to hear his account of the night's work. Long before I reached his house, I could hear the metal detector, and I had to shout twice to get him to look up from the bramble-covered hillock that he was sweeping. He bared his dreadful teeth in welcome. I was surprised to see him so cheerful. Maybe he had found something after all.

"*Salut!*" He shouldered the metal detector like a gun and waded toward me through the undergrowth, still smiling. I said he looked like a man who had been lucky.

Not yet, he said. He had been obliged to stop the previous night because my neighbors had shouted at him, complaining about the noise. I didn't understand. Their house is 250 yards away from where he had been working. What had he been doing to keep them awake?

"*Pas moi,*" he said. "*Lui,*" and he tapped the metal detector. "Wherever I went, he found something—*tak tak tak tak tak.*"

But no gold, I said.

Massot leaned so close that for one awful moment I thought he was going to kiss me. His nose twitched, and his voice dropped to a wheezing whisper. "I know where it is." He drew back and took a deep breath. "*Beh oui.* I know where it is."

Although we were standing in the forest, with the nearest human being at least a kilometer away, Massot's fear of being overheard was contagious, and I found myself whispering too.

"Where is it?"

"At the end of the *piscine.*"

"Under the roses?"

"Under the *dallage.*"

"Under the *dallage?*"

"*Oui. C'est certaing.* On my grandmother's head."

This was not the straightforward good news that Massot obviously thought it was. The *dallage* around the pool was made up of flagstones nearly three inches thick. They had been laid on a bed of reinforced concrete, as deep as the flagstones were thick. It would be a demolition job just to get down to the earth. Massot sensed what I was thinking, and put the metal detector down so that he could talk with both hands.

"In Cavaillon," he said, "you can rent a *marteau-piqueur.* It will go through anything. *Paf!*"

He was quite right. A miniature jackhammer would go through the flagstones, the reinforced concrete, the pipes feeding the pool, and the electric cables leading from the filtration pump in no time at all. *Paf!* And maybe even *Boum!*

And when the dust had settled, we might very easily find nothing more than another sickle blade to add to our collection. I said no. With infinite regret, but no.

Massot took the decision well, and was pleased with the bottle of *pastis* I gave him for his trouble. But I see him from time to time standing on the path at the back of the house, looking down at the swimming pool, sucking thoughtfully at his moustache. God knows what he might do one drunken night if someone ever gave him a *marteau-piqueur* for Christmas.

# As Advertised
## in *Vogue*

Perhaps because he still has memories of his earlier life as a homeless, hungry stray, Boy takes every opportunity to make himself as agreeable as possible around the house. He brings gifts—a fallen bird's nest, a vine root, a half-masticated espadrille that he has been saving, a mouthful of undergrowth from the forest—and deposits them under the dining table with a messy generosity that he obviously feels will endear him to us. He contributes to the housework by leaving trails of leaves and dusty paw prints on the floor. He assists in the kitchen, acting as a mobile receptacle for any scraps that may fall from above. He is never more than a few feet away, desperately, noisily, clumsily anxious to please.

His efforts to charm are not confined exclusively to us, and he has his own unorthodox but well-meaning style of greeting visitors to the house. Dropping the tennis ball that he normally keeps tucked in one side of his enormous mouth, he buries his equally enormous head in the groin of anyone who comes through the door. It's his version of a manly handshake, and our friends have come to expect it. They carry on talking, and Boy, his social duties done, retires to collapse on the nearest pair of feet.

The reactions to his welcome reflect, with some accuracy, the change of the seasons. During the winter, when our visitors, are, like us, people who live in the Lubéron through-out the year, the head in the groin is either ignored or patted, leaves and twigs are brushed off old corduroy trousers, and the smooth progress of glass to mouth continues without in-terruption. When this is replaced by starts of surprise, spilt drinks, and flustered attempts to fend off the questing snout from clean white clothes, we know that summer has arrived. And with it, the summer people.

Each year there are more of them, coming down for the sun and the scenery as they always have, and now encouraged by two more recent attractions.

The first is practical: Provence is becoming more accessible every year. There is talk of the TGV high-speed train from Paris cutting half an hour off its already quick four-hour service to Avignon. The tiny airport just outside the town is being extended, and will undoubtedly soon be calling itself Avignon International. A giant green model of the Statue of Liberty has been erected in front of the Marseille airport to announce direct flights twice a week to and from New York.

At the same time, Provence has been "discovered" yet again—and not only Provence in general, but the towns and villages where we shop for food and rummage through the markets. Fashion has descended upon us.

The bible of the Beautiful People, *Women's Wear Daily*, which pronounces on the proper length of hem, size of bust, and weight of earrings in New York, ventured last year into Saint-Rémy and the Lubéron. High-profile summer residents were shown squeezing their aubergines, sipping their *kirs*, admiring their barbered cypress trees, and generally getting away from it all—with each other and an attendant photographer, *bien sûr*—to revel in the pleasures of the simple country life.

In American *Vogue*, the world's most cloyingly pungent magazine, with its impregnated perfume advertisements, an article on the Lubéron was sandwiched between Athena Starwoman's horoscopes and a Paris Bistro Update. In the introduction to the article, the Lubéron was described as "the secret South of France"—a secret that lasted two lines before it was also described as the country's most fashionable area. How the two go together is a contradiction that only a plausible subeditor could explain.

The editors of French *Vogue*, of course, were in on the secret as well. Indeed, they had known about it for some time, as they made clear to the reader in the introduction to their article. In fine world-weary vein, they led off by saying *le Lubéron, c'est fini*, followed by some disparaging suggestions that it might be snobbish, expensive, and altogether *démodé*.

Could they really have meant it? No, they couldn't. Far from being finished, the Lubéron is apparently still attracting Parisians and foreigners who, according to *Vogue*, are *often famous*. (How often? Once a week? Twice a week? They didn't say.) And then we are invited to meet them. Come with us, *Vogue* says, into their very private world.

Good-bye privacy. For the next twelve pages, we are treated to photographs of the often famous with their children, their dogs, their gardens, their friends, and their swimming pools. There is a map—*le who's who*—showing where the chic members of Lubéron society are trying, rather unsuccessfully it seems, to hide themselves. But hiding is out of the question. These poor devils can't even have a swim or a drink without a photographer darting out of the bushes to capture the moment for the delectation of *Vogue*'s readers.

Among the photographs of artists, writers, decorators, politicians, and tycoons is a picture of a man who, as the caption says, knows all the houses in the area and who accepts three dinner invitations at the same time. The reader may think that this is merely the result of a deprived childhood or an insatiable craving for *gigot en croûte*, but it is nothing of the kind. Our man is working. He is a real estate agent. He needs to know who's looking, who's buying, and who's selling, and there just aren't enough dinners in the normal day to keep him *au courant*.

It's a hectic business being a real estate agent in the Lubéron, particularly now that the area is passing through a fashionable phase. Property prices have inflated like a three-dinner stomach, and even during our short time as residents we have seen increases that defy reason or belief. A pleasant old ruin with half a roof and a few acres of land was offered to some friends for three million francs. Other friends decided to build instead of converting, and were in shock for a week at the estimate: five million francs. A house with possibilities in one of the favored villages? One million francs.

Naturally, the agent's fees are geared to these zero-encrusted prices, although the exact percentage varies. We have heard of commissions ranging from 3 to 8 percent, sometimes paid by the seller, sometimes by the buyer.

It can add up to a very comfortable living. And, to the outsider, it may appear to be a congenial way to earn that living; it's always interesting to look at houses, and often the buyers and sellers are interesting as well (not always honest or reliable, as we shall see, but seldom dull). As a *métier*, being a real estate agent in a desirable part of the world theoretically offers a stimulating and lucrative way to pass the time in between dinners.

It is not, alas, without its problems, and the first of these is competition. Nearly six yellow pages in the Vaucluse telephone directory are taken up by real estate agents and their advertisements—properties of style, properties of character, exclusive properties, quality properties, hand-picked properties, properties of guaranteed charm—the house hunter is spoiled for choice and baffled by the terminology. What is the difference between character and style? Should one go for something exclusive or something hand-picked? The only way to find out is to take your dreams and your budget along to an agent and spend a morning, a day, a week among the *bastides*, the *mas*, the *maisons de charme*, and the white elephants that are currently on offer.

Finding an agent in the Lubéron is no more difficult than finding a butcher. In the old days, the village *notaire* used to be the man who knew if *Mère* Bertrand was selling off her old farm, or if a recent death had made a house empty and available. To a large extent, the *notaire*'s function as a property scout has been taken over by the agent, and almost every village has one. Ménerbes has two. Bonnieux has three. The more fashionable Gordes had, at the last count, four. (It was in Gordes that we saw competition in the raw. One agent was distributing flyers to all the cars parked in the Place du Château. He was followed at a discreet distance by a second agent who was taking the flyers off the windscreens and replacing them with his own. Unfortunately, we had to leave before seeing if the third and fourth agents were lurking behind a buttress waiting for their turn.)

Without exception, these agents are initially charming and helpful, and they have dossiers filled with photographs of ravishing properties, some of them actually priced at less than seven figures. These, inevitably, are the ones that have just been sold, but there are others—mills, nunneries, shepherd's hovels, grandiose *maisons de maître*, turreted follies, and farmhouses of every shape and size. What a selection! And this is only one agent.

But if you should go to see a second agent, or a third, you may experience a definite feeling of *déjà vu*. There is something familiar about many of the properties. The photographs have been taken from different angles, but there's no doubt about it. These are the same mills and nunneries and farmhouses that you saw in the previous dossier. And there you have the second problem that bedevils the life of a Lubéron agent: There are not enough properties to go round.

Building restrictions in most parts of the Lubéron are fairly stringent, and they are more or less observed by everyone except farmers, who seem to be able to build at will. And so the supply of what agents would call properties with *beaucoup d'allure* is limited. This situation brings out the hunting instinct, and many agents during the less busy winter months will spend days driving around, eyes and ears open for signs or rumor that an undiscovered jewel may shortly be coming on the market. If it is, and if the agent is quick and persuasive enough, there is the chance of an exclusive arrangement and full commission. What usually happens, though, is that a seller will retain two or three agents and leave them to sort out the delicate matter of how the fees should be split.

More problems. Who introduced the client? Who showed the property first? The agents may be obliged to collaborate, but the competitive streak is barely hidden, and nothing brings it out in the open faster than a little misunderstanding about the division of the spoils. Accusations and counteraccusations, heated phone calls, pointed remarks about unethical behavior—even, as a last resort, an appeal to the client to act as referee—all these unhappy complications have been known to upset liaisons that started off with such high hopes. That is why the *cher collègue* of yesterday can turn into the *escroc* of today. *C'est dommage, mais . . .* .

There are other, heavier crosses for the agent to bear, and these are the clients, with their unpredictable and frequently shady behavior. What is it that turns the outwardly trustworthy and respectable minnow into a shark? Money has a lot to do with it, obviously, but there is also a determination to do a deal, to haggle up to the last minute and down to the final light bulb, which is not so much a matter of francs and centimes as a desire to win, to outnegotiate the other side. And the agent is stuck in the middle.

The tussle over the price is probably the same throughout the world, but in the Lubéron there is an added local complication to muddy the waters of negotiation still further. More often than not, prospective buyers are Parisians or foreigners, while prospective sellers are *paysans du coin*. There is a considerable difference between the attitude that each side brings to business dealings, which can cause everyone concerned in the transaction weeks or months of exasperation.

The peasant finds it hard to take yes for an answer. If the price he has asked for his grandmother's old *mas* is agreed to without any quibbling, he has an awful suspicion that he has underpriced the property. This would cause him grief for the rest of his days, and his wife would nag him endlessly about the better price that a neighbor obtained for *his* grandmother's old *mas*. And so, just when the buyers think they have bought, the seller is having second thoughts. Adjustments will have to be made. The peasant arranges a rendezvous with the agent to clarify certain details.

He tells the agent that he may have neglected to say that a field adjoining the house—the very same field, as luck would have it, with the well in the corner and a good supply of water—is not included in the price. *Pas grand chose*, but he thought he'd better mention it.

Consternation from the buyers. The field was *undoubtedly* included in the price. In fact, it is the only possible place on the property flat enough for the tennis court. Their dismay is communicated to the peasant, who shrugs. What does he care about tennis courts? Nevertheless, he is a reasonable man. It is a fertile and valuable field, and he would hate to part with such a treasure, but he might be prepared to listen to an offer.

Buyers are usually impatient, and short of time. They work in Paris or Zurich or London, and they can't be coming down to the Lubéron every five minutes to look at houses. The peasant, on the other hand, is never in a hurry. He's not going anywhere. If the property doesn't sell this year, he'll put up the price and sell it next year.

Back and forth the discussions go, with the agent and the buyers becoming increasingly irritated. But when a deal is eventually done, as it usually is, the new owners try to put all thoughts of resentment behind them. It is, after all, a wonderful property, a *maison de rêve*, and to celebrate the purchase they decide to take a picnic and spend the day wandering through the rooms and planning the changes they're going to make.

Something, however, is not as it should be. The handsome

old cast-iron bathtub with the claw feet has disappeared from the bathroom. The buyers call the agent. The agent calls the peasant. Where is the bathtub?

The bathtub? His sainted grandmother's bathtub? The bathtub that is a family heirloom? Surely nobody would expect a rare object of such sentimental value to be included in the sale of a house? Nevertheless, he is a reasonable man, and might possibly be persuaded to consider an offer.

It is incidents such as this that have led buyers to tread warily along the path that leads to the *acte de vente* when the house will officially be theirs—sometimes behaving with the caution of a lawyer approaching an opinion. Inventories are made of shutters and door-knockers and kitchen sinks, of logs in the woodstore and tiles on the floor and trees in the garden. And in one marvelously mistrustful episode, even multiple inventories were thought to be insufficient protection against last-minute chicanery.

Fearing the worst, the buyer had engaged a local *huissier*, or legal official. His task was to verify, beyond any shadow of legal doubt, that the seller was leaving behind the lavatory paper holders. It is tempting to imagine the two of them, seller and *huissier*, jammed together in the confined space of the lavatory to conduct the formalities: "Raise your right hand and repeat after me: I solemnly swear to leave intact and functioning these fittings hereafter described . . ." The mind boggles.

Despite these and a hundred other snags, properties continue to sell at prices that would have been inconceivable 10 years ago. I recently heard Provence being enthusiastically promoted by an agent as "the California of Europe," not only because of the climate, but also because of something indefinable and yet irresistible that was originally invented in California: the Life-style.

As far as I can make out, the Life-style is achieved by transforming a rural community into a kind of sophisticated holiday camp, with as many urban conveniences as possible and, if there's any spare land, a golf course. If this had been going on in our corner of Provence, I had missed it, and so I asked the agent where I should go to see what he was talking about. Where was the nearest Life-style center?

He looked at me as though I'd been hiding in a time warp. "Haven't you been to Gordes recently?" he said.

We first saw Gordes 16 years ago, and in a region of beautiful villages it was the most spectacularly beautiful of all. Honey-colored and perched on the top of a hill, with long views across the plain to the Lubéron, it was what estate agents would call a gem, a picture postcard come to life. There was a Renaissance château, narrow streets cobbled in rectangular stone, and the modest facilities of an unspoiled village: a butcher, two bakers, a simple hotel, a seedy café, and a post office run by a man recruited, we were sure, for his unfailing surliness.

The countryside behind the village, permanently green with its covering of scrub oak and pine, was patterned with narrow paths bordered by dry stone walls. You could walk for hours without being aware of any houses except for the rare glimpse of an old tiled roof among the trees. We were told that building was so restricted as to be virtually forbidden.

That was 16 years ago. Today, Gordes is still beautiful—from a distance, at any rate. But as you reach the bottom of the road that leads up to the village, you are greeted by a ladder of signs, each rung advertising an hotel, a restaurant, a *salon de thé*—every comfort and attraction for the visitor is labeled except the *toilettes publiques*.

At regular intervals along the road are reproduction 19th-century street lamps that look spiky and incongruous against the weathered stone walls and houses. On the bend where the village comes into view, at least one car has always stopped to allow driver and passengers to take photographs. On the final bend before the village, a large area of tarmac has been laid down for car parking. If you choose to ignore this and drive up into the village, you will probably have to come back. The *Place du Château*, now also coated in tarmac, is usually fully booked with cars from all over Europe.

The old hotel is still there, but it has a new hotel as its next-door neighbor. A few meters further on, there is a sign for Sidney Food, *Spécialiste Modules Fast-Food*. Then there is a Souleiado boutique. Then the once-seedy café, now spruced up. In fact, everything has been spruced up, the curmudgeon in the post office has been retired, the *toilettes publiques* enlarged, and the village turned into a place for visitors rather than inhabitants. Official Gordes T-shirts can be bought to prove you've been there.

A kilometer or so up the road is another hotel, walled off from public view and equipped with a helicopter landing pad. The building restrictions in the *garrigue* have been relaxed and an enormous sign, subtitled in English, advertises luxury villas with electronic security entrance and fully fitted bathrooms at prices from 2,500,000 francs.

So far there are no signs to indicate where *Vogue*'s often-famous people have their country homes, so passengers in the procession of huge coaches on their way to the 12th-century Abbaye de Sénanque are left to speculate whose half-hidden house it is that they're looking at. One day someone of enterprise and vision will produce a map similar to those Hollywood guides to the houses of the stars, and then we shall feel even closer to California. Meanwhile, Jacuzzis and joggers are no longer sufficiently exotic to attract any attention, and the hills are alive with the thwack of tennis balls and the drowsy hum of the cement mixer.

It has often happened before, in many other parts of the world. People are attracted to an area because of its beauty and its promise of peace, and then they transform it into a high-rent suburb complete with cocktail parties, burglar-alarm systems, four-wheel-drive recreational vehicles, and other essential trappings of *la vie rustique*.

I don't think the locals mind. Why should they? Barren patches of land that couldn't support a herd of goats are suddenly worth millions of francs. Shops and restaurants and hotels prosper. The *maçons*, the carpenters, the landscape gardeners, and the tennis court builders have bulging order books, and everyone benefits from *le boum*. Cultivating tourists is much more rewarding than growing grapes.

It hasn't yet affected Ménerbes too much; not, at least, in an obviously visible way. The *Café du Progrès* is still resolutely unchic. The small, smart restaurant that opened two years ago has closed, and apart from a small, smart estate agent's office, the center of the village looks much the same as it did when we first saw it several years ago.

But change is in the air. Ménerbes has been awarded a sign, *Un des plus beaux villages de France*, and some of the inhabitants seem to have developed a sudden awareness of the media.

My wife came across three venerable ladies sitting in a row on a stone wall, their three dogs sitting in a row in front of them. It made a nice picture, and my wife asked if she could take a photograph.

The senior old lady looked at her and thought for a moment.

"What's it for?" she said. Obviously, *Vogue* had been there first.

# Mainly Dry Periods,
# with Scattered Fires

Like some of our agricultural neighbors in the valley, we subscribe to a service provided by the meteorological station at Carpentras. Twice a week we receive detailed weather forecasts on mimeographed sheets. They predict, usually very accurately, our ration of sun and rain, the likelihood of storms and *mistral*, and the temperature ranges throughout the Vaucluse.

As the early weeks of 1989 went by, the forecasts and statistics began to show ominous signs that the weather was not behaving as it should. There was not enough rain, not nearly enough.

The previous winter had been mild, with so little snow in the mountains that the torrents of spring would be no more than dribbles. Winter had also been dry. January's rainfall was 9.5 millimeters; normally it is just over 60 millimeters. February's rainfall was down. The same in March. Summer fire regulations—no burning in the fields—were put into effect early. The traditionally wet Vaucluse spring was only moist, and early summer wasn't even moist. Cavaillon's May rainfall was one millimeter, compared with the average 54.6; seven millimeters in June, compared with the average 44. Wells were going dry, and there was a significant drop in the water level of the Fontaine de Vaucluse.

Drought in the Lubéron hangs over the farmers like an overdue debt. Conversations in the fields and in the village streets are gloomy as the crops bake and the earth turns brittle and crusty. And there is always the risk of fire, terrible to think about but impossible to forget.

All it takes is a spark in the forest—a carelessly dropped cigarette end, a smouldering match—and the *mistral* will do the rest, turning a flicker into a fire, and then into an explosion of flame that rips through the trees faster than a running man. We had heard about a young *pompier* who died in the spring, near Murs. He had been facing the flames when a flying spark, maybe from a pine cone that had burst into red-hot fragments, had landed in the trees behind him, cutting him off. It had happened in seconds.

That is tragic enough when the cause of the fire is accidental, but sickening when it is deliberate. Sadly, it often is. Droughts attract pyromaniacs, and they could hardly have asked for better conditions than the summer of 1989. One man had been caught in the spring setting fire to the *garrigue*. He was young, and he wanted to be a *pompier*, but the fire service had turned him down. He was taking his revenge with a box of matches.

Our first sight of smoke was on the hot, windy evening of the 14th of July. Overhead was cloudless, the clean, burnished blue sky that the *mistral* often brings, and it accentuated the black stain that was spreading above the village of Roussillon, a few miles away across the valley. As we watched it from the path above the house, we heard the drone of engines, and a formation of Canadair planes flew low over the Lubéron, ponderous with their cargoes of water. Then helicopters, the *bombardiers d'eau*. From Bonnieux came the insistent, panicky blare of a fire siren, and we both looked nervously behind us. Less than a hundred yards separates our house from the tree line, and a hundred yards is nothing to a well-stoked fire with a gale-force wind at its back.

That evening, as the Canadairs, heavy-bellied and slow, ferried between the fire and the sea, we had to face the possibility that the next stretch of forest to go up in flames might be closer to home. The *pompiers* who had come with their calendars at Christmas had told us what we were supposed to do: cut off the electricity, close the wooden shutters, hose them down, stay in the house. We had joked about taking refuge in the wine cellar with a couple of glasses and a corkscrew—better to be roasted drunk than sober. It no longer seemed funny.

The wind dropped as night came, and the glow over Roussillon might have been no more than floodlights on the village *boules* court. We checked on the weather forecast before going to bed. It was not good; *beau temps très chaud et ensoleillé, mistral fort.*

The next day's copy of *Le Provençal* carried details of the Roussillon fire. It had destroyed more than a hundred acres of the pine woods around the village before 400 *pompiers*, 10 aircraft, and the *soldats du feu* from the army had put it out. There were photographs of horses and a herd of goats being led to safety, and of a solitary *pompier* silhouetted against a wall of flame. Three smaller fires were reported in the same article. It would probably have made the front page except for the arrival of the *Tour de France* in Marseille.

We drove across to Roussillon a few days later. What had

been pine green and beautiful was now desolate—charred, ugly tree stumps jutting like rotten teeth from the ochre-red earth of the hillsides. Miraculously, some of the houses seemed untouched despite the devastation that surrounded them. We wondered if the owners had stayed inside or run, and tried to imagine what it must have been like to sit in a dark house listening to the fire coming closer and closer, feeling its heat through the walls.

July's rainfall was five millimeters, but the wise men of the café told us that the storms of August would soak the Lubéron and allow the *pompiers* to relax. Always, we were told, *le quinze août* brought a downpour, swilling campers out of their tents, flooding roads, drenching the forest, and, with luck, drowning the pyromaniacs.

Day after day we looked for rain, and day after day we saw nothing but sun. Lavender that we had planted in the spring died. The patch of grass in front of the house abandoned its ambitions to become a lawn and turned the dirty yellow of poor straw. The earth shrank, revealing its knuckles and bones, rocks and roots that had been invisible before. The luckier peasants who had powerful irrigation systems began to water their vines. Our vines drooped. Faustin, on his tours of inspection in the vineyard, drooped also.

The pool was as warm as soup, but at least it was wet, and one evening the scent of water attracted a tribe of *sangliers*. Eleven of them came out of the forest and stopped fifty yards from the house. One boar took advantage of the halt and mounted his mate, and Boy, showing uncharacteristic bravado, went dancing toward the happy couple, his bark soprano with excitement. Still joined together like competitors in a wheelbarrow race, they chased him off, and he

returned to the door of the courtyard where he could be noisy
and brave in safety. The *sangliers* changed their minds about
the pool, and filed away through the vines to eat Jacky's
melons in the field on the other side of the road.

*Le quinze août* was as dry as the first half of the month had
been, and every time the *mistral* blew we waited for the sound
of the sirens and the Canadairs. A pyromaniac had actually
telephoned the *pompiers*, promising another fire as soon as
there was enough wind, and there were daily helicopter pa-
trols over the valley.

But they didn't see him when he did it again, this time
near Cabrières. Ashes carried by the wind fell in the courtyard, and the sun was blotted out by smoke. The smell of it
spooked the dogs, who paced and whined and barked at gusts
of wind. The red and pink evening sky was hidden behind a
smear of grey, faintly luminous, somber, and frightening.

A friend who was staying in Cabrières came over to see us
that night. Some houses on the edge of the village had been
evacuated. She had brought her passport with her, and a
spare pair of knickers.

We saw no fires after that, although the pyromaniac had
made more phone calls, always threatening the Lubéron. August ended. The rainfall reported for our area was 0.0 millimeters, compared with the average of 52. When a half-
hearted shower came in September, we stood out in it and
took great breaths of cool, damp air. For the first time in
weeks, the forest smelled fresh.

With the immediate danger of fire behind them, the local
inhabitants felt sufficiently relieved to complain about the
effects of the drought on their stomachs. With the exception
of the year's wine, which in Châteauneuf was announced as

spectacularly good, the gastronomic news was disastrous. The lack of rain in July would mean a miserable truffle crop in the winter, few in number and small in size. Hunters would have to shoot each other for sport; game that had left the parched Lubéron to look for water further north was unlikely to come back. Autumn at the table would not be the same, *pas du tout normal.*

Our education suffered. Monsieur Menicucci, whose many talents included an ability to detect and identify the wild mushrooms in the forest, had promised to take us on an expedition—kilos of mushrooms, he said, would be there for the taking. He would instruct us, and supervise afterwards in the kitchen, assisted by a bottle of Cairanne.

But October came and the hunt had to be cancelled. For the first time in Menicucci's memory, the forest was bare. He came to the house one morning, knife, stick, and basket at the ready, snakeproof boots tightly laced, and spent a fruitless hour poking among the trees before giving up. We would have to try again next year. Madame his wife would be disappointed, and so would his friend's cat, who was a great *amateur* of wild mushrooms.

A cat?

*Beh oui*, but a cat with an extraordinary nose, able to pick out dangerous or deadly mushrooms. Nature is mysterious and wonderful, said Menicucci, and often cannot be explained in a scientific manner.

I asked what the cat did with edible mushrooms. He eats them, said Menicucci, but not raw. They must be cooked in olive oil and sprinkled with chopped parsley. That is his little weakness. *C'est bizarre, non?*

. . .

The forest was officially recognized as a tinderbox in November, when it was invaded by the *Office National des Forêts*. One dark, overcast morning I was about two miles from the house when I saw a billow of smoke and heard the rasp of brushcutters. In a clearing at the end of the track, army trucks were parked next to an enormous yellow machine, perhaps 10 feet high, a cross between a bulldozer and a mammoth tractor. Men in olive-drab fatigue uniforms moved through the trees, sinister in their goggles and helmets, hacking away the undergrowth and throwing it on the fire that hissed with sizzling sap from the green wood.

An officer, hard-faced and lean, looked at me as though I was trespassing and barely nodded when I said *bonjour*. A bloody civilian, and a foreigner as well.

I turned to go home, and stopped to look at the yellow monster. The driver, a fellow civilian from the look of his cracked leather waistcoat and nonregulation checked cap, was cursing as he tried to loosen a tight nut. He exchanged his wrench for a mallet—the all-purpose Provençal remedy for obstinate mechanical equipment—which made me sure he wasn't an army man. I tried another *bonjour*, and this time it was more amiably received.

He could have been Santa Claus's younger brother; without the beard, but with ruddy round cheeks and bright eyes and a moustache that was flecked with the sawdust that was blowing in the wind. He waved his mallet in the direction of the extermination squad in the trees. *"C'est comme la guerre, eh?"*

He called it, in correct military style, *opération débroussaillage*. Twenty meters on either side of the track that led towards Ménerbes were to be cleared of undergrowth and thinned out to reduce the risk of fire. His job was to follow the men in his machine and shred everything they hadn't burned. He banged its yellow side with the flat of his hand. "This will eat a tree trunk and spit it out as twigs."

It took the men a week to cover the distance to the house. They left the edge of the forest shorn, the clearings smudged with pools of ashes. And following on, chewing and spitting a few hundred meters each day, came the yellow monster with its relentless, grinding appetite.

The driver came down to see us one evening, asking for a glass of water, easily persuaded into a glass of *pastis*. He apologized for parking at the top of the garden. Parking was a daily problem, he said; with a top speed of 10 kilometers an hour he could hardly take what he described as his little toy back home to Apt each night.

He took off his cap for the second glass of *pastis*. It was good to have someone to talk to, he said, after a day on his own with nothing to listen to but the racket of his machine. But it was necessary work. The forest had been left untended too long. It was choked with dead wood, and if there was another drought next year . . . *pof!*

We asked him if the pyromaniac had ever been caught, and he shook his head. The madman with the *briquet*, he called him. Let's hope he spends his holidays in the Cévennes next year.

The driver came again the following evening and brought us a Camembert, which he told us how to cook—the way he did when he was in the forest during the winter and needed something to keep out the cold.

"You make a fire," he said, arranging imaginary branches on the table in front of him, "and you take the cheese from the box and remove the paper wrapping. And then you put it back, *d'accord?*" To make sure we had understood, he held up the Camembert and tapped its thin wooden box.

"*Bon.* Now you put the box in the embers of the fire. The box burns. The rind of the cheese turns black. The cheese melts, but" . . . an instructive finger was raised for emphasis . . . "he is sealed inside the rind. He cannot escape into the fire."

A swig of *pastis*, the moustache wiped with the back of the hand.

"*Alors*, you take your *baguette* and split it all the way down. Now—*attention aux doigts*—you take the cheese from the fire, you make a hole in the rind, and you pour the melted cheese into the bread. *Et voilà!*"

He grinned, his red cheeks bunching under his eyes, and patted his stomach. Sooner or later, as I had learned, every conversation in Provence seems to turn to food or drink.

At the beginning of 1990, we were sent the weather statistics for the previous year. Despite an unusually wet November, our annual rainfall was less than half the normal amount.

There has been another mild winter. The water levels are still below what they should be, and it is estimated that as much as 30 percent of the undergrowth in the forest is dead, and therefore dry. The first big fire of summer destroyed more than 6,000 acres near Marseille, cutting off the *auto-route* in two places. And the madman with the *briquet* is still at large; probably, like us, taking a keen interest in the weather forecasts.

We have bought a heavy-gauge tin box to hold all those pieces of paper—passports, *attestations*, birth certificates, *con-*

*trats, permis*, old electricity bills—that are essential in France to prove your existence. To lose the house in a fire would be a disaster, but to lose our identities at the same time would make life impossible. The tin box is going in the farthest corner of the *cave*, next to the Châteauneuf.

Every time it rains we're delighted, which Faustin takes as a promising sign that we are becoming less English.

# Dinner with Pavarotti

The publicity preceded the event by months. Pictures of a bearded face, crowned by a beret, appeared in newspapers and on posters, and from spring onward anyone in Provence with half an ear for music had heard the news: Imperator Pavarotti, as *Le Provençal* called him, was coming this summer to sing for us. More than that, it would be the concert of a lifetime, because of where he had chosen to perform. Not in the Opera House in Avignon or the *salle de fêtes* in Gordes, where he would be protected from the elements, but in the open air, surrounded by ancient stones laid by his fellow Italians 19 centuries ago when they constructed the Antique Theatre of Orange. Truly, *un événement éblouissant*.

Even empty, the Antique Theatre is overwhelming, a place of colossal, almost unbelievable scale. It is in the form of a D, and the straight wall that joins the two ends of the semi-circle is 335 feet long, 120 feet high, and completely intact. Apart from the patina left on the stone by nearly 2000 years of weather, it could have been built yesterday. Behind the wall, scooped out of a hillside whose slope lends itself naturally to stepped seating, curved banks of stone can accommodate about 10,000 spectators.

Originally they were seated according to class: magistrates and local senators in the front, priests and members of the trading guilds behind them, then the man in the street and his wife, and finally, high up and far away from respectable folk, the *Pullati*, or beggars and prostitutes. By 1990 the rules had changed, and the allocation of seats depended not so much on class as speed off the mark. The concert was a foregone sellout; swift and decisive action was necessary to secure tickets.

It was taken, while we were still dithering, by our friend Christopher, a man who operates with military precision when it comes to the big night out. He arranged everything, and gave us our marching orders: on parade at 1800 hours, dinner in Orange under a magnolia tree at 1930 hours, seated in the theater by 2100 hours. All ranks to be equipped with cushions to protect buttocks from stone seats. Liquid rations provided for the intermission. Return to base approximately 0100 hours.

There are times when it is a relief and a pleasure to be told exactly what to do, and this was one of them. We left at six sharp, arriving in Orange an hour later to find the town in a festival mood. Every café was full and humming, with extra tables and chairs edging out into the streets to make driving a test of how many waiters you could avoid bumping into. Already, more than two hours before the performance, hundreds of people with cushions and picnic baskets were streaming toward the theater. The restaurants displayed special menus for the *soirée Pavarotti*. *Le tout Orange* was rubbing its hands in anticipation. And then it started to rain.

The whole town looked upward—waiters, drivers, cushion-carriers, and no doubt the maestro himself—as the first few drops landed on dusty streets that had been dry for weeks. *Quelle catastrophe!* Would he sing under an umbrella? How could the orchestra play with damp instruments, the conductor conduct with a dripping baton? For as long as the shower lasted, you could almost feel thousands of people holding their breath.

But by nine o'clock the rain had long since gone and the first stars were coming out above the immense wall of the theater as we joined the throng of music lovers and shuffled past the display of Pavarottiana on sale beside the entrance. Compact discs, tapes, posters, T-shirts—all the products of pop merchandising were there, apart from I Love Luciano bumper stickers.

The line kept stopping, as though there were an obstruction beyond the entrance, and when we came through into the theater I realized why. You stood still—you had to stand still—for a few seconds to take in the view from the front of the stage, the view that Pavarotti would see.

Thousands and thousands of faces, pale against the darkness, made row after blurred row of semicircles, which disappeared up into the night. From ground level, there was a feeling of reverse vertigo. The angle of the seating seemed impossibly steep, the spectators perched and precarious, on the brink of losing their balance and toppling down into the pit. The sound they made was uncanny—above a whisper, but below normal speech, a continuous, quiet buzz of conversation that was contained and magnified by the stone walls. I felt as though I had stepped into a human beehive.

We climbed to our seats, a hundred feet or so above the stage, exactly opposite a niche high in the wall where a floodlit statue of Augustus Caesar, in his imperial toga, stood with his arm outstretched to the crowd. In his day, the population of Orange had been about 85,000; it is now fewer than 30,000, and most of them seemed to be trying to find a few spare inches of stone to sit on.

A woman of operatic girth, blowing hard after scaling the steps, collapsed on her cushion next to me and fanned herself with a program. She was from Orange, round-faced and jolly, and she had been to the theater many times before. But she had never seen an audience like this, she said. She surveyed the heads and made her calculations: 13,000 people, she was sure of it. *Dieu merci* that the rain had stopped.

There was a sudden crack of applause as the members of the orchestra filed on stage and began to tune up, musical fragments that came sharp and clear through the expectant hum of the crowd. With a closing rumble from the kettle drums, the orchestra stopped, and looked, as everyone in the theater looked, toward the back of the stage. Directly below the statue of Augustus, the central entrance had been draped with black curtains. The rows of heads around us leaned forward in unison, as though they'd been rehearsed, and from behind the black curtain came the black and white figure of the conductor.

Another explosion of hands, and a shrill, ragged chorus of whistles from the seats far behind and above us. Madame next door tut-tutted. This was not a football match. *Épou-vantable* behavior. In fact, it was probably in accordance with tradition, since the whistling was coming from the beggars and prostitutes' seats, not an area where one would expect to hear genteel applause.

The orchestra played a Donizetti overture, the music floating and dipping in the night air, undistorted and naturally amplified, bathing the theater in sound. The acoustics were mercilessly revealing. If there were any false notes tonight, most of Orange would know.

The conductor bowed and walked back toward the curtain, and there was a moment—hardly more than a second—when 13,000 people were silent. And then, to a roar that must have felt like a physical blow, the man himself appeared, black hair, black beard, white tie and tails, a voluminous white handkerchief floating from his left hand. He spread his arms to the crowd. He put his palms together and bowed his head. Pavarotti was ready to sing.

Up in the beggars and prostitutes' section, however, they were not ready to stop whistling—piercing, two-fingers-in-the-mouth whistles that could have hailed a taxi on the other side of Orange. Madame next door was scandalized. Opera hooligans, she called them. *Shhhhh*, she went. *Shhhh*, went thousands of others. Renewed whistling from the beggars and prostitutes. Pavarotti stood waiting, head down, arms by his side. The conductor's baton was up. To the accompaniment of a few last defiant whistles, they began.

"*Quanto e cara, quanto e bella*," sang Pavarotti. It sounded so easy, the size of his voice reducing the theater to the size of a room. He stood very still, his weight on his right leg, the heel of his left foot raised slightly from the ground, hand-kerchief rippling in the breeze—a relaxed, perfectly controlled performance.

He finished with a ritual that he would repeat throughout the evening: an upward flick of the head at the end of the final note, a vast grin, arms spread wide before bringing his palms together and bowing his head, a handshake with the conductor while the applause thundered down to crash against the back wall.

He sang again, and before the applause had died away he was escorted by the conductor to the curtained entrance and disappeared. I imagined he had gone to rest his vocal cords and have a restorative spoonful of honey. But Madame next door had a different explanation, and it intrigued me for the next two hours.

"*À mon avis*," she said, "he is taking a light dinner between arias."

"Surely not, Madame," I said.

"*Shhhh*. Here is the flutist."

At the end of the piece, Madame returned to her theory. Pavarotti, she said, was a big man and a famous gourmet. The performance was long. To sing as he sang, *comme un ange*, was hard, demanding work. It was altogether logical that he should sustain himself during the periods when he was not on stage. If I were to study the program, I would see that it might have been constructed to allow for a well-spaced five-course snack to be consumed while the orchestra diverted the audience. *Voilà!*

I looked at the program, and I had to admit that Madame had a point. It was entirely possible, and reading between the arias, a menu appeared:

**DONIZETTI**
*(Insalata di carciofi)*

**CILEA**
*(Zuppa di fagioli alla Toscana)*

**ENTRACTE**
*(Sogliole alla Veneziana)*

## Dinner with Pavarotti

**PUCCINI**
*(Tonnelini con funghi e piselli)*

**VERDI**
*(Formaggi)*

**MASSENET**
*(Granita di limone)*

**ENCORE**
*(Caffè e grappa)*

There was another, more visible sign that the singing supper might not be just a figment of Madame's imagination. Like everyone else, I had assumed that the white square draped elegantly through the fingers of Pavarotti's left hand was a handkerchief. But it was larger than a handkerchief, much larger. I mentioned it to Madame, and she nodded. "*Évidemment,*" she said, "*c'est une serviette.*" Having proved her case, she settled back to enjoy the rest of the concert.

Pavarotti was unforgettable, not only for his singing but for the way in which he played to the audience, risking the occasional vocal departure from the score, patting the conductor on the cheek when it came off, making his exits and entrances with faultless timing. After one of his periods behind the curtain, he returned wearing a long blue scarf wrapped around his neck and reaching to his waist—against the cool night air, or so I thought.

Madame, of course, knew better. He has had a small accident with some sauce, she said, and the scarf is there to conceal the spots on his white waistcoat. Isn't he divine?

The official program ended, but the orchestra lingered on. From the beggars and prostitutes' section came an insistent chant—*Ver-di! Ver-di! Ver-di!*—and this time it spread through the crowd until Pavarotti emerged to give us a second helping of encores: *Nessun Dorma, O Sole Mio,* rapture in the audience, bows from the orchestra, one last salute from the star, and then it was over.

It took us half an hour to clear the exit, and as we came out we saw two enormous Mercedes pulling away from the theater. "I bet that's him," said Christopher. "I wonder where he's going to have dinner." He wasn't to know, because he hadn't been sitting next to Madame, what had been going on behind the black curtain. Thirteen thousand people had been to dinner with Pavarotti without realizing it. I hope he comes to Orange again, and I hope that next time they print the menu in the program.

# A *Pastis* Lesson

Tin tables and scuffed wicker chairs are set out under the shade of massive plane trees. It is close to noon, and the motes of dust kicked up by an old man's canvas boots as he shuffles across the square hang for a long moment in the air, sharply defined in the glare of the sun. The café waiter looks up from his copy of *L'Équipe* and saunters out to take your order.

He comes back with a small glass, maybe a quarter full if he's been generous, and a beaded carafe of water. The glass turns cloudy as you fill it up, a color somewhere between yellow and misty grey, and there is the sharp, sweet smell of aniseed.

*Santé.* You are drinking *pastis*, the milk of Provence.

For me, the most powerful ingredient in *pastis* is not aniseed or alcohol but *ambiance*, and that dictates how and where it should be drunk. I cannot imagine drinking it in a hurry. I cannot imagine drinking it in a pub in Fulham, a bar in New York, or anywhere that requires its customers to wear socks. It wouldn't taste the same. There has to be heat and sunlight and the illusion that the clock has stopped. I have to be in Provence.

Before moving here, I had always thought of *pastis* as a commodity, a French national asset made by two giant institutions. There was Pernod, there was Ricard, and that was it.

Then I started to come across others—Casanis, Janot, Granier—and I wondered how many different *marques* there were. I counted five in one bar, seven in another. Every Provençal I asked was, of course, an expert. Each of them gave me a different, emphatic, and probably inaccurate answer, complete with disparaging remarks about the brands that he personally wouldn't give to his mother-in-law.

It was only by chance that I found a professor of *pastis*, and since he also happens to be a very good chef, attending class was no hardship.

Michel Bosc was born near Avignon and emigrated to Cabrières, a few miles away. For 12 years now he has run a restaurant in the village, *Le Bistrot à Michel*, and each year he has put his profits back into the business. He has added a large terrace, expanded the kitchens, put in four bedrooms for overtired or overindulged customers, and generally turned *chez Michel* into a comfortable, bustling place.

But despite all the improvements, and the occasional outbreaks of rampant chic among the summer clientele, one thing hasn't changed. The bar at the front of the restaurant is still the village bar. Every evening there will be half a dozen men with burned faces and work clothes who have dropped in, not to eat, but to argue about *boules* over a couple of drinks. And the drinks are invariably *pastis*.

We arrived one evening to find Michel behind the bar, presiding over an informal *dégustation*. Seven or eight different

brands were being put through their paces by the local en-
thusiasts, some of them brands I had never seen.

A *pastis* tasting is not the hushed, almost religious ritual
that you might find in the cellars of Bordeaux or Burgundy,
and Michel had to raise his voice to make himself heard over
the smacking of lips and the banging of glasses on the bar.

"Try this," he said. "It's just like mother used to make. It
comes from Forcalquier." He slid a glass across the bar and
topped it up from a sweating metal jug rattling with ice cubes.

Good grief. This is what mother used to make? Two or
three of these and I'd be lucky to make it upstairs to one of
the bedrooms on my hands and knees. I said it seemed strong,
and Michel showed me the bottle: 45 percent alcohol, stronger
than brandy, but not above the legal limit for *pastis*, and
positively mild in comparison with one that Michel had once
been given. Two of those, he said, would make a man fall
straight backward with a smile on his face, *plof*! But it was
something special, that one, and I gathered from Michel's
half-wink that it was not altogether legal.

He left the bar suddenly, as if he'd remembered a *soufflé*
in the oven, and came back with some objects that he put in
front of me on the bar.

"Do you know what those are?"

There was a tall, spiral-patterned glass on a short, thick
stem; a smaller, chunky glass, as narrow as a thimble and
twice as high; and what looked like a flattened tin spoon
decorated with symmetrical rows of perforations. On the stem
just behind the flat head was a U-shaped kink.

"This place used to be a café long before I took it over,"
said Michel. "I found these when we were knocking through
a wall. You've never seen them before?"

I had no idea what they were.

"In the old days, all the cafés had them. They're for *absinthe*." He curled an index finger around the end of his nose and twisted, the gesture for drunkenness. He picked up the smaller of the two glasses. "This is the *dosette*, the old measure for *absinthe*." It was solid and tactile, and felt as heavy as a slug of lead when he passed it to me. He took the other glass and balanced the spoon on top of it, the kink in the stem fitting snugly over the rim.

"*Bon*. On here"—he tapped the blade of the spoon—"you put sugar. Then you pour water over the sugar and it drips through the holes and into the *absinthe*. At the end of the last century, this was a drink very much *à la mode*."

*Absinthe*, so Michel told me, was a green liqueur originally distilled from wine and the wormwood plant. Very bitter, stimulating and hallucinogenic, addictive and dangerous. It was 68 percent alcohol, and could cause blindness, epilepsy, and insanity. Under its influence, Van Gogh is said to have cut off his own ear, and Verlaine to have shot Rimbaud. It gave its name to a particular disease—*absinthisme*—and the addict would quite often *"casser sa pipe"* and die. For this reason, it was made illegal in 1915.

One man who would not have been pleased to see it go was Jules Pernod, who had an *absinthe* factory at Montfavet, near Avignon. But he adapted to the times by changing his production over to a drink based on the legally authorized *anis*. It was an immediate success, with the considerable advantage that customers would live to come back for more.

"So you see," said Michel, "commercial *pastis* was born in Avignon, like me. Try another one."

He took a bottle of Granier from the shelf, and I was able to say that I had the same brand at home. Granier, *"Mon pastis"* as it says on the label, is made in Cavaillon. It has a more gentle color than Pernod's rather fierce greenish tinge, and I find it a softer drink. Also, I'm inclined to support local endeavors whenever they taste good.

The Granier went down and I was still standing up. To continue my first lesson, Michel said, it was necessary to try another, a *grande marque*, so that I could make a considered judgment across a range of slight variations in taste and color. He gave me a Ricard.

By this time it was becoming rather difficult to maintain a detached and scholarly attitude to the comparison of one *pastis* against another. I liked them all—clean-tasting, smooth, and insidious. One might have had a drop more licorice than the rest, but the palate develops a certain numbness after a few highly flavored and highly alcoholic shots. It's a pleasant numbness, and it stimulates a roaring appetite, but any traces of critical appraisal I might have started with had vanished somewhere between the second and third glasses. As a *pastis* connoisseur, I was hopeless. Happy and hungry, but hopeless.

"How was the Ricard?" asked Michel. I said that the Ricard was fine, but perhaps I had absorbed enough education for one night.

For days afterward, I kept scribbling down questions that I wanted to ask Michel. I found it curious, for instance, that the word was so well known and had such strong associations, and yet its origins seemed as cloudy as the drink itself. Who had invented *pastis* before Pernod had taken it over? Why was it so firmly rooted in Provence, rather than Burgundy or the Loire? I went back to the professor.

Whenever I have asked a Provençal about Provence—whether about climate, food, history, the habits of animals, or the oddities of humans—I have never been short of answers. The Provençal loves to instruct, usually with a great deal of personal embroidery, and preferably around a table. And so it was this time. Michel arranged a lunch, on the one day of the week when his restaurant is normally closed, with a few friends he described as *"hommes responsables"* who would be happy to lead me down the path of knowledge.

Eighteen of us gathered under the big white canvas umbrella in Michel's courtyard, and I was introduced to a blur of faces and names and descriptions: a government official from Avignon, a wine grower from Carpentras, two executives from Ricard, some stalwarts from Cabrières. There was even a man wearing a tie, but he slipped it off after five minutes and hung it in a noose over the drinks trolley. That was the beginning and the end of any formality.

Most of the men shared Michel's passion for *boules*, and the wine grower from Carpentras had brought with him a few cases of his special *cuvée*, with labels showing a game in progress. While the *rosé* was being chilled and the red uncorked, there was a generous dispensation of the sporting drink and the *boules* player's standby, *le vrai pastis de Marseille, le pastis Ricard*.

Born in 1909 and, according to one of his executives, still looking for trouble, Paul Ricard's success is a classic case of energetic and intelligent exploitation. His father was a wine merchant, and young Paul's work took him into the bars and *bistrots* of Marseille. In those days the laws of concoction were not stringent, and many bars made their own *pastis*. Ricard decided to make his, but he added an ingredient that the others lacked, which was a genius for promotion. *Le vrai pastis de Marseille* may not have been very different from the others, but it was good, and made better by Ricard's talent for marketing. It was not long before his *pastis* was the most popular *pastis*, at least in Marseille.

Ricard was ready to expand, and he made a decision that probably accelerated his success by several years. The area around Marseille was a competitive market; *pastis* was everywhere, a commonplace drink. And Marseille itself didn't enjoy the best of reputations among its neighbors. (Even today, a Marseillais is regarded as a *blagueur*, an exaggerator, a man who will describe a sardine as a whale, not entirely to be believed.)

Further north, however, *pastis* could be sold as something exotic, and distance lent improvement to Marseille's reputation. It could be invested with the charm of the south—a slightly raffish, relaxed, sunny charm that would appeal to a northerner used to freezing winters and grey skies. So Ricard went north, first to Lyon and then to Paris, and the formula worked. Today it would be unusual to find a bar anywhere in France without its bottle of *le vrai pastis de Marseille*.

The man from Ricard who was telling me this talked about his *patron* with genuine liking. Monsieur Paul, he said, was *un original*, someone who looked for a challenge every day. When I asked if he was involved, like many powerful businessmen, in politics, there was a snort of laughter. "Politicians? He vomits on them all." I had some sympathy for the sentiment, but in a way I thought it was a pity. The idea of a *pastis* baron as President of France appealed to me, and he would probably have been elected on his advertising slogan: *Un Ricard, sinon rien.*

But Ricard hadn't invented *pastis*. Like Pernod, he had bottled and marketed something that had been there before. Where had it come from? Who had first mixed the *anis*, the licorice, the sugar, and the alcohol? Was there a monk (monks, for some reason, have an affinity for alcoholic invention, from champagne to Benedictine) who had made the discovery one blessed day in the monastery kitchens?

Nobody around the table knew exactly how the first glass of *pastis* had come into a thirsty world, but lack of precise knowledge never inhibits a Provençal from expressing an opinion as fact, or a legend as reliable history. The least plausible, and therefore favorite, explanation was the hermit theory—hermits, of course, being almost up to monk standard when it comes to the invention of unusual *apéritifs*.

This particular hermit lived in a hut deep in the forest on the slopes of the Lubéron. He collected herbs, which he stewed in a giant pot, the traditional bubbling cauldron favored by witches, wizards, and alchemists. The juices left in the cauldron after boiling had remarkable properties, not only quenching the hermit's thirst, but protecting him from an outbreak of plague that was threatening to decimate the population of the Lubéron. The hermit was a generous fellow, and shared his mixture with sufferers from the plague, who immediately recovered. Sensing, perhaps like Paul Ricard long after him, the wider possibilities for his miraculous drink, he left his forest hut and did what any businesslike hermit would have done: He moved to Marseille and opened a bar.

The less picturesque but more likely reason for Provence being the home of *pastis* is that the ingredients were easy to come by. The herbs were cheap, or free. Most peasants made their own wine and distilled their own head-splitting liqueurs, and until fairly recently the right of distillation was a family asset that could be passed down from father to son. That right has been revoked, but there are some surviving *distillateurs* who, until they die, are legally entitled to make what they drink, and *pastis maison* still exists.

Madame Bosc, Michel's wife, was born near Carpentras and remembers her grandfather making a double-strength *pastis*, 90 percent alcohol, a drink that could make a statue fall down. One day he received a visit from the village *gendarme*. An official visit, on the official *moto*, in full uniform, never a good sign. The *gendarme* was persuaded into one of grandfather's virulent glasses of *pastis*, then another, then a third. The purpose of the visit was never discussed, but grandfather had to make two trips to the *gendarmerie* in his van: the first was to deliver the unconscious policeman and his bike; the second, to deliver his boots and his *pistolet*, which had been discovered later under the table.

Those were the days. And somewhere in Provence, they probably still are.

# The *Flic*

It was bad luck that I had no change for the parking meter on one of the few days that the Cavaillon traffic control authorities were out in force. There are two of them, well-padded and slow-moving men who do their best to look sinister in their peaked caps and sunglasses as they move with immense deliberation from car to car, looking for a *contravention*.

I had found a vacant meter that needed feeding, and I went into a nearby café for some one-franc pieces. When I returned to the car, a portly figure in blue was squinting suspiciously at the dial on the meter. He looked up and aimed his sunglasses at me, tapping the dial with his pen.

"He has expired."

I explained my problem, but he was not in the mood to consider any mitigating circumstances.

"*Tant pis pour vous,*" he said. "*C'est une contravention.*"

I looked around and saw that there were half a dozen cars double-parked. A *maçon's* truck, brimming with rubble, was abandoned at the corner of a side street, completely blocking the exit. A van on the other side of the road had been left straddling a pedestrian crossing. My crime seemed relatively minor compared with these flagrant abuses, and I was unwise enough to say so.

I then became officially invisible. There was no reply except a sniff of irritation, and the guardian of the highways walked around me so that he could take down the number of the car. He unsheathed his notebook and consulted his watch.

He was starting to commit my sins to paper—probably adding on a bonus fine for impertinence—when there was a bawl from the café where I had been for change.

*"Eh, toi! Georges!"*

Georges and I looked around to see a stocky man making his way through the tables and chairs on the pavement, one finger wagging from side to side in the Provençal shorthand that expresses violent disagreement.

For five minutes, Georges and the stocky man shrugged and gesticulated and tapped each other sternly on the chest while my case was discussed. It was true, said the newcomer. Monsieur had just arrived, and he had indeed been into the café to get change. There were witnesses. He flung his arm back toward the café, where three or four faces were turned toward us from the twilight of the bar.

The law is the law, said Georges. It is a clear *contravention*. Besides, I have started to write the form, and so nothing can be done. It is irrevocable.

*Mais c'est de la connerie, ça.* Change the form, and give it to that woodenhead who is blocking the street with his truck.

Georges weakened. He looked at the truck and his notebook, gave another sniff, and turned to me so that he could have the last word. "Next time, have change." He looked at me intently, no doubt committing my criminal features to memory in case he might need to pull in a suspect one day, and moved off along the pavement toward the *maçon*'s truck.

My rescuer grinned and shook his head. "He has *pois chiches* for brains, that one." He repeated the insult. Chickpeas, from ear to ear.

I thanked him. Could I buy him a drink? We went into the café together and sat at a dark table in the corner, and I was there for the next two hours.

Robert was his name. He was not quite short, not quite fat, broad across the chest and stomach, thick-necked, dark-faced, dashingly moustached. His smile was a contrast in gold fillings and nicotine-edged teeth, and his brown eyes were lively with amusement. There was an air of faintly unreliable charm about him, the charm of an engaging scamp. I could imagine him in the Cavaillon market selling guaranteed indestructible crockery and almost genuine Levi's, whatever might have fallen off the back of the *camion* the night before.

As it turned out, he had been a policeman, which was how he had come to know and dislike Georges. Now he was a security consultant, selling alarm systems to owners of second homes in the Lubéron. *Cambrioleurs* were everywhere nowadays, he said, looking for the open window or the unlocked door. It was wonderful for business. Did I have an alarm system? No? *Quelle horreur!* He slipped a card across the table. There was his name and a slogan that read Alarm Technology of the Future, a message that was somewhat at odds with his trademark—a small drawing of a parrot on a perch squawking "*Au voleur!*"

I was interested in his work with the police, and why he had left. He settled back in a cloud of *Gitanes* smoke, waved his empty glass at the barman for more *pastis*, and started to talk.

In the beginning, he said, it had been a little slow. Waiting for promotion, just like everyone else, trudging through the routine work, getting bored with the desk jobs, not the kind of excitement he had hoped for. And then came the break, one weekend in Fréjus, where he was taking a few days' leave.

Every morning he went for breakfast to a café overlooking the sea, and every morning at the same time a man came down to the beach for windsurfing lessons. With the idle half-interest of a holidaymaker, Robert watched as the man got up on his windsurfer, fell off, and got up again.

There was something familiar about the man. Robert had never met him, he was sure, but he had seen him somewhere. There was a prominent mole on his neck and a tattoo on his left arm, the kind of small distinguishing marks that a policeman is trained to notice and remember. It was the windsurfer's profile that stirred Robert's memory, the mole on the neck and his slightly hooked nose.

After two days, it came to him. He had seen the profile in black and white with a number underneath it; an identity photograph, a police mug shot. The windsurfer had a record.

Robert went to the local *gendarmerie*, and within half an hour he was looking at the face of a man who had escaped from prison the year before. He was the leader of *le gang de Gardanne*, and known to be dangerous. Physical characteristics included a mole on the neck and a tattoo on the left arm.

A trap was set, which Robert described with some difficulty through his laughter. Twenty officers, disguised in swimming trunks, appeared on the beach bright and early and attempted to look inconspicuous despite the curious similarity of their *bronzage*—the policeman's suntan of brown forearms, brown vee at the neck, and brown face, with everywhere else, from toes to forehead, an unweathered white.

Fortunately, the fugitive was too busy getting aboard his windsurfer to notice anything suspicious about twenty pale men loitering with intent until they surrounded him in shallow water and took him away. A subsequent search of his studio apartment in Fréjus produced two .357 Magnum handguns and three grenades. Robert was credited with the collar, and seconded to plainclothes duty at Marignane airport, where his powers of observation could be fully exploited.

I stopped him there for a moment, because I had always been puzzled by the apparent lack of official surveillance at Marseille. Arriving passengers can leave their hand luggage with friends while they go to the baggage claim area, and if all they have is hand luggage they don't need to pass through customs at all. Given Marseille's reputation, this seemed strangely casual.

Robert tilted his head and laid a stubby finger along the side of his nose. It is not quite as *décontracté* as it appears, he said. Police and *douaniers*, sometimes dressed as business executives, sometimes in jeans and T-shirts, are always there, mingling with the passengers, strolling through the parking areas, watching and listening. He himself had caught one or two petty smugglers—nothing big, just amateurs who thought that once they were in the car park they'd be safe, that they could slap each other on the back and talk about it. Crazy.

But there were weeks when nothing much happened, and in the end boredom had got to him. That, and his *zizi*. He grinned, and pointed with his thumb down between his legs.

He'd stopped a girl—a good-looking girl, well dressed, travelling alone, the classic drug "mule"—as she was getting into a car with Swiss plates. He asked her the standard question, how long the car had been in France. She became nervous, then friendly, then very friendly, and the two of them spent the afternoon together in the airport hotel. Robert had been seen coming out with her, and that was it. *Fini*. Funnily enough, it had been the same week that a warden in the Beaumettes jail had been caught passing Scotch in doctored yogurt pots to one of the prisoners. *Fini* for him too.

Robert shrugged. It was wrong, it was stupid, but policemen weren't saints. There were always the *brebis galeuses*, the black sheep. He looked down at his glass, the picture of a penitent man regretting past misdeeds. One slip, and a career in ruins. I started to feel sorry for him, and said so. He reached across the table and patted my arm, and then spoiled the effect by saying that another drink would make him feel much better. He laughed, and I wondered how much of what he'd told me was the truth.


In a moment of *pastis*-scented *bonhomie*, Robert had said that he would come up to the house one day to advise us on our security arrangements. There would be no obligation, and if we should decide to make ourselves impregnable, he would install the most technically advanced booby traps at a *prix d'ami*.

I thanked him and forgot about it. Favors offered in bars should never be taken too seriously, particularly in Provence, where the most sober of promises is likely to take months to materialize. In any case, having seen how carefully members of the public ignore the shriek of car alarm systems in the streets, I was not convinced that electronic devices were much of a deterrent. I had more faith in a barking dog.

To my surprise, Robert came as he said he would, in a

silver BMW abristle with antennae, dressed in perilously tight trousers and a black shirt, humming with a musky and aggressive after-shave. The splendor of his appearance was explained by his companion, whom he introduced as his friend Isabelle. They were going to have lunch in Gordes, and Robert thought it was a chance to combine business with pleasure. He managed to make it sound infinitely suggestive.

Isabelle was no more than twenty. A blonde fringe brushed the rims of gigantic sunglasses. A minimal part of her body was coated with hot-pink spandex, an iridescent tube that ended well above mid-thigh. The courtly Robert insisted that she lead the way up the steps to the house, and he clearly relished every step. He was a man who could give lessons in leering.

While Isabelle busied herself with the contents of her makeup bag, I took Robert around the house, and he gave me a predictably disturbing assessment of the opportunities that our home provided for any larcenous idiot with a screwdriver. Windows and doors and shutters were all inspected and dismissed as being next to useless. And the dogs? *Aucun problème.* They could be taken care of with a few scraps of drugged meat, and then the house would be at the mercy of the thieves. Robert's overwhelming after-shave gusted over me as he pinned me against the wall. *You have no idea what these animals do.*

His voice became low and confidential. He wouldn't want Madame my wife to overhear what he was about to tell me, since it was rather indelicate.

Burglars, he said, are often superstitious. In many cases —he had seen it more times than he liked to think about— they feel it necessary before leaving a ransacked house to defecate, usually on the floor, preferably on fitted carpet. In this way, they think that any bad luck will remain in the house instead of with them. *Merde partout*, he said, and made the word sound as if he'd just stepped in it. *C'est désagréable, non?* It certainly was. *Désagréable* was a mild way of putting it.

But, said Robert, life was sometimes just. An entire group of *cambrioleurs* had once been apprehended because of this very superstition. The house had been picked clean, the swag loaded into a truck, and all that remained was to perform the parting gesture, for good luck's sake. The head of the gang, however, experienced considerable difficulty in making his contribution. Try as he might, nothing happened. He was *très, très constipé*. And he was still there, crouched and cursing, when the police arrived.

It was a heartening story, although I realized that according to the national average we had only a one in five chance of being visited by a constipated burglar. We couldn't count on it.

Robert took me outside and began to propose his plans for turning the house into a fortress. At the bottom of the drive there should be electronically operated steel gates. In front of the house, a pressure-activated lighting system; anything heavier than a chicken coming up the drive would be caught in the glare of a battery of floodlights. This was often enough to make burglars give up and run for it. But to be totally protected, to be able to sleep like an innocent child, one should also have the last word in repellents—*la maison hurlante*, the howling house.

Robert paused to gauge my reaction to this hideous novelty, and smiled across at Isabelle, who was peering over her sunglasses at her nails. They were a perfect hot-pink match for her dress.

*"Ça va, chou-chou?"*

She twitched a honey-colored shoulder at him, and it was with a visible effort that he turned his thoughts back to howling houses.

*Alors*, it was all done with electronic beams, which protected every door, every window, every orifice larger than a chink. And so if a determined and light-footed burglar managed to scale the steel gates and tiptoe through the floodlights, the merest touch of his finger on window or door would set the house screaming. One could also, *bien sûr*, enhance the effect by installing an amplifier on the roof so that the screams could be heard for several kilometers.

But that wasn't the end of it. At the same time, a partner of Robert's near Gordes, whose house was linked to the system, would drive over instantly with his loaded *pistolet* and his large Alsatian. Secure behind this multilayered protection, I would be perfectly *tranquille*.

It sounded anything but *tranquille*. I immediately thought of Faustin in his tractor, pounding on the steel gates at six in the morning to get to the vines; of the floodlights going on all through the night as foxes or *sangliers* or the cat next door crossed the drive; of setting off the howling mechanism by accident, and having to apologize fast to an irritated man with a gun before his dog ripped me to pieces. Life in Fort Knox would be a permanent, dangerous hell. Even as a barricade against the August invasion, it simply wouldn't be worth the nervous wear and tear.

Luckily, Robert was distracted from pressing for a sale. Isabelle, now satisfied with the state of her nails, the positioning of her sunglasses, and the overall adhesion of her tubelet, was ready to go. She cooed across the courtyard at him. *"Bobo, j'ai faim."*

*"Oui, oui, chérie. Deux secondes."* He turned to me and tried to revert to business, but his howling mechanism had been activated and our domestic security was not the pressing priority of the moment.

I asked him where he was going to have lunch.

*"La Bastide,"* he said. "Do you know it? It used to be the *gendarmerie*. Once a *flic*, always a *flic*, eh?"

I said I'd heard that it was also a hotel, and he winked. He was a very expressive winker. This was a wink of the purest lubricity.

"I know," he said.

# Mouthful for Mouthful with the Athlete Gourmet

We heard about Régis from some friends. They had invited him to dinner at their house, and during the morning he had called to ask what he would be given to eat. Even in France, that shows a greater interest than normal in the menu, and his hostess was curious. Why was he asking? There were cold stuffed *moules*, there was pork with truffle gravy, there were cheeses, there were homemade sorbets. Were any of these a problem? Had he developed allergies? Become a vegetarian? Gone, God forbid, on a diet?

Certainly not, said Régis. It all sounded delicious. But there was *un petit inconvénient*, and it was this: He was suffering from a sharp attack of piles, and found it impossible to sit through an entire dinner. A single course was all that he could manage without discomfort, and he wanted to pick the course that tempted him most. He was sure that his hostess would sympathize with his predicament.

As it was Régis, she did. Régis, so she told us later, was a man whose life was dedicated to the table—knowledgeably, almost obsessively concerned with eating and drinking. But not as a glutton. No, Régis was a gourmet who happened to have a huge and extremely well-informed appetite. Also, she said, he was amusing about his passion, and he had some views that we might find interesting about the English attitude toward food. Perhaps we would like to meet him once he had recovered from his *crise postérieure.*

And, one evening a few weeks later, we did.

He arrived in haste, nursing a cold bottle of Krug champagne, not quite cold enough, and spent the first five minutes fussing with an ice bucket to bring the bottle to the correct drinking temperature, which he said had to be between 37 and 45 degrees. While he rotated the bottle gently in the bucket, he told us of a dinner party he had been to the previous week that had been a gastronomic disaster. His only enjoyable moment, he said, had come at the end, when one of the female guests was saying good-bye to her hostess.

"What an unusual evening," she had said. "Everything was cold except the champagne."

Régis quivered with laughter and eased the cork out so carefully that there was nothing but a quiet, effervescent sigh to mark the opening.

He was a large man, dark and fleshy, with the deep blue eyes that are sometimes found, rather surprisingly, in swarthy Provençal faces. Unlike the rest of us in our conventional clothes, he was dressed in a tracksuit—pale grey, trimmed in red, with *Le Coq Sportif* embroidered on the chest. His shoes were equally athletic—complicated creations with multicolored layers of rubber sole, more suitable for a marathon than an evening under the dinner table. He saw me looking at them.

"I must be comfortable when I eat," he said, "and nothing is more comfortable than the clothing of athletes. Also" . . .

he pulled his waistband in and out . . . "one can make a place for the second helping. *Très important*." He grinned, and raised his glass. "To England and the English, as long as they keep their cooking to themselves."

Most of the French people we had met were more or less disdainful of *la cuisine Anglaise* without knowing very much about it. But Régis was different. He had made a study of the English and their eating habits, and during dinner he told us exactly where we went wrong.

It starts, he said, at babyhood. The English baby is fed on bland mush, the kind of pabulum one would give to an undiscriminating chicken, *sans caractère, sans goût*. The French infant, however, even before he has teeth, is treated as a human being with taste buds. As evidence, Régis described the menu offered by Gallia, one of the leading baby food manufacturers. It included brains, fillet of sole, *poulet au riz*, tuna, lamb, liver, veal, Gruyère, soups, fruits, vegetables, puddings of quince and bilberry, *crème caramel*, and *fromage blanc*. All of that and more, said Régis, before the child is 18 months old. You see? The palate is being educated. He paused to lower his head over the chicken in tarragon that had just been put in front of him, inhaled, and adjusted the napkin tucked in the collar of his tracksuit.

He then moved on a few years to the point where the budding gourmet goes to school. Did I remember, he asked me, the food I ate at school? I did indeed, with horror, and he nodded understandingly. English school food, he said, is famously horrible. It is grey and *triste* and mysterious, because you never know what it is you're trying to force yourself to eat. But at the village school attended by his five-year-old daughter, the menu for the week is posted on the notice board, so that meals won't be duplicated at home, and each day there is a three-course lunch. Yesterday, for instance, little Mathilde had eaten a celery salad with a slice of ham and cheese *quiche, riz aux saucisses*, and baked bananas. *Voilà!* The palate continues its education. And so it is inevitable that the French adult has a better appreciation of food, and higher expectations, than the English adult.

Régis sliced a fat pear to eat with his cheese, and pointed his knife at me as if I had been responsible for the badly educated English palate. We now come, he said, to restaurants. He shook his head sorrowfully, and placed his hands wide apart on the table, palms upward, fingers bunched together. Here—the left hand was raised a couple of inches—you have *le pub*. Picturesque, but with food only as a sponge for beer. And here—the other hand was raised higher—you have expensive restaurants for *hommes d'affaires* whose companies pay for what they eat.

And in the middle? Régis looked at the space between his two hands, the corners of his mouth turned down, an expression of despair on his plump face. In the middle is a desert, *rien*. Where are your *bistrots*? Where are your honest *bourgeois* restaurants? Where are your *relais routiers*? Who but a rich man can afford to go out and eat well in England?

I would have liked to argue with him, but I didn't have the ammunition. He was asking questions that we had asked ourselves many times when we were living in the country in England, where the choice was limited to pubs or tarted-up restaurants with delusions of adequacy and London-sized bills. In the end, we had given up, defeated by microwaved specialities and table wine served in ceremonial baskets by charming but incompetent people called Justin or Emma.

Régis stirred his coffee and hesitated for a moment between Calvados and the tall, frosted bottle of *eau de vie de poires* from Manguin in Avignon. I asked him about his favorite restaurants.

"There is always Les Baux," he said. "But the bill is spectacular." He shook his hand from the wrist as if he had burnt his fingers. "It is not for every day. In any case, I prefer places more modest, less international."

In other words, I said, more French.

"*Voilà!*" said Régis. "More French, and where one finds a *rapport qualité–prix*, a value for money. That still exists here, you know, at every level. I have made a study of it." I was sure he had, but he still hadn't given me any names apart from Les Baux, which we were saving until we won the national lottery. How about something a little less grand?

"If you like," said Régis, "it would be amusing to have lunch at two restaurants, very different, but both of a high standard." He poured another nip of Calvados—"for the digestion"—and leaned back in his chair. "Yes," he said, "it will be my contribution to the education of *les Anglais*. Your wife will come, *naturellement*." Of course she would come. The wife of Régis, unfortunately, would not be with us. She would be at home, preparing dinner.

He told us to meet him in Avignon, at one of the cafés in the Place de l'Horloge, when he would reveal the first of his two chosen restaurants. He kissed his fingers noisily over the phone, and advised us not to make any arrangements for the afternoon. After a lunch such as the one he planned, nothing more energetic than a *digestif* would be possible.

We watched him as he billowed toward us across the *place*, moving lightly for such a big man in his black basketball boots and what must have been his most formal tracksuit, also black, with UCLA in pink letters on one meaty thigh. He was carrying a shopping basket and a zip-striped handbag of the kind that French executives use for their personal documents and emergency bottles of *eau de cologne*.

He ordered a glass of champagne and showed us some baby melons, no bigger than apples, that he had just bought in the market. They were to be scooped clean, dosed with a ratafia of grape juice and brandy, and left for 24 hours in the refrigerator. They would taste, so Régis assured us, like a young girl's lips. I had never thought of melons in quite that way before, but I put that down to the shortcomings of my English education.

With a final fond squeeze of their tiny green bottoms, Régis put the melons back in the basket and addressed himself to the business of the day.

"We are going," he said, "to Hiély, just over there in the Rue de la République. Pierre Hiély is a prince of the kitchen. He has been at the ovens for twenty, twenty-five years, and he is a prodigy. Never a disappointing meal." Régis wagged his finger at us. *"Jamais!"*

Apart from a small framed menu at the entrance, Hiély makes no attempt to entice the passerby. The narrow door opens into a narrow corridor, and the restaurant is up a flight of stairs. It's a big room with a handsome herringbone parquet floor, decorated in sober colors, tables spaced comfortably far apart. Here, as in most good French restaurants, the solitary client is treated as well as a party of half a dozen. Tables for one are not wedged into a dead corner as an afterthought, but in windowed alcoves overlooking the street. These were already occupied by men in suits, presumably local businessmen who had to snatch their lunch in a mere two hours before going back to the office. The other clients, all French except for us, were less formally dressed.

I remembered being turned away from a restaurant with airs and graces in Somerset because I wasn't wearing a tie, something that has never happened to me in France. And here was Régis, resembling a refugee from the weight watchers' gym in his tracksuit, being welcomed like a king by Madame as he checked in his shopping basket and asked if Monsieur Hiély was on form. Madame allowed herself a smile. *"Oui, comme toujours."*

Régis beamed and rubbed his hands together as we were shown to our table, sniffing the air to see if he could pick up any hints of what was to come. In another of his favorite restaurants, he said, the chef allowed him into the kitchen, and he would close his eyes and select his meal by nose.

He tucked his napkin under his chin and murmured to the waiter. *"Un grand?"* said the waiter. *"Un grand,"* said Régis, and sixty seconds later a large glass pitcher, opaque with cold, was placed in front of us. Régis became professorial; our lesson was about to commence. "In a serious restaurant," he said, "one can always have confidence in the house wines. This is a Côtes-du-Rhône. *Santé.*" He took a gargantuan sip and chewed on it for a few seconds before expressing his satisfaction with a sigh.

*"Bon.* Now, you will permit some advice on the menu? As you see, there is a *dégustation* which is delicious, but possibly a little long for a simple lunch. There is a fine choice *à la carte.* But we must remember why we are here." He looked at us over the top of his wine glass. "It is so that you can experience the *rapport qualité–prix.* Any good chef can feed you well for 500 francs a head. The test is how well you can

eat for less than half that, and so I propose the short menu. *D'accord?"*

We were *d'accord.* The short menu was enough to make a Michelin inspector salivate, let alone two English amateurs like us. With some difficulty, we made our decisions while Régis hummed quietly over the wine list. He beckoned over the waiter for another reverent exchange of murmurs.

"I break my own rule," said Régis. "The red house wine is, of course, faultless. But here," he tapped the page in front of him, "here is a little treasure, *pas cher,* from the Domaine de Trévallon, north of Aix. Not too heavy, but with the character of a big wine. You will see."

As one waiter departed for the cellar, another arrived with a snack to keep us going until the first course was ready— small ramekins, each filled with a creamy *brandade* of cod, topped with a tiny, perfectly fried quail's egg and garnished with black olives. Régis was silent with concentration, and I could hear the moist creak of corks being eased from bottles, the low voices of the waiters, and the subdued chink of knives and forks against thin china plates.

Régis wiped his ramekin clean with a scrap of bread—he used bread like an implement to guide food to his fork—and poured some more wine. *"Ça commence bien, eh?"*

And lunch continued as it had begun, *bien.* A flan of *foie gras* in a thick but delicate sauce of wild mushrooms and asparagus was followed by homemade sausages of Sisteron lamb and sage with a *confiture* of sweet red onions and, in a separate flat dish, a gratin of potato that was no thicker than my napkin, a single crisp layer that dissolved on the tongue.

Now that the edge was off his appetite, Régis was able to resume conversation, and he told us about a literary project that he was considering. He had read in the paper that an international center for Marquis de Sade studies was to be opened during the Avignon arts festival. There would also be an opera performed in honor of *le divin marquis*, and a champagne named after him. These events indicated a renewal of public interest in the old monster and, as Régis pointed out, even sadists have to eat. His idea was to give them their very own recipes.

"I shall call it *Cuisine Sadique: The Marquis de Sade's Cookbook*," he said, "and all the ingredients will be beaten, whipped, trussed, crushed, or seared. There will be many painful words used in the descriptions and so I am sure it will be a *succès fou* in Germany. But you must advise me about England." He leaned forward and his voice became confidential. "Is it true that all men who have been to English public schools are fond of . . . *comment dirais-je* . . . a little punishment?" He sipped his wine and raised his eyebrows. "*Le spanking, non?*"

I said that he should try to find a publisher who had been to Eton, and to devise a recipe that included flogging.

"*Qu'est-ce que ça veut dire*, flogging?"

I explained as best I could, and Régis nodded. "*Ah, oui.* Maybe with a breast of chicken one could do flogging, with a very sharp sauce of *citron*. *Très bien.*" He made notes in a small, neat hand on the back of his checkbook. "*Un bestseller, c'est certain.*"

The bestseller was put aside while Régis took us on a tour of the cheese trolley, stopping frequently en route to instruct us and the waiter on the correct balance between hard and soft, *piquant* and *doux*, fresh and aged. He chose five out of the twenty or more cheeses on offer, and congratulated himself on having had the foresight to predict that we would need a second bottle of Trévallon.

I bit into a peppery goat's cheese, and felt a prickle of perspiration on the bridge of my nose under my glasses. The wine slipped down like silk. It had been a wonderful meal, completely satisfying, served with easy efficiency by highly professional waiters. I told Régis how much I had enjoyed it, and he looked at me with surprise.

"But we haven't finished. There is more." A plate of tiny meringues was put on the table. "Ah," he said, "these are to help us prepare for the desserts. They taste like clouds." He ate two in quick succession, and looked around to make sure the dessert waiter hadn't forgotten us.

A second vehicle, larger and more loaded than the cheese trolley, was wheeled carefully up to the table and parked in front of us. It would have caused deep distress to anyone with a weight problem: bowls of fresh cream and *fromage blanc*, truffled chocolate cake covered in more chocolate, pastries, *vacherins*, rum-soaked *babas*, tarts, sorbets, *fraises des bois*, fruits bathed in syrup—it was all too much for Régis to take in while sitting down, and so he got up and prowled around to make sure that nothing was hiding behind the fresh raspberries.

My wife chose ice cream made with local honey, and the waiter took a spoon from its pot of hot water, scooping the ice cream from the bowl with a graceful roll of the wrist. He stood with plate and spoon, poised for further instructions. *"Avec ça?"*

*"C'est tout, merci."*

Régis made up for my wife's restraint with what he called a selection of textures—chocolate, pastry, fruit, and cream —and pushed the sleeves of his tracksuit up above his elbows. Even on him, the pace was beginning to tell.

I ordered coffee. There was a moment of shocked silence while Régis and the waiter looked at me.

"*Pas de dessert?*" said the waiter.

"It's part of the menu," said Régis.

Both of them seemed worried, as though I had suddenly been taken ill, but it was no good. Hiély had won by a knock-out.

The bill was 230 francs a head, plus wine. It was astonishing value for the money. For 280 francs, we could have had the long *menu dégustation*. Maybe next time, said Régis. Yes, maybe next time, after three days of fasting and a 10-mile walk.


The second half of the gastronomy course was postponed to allow Régis to take his annual cure. For two weeks, he ate sparingly—three-course meals instead of his customary five courses—and soaked his liver in mineral water. This was essential for the rejuvenation of his system.

To celebrate the end of the *régime*, he proposed lunch at a restaurant called *Le Bec Fin*, and told me to meet him there no later than quarter to twelve to be sure of a table. I should be able to find it easily enough, he said. It was on the RN 7 at Orgon, recognizable by the number of trucks in the car park. It would not be necessary to wear a jacket. My wife, wiser than I in the heat, decided to stay and guard the pool.

By the time I arrived, the restaurant was completely surrounded by trucks, their cabins jammed tight against tree trunks to take advantage of the scraps of shade. Half a dozen car transporters were drawn up, nose to tail, on the hard shoulder opposite. A latecomer cruised off the road, squeezed into a narrow strip next to the dining room, and stopped with a hydraulic hiss of relief. The driver stood for a moment in the sun and eased his back, the shape of his arched spine repeated exactly in the generous swell of his stomach.

The bar was full and loud; big men, big moustaches, big bellies, big voices. Régis, standing in a corner with a glass, looked almost svelte by comparison. He was dressed for July, in running shorts and a sleeveless vest, his handbag looped over one wrist.

"*Salut!*" He tidied up the last of his *pastis* and ordered two more. "*C'est autre chose, eh? Pas comme Hiély.*"

It could hardly have been less like Hiély. Behind the bar, damp from the wet cloth that Madame was using in great swoops, was a notice that said DANGER! RISQUE D'ENGUE-LADE!—watch out for a slanging match. Through the open door that led to the lavatory I could see another notice: DOUCHE, 8 FRANCS. From an invisible kitchen came the clatter of saucepans and the hot tang of simmering garlic.

I asked Régis how he felt after his period of self-imposed restraint, and he turned sideways to show off his belly in profile. Madame behind the bar looked up as she flicked the froth from a glass of beer with a wooden spatula. She inspected the long curve that started just below Régis's chest and ended overhanging the waistband of his running shorts. "When's it due?" she asked.

We went through to the dining room and found an empty table at the back. A small dark woman with a pretty smile and an undisciplined black brassiere strap that resisted her efforts at adjustment came to tell us the rules. For the first course, we should serve ourselves from the buffet, and then there was a choice of beef, calamari, or *poulet fermier*. The wine list was brief—red or *rosé*, which came in a liter bottle with a plastic stopper and a bowl of ice cubes. The waitress wished us *bon appétit*, performed a little bob that was almost a curtsy, hitched up her bra strap, and went off with our order.

Régis opened the wine with mock ceremony and sniffed the plastic stopper. "From the Var," he said, "*sans prétention, mais honnête.*" He took a sip and drew it slowly through his front teeth. "*Il est bon.*"

We joined the line of truck drivers at the buffet. They were achieving small miracles of balance, piling their plates with an assortment that was a meal in itself: two kinds of *saucisson*, hard-boiled eggs in mayonnaise, moist tangles of *celeri rémoulade*, saffron-colored rice with red peppers, tiny peas and sliced carrots, a pork *terrine* in pastry, *rillettes*, cold squid, wedges of fresh melon. Régis grumbled at the size of the plates and took two, resting the second with a waiter's expertise on the inside of his forearm as he plundered each of the serving bowls.

There was a moment of panic when we returned to the table. Impossible even to think of eating without bread. Where was the bread? Régis caught the eye of our waitress and raised a hand to his mouth, making biting motions with bunched fingers against his thumb. She pulled a *baguette* from the brown paper sack standing in the corner and ran it through the guillotine with a speed that made me wince. The slices of bread were still reflating after the pressure of the blade when they were put in front of us.

I told Régis that he might be able to use the bread guillotine in his Marquis de Sade cookbook, and he paused in mid-*saucisson*.

"*Peut-être*," he said, "but one must be careful, above all with the American market. Have you heard about the difficulty with the champagne?"

Apparently, so Régis had read in a newspaper article, the champagne of the Marquis de Sade had not been welcome in the land of the free because of its label, which was decorated with a drawing of the top half of a well-endowed young woman. This might not have been a problem, except that a sharp-eyed guardian of public morality had noticed the position of the young woman's arms. It was not explicit, not depicted on the label itself, but there was the merest hint of a suggestion that the arms *might have been pinioned*.

*Oh là là.* Imagine the effect of such degeneracy on the youth of the country, not to mention some of the more susceptible adults. The fabric of society would be ripped asunder, and there would be champagne and bondage parties all the way from Santa Barbara to Boston. God only knows what might happen in Connecticut.

Régis resumed eating, his paper napkin tucked in the top of his vest. At the next table, a man on his second course unbuttoned his shirt to let the air circulate, and revealed a stupendous mahogany paunch with a gold crucifix suspended neatly between furry bosoms. Very few people were picking at their food, and I wondered how they could manage to stay alert at the wheel of a 50-ton truck all afternoon.

We wiped our empty plates with bread, and then wiped our knives and forks the same way. Our waitress came with three oval stainless steel dishes, burning hot. On the first were two halves of a chicken in gravy; on the second, tomatoes stuffed with garlic and parsley; on the third, tiny potatoes that had been roasted with herbs. Régis sniffed everything before serving me.

"What do the *routiers* in England eat?"

Two eggs, bacon, chips, sausages, baked beans, a fried slice, a pint of tea.

"No wine? No cheese? No desserts?"

I didn't think so, although my *routier* experience had been very limited. I said they might stop at a pub, but the law about drinking and driving was severe.

Régis poured some more wine. "Here in France," he said, "I am told that one is permitted an *apéritif*, half a bottle of wine, and a *digestif*."

I said that I had read somewhere about the accident rate in France being higher than anywhere in Europe, and twice as high as in America.

"That has nothing to do with alcohol," said Régis. "It is a question of national *esprit*. We are impatient, and we love speed. *Malheureusement*, not all of us are good drivers." He mopped his plate and changed the conversation back to more comfortable ground.

"This is a high quality chicken, don't you think?" He picked up a bone from his plate and tested it between his teeth. "Good strong bones. He has been raised properly, in the open air. The bones of an industrial chicken are like *papier-mâché*."

It was indeed a fine chicken, firm but tender, and perfectly cooked, like the potatoes and the garlicky tomatoes. I said that I was surprised not only at the standard of cooking, but the abundance of the portions. And I was sure the bill wasn't going to be painful.

Régis cleaned his knife and fork again, and signaled the waitress to bring cheese.

"It's simple," he said. "The *routier* is a good client, very faithful. He will always drive the extra fifty kilometers to eat well at a correct price, and he will tell other *routiers* that the restaurant is worth a detour. As long as the standard is maintained, there will never be empty tables." He waved a forkful of Brie at the dining room. *"Tu vois?"*

I looked around, and gave up counting, but there must have been close to a hundred men eating, and maybe thirty more in the bar.

"It is a solid business. But if the chef becomes mean, or starts cheating, or the service is too slow, the *routiers* will go. Within a month, there will be nobody, a few tourists."

There was a rumble outside, and the room became sunny as a truck pulled away from its place next to the window. Our neighbor with the crucifix put on his sunglasses to eat his dessert, a bowl of three different ice creams.

*"Glaces, crème caramel, ou flan?"* The black bra strap was hitched into place, only to slip out again as the waitress cleared our table.

Régis ate his *crème caramel* with soft sucking sounds of enjoyment, and reached for the ice cream that he had ordered for me. I'd never make a *routier*. I didn't have the capacity.

It was still early, well before two, and the room was beginning to clear. Bills were being paid—huge fingers opening dainty little purses to take out carefully folded banknotes, the waitress bobbing and smiling and hitching as she brought change and wished the men *bonne route*.

We had double-strength coffee, black and scalding beneath its scum of brown bubbles, and Calvados in rotund little glasses. Régis tipped his glass until its rounded side touched the table and the gold liquid exactly reached the rim—the old way, he said, of judging a true measure.

The bill for us both was 140 francs. Like our lunch at Hiély, it was wonderful value for the money, and I had only one regret as we went outside and felt the hammer of the sun. If I'd brought a towel, I could have had a shower.

"Well," said Régis, "that will hold me until tonight." We shook hands, and he threatened me with a *bouillabaisse* in Marseille on our next educational outing.

I went back into the bar for some more coffee, and to see if I could rent a towel.

# Fashion and Sporting Notes from the Ménerbes Dog Show

The Ménerbes stadium, a level field among the vines, is normally the setting for loud and enthusiastic matches played by the village soccer team. There might be a dozen cars parked under the pine trees, and supporters divide their attention between the game and their copious picnics. But for one day a year, usually the second Sunday in June, the *stade* is transformed. Bunting, in the Provençal blood and guts colors of red and yellow, is strung across the forest paths. An overgrown hollow is cleared to provide extra parking, and a screen of split bamboo *canisse* is erected along the side of the road so that passersby can't watch the proceedings without paying their 15-franc entrance fee. Because this is, after all, a major local event, a mixture of Crufts dog show and Ascot, the *Foire aux Chiens de Ménerbes*.

This year it started early and noisily. Just after seven, we were opening the doors and shutters and enjoying the one morning of the week when our neighbor's tractor stays in bed. The birds were singing, the sun was shining, the valley was still. Peace, perfect peace. And then, half a mile away over the hill, the *chef d'animation* began his loudspeaker trials with an electronic yelp that ricochetted through the mountains and must have woken up half the Lubéron.

"*Allo allo, un, deux, trois, bonjour Ménerbes!*" He paused to cough. It sounded like an avalanche. "*Bon,*" he said, "*ça marche.*" He turned the volume down a notch and tuned in to Radio Monte Carlo. A quiet morning was out of the question.

We had decided to wait until the afternoon before going to the show. By then the preliminary heats would be over, mongrels and dogs of dubious behavior would be weeded out, a good lunch would have been had by all, and the best noses in the business would be ready to do battle in the field trials.

On the stroke of noon, the loudspeaker went dead and the background chorus of barking was reduced to the occasional plaintive serenade of a hound expressing unrequited lust or boredom. The valley was otherwise silent. For two hours, dogs and everything else took second place to stomachs.

"*Tout le monde a bien mangé?*" bellowed the loudspeaker. The microphone amplified a half-suppressed belch. "*Bon. Alors, on recommence.*" We started off along the track that leads to the *stade*.

A shaded clearing above the car park had been taken over by an elite group of dealers who were selling specialist breeds, or hybrids, dogs of particular and valuable skills—trackers of the wild *sanglier*, hunters of rabbits, detectors of quail and woodcock. They were strung like a living necklace on chains beneath the trees, twitching in their sleep. Their owners looked like gypsies: slender, dark men with gold teeth flashing through dense black moustaches.

One of them noticed my wife admiring a wrinkled black-and-tan specimen who was scratching his ear lazily with a huge back paw. *"Il est beau, eh?"* said the owner, and shone his teeth at us. He bent down and took hold of a handful of loose skin behind the dog's head. "He comes in his own *sac à main*. You can carry him home." The dog raised his eyes in resignation at having been born with a coat several sizes too big, and his paw stopped in mid-scratch. My wife shook her head. "We already have three dogs." The man shrugged, and let the skin drop in heavy folds. "Three, four—what's the difference?"

A little further along the track, the sales presentation became more sophisticated. On top of a hutch made from plywood and wire netting, a printed card announced: *Fox-terrier, imbattable aux lapins et aux truffes. Un vrai champion.* The champion, a short, stout brown and white dog, was snoring on his back, all four stumpy legs in the air. We barely slowed down, but it was enough for the owner. *"Il est beau, eh?"* He woke the dog up and lifted him from the hutch. *"Régardez!"* He put the dog on the ground and took a slice of sausage from the tin plate that was next to the empty wine bottle on the bonnet of his van.

*"Chose extraordinaire,"* he said. "When these dogs are hunting, nothing will distract them. They become *rigide*. You press the back of the head and the rear legs will rise into the air." He put the sausage down, covered it with leaves and let the dog root for it, then placed his foot on the back of the dog's head and pressed. The dog snarled and bit him on the ankle. We moved on.

The *stade* was recovering from lunch, the small folding tables under the trees still scattered with scraps of food and empty glasses. A spaniel had managed to jump onto one of the tables and clear it up, and was asleep with its chin in a plate. Spectators moved with the slowness that comes from a full belly and a hot day, picking their teeth as they inspected the offerings of the local arms dealer.

On a long trestle table, 30 or 40 guns were laid neatly in a row, including the new sensation that was attracting great interest. It was a matte black pump-action riot gun. If there were ever to be a mass uprising of bloodthirsty killer rabbits in the forest, this was undoubtedly the machine one needed to keep them in order. But some of the other items puzzled us. What would a hunter do with brass knuckle-dusters and sharpened steel throwing stars, as used, so a hand-printed card said, by the Japanese Ninja? It was a selection that contrasted violently with the rubber bones and squeaky toys on sale at English dog shows.

It is always possible, when dogs and owners gather together en masse, to find living proof of the theory that they grow to resemble each other. In other parts of the world, this may be confined to physical characteristics—ladies and basset hounds with matching jowls, whiskery little men with bushy eyebrows and scotties, emaciated ex-jockeys with their whippets. But, France being France, there seems to be a deliberate effort to emphasize the resemblance through fashion, by choosing *ensembles* that turn dog and owner into coordinated accessories.

There were two clear winners in the Ménerbes *Concours d'Élégance*, perfectly complementary and visibly very pleased with the attention they were attracting from less modish spectators. In the ladies' section, a blonde with a white shirt, white shorts, white cowboy boots, and a white miniature poodle on a white lead picked her way fastidiously through the dust to sip, with little finger cocked, an Orangina at the bar. The ladies of the village, sensibly dressed in skirts and flat shoes, looked at her with the same critical interest they usually reserve for cuts of meat at the butcher's.

The male entries were dominated by a thickset man with a waist-high Great Dane. The dog was pure, shiny black. The man wore a tight black T-shirt, even tighter black jeans, and black cowboy boots. The dog wore a heavy chain-link collar. The man wore a necklace like a small hawser, with a medallion that thudded against his sternum with every step, and a similarly important bracelet. By some oversight, the dog wasn't wearing a bracelet, but they made a virile pair as they posed on the high ground. The man gave the impression of having to control his massive beast by brute force, yanking on the collar and growling. The dog, as placid as Great Danes normally are, had no idea he was supposed to be vicious or restive, and observed smaller dogs passing underneath him with polite interest.

We were wondering how long the Great Dane's good humor would last before he ate one of the tiny dogs that clustered like flies around his back legs when we were ambushed by Monsieur Mathieu and his tombola tickets. For a mere 10 francs, he was offering us a chance to win one of the sporting and gastronomic treasures donated by local tradesmen: a mountain bike, a microwave oven, a shotgun, or a *maxi saucisson*. I was relieved that puppies weren't among the prizes. Monsieur Mathieu leered. "You never know what might be in the *saucisson*," he said. And then, seeing the horror on my wife's face, he patted her. *"Non, non. Je rigole."*

In fact, there were enough puppies on display to make a mountain of *saucissons*. They lay or squirmed in piles under almost every tree, on blankets, in cardboard cartons, in home-made kennels, and on old sweaters. It was a testing time as we went from one furry, multilegged heap to the next. My wife is highly susceptible to anything with four feet and a wet nose, and the sales tactics of the owners were shameless. At the slightest sign of interest they would pluck a puppy from the pile and thrust it into her arms, where it would promptly go to sleep. *"Voilà! Comme il est content!"* I could see her weakening by the minute.

We were saved by the loudspeaker introducing the expert who was to give the commentary on the field trials. He was in *tenue de chasse*—khaki cap, shirt, and trousers—with a deep tobacco voice. He was unused to speaking into a microphone and, being Provençal, he was unable to keep his hands still. Thus his explanation came and went in intermittent snatches as he pointed the microphone helpfully at various parts of the field while his words disappeared into the breeze.

The competitors were lined up at the far end, half a dozen pointers and two mud-colored dogs of impenetrable ancestry. Small clumps of brushwood had been placed at random around the field. These were the *bosquets* in which the game —a live quail that was held aloft by the quail handler for inspection—was to be hidden.

The *chasseur*'s microphone technique improved enough for us to hear him explain that the quail would be tethered in a different *bosquet* for each competitor, and that it would not be killed (unless it was scared to death) by the dogs. They would simply indicate the hiding place, and the fastest find would win.

The quail was hidden, and the first competitor unleashed. He passed by two clumps with barely a sniff and then, still yards away from the third, stiffened and stopped.

*"Aha! Il est fort, ce chien,"* boomed the *chasseur*. The dog looked up for a second, distracted by the noise, before con-

tinuing his approach. He was now walking in slow motion, placing one paw on the ground with exaggerated care before lifting another, his neck and head stretched toward the *bosquet*, unwavering despite the *chasseur*'s admiring comments about his concentration and the delicacy of his movements.

Three feet away from the petrified quail, the dog froze, one front paw raised, with head, neck, back, and tail in a perfect straight line.

"*Tiens! Bravo!*" said the *chasseur*, and started to clap, forgetting that he had a microphone in one hand. The owner retrieved his dog, and the two of them returned to the starting point in a triumphant competition trot. The official time-keeper, a lady in high heels and an elaborate black and white dress with flying panels, marked the dog's performance on a clipboard. The quail handler dashed out to replant the quail in another *bosquet*, and the second contestant was sent on his way.

He went immediately to the *bosquet* recently vacated by the quail, and stopped.

"*Beh oui,*" said the *chasseur*, "the scent is still strong there. But wait." We waited. The dog waited. Then he got tired of waiting, and possibly annoyed at being sent out on a fool's errand. He lifted his leg on the *bosquet* and went back to his owner.

The quail handler moved the unfortunate quail to a new hiding place, but it must have been a particularly pungent bird, because dog after dog stopped at one or the other of the empty clumps, head cocked and paw tentatively raised, before giving up. An old man standing next to us explained the problem. The quail, he said, should have been walked on its lead from one *bosquet* to the next so that it left a scent. How else could a dog be expected to find him? Dogs are not *clair-*

*voyants*. The old man shook his head and made soft clicking noises of disapproval with his tongue against his teeth.

The final competitor, one of the mud-colored dogs, had been showing signs of increasing excitement as he watched the others being sent off, whining with impatience and tugging at his lead. When his turn came, it was obvious that he had misunderstood the rules of the competition. Disregarding the quail and the *bosquets*, he completed a circuit of the *stade* at full speed before racing into the vines, followed by his bellowing owner. *"Oh là là,"* said the *chasseur. "Une locomotive. Tant pis."*

Later, as the sun dipped and the shadows grew longer, Monsieur Dufour, president of *Le Philosophe* hunting club, presented the prizes before settling down with his colleagues to a gigantic paella. Long after dark, we could hear the distant sounds of laughter and clinking glasses and, somewhere in the vines, the man shouting for his mud-colored dog.

# Inside the Belly
# of Avignon

Place Pie, in the center of Avignon, is a forlorn sight in the dingy grey moments that come just before dawn. It is an architectural mongrel of a square, with two sides of seedy but elegant old buildings looking across at a hideous monument to modern town planning. A graduate of the *béton armé* school of construction has been given a free hand, and he has made the worst of it.

Benches, crude slabs, have been dumped around a central eyesore. On those benches, the weary sightseer can rest and contemplate a second, much more imposing eyesore, three stained concrete stories that on weekdays are crammed with cars by eight in the morning. The reason for the cars, and the reason I was in the Place Pie in time to see dawn's rosy flush come up on the concrete, is that the best food in Avignon is displayed and sold under the car park, in *Les Halles*.

I arrived there a few minutes before six and parked in one of the few free places on the second level. Below me on the *place* I saw two derelicts with skin the same color as the bench they were sitting on. They were sharing a liter of red wine, taking turns swigging from the bottle. A *gendarme* came up to them and gestured to them to move on, then stood with his hands on his hips, watching. They walked in the slouched, defeated way of men with nothing to hope for and nowhere to go, and sat on the pavement on the other side of the *place*. The *gendarme* shrugged and turned away.

The contrast between the quiet, dull emptiness of the *place* and the interior of *Les Halles* was sudden and total. On one side of the door was a town still asleep; on the other, bright lights and bright colors, pandemonium and shouting and laughter, a working day in full and noisy swing.

I had to jump aside to avoid collision with a trolley piled to head height with crates of peaches, pushed by a man chanting "*Klaxon! Klaxon!*" as he careered round the corner. Other trolleys were behind him, their loads swaying. I looked for somewhere to escape from high-velocity fruit and vegetables, and made a dash for a sign that read *buvette*. If I was going to be run over, I would rather the tragedy occurred at a bar.

Jacky and Isabelle, so the sign said, were the owners, and they were in a state of siege. The bar was so crowded that three men were reading the same newspaper, and all the tables nearby were taken up with the first sitting for breakfast, or possibly lunch. It was difficult to tell by looking at the food which meal was being eaten. *Croissants* were being dipped into thick, steaming cups of *café crème* next to tumblers of red wine and sausage sandwiches as long as a forearm, or beer and crusty squares of warm pizza. I felt a twinge of longing for the breakfast of champions, the half-pint of red wine and the sausage sandwich, but drinking at dawn is the reward for working all night. I ordered coffee, and tried to see some semblance of order in the surrounding chaos.

*Les Halles* takes up an area perhaps seventy yards square, and very few inches are wasted. Three main passageways separate the *étaux*, stalls of varying sizes, and at that time in the morning it was hard to imagine customers being able to reach them. Crates, mangled cardboard boxes, and wispy clumps of paper straw were stacked high in front of many of the counters, and the floor was garnished with casualties— lettuce leaves, squashed tomatoes, errant *haricots*—that had been unable to cling on during the last breakneck stage of delivery.

The stallholders, too busy writing up the day's prices and arranging their produce to spare five minutes for a visit to the bar, bellowed for coffee, which was served to them by Isabelle's waitress, an acrobatic girl over the crates and a steady hand with her tray. She even managed to keep her footing in the high-risk zone of the fishsellers, where the floor was slick with the ice that men with raw, nicked hands and rubber aprons were shovelling onto the steel display shelves.

It made a noise like gravel on glass, and there was another, more painful sound that cut through the hubbub as the butchers sawed at bones and severed tendons with decisive, dangerously fast chops of their cleavers. I hoped for their fingers' sake that they hadn't had wine for breakfast.

After half an hour it was safe to leave the bar. The piles of crates had been removed, the trolleys parked; the traffic was on legs now instead of wheels. An army of brooms had whisked away the scraps of fallen vegetables, prices had been marked on spiked plastic labels, tills unlocked, coffee drunk. *Les Halles* was open for business.

I have never seen so much fresh food and so much variety in such a confined space. I counted fifty stalls, many of them entirely devoted to a single speciality. There were two stalls

selling olives—just olives—in every conceivable style of prep-
aration: olives *à la grecque*, olives in herb-flavored oil, olives
mixed with scarlet shards of pimento, olives from Nyons,
olives from Les Baux, olives that looked like small black plums
or elongated green grapes. They were lined up in squat
wooden tubs, gleaming as though each one had been individ-
ually polished. At the end of the line were the only nonolives
to be seen, a barrel of anchovies from Collioure, packed in
tighter than any sardines, sharp and salty when I leaned down
to smell them. Madame behind the counter told me to try
one, with a plump black olive. Did I know how to make
*tapenade*, the olive and anchovy paste? A pot of that every day
and I'd live to be a hundred.

Another stall, another specialist: anything with feathers.
Pigeons, plucked and trussed, capons, breasts of duck and
thighs of duckling, three different members of the chicken
aristocracy, with the supreme chickens, the *poulets de Bresse*,
wearing their red, white, and blue labels like medals. *Lé-
galement contrôlée*, said the labels, by the *Comité Interprofes-
sionnel de la Volaille de Bresse*. I could imagine the chosen
chickens receiving their decorations from a dignified committee member, almost certainly with the traditional kiss on
each side of the beak.

And then there were fish, laid out gill to gill on a row of
stalls that extended along the length of one wall, 40 yards or
more of glistening scales and still-bright eyes. Banks of
crushed ice, smelling of the sea, separated the squid from
the blood-darkened tuna, the *rascasses* from the *loups de mer*,
the cod from the skate. Pyramids of clams, of the molluscs
called *seiches*, of winkles, tiny grey shrimp, and monster *gam-
bas*, fish for *friture*, fish for *soupe*, lobsters the color of dark
steel, jolts of yellow coming from the dishes of fresh lemons

on the counter, deft hands with long thin knives cutting and gutting, the squelch of rubber boots on the wet stone floor.

It was coming up to seven o'clock, and the first housewives were starting to investigate, with prods and squeezes, what they would be cooking that night. The market opens at 5:30, and the first half-hour is officially reserved for the *commerçants* and restaurant owners, but I couldn't see anyone being courageous enough to stand in the way of a determined Avignon matron who wanted to get her errands done before six. Shop early for the best, we had often been told, and wait until just before the market closes for the cheapest.

But who could wait that long, surrounded by temptation like this? In one short stretch, I had eaten mentally a dozen times. A bowl of brown free-range eggs turned into a *piperade*, with Bayonne ham from the stall next door and peppers from a few feet further on. That kept me going until I reached the smoked salmon and caviar. But there were the cheeses, the *saucissons*, the rabbit and hare and pork *pâtés*, the great pale scoops of *rillettes*, the *confits de canard*—it would be madness not to try them all.

I very nearly stopped my research to have a picnic in the car park. Everything I needed—including bread from one stall, wine from another—was within 20 yards, fresh and beautifully presented. What could have been a better way to start the day? I realized that my appetite had adjusted to the environment, leapfrogging several hours. My watch said 7:30. My stomach whispered lunch, and to hell with the time. I went to look for the liquid moral support of more coffee.

There are three bars in *Les Halles*—Jacky and Isabelle, Cyrille and Evelyne, and, the most dangerous of the three, *Chez Kiki*, where they start serving champagne long before most people get up. I saw two burly men toasting each other, their *flûtes* of champagne held delicately between thick fingers, earth under their fingernails, earth on their heavy boots. Obviously they had sold their lettuces well that morning.

The passageways and stalls were now crowded with members of the public, shopping with the intent, slightly suspicious expressions of people who were determined to find the most tender, the juiciest, the best. A woman put on her reading glasses to inspect a row of cauliflowers that, to me, looked identical. She picked one up, hefted it in her hand, peered at its tight white head, sniffed it, put it down. Three times she did this before making her choice, and then she watched the stallholder over the top of her glasses to make sure he didn't try to substitute it for a less perfect specimen in the back row. I remembered being told not to handle the vegetables in a London greengrocer's. There would have been outrage here if the same miserable ruling were introduced. No fruits or vegetables are bought without going through trial by touch, and any stallholder who tried to discourage the habit would be pelted out of the market.

Avignon has had its *Halles* since 1910, although the site under the car park has been in operation only since 1973. That was as much information as the girl in the office could give me. When I asked about the amount of food sold in a day or a week, she just shrugged and told me *beaucoup*.

And *beaucoup* there certainly was, being stuffed and piled into every kind of receptacle from battered suitcases to handbags seemingly capable of infinite expansion. An elderly, bandy-legged man in shorts and a crash helmet wheeled his *mobylette* up to the entrance and came in to collect his morning's shopping—a plastic *cageot* of melons and peaches, two enormous baskets straining to contain their contents, a cotton sack with a dozen *baguettes*. He distributed the weight carefully around his machine. The crate of fruit was secured with elastic straps to the rack behind the saddle, the baskets hung on the handlebars, the bread sack slung across his back. As he wheeled his load—enough food for a week—away from the market, he shouted at one of the stallholders, "*À demain!*"

I watched him as he joined the traffic in the Place Pie, the tiny engine of his bike spluttering with effort, his head bent forward over the handlebars and the *baguettes* sticking up like a quiver of fat golden arrows. It was 11:00, and the café opposite the market had tables on the pavement set for lunch.

# Postcards from Summer

It has taken us three years to accept the fact that we live in the same house, but in two different places.

What we think of as normal life starts in September. Apart from market days in the towns, there are no crowds. Traffic on the back roads is sparse during the day—a tractor, a few vans—and virtually nonexistent at night. There is always a table in every restaurant, except perhaps for Sunday lunch. Social life is intermittent and uncomplicated. The baker has bread, the plumber has time for a chat, the postman has time for a drink. After the first deafening weekend of the hunting season, the forest is quiet. Each field has a stooped, reflective figure working among the vines, very slowly up one line, very slowly down the next. The hours between noon and two are dead.

And then we come to July and August.

We used to treat them as just another two months of the year; hot months, certainly, but nothing that required much adjustment on our part except to make sure that the afternoon included a siesta.

We were wrong. Where we live in July and August is still the Lubéron, but it's not the same Lubéron. It is the Lubéron *en vacances*, and our past efforts to live normally during abnormal times have been miserably unsuccessful. So unsuccessful that we once considered cancelling summer altogether and going somewhere grey and cool and peaceful, like the Hebrides.

But if we did, we would probably miss it, all of it, even the days and incidents that have reduced us to sweating, irritated, overtired zombies. So we have decided to come to terms with the Lubéron in the summer, to do our best to join the rest of the world on holiday and, like them, to send postcards telling distant friends about the wonderful times we are having. Here are a few.


*Saint-Tropez*

*Cherchez les nudistes!* It is open season for nature lovers, and there is likely to be a sharp increase in the number of applicants wishing to join the Saint-Tropez police force.

The mayor, Monsieur Spada, has flown in the face of years of tradition (Saint-Tropez made public nudity famous, after all) and has decreed that in the name of safety and hygiene there will be no more naked sunbathing on the public beaches. "*Le nudisme intégral est interdit*," says Monsieur Spada, and he has empowered the police to seize and arrest any offenders. Well, perhaps not to seize them, but to track them down and fine them 75 francs, or as much as 1500 francs if they have been guilty of creating a public outrage. Exactly where a nudist might keep 1500 francs is a question that is puzzling local residents.

Meanwhile, a defiant group of nudists has set up headquarters in some rocks behind *la plage de la Moutte*. A spokes-woman for the group has said that under no circumstances would bathing suits be worn. Wish you were here.

## The Melon Field

Faustin's brother Jacky, a wiry little man of sixty or so, grows melons in the field opposite the house. It's a large field, but he does all the work himself, and by hand. In the spring I have often seen him out there for six or seven hours, back bent like a hinge, his hoe chopping at the weeds that threaten to strangle his crop. He doesn't spray—who would eat a melon tasting of chemicals?—and I think he must enjoy looking after his land in the traditional way.

Now that the melons are ripening, he comes to the field at 6:00 every morning to pick the ones that are ready. He takes them up to Ménerbes to be packed in shallow wooden crates. From Ménerbes they go to Cavaillon, and from Cavaillon to Avignon, to Paris, everywhere. It amuses Jacky to think of people in smart restaurants paying *une petite fortune* for a simple thing like a melon.

If I get up early enough I can catch him before he goes to Ménerbes. He always has a couple of melons that are too ripe to travel, and he sells them to me for a few francs.

As I walk back to the house, the sun clears the top of the mountain and it is suddenly hot on my face. The melons, heavy and satisfying in my hands, are still cool from the night air. We have them for breakfast, fresh and sweet, less than ten minutes after they have been picked.

*Behind the Bar*

There is a point at which a swimming pool ceases to be a luxury and becomes very close to a necessity, and that point is when the temperature hits 100 degrees. Whenever people ask us about renting a house for the summer, we always tell them this, and some of them listen.

Others don't, and within two days of arriving they are on the phone telling us what we told them months before. It's so *hot*, they say. Too hot for tennis, too hot for cycling, too hot for sightseeing, too hot, too hot. Oh, for a pool. You're so lucky.

There is a hopeful pause. Is it my imagination, or can I actually hear the drops of perspiration falling like summer rain on the pages of the telephone directory?

I suppose the answer is to be callous but helpful. There is a public swimming pool near Apt, if you don't mind sharing the water with a few hundred small brown dervishes on their school holidays. There is the Mediterranean, only an hour's drive away; no, with traffic it could take two hours. Make sure you have some bottles of Evian in the car. It wouldn't do to get dehydrated.

Or you could close the shutters against the sun, spend the day in the house, and spring forth refreshed into the evening air. It would be difficult to acquire the souvenir suntan, but at least there would be no chance of heatstroke.

These brutal and unworthy suggestions barely have time to cross my mind before the voice of despair turns into the voice of relief. Of course! We could come over in the morning for a quick dip without disturbing you. Just a splash. You won't even know we've been.

They come at noon, with friends. They swim. They take the sun. Thirst creeps up on them, much to their surprise, and that's why I'm behind the bar. My wife is in the kitchen, making lunch for six. *Vivent les vacances.*

## The Night Walk

The dogs cope with the heat by sleeping through it, stretched out in the courtyard or curled in the shade of the rosemary hedge. They come to life as the pink in the sky is turning to darkness, sniffing the breeze, jostling each other around our feet in their anticipation of a walk. We take the flashlight and follow them into the forest.

It smells of warm pine needles and baked earth, dry and spicy when we step on a patch of thyme. Small, invisible creatures slither away from us and rustle through the leaves of the wild box that grows like a weed.

Sounds carry: *cigales* and frogs, the muffled thump of music through the open window of a faraway house, the clinks and murmurs of dinner drifting up from Faustin's terrace. The hills on the other side of the valley, uninhabited for 10 months a year, are pricked with lights that will be switched off at the end of August.

We get back to the house and take off our shoes, and the warmth of the flagstones is an invitation to swim. A dive into dark water, and then a last glass of wine. The sky is clear except for a jumble of stars; it will be hot again tomorrow. Hot and slow, just like today.

## Knee-deep in Lavender

I had been cutting lavender with a pair of pruning shears and I was making a slow, amateurish job of it, nearly an hour to do fewer than a dozen clumps. When Henriette arrived at the house with a basket of aubergines, I was pleased to have the chance to stop. Henriette looked at the lavender, looked at the pruning shears, and shook her head at the ignorance of her neighbor. Didn't I know how to cut lavender? What was I doing with those pruning shears? Where was my *faucille*?

She went to her van and came back with a blackened sickle, its needle-sharp tip embedded in an old wine cork for safety. It was surprisingly light, and felt sharp enough to shave with. I made a few passes with it in the air, and Henriette shook her head again. Obviously, I needed a lesson.

She hitched up her skirt and attacked the nearest row of lavender, gathering the long stems into a tight bunch with one arm and slicing them off at the bottom with a single smooth pull of the sickle. In five minutes she had cut more than I had in an hour. It looked easy; bend, gather, pull. Nothing to it.

"*Voilà!*" said Henriette. "When I was a little girl in the Basses-Alpes, we had hectares of lavender, and no machines. Everyone used the *faucille*."

She passed it back to me, told me to mind my legs, and went off to join Faustin in the vines.

It wasn't as easy as it looked, and my first effort produced a ragged, uneven clump, more chewed than sliced. I realized that the sickle was made for right-handed lavender cutters, and had to compensate for being left-handed by slicing away from me. My wife came out to tell me to mind my legs. She doesn't trust me with sharp implements, and so she was reassured to see me cutting away from the body. Even with my genius for self-inflicted wounds there seemed to be little risk of amputation.

I had just come to the final clump when Henriette came back. I looked up, hoping for praise, and sliced my index finger nearly through to the bone. There was a great deal of blood, and Henriette asked me if I was giving myself a manicure. I sometimes wonder about her sense of humor. Two days later she gave me a sickle of my very own, and told me that I was forbidden to use it unless I was wearing gloves.

## The Alcoholic Tendencies of Wasps

The Provençal wasp, although small, has an evil sting. He also has an ungallant, hit-and-run method of attack in the swimming pool. He paddles up behind his unsuspecting victim, waits until an arm is raised, and—*tok!*—strikes deep into the armpit. It hurts for several hours, and often causes people who have been stung to dress in protective clothing before they go swimming. This is the local version of the Miss Wet T-shirt contest.

I don't know whether all wasps like water, but here they love it—floating in the shallow end, dozing in the puddles on the flagstones, keeping an eye out for the unguarded armpit and the tender extremity—and after one disastrous day during which not only armpits but inner thighs received direct hits (obviously, some wasps can hold their breath and operate under water), I was sent off to look for wasp traps.

When I found them, in a *droguerie* in the back alleys of Cavaillon, I was lucky enough to find a wasp expert behind the counter. He demonstrated for me the latest model in traps, a plastic descendant of the old glass hanging traps that can sometimes be found in flea markets. It had been specially designed, he said, for use around swimming pools, and could be made irresistible to wasps.

It was in two parts. The base was a round bowl, raised off the ground by three flat supports, with a funnel leading up from the bottom. The top fitted over the lower bowl and prevented wasps who had made their way up the funnel from escaping.

But that, said the wasp expert, was the simple part. More difficult, more subtle, more artistic, was the bait. How does one persuade the wasp to abandon the pleasures of the flesh and climb up the funnel into the trap? What could tempt him away from the pool?

After spending some time in Provence, you learn to expect a brief lecture with every purchase, from an organically grown cabbage (two minutes) to a bed (half an hour or more, depending on the state of your back). For wasp traps, you should allow between 10 and 15 minutes. I sat on the stool in front of the counter and listened.

Wasps, it turned out, like alcohol. Some wasps like it *sucré*, others like it fruity, and there are even those who will crawl anywhere for a drop of *anis*. It is, said the expert, a matter of experimentation, a balancing of flavors and consistencies until one finds the blend that suits the palate of the local wasp population.

He suggested a few basic recipes: sweet vermouth with honey and water, diluted *crème de cassis*, dark beer spiked with *marc*, neat *pastis*. As an added inducement, the funnel can be lightly coated with honey, and a small puddle of water should always be left immediately beneath the funnel.

The expert set up a trap on the counter, and with two fingers imitated a wasp out for a stroll.

He stops, attracted by the puddle of water. The fingers stopped. He approaches the water, and then he becomes aware of something delicious above him. He climbs up the funnel to investigate, he jumps into his cocktail, *et voilà!*— he is unable to get out, being too drunk to crawl back down the funnel. He dies, but he dies happy.

I bought two traps, and tried out the recipes. All of them worked, which leads me to believe that the wasp has a serious drinking problem. And now, if ever a guest is overcome by strong waters, he is described as being as pissed as a wasp.


## *Maladie du Lubéron*

Most of the seasonal ailments of summer, while they may be uncomfortable or painful or merely embarrassing, are at least regarded with some sympathy. A man convalescing after an explosive encounter with one *merguez* sausage too many is not expected to venture back into polite society until his constitution has recovered. The same is true of third-degree sunburn, *rosé* poisoning, scorpion bites, a surfeit of garlic, or the giddiness and nausea caused by prolonged exposure to French bureaucracy. One suffers, but one is allowed to suffer alone and in peace.

There is another affliction, worse than scorpions or rogue sausages, which we have experienced ourselves and seen many times in other permanent residents of this quiet corner of France. Symptoms usually appear some time around mid-July and persist until early September: glazed and bloodshot eyes, yawning, loss of appetite, shortness of temper, lethargy, and a mild form of paranoia that manifests itself in sudden urges to join a monastery.

This is the *maladie du Lubéron*, or creeping social fatigue, and it provokes about the same degree of sympathy as a millionaire's servant problems.

If we examine the patients—the permanent residents— we can see why it happens. Permanent residents have their work, their local friends, their unhurried routines. They made a deliberate choice to live in the Lubéron instead of one of the cocktail capitals of the world because they wanted, if not to get away from it all, to get away from most of it. This eccentricity is understood and tolerated for 10 months a year.

Try to explain that in July and August. Here come the visitors, fresh from the plane or hot off the *autoroute*, panting for social action. Let's meet some of the locals! To hell with the book in the hammock and the walk in the woods. To hell with solitude; they want people—people for lunch, people for drinks, people for dinner—and so invitations and counterinvitations fly back and forth until every day for weeks has its own social highlight.

As the holiday comes to an end with one final multibottle dinner, it is possible to see even on the visitors' faces some traces of weariness. They had no idea it was so lively down here. They are only half-joking when they say they're going to need a rest to get over the whirl of the past few days. Is it always like this? How do you keep it up?

It isn't, and we don't. Like many of our friends, we collapse in between visitations, guarding empty days and free evenings, eating little and drinking less, going to bed early. And every year, when the dust has settled, we talk to other members of the distressed residents' association about ways of making summer less of an endurance test.

We all agree that firmness is the answer. Say no more often than yes. Harden the heart against the surprise visitor who cannot find a hotel room, the deprived child who has no swimming pool, the desperate traveler who has lost his wallet. Be firm; be helpful, be kind, be rude, but above all *be firm*.

And yet I know—I think we all know—that next summer will be the same. I suppose we must enjoy it. Or we would, if we weren't exhausted.

## Place du Village

Cars have been banned from the village square, and stalls or trestle tables have been set up on three sides. On the fourth, a framework of scaffolding, blinking with colored lights, supports a raised platform made from wooden planks. Outside the café, the usual single row of tables and chairs has been multiplied by 10, and an extra waiter has been taken on to serve the sprawl of customers stretching from the butcher's down to the post office. Children and dogs chase each other through the crowd, stealing lumps of sugar from the tables and dodging the old men's sticks that are waved in mock anger. Nobody will go to bed early tonight, not even the children, because this is the village's annual party, the *fête votive*.

It begins in the late afternoon with a *pot d'amitié* in the square and the official opening of the stalls. Local artisans, the men's faces shining from an afternoon shave, stand behind their tables, glass in hand, or make final adjustments to their displays. There is pottery and jewelry, honey and lavender essence, hand-woven fabrics, iron and stone artifacts, paintings and wood carvings, books, postcards, tooled leatherwork, corkscrews with twisted olive-wood handles, patterned sachets of dried herbs. The woman selling pizza does brisk business as the first glass of wine begins to make the crowd hungry.

People drift off, eat, drift back. The night comes down, warm and still, the mountains in the distance just visible as deep black humps against the sky. The three-man accordion band tunes up on the platform and launches into the first of many *paso dobles* while the rock group from Avignon that will follow later rehearses on beer and *pastis* in the café.

The first dancers appear—an old man and his granddaughter, her nose pressed into his belt buckle, her feet balanced precariously on his feet. They are joined by a mother, father, and daughter dancing *à trois*, and then by several elderly couples, holding each other with stiff formality, their faces set with concentration as they try to retrace the steps they learned fifty years ago.

The *paso doble* session comes to an end with a flourish and a ruffle of accordions and drums, and the rock group warms up with five minutes of electronic tweaks that bounce off the old stone walls of the church opposite the platform.

The group's singer, a well-built young lady in tight black Lycra and a screaming orange wig, has attracted an audience before singing a note. An old man, the peak of his cap almost meeting the jut of his chin, has dragged a chair across from the café to sit directly in front of the microphone. As the singer starts her first number, some village boys made bold by his example come out of the shadows to stand by the old man's chair. All of them stare as though hypnotized at the shiny black pelvis rotating just above their heads.

The village girls, short of partners, dance with each other, as close as possible to the backs of the mesmerized boys. One of the waiters puts down his tray to caper in front of a pretty girl sitting with her parents. She blushes and ducks her head, but her mother nudges her to dance. Go on. The holiday will soon be over.

After an hour of music that threatens to dislodge the windows of the houses around the square, the group performs its finale. With an intensity worthy of Piaf on a sad night, the singer gives us *"Comme d'habitude,"* or "My Way," ending with a sob, her orange head bent over the microphone. The old man nods and bangs his stick on the ground, and the dancers go back to the café to see if there's any beer left.

Normally, there would have been *feux d'artifice* shooting up from the field behind the war memorial. This year, because of the drought, fireworks are forbidden. But it was a good *fête*. And did you see how the postman danced?

# Arrest That Dog!

A friend in London who occasionally keeps me informed about subjects of international importance that might not be reported in *Le Provençal* sent me a disturbing newspaper clipping. It was taken from the *Times*, and it revealed an enterprise of unspeakable villainy, a knife thrust deep into the most sensitive part of a Frenchman's anatomy.

A gang of scoundrels had been importing white truffles (sometimes contemptuously referred to as "industrial" truffles) from Italy and staining them with walnut dye until their complexions were dark enough to pass as black truffles. These, as every gourmet knows, have infinitely more flavor than their white cousins, and cost infinitely more money. The *Times* reporter, I think, had seriously underestimated the prices. He had quoted 400 francs a kilo, which would have caused a stampede at Fauchon in Paris, where I had seen them arranged in the window like jewels at 7000 francs a kilo.

But that wasn't the point. It was the nature of the crime that mattered. Here were the French, self-appointed world champions of gastronomy, being taken in by counterfeit delicacies, their taste buds hoodwinked and their wallets plucked clean. Worse still, the fraud didn't even depend on second-class domestic truffles, but on pallid castoffs from Italy—*Italy*, for God's sake!

I had once heard a Frenchman express his opinion of Italian food in a single libelous phrase: After the noodle, there is nothing. And yet hundreds, maybe thousands, of dusky Italian impersonators had found their way into knowledgeable French stomachs under the crudest of false pretences. The shame of it was enough to make a man weep all over his *foie gras*.

The story reminded me of Alain, who had offered to take me for a day of truffle hunting below Mont Ventoux, and to demonstrate the skills of his miniature pig. But when I called him, he told me he was having a very thin season, the result of the summer drought. *En plus*, the experiment with the pig had been a failure. She was not suited to the work. Nevertheless, he had a few truffles if we were interested, small but good. We arranged to meet in Apt, where he had to see a man about a dog.

There is one café in Apt that is filled on market day with men who have truffles to sell. While they wait for customers, they pass the time cheating at cards and lying about how much they were able to charge a passing Parisian for 150 grams of mud and fungus. They carry folding scales in their pockets, and ancient wooden-handled Opinel knives, which are used to cut tiny nicks in the surface of a truffle to prove that its blackness is more than skin deep. Mixed in with the café smell of coffee and black tobacco is the earthy, almost putrid scent that comes from the contents of the shabby linen bags on the tables. Early morning glasses of *rosé* are sipped, and conversations are often conducted in secretive mutters.

While I waited for Alain, I watched two men crouched over their drinks, their heads close together, glancing around between sentences. One of them took out a cracked Bic pen and wrote something on the palm of his hand. He showed what he had written to the other man and then spat into his palm and carefully rubbed out the evidence. What could it have been? The new price per kilo? The combination of the vault in the bank next door? Or a warning? *Say nothing. A man with glasses is staring at us.*

Alain arrived, and everyone in the café looked at him, as they had looked at me. I felt as though I was about to do something dangerous and illegal instead of buying ingredients for an omelet.

I had brought with me the clipping from the *Times*, but it was old news to Alain. He had heard about it from a friend in the Périgord, where it was causing a great deal of righteous indignation among honest truffle dealers, and grave suspicions in the minds of their customers.

Alain had come to Apt to begin negotiations for the purchase of a new truffle dog. He knew the owner, but not well, and therefore the business would take some time. The asking price was substantial, 20,000 francs, and nothing could be taken on trust. Tests in the field would have to be arranged. The dog's age would have to be established, and his stamina and scenting skills demonstrated. One never knew.

I asked about the miniature pig. Alain shrugged, and drew his index finger across his throat. In the end, he said, unless one was prepared to accept the inconvenience of a full-sized pig, a dog was the only solution. But to find the right dog, a dog that would be worth its weight in banknotes, that was not at all straightforward.

There is no such breed as a truffle hound. Most of the

truffle dogs that I had seen were small, nondescript, yappy creatures that looked as though a terrier might have been briefly involved in the bloodline many generations ago. Alain himself had an old Alsatian which, in its day, had worked well. It was all a question of individual instinct and training, and there were no guarantees that a dog who performed for one owner would perform for another. Alain remembered something and smiled. There was a famous story. I refilled his glass, and he told me.

A man from St. Didier once had a dog who could find truffles, so he said, where no other dog had found them before. Throughout the winter, when other hunters were coming back from the hills with a handful, or a dozen, the man from St. Didier would return to the café with his satchel bulging. The dog was a *merveille*, and the owner never stopped boasting about his little Napoléon, so called because his nose was worth gold.

Many men coveted Napoléon, but each time they offered to buy him, the owner refused. Until one day a man came into the café and put four *briques* on the table, four thick wads pinned together, 40,000 francs. This was an extraordinary price and, with a show of reluctance, it was finally accepted. Napoléon went off with his new master.

For the remainder of the season, he didn't find a single truffle. The new owner was *en colère*. He brought Napoléon to the café and demanded his money back. The old owner told him to go away and learn how to hunt properly. Such an *imbécile* didn't deserve a dog like Napoléon. Other unpleasant words were exchanged, but there was no question of the money being refunded.

The new owner went into Avignon to find a lawyer. The

lawyer said, as lawyers often do, that it was a grey area. There was no precedent to refer to, no case in the long and meticulously documented history of French law that touched on the matter of a dog being derelict in his duty. It was without doubt a dispute that would have to be decided by a learned judge.

Months and many consultations later, the two men were instructed to appear in court. The judge, being a thorough and conscientious man, wanted to be sure that all the principals in the case were present. A gendarme was sent to arrest the dog and bring him to court as a material witness.

Whether or not the dog's presence in the witness box helped the judge in his deliberations is not known, but he handed down the following verdict: Napoléon was to be returned to his old owner, who would repay half the purchase price, being allowed to keep the other half as compensation for the loss of the dog's services.

Now reunited, Napoléon and his old owner moved from St. Didier to a village north of Carpentras. Two years later, an identical case was reported, although due to inflation the amount of money had increased. Napoléon and his owner had done it again.

But there was something I didn't understand. If the dog was such a virtuoso truffle hunter, surely his owner would make more money by working him than selling him, even though he ended up keeping the dog and half the money each time he went to court.

Ah, said Alain, you have assumed, like everyone else, that the truffles in the satchel were found by Napoléon on the days they were brought into the café.

*Non?*

*Non.* They were kept in the *congélateur* and brought out once or twice a week. That dog couldn't find a pork chop in a *charcuterie*. He had a nose of wood.

Alain finished his wine. "You must never buy a dog in a café. Only when you have seen him work." He looked at his watch. "I have time for another glass. And you?"

Always, I said. Did he have another story?

"This you will like, being a writer," he said. "It happened many years ago, but I am told it is true."

A peasant owned a patch of land some distance from his house. It was not a big patch, less than two *hectares*, but it was crowded with ancient oaks, and each winter there were many truffles, enough to allow the peasant to live in comfortable idleness for the rest of the year. His pig barely needed to search. Year after year, truffles grew more or less where they had grown before. It was like finding money under the trees. God was good, and a prosperous old age was assured.

One can imagine the peasant's irritation the first morning he noticed freshly displaced earth under the trees. Something had been on his land during the night, possibly a dog or even a stray pig. A little further on, he noticed a cigarette end crushed into the earth—a modern, filter-tipped cigarette, not of the kind he smoked. And certainly not dropped by a stray pig. This was extremely alarming.

As he went from tree to tree, so his alarm increased. More earth had been disturbed, and he saw fresh grazes on some rocks that could only have been made by a truffle pick.

It wasn't, it couldn't have been, one of his neighbors. He had known them all since childhood. It must have been a foreigner, someone who didn't know that this precious patch was his.

Since he was a reasonable man, he had to admit that there

was no way a foreigner could tell if the land was privately owned or not. Fences and signs were expensive, and he had never seen the need for them. His land was his land; everyone knew that. Clearly, times had changed and strangers were finding their way into the hills. He drove to the nearest town that afternoon and bought an armful of signs: PROPRIÉTÉ PRIVÉE, DÉFENSE D'ENTRER, and, for good measure, three or four that read CHIEN MÉCHANT. He and his wife worked until dark nailing them up around the perimeter of the land.

A few days went by without any further signs of the trespasser with the truffle pick, and the peasant allowed himself to relax. It had been an innocent mistake, although he did wonder why an innocent man would hunt truffles at night.

And then it happened again. The signs had been ignored, the land violated, and who knows how many fat black nuggets taken from the earth under cover of darkness. It could no longer be excused as the mistake of an ignorant enthusiast. This was a *braconnier*, a poacher, a thief in the night who hoped to profit from an old man's only source of income.

The peasant and his wife discussed the problem that night as they sat in the kitchen and ate their *soupe*. They could, of course, call in the police. But since the truffles—or at least, the money made from selling the truffles—did not officially exist, it might not be prudent to involve the authorities. Questions would be asked about the value of what had been stolen, and private information such as this was best kept private. Besides, the official penalty for truffle poaching, even if it were a spell in jail, would not replace the thousands of francs that were even now stuffed in the poacher's deep and dishonest pockets.

And so the couple decided to seek tougher but more satisfactory justice, and the peasant went to see two of his neighbors, men who would understand what needed to be done.

They agreed to help him, and for several long, cold nights the three of them waited with their shotguns among the truffle oaks, coming home each dawn slightly tipsy from the *marc* that they had been obliged to drink to keep out the chill. At last, one night when the clouds scudded across the face of the moon and the *mistral* bit into the faces of the three men, they saw the headlights of a car. It stopped at the end of a dirt track, two hundred meters down the hill.

The engine stopped, lights were extinguished, doors were opened and quietly closed. There were voices, and then the glow of a flashlight, which came slowly up the hill toward them.

First into the trees was a dog. He stopped, picked up the scent of the men, and barked—a high, nervous bark, followed at once by *ssssst!* as the poacher hissed him quiet. The men flexed their numb fingers for a better grip on their guns, and the peasant took aim with the flashlight he had brought especially for the ambush.

The beam caught them as they came into the clearing: a couple, middle-aged and unremarkable, the woman carrying a small sack, the man with flashlight and truffle pick. Red-handed.

The three men, making great display of their artillery, approached the couple. They had no defense, and with gun barrels under their noses quickly admitted that they had been there before to steal truffles.

How many truffles? asked the old peasant. Two kilos? Five kilos? More?

Silence from the poachers, and silence from the three men as they thought about what they should do. Justice must be done; more important than justice, money must be repaid. One of the men whispered in the old peasant's ear, and he nodded. Yes, that is what we will do. He announced the verdict of the impromptu court.

Where was the poacher's bank? Nyons? *Ah bon*. If you start walking now you will be there when it opens. You will take out 30,000 francs, which you will bring back here. We shall keep your car, your dog, and your wife until you return.

The poacher set off on the four-hour walk to Nyons. His dog was put in the boot of the car, his wife in the back seat. The three men squeezed in too. It was a cold night. They dozed through it in between tots of *marc*.

Dawn came, then morning, then noon . . .

Alain stopped his story. "You're a writer," he said. "How do you think it ended?"

I made a couple of guesses, both wrong, and Alain laughed.

"It was very simple, not at all *dramatique*," he said. "Except perhaps for the wife. The poacher went to his bank in Nyons and took out all the money he possessed, and then—*pouf!*— he disappeared."

"He never came back?"

"Nobody ever saw him again."

"Not his wife?"

"Certainly not his wife. He was not fond of his wife."

"And the peasant?"

"He died an angry man."

Alain said he had to go. I paid him for the truffles, and wished him luck with his new dog. When I got home, I cut one of the truffles in half to make sure it was the genuine, deep black all the way through. He seemed like a good fellow, Alain, but you never know.

# Life Through Rosé-Tinted Spectacles

Going native.

I don't know whether it was meant as a joke, an insult, or a compliment, but that was what the man from London said. He had dropped in unexpectedly on his way to the coast, and stayed for lunch. We hadn't seen him for five years, and he was obviously curious to see what effects life in Provence was having on us, examining us thoughtfully for signs of moral and physical deterioration.

We weren't conscious of having changed, but he was sure of it, although there was nothing he could put his finger on. For lack of any single change as plain as delirium tremens, rusty English, or premature senility, he put us in the vague, convenient, and all-embracing pigeonhole marked "going native."

As he drove away in his clean car, telephone antenna fluttering gaily in the breeze, I looked at our small and dusty Citroën, which was innocent of any communications facility. That was certainly a native car. And, in comparison with our visitor's Côte d'Azur outfit, I was wearing native dress—old shirt, shorts, no shoes. Then I remembered how often he had looked at his watch during lunch, because he was meeting friends in Nice at 6:30. Not later in the day, not sometime that evening, but at 6:30. Precisely. We had long ago abandoned timekeeping of such a high standard due to lack of local support, and now lived according to the rules of the approximate rendezvous. Another native habit.

The more I thought about it, the more I realized that we must have changed. I wouldn't have called it going native, but there are dozens of differences between our old life and our new life, and we have had to adjust to them. It hasn't been difficult. Most of the changes have taken place gradually, pleasantly, almost imperceptibly. All of them, I think, are changes for the better.

We no longer watch television. It wasn't a self-righteous decision to give us time for more intellectual pursuits; it simply happened. In the summer, watching television can't begin to compare with watching the evening sky. In the winter, it can't compete with dinner. The television set has now been relegated to a cupboard to make space for more books.

We eat better than we used to, and probably more cheaply. It is impossible to live in France for any length of time and stay immune to the national enthusiasm for food, and who would want to? Why not make a daily pleasure out of a daily necessity? We have slipped into the gastronomic rhythm of Provence, taking advantage of the special offers provided by nature all through the year: asparagus, tiny *haricots verts* barely thicker than matchsticks, fat *fèves*, cherries, aubergines, *courgettes*, peppers, peaches and apricots and melons and grapes, *blettes*, wild mushrooms, olives, truffles—every season brings its own treat. With the expensive exception of the truffle, nothing costs more than a few francs a kilo.

Meat is a different matter, and butchers' prices can make the visitor wince. Provence is not cattle country, and so the Englishman in search of his roast beef on Sunday had better take his checkbook and be prepared for disappointment, because the beef is neither cheap nor tender. But lamb, above all from the area around Sisteron where the sheep season themselves with herbs, has a taste that would be a crime to disguise with mint sauce. And every part of the pig is good.

Even so, we now eat less meat. An occasional *appellation contrôlée* chicken from Bresse, the wild rabbits that Henriette brings in the winter, a cassoulet when the temperature drops and the *mistral* howls around the house—meat from time to time is wonderful. Meat every day is a habit of the past. There is so much else: fish from the Mediterranean, fresh pasta, limitless recipes for all those vegetables, dozens of breads, hundreds of cheeses.

It may be the change in our diet and the way it is cooked, always in olive oil, but we have both lost weight. Only a little, but enough to cause some surprise to friends who expect us to have developed the ballooning *embonpoint*—the stomach on stilts—that sometimes grows on people with good appetites who have the luck to eat in France.

Through no deliberate intention of our own, we also take more exercise. Not the grim contortions promoted by gaunt women in leotards, but the exercise that comes naturally from living in a climate that allows you to spend eight or nine months of the year outdoors. Discipline has nothing to do with it, apart from the small disciplines of country life— bringing logs in for the fire, keeping the weeds down and the ditches clear, planting, pruning, bending, and lifting. And, every day in every kind of weather, walking.

We have had people to stay who refuse to believe that

walking can be hard exercise. It's not dramatic effort, not immediately punishing, not fast, not violent. Everybody walks, they say. You can't call that exercise. Eventually, if they insist, we take them out for a stroll with the dogs.

For the first 10 minutes the going is flat, along the footpath at the bottom of the mountain, easy and undemanding. Pleasant to get a little fresh air and a view of Mont Ventoux in the distance. But exercise? They're not even short of breath.

Then we turn and go up the track leading to the cedar forest that grows along the spine of the Lubéron. The surface changes from sandy soil cushioned with pine needles to rocks and patches of scree, and we begin to climb. After five minutes, there are no more condescending remarks about walking being an old man's exercise. After 10 minutes, there are no remarks at all, only the sound of increasingly heavy breathing, punctuated by coughing. The track twists around boulders and under branches so low you have to bend double. There is no encouraging glimpse of the top; the view is limited to a hundred yards or so of narrow, stony, steeply inclined track before it disappears around the next outcrop of rock. If there is any breath to spare, there might be a curse as an ankle turns on the shifting scree. Legs and lungs are burning.

The dogs pad on ahead, with the rest of us strung out behind them at irregular intervals, the least fit stumbling along with their backs bent and their hands on their thighs. Pride usually prevents them from stopping, and they wheeze away stubbornly, heads down, feeling sick. They will never again dismiss walking as nonexercise.

The reward for this effort is to find yourself in a silent, extraordinary landscape, sometimes eerie, always beautiful. The cedars are magnificent, and magical when they are draped with great swags of snow. Beyond them, on the south face of the mountain, the land drops away sharply, grey and jagged, softened by the thyme and box that seem to be able to grow in the most unpromising wrinkle of rock.

On a clear day, when the *mistral* has blown and the air shines, the views toward the sea are long and sharply focused, almost as if they have been magnified, and there is a sense of being hundreds of miles away from the rest of the world. I once met a peasant up there, on the road the forest service made through the cedars. He was on an old bicycle, a gun slung across his back, a dog loping beside him. We were both startled to see another human being. It is normally less busy, and the only sound is the wind nagging at the trees.

The days pass slowly but the weeks rush by. We now measure the year in ways that have little to do with diaries and specific dates. There is the almond blossom in February, and a few weeks of prespring panic in the garden as we try to do the work we've been talking about doing all winter. Spring is a mixture of cherry blossom and a thousand weeds and the first guests of the year, hoping for subtropical weather and often getting nothing but rain and wind. Summer might start in April. It might start in May. We know it's arrived when Bernard calls to help us uncover and clean the pool.

Poppies in June, drought in July, storms in August. The vines begin to turn rusty, the hunters come out of their summer hibernation, the grapes have been picked, and the water in the pool nips more and more fiercely until it becomes too cold for anything more than a masochistic plunge in the middle of the day. It must be the end of October.

Winter is filled with good resolutions, and some of them are actually achieved. A dead tree is cut down, a wall is built, the old steel garden chairs are repainted, and whenever there is time to spare we take up the dictionary and resume our struggle with the French language.

Our French has improved, and the thought of spending an evening in totally French company is not as daunting as it used to be. But, to use the words that were so often used in my school reports, there is considerable room for improvement. Must try harder. And so we inch our way through books by Pagnol and Giono and de Maupassant, buy *Le Provençal* regularly, listen to the machine-gun delivery of radio newsreaders, and attempt to unravel the mysteries of what we are constantly being told is a supremely logical language.

I think that is a myth, invented by the French to bewilder foreigners. Where is the logic, for instance, in the genders given to proper names and nouns? Why is the Rhône masculine and the Durance feminine? They are both rivers, and if they must have a sex, why can't it be the same one? When I asked a Frenchman to explain this to me, he delivered a dissertation on sources, streams, and floods which, according to him, answered the question conclusively and, of course, logically. Then he went on to the masculine ocean, the feminine sea, the masculine lake, and the feminine puddle. Even the water must get confused.

His speech did nothing to change my theory, which is that genders are there for no other reason than to make life difficult. They have been allocated in a whimsical and arbitrary fashion, sometimes with a cavalier disregard for the anatomical niceties. The French for vagina is *vagin*. *Le vagin*. Masculine. How can the puzzled student hope to apply logic to a language in which the vagina is masculine?

There is also the androgynous *lui* waiting to ambush us at the threshold of many a sentence. Normally, *lui* is him. In some constructions, *lui* is her. Often, we are left in the dark as to *lui's* gender until it is made known to use some time after he or she has been introduced, as in: *"Demandez-lui,"* (ask him) *"peut-être qu'elle peut vous aidez"* (perhaps she can help you). A short-lived mystery, possibly, but one that can puzzle the novice, particularly when *lui's* first name is also a mixture of masculine and feminine, such as Jean-Marie or Marie-Pierre.

And that is not the worst of it. Strange and unnatural events take place every day within the formalities of French syntax. A recent newspaper article, reporting on the marriage of the rock singer Johnny Hallyday, paused in its description of the bride's frock to give Johnny a pat on the back. *"Il est,"* said the article, *"une grande vedette."* In the space of a single short sentence, the star had undergone a sex change, and on his wedding day too.

It is perhaps because of these perplexing twists and turns that French was for centuries the language of diplomacy, an occupation in which simplicity and clarity are not regarded as being necessary, or even desirable. Indeed, the guarded statement, made fuzzy by formality and open to several different interpretations, is much less likely to land an ambassador in the soup that plain words that mean what they say. A diplomat, according to Alex Dreier, is "anyone who thinks twice before saying nothing." Nuance and significant vagueness are essential, and French might have been invented to allow these linguistic weeds to flourish in the crevices of every sentence.

But it is a beautiful, supple, and romantic language, although it may not quite deserve the reverence that inspires a course of French lessons to be described as a *"cours de civilisation"* by those who regard it as a national treasure and a shining example of how everyone should speak. One can imagine the dismay of these purists at the foreign horrors that are now creeping into everyday French.

The rot probably started when *le weekend* slipped across the Channel to Paris at about the same time that a nightclub owner in Pigalle christened his establishment *Le Sexy*. Inevitably, this led to the naughty institution of *le weekend sexy*, to the delight of Parisian hotel owners and the despair of their counterparts in Brighton and other less erotically blessed resorts.

The invasion of the language hasn't stopped in the bedroom. It has also infiltrated the office. The executive now has *un job*. If the pressure of work becomes too much for him, he will find himself increasingly *stressé*, perhaps because of the demands of being *un leader* in the business jungle of *le marketing*. The poor, overworked wretch doesn't even have time for the traditional three-hour lunch, and has to make do with *le fast food*. It is the worst kind of Franglais, and it goads the elders of the Académie Française into fits of outrage. I can't say I blame them. These clumsy intrusions into such a graceful language are *scandaleuses*; or, to put it another way, *les pits*.

The gradual spread of Franglais is helped by the fact that there are many fewer words in the French vocabulary than in English. This has its own set of problems, because the same word can have more than one meaning. In Paris, for instance, *"je suis ravi"* will normally be taken to mean "I am delighted." In the Café du Progrès in Ménerbes, however, *ravi* has a second, uncomplimentary translation, and the same phrase can mean "I am the village idiot."

In order to disguise my confusion and to avoid at least some of the many verbal booby traps, I have learned to grunt like a native, to make those short but expressive sounds—those sharp intakes of breath, those understanding clickings of the tongue, those mutters of *beh oui*—that are used like conversational stepping-stones in between one subject and the next.

Of all these, the most flexible and therefore most useful is the short and apparently explicit phrase, *ah bon*, used with or without a question mark. I used to think this meant what it said, but of course it doesn't. A typical exchange, with the right degree of catastrophe and gloom, might go something like this:

"Young Jean-Pierre is in real trouble this time."

"*Oui?*"

"*Beh oui.* He came out of the café, got in his car, ran over a *gendarme*—completely *écrasé*—drove into a wall, went through the windscreen, split his head open, and broke his leg in fourteen places."

"*Ah bon.*"

Depending on inflection, *ah bon* can express shock, disbelief, indifference, irritation, or joy—a remarkable achievement for two short words.

Similarly, it is possible to conduct the greater part of a brief conversation with two other monosyllables—*ça va*, which literally mean "it goes." Every day, in every town and village around Provence, acquaintances will meet on the street, perform the ritual handshake, and deliver the ritual dialogue:

"*Ça va?*"

"*Oui. Ça va, ça va. Et vous?*"

"*Bohf, ça va.*"

"*Bieng. Ça va alors.*"

"*Oui, oui. Ça va.*"

"*Allez. Au 'voir.*"

"*Au 'voir.*"

The words alone do not do justice to the occasion, which is decorated with shrugs and sighs and thoughtful pauses that can stretch to two or three minutes if the sun is shining and there is nothing pressing to do. And, naturally, the same unhurried, pleasant acknowledgment of neighborhood faces will be repeated several times in the course of the morning's errands.

It is easy to be misled, after a few months of these uncomplicated encounters, into believing that you are beginning to distinguish yourself in colloquial French. You may even have spent long evenings with French people who profess to understand you. They become more than acquaintances; they become friends. And when they judge the moment is ripe, they present you with the gift of friendship in spoken form, which brings with it an entirely new set of opportunities to make a fool of yourself. Instead of using *vous*, they will start addressing you as *tu* or *toi*, a form of intimacy that has its own verb, *tutoyer*.

The day when a Frenchman switches from the formality of *vous* to the familiarity of *tu* is a day to be taken seriously. It is an unmistakable signal that he has decided—after weeks or months or sometimes years—that he likes you. It would be churlish and unfriendly of you not to return the compliment. And so, just when you are at last feeling comfortable with *vous* and all the plurals that go with it, you are thrust headlong into the singular world of *tu*. (Unless, of course, you follow the example of ex-President Giscard d'Estaing, who apparently addresses even his wife as *vous*.)

But we stumble along, committing all kinds of sins against grammar and gender, making long and awkward detours to avoid the swamps of the subjunctive and the chasms in our vocabularies, hoping that our friends are not too appalled at the mauling we give their language. They are kind enough to say that our French doesn't make them shudder. I doubt that, but there is no doubting their desire to help us feel at home, and there is a warmth to everyday life that is not just the sun.

That, at least, has been our experience. It obviously isn't universal, and some people either don't believe it, or even seem to resent it. We have been accused of the crime of cheerfulness, of turning a blind eye to minor problems, and of deliberately ignoring what is invariably described as the dark side of the Provençal character. This ominous cliché is wheeled out and festooned with words like dishonest, lazy, bigoted, greedy, and brutal. It is as if they are peculiarly local characteristics that the innocent foreigner—honest, industrious, unprejudiced, and generally blameless—will be exposed to for the first time in his life.

It is of course true that there are crooks and bigots in Provence, just as there are crooks and bigots everywhere. But we've been lucky, and Provence has been good to us. We will never be more than permanent visitors in someone else's country, but we have been made welcome and happy. There are no regrets, few complaints, many pleasures.

*Merci, Provence.*